PREHISTORIC
BELIEF

PREHISTORIC BELIEF

Shamans, Trance and the Afterlife

MIKE WILLIAMS

For Richard Bradley

In gratitude for conversations past
and in anticipation for those yet to happen

First published 2010

The History Press
The Mill, Brimscombe Port
Stroud, Gloucestershire, GL5 2QG
www.thehistorypress.co.uk

British Library Cataloguing in Publication Data.
A catalogue record for this book is available from the British Library.

ISBN 978 0 7524 4921 0

Typesetting and origination by The History Press
Printed in Great Britain
Manufacturing managed by Jellyfish Print Solutions Ltd

CONTENTS

PREFACE

To an archaeologist, origins are important: the emergence of culture, the first farmers, and the change from bronze to iron are all examples of subjects that provoke endless discussion. This idea got me thinking as to the origin of this book, and I realised that it was when I was studying for my Masters degree in archaeology at Reading University. Each week, my professor, Richard Bradley, would meet with me and another student, Kirsti Bambridge, to discuss an aspect of our course. Richard would inform us of the subject and Kirsti and I would read up on it beforehand, ready to enjoy an hour of brainstorming with Richard. In this way, week by week, we developed an understanding of a large and complex subject without ever letting the excitement, enthusiasm, or sheer pleasure of studying it escape us (and it never did, even through the subsequent years studying for my PhD). I realised that I had approached writing this book in exactly the same way: imagining that I had been set a topic to cover with each chapter and then brainstorming it into a cohesive narrative. I hope that, in this way, the book retains something of the immediacy and enthusiasm with which I wrote it.

While I was clearly drawing on the work and research of others to formulate my ideas, I realised that, from then on, I often headed in my own direction. I am quite happy, therefore, to use a generous smattering of 'perhaps' and 'possibly', because this is often as far as the evidence will allow me to go. Moreover, while I did not want to clutter the text with direct references to the works I have consulted, I felt that it was important to show interested readers where I obtained my information and the sources that I relied upon when forming my conclusions – a foil for the bolder statements that creep in. Accordingly, I have written a series of endnotes that add a little more detail to the content of the chapters and also provide references for my source material. A subsequent bibliography does the rest. The reader can consult or ignore these endnotes entirely at their own inclination; no harm will befall the remaining text either way.

At its heart, I want this book to be a good read and, while avoiding playing fast and loose with the evidence, I have always erred towards this aim. I have also been aware that, in writing this book, I could not hope to equal the works of the specialists in each field that I cover. Prehistory is vast and involves so many sub-disciplines and attendant literature that it can make the head spin. Does this mean that books such as this, which attempt a broad sweep of the human condition across many thousands of years, should never be written? That is for the reader to decide, but I feel it is beholden on a writer at least to try. Ambition should not be faulted, even if the adequacy of the result deserves criticism by the specialist.

I also want this book to challenge the way we think about the past and I have therefore added short vignettes that attempt to recreate the ancient world and allow us, even if for a few brief moments, to journey there and experience it for ourselves. For me, the past must be touched if it is to have meaning. Since the available evidence necessarily limits these vignettes, there are times when they might obscure as well as reveal what is known about the period. Flights of fancy they might be, but they remain tethered by the evidence.

As any writer knows, books are like children – you do your best bringing them up but, ultimately, you have to let them out into the world and allow them to make their own way. If you are about to embark on a journey through the following pages then it is to you, my reader, that I owe the greatest acknowledgement and debt. I sincerely hope that we will enjoy the time we spend with each other.

ACKNOWLEDGEMENTS

There are many who have touched this book over the years of its gestation and it is part of the privilege of seeing it in print that I am able to finally acknowledge their help and guidance.

The genesis of the book was with my research towards my PhD degree and so my first debt is to the Archaeology Department of the University of Reading for their help and support in nurturing my progress. John Creighton and Martin Bell sat on my advisory group and Sturt Manning, Bob Chapman, Heinrich Härke, and Steve Mithen were always extremely supportive of my work. I would like to thank the Arts and Humanities Research Board for providing a Postgraduate Studentship to cover the entire three-year research period and, additionally, the Faculty of Letters and Social Sciences at the University of Reading for a scholarship over the same period. Thomas Dowson was an illuminating examiner of my thesis and I enjoyed our conversations on all things shamanic.

The librarians of the University of Reading, the Sackler Library, the Radcliffe Science Library, and the Bodleian Library, all in Oxford, have been extremely helpful in obtaining references. Without such support, new research would cease.

Dave Yates, Dave Mason, Kirsti Bambridge, Jill York, and Debbie Wander have always been extremely generous with sharing their work and ideas and have greatly added to the book.

The credits for the illustrations are noted elsewhere but Giovanni Caselli, Helga Schültze from the National Museum of Denmark, Kurt Wehrberger from Ulmer Museum, and Julie Gardiner of Wessex Archaeology were especially helpful.

At The History Press, my grateful thanks to Wendy Logue, Fran Cantillion, and Tom Vivian for being such superb editors and Gary Chapman for his help and support for so many years.

Dave Mason, Kirsti Bambridge, and Gudrun Minton read and commented on initial drafts of the book and I am extremely grateful for their patience and diligence.

My family have always been staunch supporters of anything I embark upon and this book has been no different. In particular, I just could not write without my wife,

Vanessa, to support me. I should also thank my dog, Mabon, since he actually makes an appearance on one or two pages.

It is traditional to reserve the greatest debt until last and this book is no different. I explained at the beginning of the preface that I approached each chapter as if I was writing it for a tutorial with my MA and PhD professor, Richard Bradley. Anyone who knows Richard will understand that spending time in his company is illuminating, inspiring, and one of the best uses of time it is possible to make. His knowledge, ideas, and enthusiasm may make him one of the best prehistorians but it is his warmth, generosity, and humanity that make him one of the best people I know. I simply could not have written this book for anyone else.

Introduction

A SMILE OF ETERNITY

The man stands naked in the moonlight, his arms bound tight so that his veins curl like snakes as they emerge from the fur band around his upper arm. He does not struggle; indeed, he speaks to the people gathered around him at the side of the marsh quite calmly, as if this is his doing, his choice to die. He bends his head for the garrotte to be wrapped around his neck and the knot that will end his life is pulled tight about his throat. As the cord digs deep, the man tenses, his back arching wildly and his protruding tongue turning black. Still the cord tightens so that the man has to gasp for the last breath he will take. At the moment it seems certain he will die, a knife flashes across the darkened sky and his throat is slashed, from one ear to the other. Blood, under pressure from the tightening garrotte, erupts like a stream in spate and its thickness splatters the ground with gore. The man's legs give way as death finally claims him, but his fall is checked and he is laid gently to rest, a smile of eternity etched about his lips.

This disturbing scene was one that was played out many times at the end of the Iron Age, about 2000 years ago. To modern sensibilities, it seems unfathomable that anyone would willingly choose to die in such a gruesome fashion. It makes us realise that the gulf between us and the people of that time is far greater than the 2000 intervening years. People in the past lived differently to us, they behaved differently to us and, perhaps most importantly, they believed in different things to us. This makes any interpretation of the past fraught with difficulty: are we projecting our own beliefs and prejudices back into the past, or are we truly seeing the world as people living in those ancient times may have seen it themselves? Perhaps we will never be sure but without an awareness of what people might have believed in the past, there will always be things that remain beyond our comprehension. Just why did people paint cave walls with designs so beautiful that they make you weep for the joy of them? Why did people hold hunting ceremonies where humans became animals and animals became ghosts? Why did people honour the passing of their swords with the same dignity as a great warrior, and why did a few individuals give their life's blood to the bog so that their people should live? Without knowing the beliefs that motivated people to do these things, we shall never truly understand their lives.

The stimulus for me to explore the beliefs of the past stems from my participation with modern Druid orders and my practice of shamanism. This is not to say that my involvement gives me any special insight into the past – the path that I follow is most assuredly a modern reinvention – but my experience of ritual and of journeying to the otherworld in a shamanic trance shows me that there can be far more happening than appears on the surface.

The point of most religious ritual is to touch, however briefly, the unseen forces of the world, the ineffability of the sacred. For a shamanic journey, the intention is to reach the otherworld and experience another sort of reality. Sometimes these encounters can be incredible, perhaps even life-changing, and they can certainly leave participants with a new view of existence, altering their beliefs about the reality of the world. However, to an observer merely watching proceedings, very little appears to happen. In fact, the whole thing can even look a little ridiculous.

When recording a shaman's otherworldly journey to the spirits, for example, it is easy to dismiss his or her first-hand account of what happened. Hearing that the shaman passed through gates of fire, fought the demons of the west, obtained guidance from helper spirits, and retrieved a lost soul, gathering it into a piece of crystal before bringing it back into this world, defies rational explanation. It is far easier to concentrate on what the shaman wore for the ceremony, the type of drum that he or she played, and any special equipment that was used, such as the crystal soul-catcher, if that even existed in this reality. Later, however, when the shaman starts to explain the layout of the village, with gates of fire leading into the wildness of the forest, with talismans buried to the west to keep the demons at bay, and with offerings left every morning for the helper spirits, each mirroring the reality found in the otherworlds, nothing quite makes sense and it all looks, well, a little ridiculous. Without an understanding of the entire bounds of existence for the shaman, including the reality of the otherworlds (and possibly even experiencing it oneself), there is insufficient context for an observer to make sense of very much at all.

The same is true for the past, except that there is nobody from that time to whom we can address our questions, and participation becomes fraught when it involves volunteering for being brutally slaughtered and laid for eternity in a bog. To those in the past, however, who *were* willing to offer up their lives, their sacrifice made perfect sense within their beliefs about the world and the reality that they inhabited. Moreover, to offer up one's life to such beliefs suggests that these were no passing impulse but rather a deep-seated and persuasive way of understanding existence. To find out just how ingrained these beliefs were, we need to follow them back or, as this book does, follow them forward from the time that they first surfaced. Nevertheless, just how far back is it necessary to go?

If, as for the shaman of the village, beliefs emerge both from this world and also from the unseen influences of trance, dreams, and flights of imagination, then we need to start when these first began, and that is an extremely long time ago. Within Europe, which is the subject of this book, it means returning to the time when a new species of human emerged from Africa, some 40,000 years ago. These were

Homo sapiens, the 'thinking humans' – us. However, in settling the continent, these new humans displaced an even older species, Neanderthals, which showed traits of forming their own beliefs about the world. Just how complex these beliefs were is something we will shortly find out.

To explore the Neanderthals further, however, we must leave behind the twenty-first-century world and move into theirs. Reading about evidence and explanation, while invaluable in our quest, will not be enough; we need to inhabit the same reality as the people of the distant past. We need to see what they saw, feel what they felt; only then will we begin to discern what they might have believed about their world. We need to embark on a journey to the past, 40,000 years ago, to a cave somewhere in Europe.

Ice sheets cover the far north and the ground freezes solid for half the year. Night is coming on and we urgently need shelter. You notice a cave ahead just as the first sheets of hail begin to cloud our vision. We struggle on, wondering just what we might find …

PART ONE

IN THE GRIP OF THE ICE: THE PALAEOLITHIC

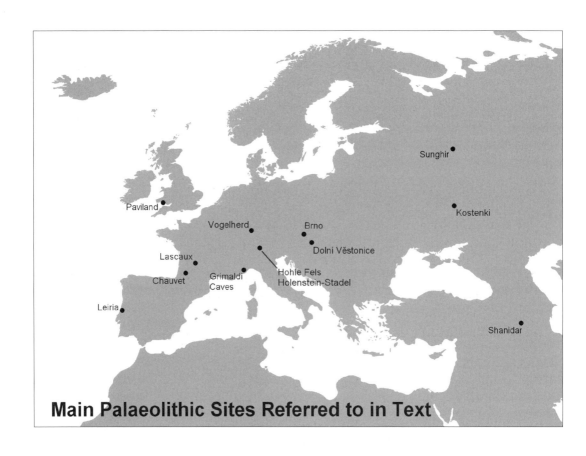

Main Palaeolithic Sites Referred to in Text

Chapter 1

ANCIENT RITES IN AN ANCIENT CAVE

All about us is a landscape of ice and snow; the wind tugs at the furs wrapped around us and the chill grips our bodies like a fist. You gesture to the cave and we move inside. It is strangely lit and we realise with a start that there is a fire towards the rear and large shapes moving around it. They are people, but not like any we have ever seen before. Large, squat, and powerfully built; we catch glimpses of their faces and cannot help but stare at their pronounced noses and brows. We have entered the lair of the Neanderthals. Moving closer, we notice that they are filling a pit with stones and loose earth. They are covering something but we cannot quite make it out. You creep closer still and point to a shape sticking out of the soil. It is an arm; the Neanderthals have just buried one of their dead. All at once there is a low sound that fills the cave; it is mournful but strangely rhythmic. We realise that it is the Neanderthals singing; is this how they lament their dead?

It is difficult to establish when Neanderthals first colonised Europe, as the fossil remains of the earliest examples are difficult to tell apart from earlier species of humans. It was thought that 300,000 years ago was the absolute earliest that Neanderthals had evolved as a separate species but new excavations at Atapuerca, in northern Spain, have suggested that it might be closer to 400,000 years ago, although whether these fragmentary remains are of Neanderthals or of an even earlier species of human is still debated.[1] However, from the remains of several individuals found at Ehringsdorf in Germany, and (more securely dated but far scantier in terms of remains), Pontnewydd Cave in Wales, it seems certain that Neanderthals had colonised most of Europe by at least 230,000 years ago.[2] They were to last another 200,000 years.

The landscape inhabited by the Neanderthals was one of wildly fluctuating temperatures. Although supremely adapted for the Ice Age, which affected Europe for much of the time that they were around, Neanderthals also had to cope with sudden periods of warming and even, on occasions, sub-tropical environments. During the last inter-glacial period (the warmer period between Ice Ages), between 128,000 and 118,000 years ago, there were even hippos living in southern England. Sudden climate change was nothing new to the Neanderthals and they coped with it remarkably well.[3]

Although Neanderthals certainly looked very like us, just how human their behaviour actually was is hotly debated, especially when it comes to burial. Caring for the dead is a very human trait since the focus is on the presumed soul of the individual and its journey to the afterlife – concepts requiring imagination and belief, which some think were beyond the reach of Neanderthals. Had we arrived slightly earlier in the cave, we may have witnessed how the Neanderthals had conducted the burial of their dead: whether they had spoken any words to the corpse, whether they had put any offerings in the grave, and whether the body had been laid out with respect. We certainly heard what sounded like singing but was this part of a mourning ritual or just a spontaneous outpouring of grief? Evidence of Neanderthal burial is tantalisingly scant and these are issues that archaeologists continue to debate.

Although some 500 Neanderthal bodies are known, most are very fragmentary and only around 20 are reasonably whole. Of these, even fewer were buried.[4] However, in the few cases where a pit had been dug to hold the body (interpreted as a sign of deliberate action on the part of the survivors) many of the remains were positioned in a foetal position, as if they had been placed with respect. Moreover, at La Ferrassie in France, two bodies were laid head-to-head, perhaps mirroring the relationship the individuals had in life.[5]

Possibly the most celebrated Neanderthal burials were found within caves at Shanidar, in modern-day Iraq. Rose and Ralph Solecki, a husband and wife team, found several burials between 1953 and 1960, including a man who had been crushed on the right side of his body, perhaps from a rock-fall, leading to partial paralysis and infection. That he lived for several months after the accident shows that the others in the group must have cared for him, and were evidently not thuggish brutes, but it did not prove that they honoured him after death.[6] Elsewhere in the cave, a Neanderthal burial was surrounded by flower pollen.[7] Could this have come from bouquets left by distraught loved ones? This would have been a typically human gesture to mark mourning and loss, and it would also indicate, as the excavator put it, that Neanderthals had a love of beauty.[8] The idea seemed to echo the preoccupation with 'flower power' at the time of excavation.

At another Neanderthal burial site at Teshik-Tash in Uzbekistan, a young boy was laid in a cave surrounded by six pairs of horns from local mountain goats.[9] The brief lighting of a fire next to the body seems to suggest that maybe this was part of a funeral ritual. At other sites, items appear to have been left with the bodies, perhaps indicating that these were offerings for the deceased to use in the afterlife. Particularly striking were the cattle bones left next to a body at Chapelle-aux-Saints in France.[10] If these were once joints of meat, could they have been provisions for the afterlife? Similarly, at Amud, in Israel, a red deer jawbone seemed to have been deliberately placed next to the pelvis of an infant.[11] Was there some symbolism associated with this act?

In our cave, we watch as the last stones are placed on the grave and the Neanderthals turn their attention back to the fire. One leans forward and throws another branch to land in its heart. There is a sharp hiss and the flames leap momentarily higher. The Neanderthal nearest the fire is briefly lit and we notice that he is sawing something with a flint knife, holding the item tightly between his front teeth. We also notice a thread around his neck. It is a sinew necklace holding a small shiny object, possibly a shell; the fire has dimmed again and it is difficult to tell. With a start, we realise that the object rests on the swell of a breast. This is a Neanderthal woman! We grin at each other in embarrassment but there is no need to apologise for our mistake. Through the gloom and smoke of the cave, both sexes look remarkably alike.

Wearing jewellery at this time was almost certainly symbolic: it portrayed a message. Could the Neanderthal woman have been saying something about herself? The shell may have marked her out as having travelled to the sea, or that she had relatives in that part of the world. Nevertheless, would the others have understood the message? What this demands is abstract thought, an advanced form of intelligence thought to be held exclusively by modern humans. In effect, the shell stands for so much more than merely a shell; it becomes a metaphor for a host of other ideas and thoughts. To understand it fully requires a degree of comprehension that brings together a variety of disparate ideas and links them with symbolic connections. Could the Neanderthals have done this, or was a shell merely a shell?

However, shell jewellery is not the only evidence for symbolic thought attributed to Neanderthals. Art is usually assumed to be an indication of advanced thought: making something stand for something else. Although the evidence for Neanderthal art is vanishingly small, some claim to have found it. At Berekhat, in Israel, a small figure of what might be a woman was certainly made by Neanderthals, as microscopic analysis of the cut marks demonstrates.[12] Elsewhere, at La Roche-Cotard in France, other excavators have claimed that a lump of flint was modified with the addition of a bone splinter to resemble a face.[13] As with most art, however, its veracity is most certainly in the eye of the beholder. Although there are no caves that were painted by the Neanderthals, they gathered lumps of pigment, particularly red ochre and black manganese dioxide.[14] The most likely explanation is that the pigment was for painting their bodies, although whether this was for decoration or merely to fend off the strong sun is a moot point.

Although we thought we heard the Neanderthals singing, some think that they went further still and actually made musical instruments. Moreover, an appreciation of music would support the view that Neanderthals had an advanced level of intelligence. At Divje Babe Cave in Slovakia, the excavator, Ivan Turk, found an 11cm hollow thigh bone from a bear with two or more holes pierced into its surface. It looked just like a flute and since it was found near to what may have been a fire, images of Neanderthals gathered around the blaze and enjoying an impromptu music recital caught the imagination.[15]

In some caves, although not all with Neanderthal remains, archaeologists have found piles of cave-bear bones and skulls, some seemingly placed in stone-lined pits.[16]

At Régordou, the bones were from the brown bear but at Drachenloch, in the Swiss Alps, the bones were from the now extinct cave bear, a huge and ferocious predator, much bigger than a modern grizzly bear. Did the Neanderthals recognise its strength and collect the skulls in homage to it? Were the bone caches actually shrines for worship in some primitive cult of the cave bear?

As we leave the cave of the Neanderthals, we have discovered little that is new. These people remain enigmatic. They certainly looked like humans but did they think in the same way that we do? It is impossible to say outright but the evidence, albeit circumstantial, is persuasive. Surely we can draw some conclusions? Well, sadly not. For every step towards revealing Neanderthal beliefs, there seem to be two steps back. In the grave at Shanidar, 'flower power', as we shall see, had more to do with mouse than man.

Chapter 2

MORE MOUSE THAN MAN

The famous Shanidar flower burial may not have been all that it first appears to be. The Persian jird, a small gerbil-like rodent, also likes to visit the same caves that the Neanderthals inhabited – they make their nests in them. These nests are then provisioned with their favourite food, flower heads, which the jird stores in great numbers. In fact, the larder of the Persian jird would be more than enough to account for all of the flower pollen found with the Shanidar burial. The bouquets of mourning Neanderthal relatives may have been nothing more than a rodent's food store.[1]

Although the goat horns around the young boy at Teshik-Tash were certainly placed there by the Neanderthals themselves, they may be less extraordinary than they first appear. Of the 768 non-rodent bones in the cave, that is, bones that would have probably been brought in by the Neanderthals rather than occurring naturally, 760 were from mountain goats.[2] Clearly, goat featured regularly on the menu and the horns may have been lying around anyway, providing a convenient digging pick to fashion the grave pit. There was no symbolism involved in the act, merely a straightforward approach to solving a practical problem: how to dig the grave. The haunches of meat at Chapelle-aux-Saints and even the red deer jawbone at Amud may have been chance occurrences; bones moved about in the cave by scavengers or the movement of sediments over thousands of years, leaving a picture whose apparent story is false.

Similarly, under scrutiny, the bear skulls that appear to have been cached in the stone-lined pits reveal no cut marks, indicating that the heads fell off naturally after death. Indeed, in some caves with bear bones, no Neanderthal presence has ever been detected. The remains seem to be no more than a striking coincidence when a number of skulls and bones were moved about by water flowing into the cave and were caught up within some blocks of stone that had fallen from the ceiling. It may have even been a hibernating bear itself that swung its paw over the cave floor to make some room for its bed and swept the remains of its distant relations into the corner. These were not shrines of an ancient bear cult, but rather natural accumulations of bones that were big enough to have become trapped together.[3]

Finally, the shell necklace that we saw was probably just a crude copy from a more recent occupant of those snowy lands: modern humans. Although Neanderthals had Europe to themselves for thousands and thousands of years, from about 40,000 years ago to when they finally died out around 30,000 years ago, they shared the continent with our earliest forebears. The last Neanderthals seem to have copied these modern people, fashioning similar tools and even wearing similar body decorations.[4] There are two explanations for this. A minority see the Neanderthals as having reached a degree of sophistication whereby they had begun to develop the advanced patterns of thought necessary to understand and appreciate art, culture, and symbolic representation.[5] The other view is that it is just too coincidental that this happened only when modern humans appeared. Rather than developing these behaviours themselves, the Neanderthals were mimicking what they saw modern people do.[6] Whether they ever understood the symbolic importance of what they were doing is extremely unlikely. In short, their brains were just not up to it.

Neanderthals had bodies far more adapted to the cold environment than ours. Their frames were stocky with short limbs to conserve heat, their noses were large and flared to warm and humidify the cold air that they breathed, and their brains were larger than those of modern humans.[7] However, despite its size, it is unlikely that the Neanderthal brain had the myriad of neural connections that are contained within a modern human brain and it is these connections that are crucial to advanced intelligence. Neanderthals probably had little conception of the past or even of the future; they lived only in the present moment.[8] The abundance of tools found in some Neanderthal encampments suggest that they would make a tool for a particular purpose but then would just as readily abandon it when their task was completed. Similarly, many of the tools that they made were generic rather than specialised for a particular task – a one-size-fits-all solution. There appears to have been little forward planning in their world.

It was not that the Neanderthals did not have a store of wisdom that they could draw upon in their everyday lives, but that, rather, this is all that they had.[9] They could remember (and presumably learn from a parent) how to do a certain task but they could not innovate to find a better way of doing it. This is why their tools and way of living remained essentially unchanged for thousands of years. This lack of joined-up thought makes it seem almost impossible that they could think symbolically. An object, such as shell, could only ever be a shell; it could not stand for something else, such as a far-away relative, a memory of a visit to the sea, or a symbol of belonging to a family group. This type of thought was beyond a Neanderthal. When we saw the Neanderthal wearing the shell necklace, she had almost certainly copied (or even obtained) it from a modern human; she must have liked wearing it but likely had no thoughts beyond that. To a Neanderthal, such jewellery had no symbolic meaning at all. This is probably true for all the suggested examples of Neanderthal art. The objects were certainly made by Neanderthals but were probably aborted tools or random marks created in ways that are now lost to us. They were neither symbolic nor were they created for their beauty. Even the flute, on closer inspection, has been revealed to have been formed when a carnivore bit the bone and left two round puncture marks with its teeth.[10] If the Neanderthals did ever sit around the fire on an evening, it certainly was not to listen to music.

If Neanderthals had no symbolic thought, it is very unlikely that they had developed that pinnacle of symbolic usage: speech. Words are perhaps the ultimate symbol, since a series of sounds always stands for something else. Steve Mithen makes a convincing argument that, although Neanderthals would have used sounds for communication (and may have even sung at times of social stress, such as burials) they were not refined into speech as we would know it.[11] In the same way as I understand that different barks from my dog mean different things, and might therefore comprehend his meaning, so Neanderthals probably understood what another was communicating to them. However, just as my dog might bark that he is hungry or bark that there is someone at the door, he would never be able to bark that there is somebody hungry at the door; such joined up meanings would be beyond him and were likely to have been beyond Neanderthals.

Of course, this is to judge Neanderthals compared to our own species rather than accepting them on their own terms; they were supremely adapted to their frozen environment and were undoubtedly the first pan-European people.[12] They survived for almost a quarter of a million years and toughed out a succession of Ice Ages and the occasional warmer interlude. They might be around still if it was not for the arrival of the other species of human around at the time: us. However, this was not some colonialist policy of extermination on our part but rather a gradual out-competing, in a similar way that the grey squirrel has ousted the red from much of its former haunts. Ezra Zubrow, an expert on the effects of varying rates of reproduction on populations, has calculated that a difference in infant mortality between Neanderthals and modern humans of only 2 per cent would have wiped out the Neanderthals in 30 generations, or about 1000 years.[13]

Such a difference could easily have been caused by climatic changes. Neanderthals were used to the odd warming of the earth and, before modern humans were around, they could muddle through by themselves. Once they had competition, however, it appears that they lost out. All the evidence suggests that Neanderthals were big meat eaters; preying on large herbivores was almost the only survival strategy that they knew. We have already seen the abundance of mountain goats at Teshik-Tash and this seems typical of their diet: monotonous, meat-rich, and taken from a narrow range of species.[14] Modern humans, by contrast, took their nutrition from a far wider range of sources: small mammals, birds, fish, and vegetation.[15] When the climate warmed, and the larger game animals were perhaps less abundant, modern humans had the edge. Not only could they fashion specialist tools to make the remaining large game animals easier to catch, they could also fall back upon other sources of food. When episodes of warming had happened before, the Neanderthals had retreated to areas where they could wait out the conditions before bouncing back. This time, however, there was no place to go.[16] Out-competed in obtaining food, their birth rate declined and, as Ezra Zubrow has shown, this would very

rapidly prove fatal. By sometime around 30,000 years ago, Neanderthals were effectively extinct.

So, what can we conclude about Neanderthal beliefs? Did they have any?
Certainly, the flowers, the bear skulls, the flute, and even the jewellery came to nothing, but what of the burials themselves? Surely these provide evidence of care of the
dead, evidence that could be extended to imply a belief in the soul's journey to an
afterlife? Once again, probably not. Just because Neanderthals sometimes buried
their dead, it does not necessarily imply that there was any symbolic or ideological
reason for doing so.[17] It is just as likely that the dead were buried to get them out
of the way, rather as they might have buried bones and food waste to maintain a
relative level of sanitation within the cave.[18] This is not to suggest that Neanderthals
were treating dead bodies as potential food. Although there are signs that some
early Neanderthals ate their dead, such as the cave at Krapína in Croatia where 800
Neanderthal bones (out of 850) had been butchered and cracked open to obtain
the meat and marrow (something only other Neanderthals could have done), no
creature survives long as a cannibal. It is likely that cannibalism supplemented rather
than comprised the Neanderthal diet.[19] Furthermore, burials in caves are extremely
rare and probably represent only the few who died while inside them.[20] For the
others, out in the world, they were probably just left where they fell.[21] Neanderthals
likely buried their dead since it was the most practical thing to do with them; that
they chose to place them in the foetal position only saved them from digging a
larger pit. The grief that they felt may not have moved beyond an immediate feeling
of bewilderment and loss, and certainly did not lead to complex thoughts about
where the soul went after death.

However, there is one burial at Leiria, in Portugal, where a young Neanderthal
child was buried with a great deal of care. Several objects were placed in the grave,
including a seashell pendant and the bones of red deer and rabbit, and the body was
wrapped in a shroud, stained red with ochre.[22] Surely these items were not for use by
the child but rather for its soul after death? Is this, finally, evidence of Neanderthal
belief? A careful analysis of the bones suggests otherwise. Whereas the trunk and leg
bones are of the usual Neanderthal stockiness, the arms are gracile and more akin to
a modern human. The evidence for a chin seems to confirm that one of the parents
of this child was Neanderthal, perhaps the mother, but that the father was a modern
human. The child was of mixed species.[23] How the parents met and raised a child
is not something we will ever know, nor how the child was treated in life, whether
as a Neanderthal or as a modern human. Nevertheless, the evidence in the grave is
unmistakable. This is like no other Neanderthal burial we know. In death, the child
achieved what no Neanderthal had done before: its soul journeyed to the afterlife,
where it might enjoy the items that were buried with the body, or so those left
behind probably believed. To discover more about these wonderful new beliefs, we
must now leave the Neanderthals behind and join our own kind: the first modern
humans in Europe.

Chapter 3

DAWN OF THE SPIRITS

We find ourselves by another grave (this far back in time, graves are often the only evidence we have that people lived here at all). It is bitterly cold, although the men who have just finished digging the shallow pit are sweating hard. We move away from them, finding the powerful odour of their bodies almost unbearable. We stop at a small group crouched around the body of a boy. He looks young, barely a teenager, and he is dressed in the most amazing clothes. Draped about him and sewn into his tunic are strings of beads and polished teeth. They must have taken hours and hours to make. A pendant lies on his chest and you point out an animal carved from ivory by his side, a mammoth perhaps. There is also a mammoth tusk and what appears to be the leg bone from a human, now yellowed with age. These items are all destined for the grave. We wonder at the wealth of these people, that they can confine such riches to the ground. Why would they do such a thing? We look at each other in awe.

Although we did not see it ourselves, next to the newly dug grave of the boy was another grave, this one holding a girl of around eight years old. The two graves were part of a group of five from Sunghir, in eastern Russia.[1] The girl had been dressed in a similar way to the boy, with over 5000 beads attached to her clothes. She wore a beaded cap and had ivory discs and lances by her side. She also had two pierced antler batons, which are variously described as spear straighteners or ceremonial objects. In this instance, the latter makes more sense. As we have seen, the boy had a similar number of ivory beads sewn into his clothing, a beaded cap, an ivory pendant, a mammoth sculpture, and a whole tusk by his side. He also had a human leg bone stuffed full of ochre and, unlike the girl, had a number of fox teeth sewn into his belt.[2] Perhaps fox teeth were specific to males? It has been estimated that each ivory bead took 45 minutes to make; this means the entire number worn by the girl would have taken in excess of 3750 hours.[3] This was a massive investment of time; the modern equivalent in terms of value would be almost too enormous to quantify. In fact, the task could probably have only been undertaken by an entire community working together. To dress individuals in this way and then put them in the earth only makes sense if there is an expectation that the person will be able to make use of the clothes and the objects after they are dead. It is the first sign we have that people believed not only that a person's soul survived them after death, but that the soul also continued its existence somewhere else: the afterlife.

The other aspect of the Sunghir burials that appears strange is that children were singled out for such elaborate burials. The other burials from the group, a male placed directly above the children, a skull from another individual, and various limb-bone fragments, had far poorer burials. Why were these children so special? They may have been the offspring of an important person, perhaps the chief, but since the interval between the two burials could have been up to 200 years, this seems unlikely (we might expect the children of intervening chiefs to be buried in a similar fashion but no further child burials have been found). More likely perhaps, is that the children were judged to have special powers. They may have had prophetic dreams, suffered from epilepsy (an illness often singled out as demonstrating unusual ability), or were otherwise deemed to be in touch with hidden, supernatural forces.

Other burials at this time also seem to have been special in some way. At Paviland, in Wales, the 'Red Lady' burial has recently been re-dated as one of the earliest in Europe. If I had been writing this a short time ago, I would have stated that the burial took place about 26,000 years ago, when the Ice Age was at its height. Following more sophisticated dating techniques, however, this age has increased by 3000 years to mean that the burial actually occurred during one of the warmer interludes, a far more reasonable proposition.[4] The people of the time took one of their dead, a man of about 27 years old, and brought him to a remote cave to be buried.[5] Unlike the Neanderthals, who only used caves for burials because they were convenient, the 'Red Lady' was deliberately brought to a cave to be buried there. Perhaps the cave was considered a special, even a sacred place, and the man was correspondingly considered equally special. He was dressed in leather clothes – shirt, trousers, and moccasins – and buried in a shallow pit with a stone on which to rest his head and feet.[6] A skull of a mammoth sat nearby, perhaps watching over the dead man, and a number of broken ivory rods and bracelets were placed on his chest. Maybe the rods were even used in the burial ritual, rather like magic wands or, perhaps, more prosaically, they were blanks for cutting beads. A bag decorated with periwinkles also lay on the man's thigh. Before the body was covered, it was liberally sprinkled with red ochre, staining the clothes and even the bones a deep red. Many years after the burial, the cave was intermittently reused and more items were left there, including carved human figures. It seems that the sanctity of the cave persisted.

At Brno, in the Czech Republic, another man was buried far from any settlement site, indicating that the place must have been chosen for other reason, perhaps because it too was considered special or sacred.[7] Again, the man was strewn with ochre and had a head covering with 600 dentalium shells sewn into it. He also had mammoth tusks, a rhino skull, the teeth of a horse, and stone discs accompanying him in the grave. However, there was also a unique item: an ivory marionette of a human figure, the arms and legs joined to the body so that they could move independently. It is possible that the man used the marionette in magical performances and the addition of a possible drumstick in the grave adds another element to these performances. Similar marionettes are used in another culture, far removed in time but perhaps not in focus, since the Inuit peoples carve figurines of humans for use in their shamanic rituals.[8] As the Brno man was clearly very closely identified with these items (after all, they were confined to his grave) it is possible that he was a shaman[9] or, at least, the Palaeolithic equivalent of a shaman.[10]

After Sunghir, we are back at another grave, this time at a place called Dolní Věstonice in the Czech Republic. We watch as three bodies are laid in a large but very shallow pit: a woman between two young men. The people conducting the burial take care to arrange the bodies, and each is positioned to touch another. We recognise the beads and pierced teeth the bodies wear, although not as many as we saw at Sunghir, and the few items that are placed next to them, mostly ornaments and tools. You point at an approaching woman as the others move back to let her through. She holds a small container of something red, which we recognise as ochre. She sprinkles the ochre liberally over the heads of the dead bodies, and then across the groin of the woman; as she does so, we notice that the woman was badly disabled in life, her leg deformed and her spine crooked. There is a low murmuring as the woman's groin is coloured red and, again, it seems as if this means something to the assembled mourners. Finally, branches are placed on top of the bodies and, all of a sudden, set alight. We feel the momentary heat of the blaze as each person throws handfuls of earth onto the grave, extinguishing the flames as quickly as they arose. You look at me and I shrug – who knows what all of this means to the people around us.

The ochre we saw sprinkled over the bodies was mirrored at Paviland, where the body was stained red as a result, and also at Brno. At Sunghir, the human leg bone buried with the boy was filled with ochre. In all, 27 burials at this time, a remarkably high percentage, have colourant in the grave, mostly ochre.[11] The clear similarity between the colour of the pigment and the colour of blood suggests that ochre was considered to contain some sort of life force. Perhaps it was designed to mark the soul's transition to an existence in the afterlife and further reaffirmed people's belief in this alternative realm. The sudden spark of flame at Dolní Věstonice may represent much the same thing. Moreover, the covering of the woman's groin with pigment suggests that there may even have been a fourth human in the grave: a foetus, its remains lost to the ravages of time.[12]

The badly disabled woman at Dolní Věstonice[13] is mirrored by the man at Brno, who suffered from the bone disease periostitis, and also by other burials at this time, which contain individuals who were disabled in some way.[14] If these people were singled out for special treatment (and, from their burials, it is clear that they were), it was despite their terrible disabilities or perhaps even because of them. Shamans from more recent times are often disabled or are otherwise distinguished through an initiatory illness and it is possible that this attitude has roots that stretch back into the Palaeolithic.[15]

The burial of three individuals together at Dolní Věstonice also has its echo in other burials of the time. At Sunghir, we have seen how a boy and a girl were buried head-to-head in a long grave, although not at the same time. Similarly, within the caves at Barma Grande, in Italy, an adult male was buried with two adolescents, a male and a female.[16] Although this triple burial was transverse to the cave, other burials follow the axis of the cave in their alignment, as if it was important that the location be reflected in the positioning of the individual.[17] If these places were considered special in their own right, then perhaps this is not surprising. At Předmostí in the Czech Republic, there is a large burial of some eight adults and 12 children but with a trail of single human bones and assorted animal bones leading to the south and south-east.[18] The south-east is the direction from which the midwinter sun rises and this may be the first indication that early people were watching the sunrise and orientating parts of their world around it. As we shall see, this will take on far greater importance as time progresses.

At Dolní Věstonice, close to the triple burial, were fragments of a limestone rod, marked with 29 scratched lines. The arrangement of these lines may refer to the phases of the moon.[19] If so, then it is yet another indication that people of the Palaeolithic were concerned with things beyond this world. If the people in the graves were the shamans of the time, then the moon phase rods at Dolní Věstonice give an indication of the knowledge that they held.

As with many recent shamans, there are signs that people feared them and the power that they wielded. Many of the burials were covered; we saw at Dolní Věstonice how the bodies were obscured by wooden branches and how these were set alight before being covered with earth. In other cases, the shoulder blades from mammoths covered the bodies.[20] In addition, at Kostenki in Russia and at other burials at Dolní Věstonice, the remains were tightly bound, with arms and legs tied close to the body.[21] If these people were feared in life, perhaps their souls were also feared in death and the bodies were covered and bound to keep them from rising again and disturbing the living.[22]

If these burials do represent the shamans of the Ice Age, then these shamans would have spent their lives interacting with the supernatural and speaking of things that others could not see. That people understood and respected the shamans seems borne out in the lavish way that they furnished their graves, leaving items of incredible value that the deceased could take with them to the afterlife. The Neanderthals we met in the previous chapters could never have conceived of such a thing; their brains were simply not up to it. But why not? What makes people like us so special?

Chapter 4

REMEMBERING THE DREAM

On 24 November 1974, Don Johanson was going to have a quiet day writing up his field notes in his camp, a simple arrangement located in the Hadar region of Ethiopia. One of his students, Tom Gray, had other ideas and persuaded Johanson to join him on another hunt for the fossil remains of our earliest ancestors. Little was either of them to know that the day would go down in history, for among the baked and blistered earth was a scattering of bones. Almost complete, and named Lucy by the team, she is one of the most important hominin remains to have ever been found.[1]

However, Lucy was a long way from what we would regard as 'human'.[2] Belonging to a species called *Australopithecine afarensis* (meaning 'southern ape from afar' and dating to between 3.3 to 2.8 million years ago), she would have walked upright (thereby confirming her claim to be an early hominin) but, apart from that, she was essentially an ape. She probably foraged for food on the ground and in trees like any modern-day chimpanzee but, when she crossed the open savannah, she would have walked bipedally, on two legs, just like we do. Lucy is not the oldest hominin species: that distinction belongs to *Australopithecine anamensis*, who was walking upright from about 4.2 million years ago. The first remains of *A. anamensis* were only identified a little over a decade ago.[3]

Lucy's species led to *Australopithecine africanus* (meaning 'southern ape from Africa' and dating from between 3 to 2 million years ago). The most celebrated remains came from Taung in South Africa and were studied by Raymond Dart, the newly appointed Professor of Anatomy for the region.[4] Due to Dart's perceived inexperience, the find was ignored for almost a decade until more fossils emerged from the same site and were recognised for what they were: a new species of early hominin. Although Dart claimed that *A. africanus* were hunters, it is more likely that they were the hunted and lived on their wits to avoid the large predators that abounded at the time. They were also unlikely to have used fire or even made stone tools. Although *A. africanus* was on the way to becoming human, it still had a long road to travel.

All the *Australopithecine* species we have looked at so far are called 'gracile' because that is what they were: small and lightly built. However, there was another type of *Australopithecine* around at the time, called *Australopithecine robustus*.[5] These were heavier and thicker set, although the bite marks in the back of the remains of a skull from Swartkrans in South Africa shows that they were still hunted. Despite their stature, *A. robustus* went extinct, perhaps as a result of environmental pressures but perhaps because they were hunted by something other than leopards. While *A. robustus* was trying to make its way in the world, the graciles had developed into a completely new species: *Homo*, human.

Olduvai Gorge in Kenya had yielded many tools over the years but no evidence of their maker. That was until 1960, when Louis and Mary Leaky thrilled the world by finding a skull that was far more human-like than *Australopithecine*.[6] Called *Homo habilis* (meaning 'handy human', due to its tool-making ability) it lived between 2.2 and 1.6 million years ago. Since *H. habilis* was discovered, new intermediate species have surfaced, but the next big leap seems to have been to *Homo erectus* (meaning 'upright human', and dating to between 1.6 million to 500,000 years ago). Moreover, this species did something that no other had done before: it travelled. Found as far away as Java and China, it clearly spread out of Africa.[7] However, despite being found in Georgia, it seems that *H. erectus* did not colonise Europe.[8] Perhaps the altering seasons were more than it could cope with or perhaps the large carnivores were too much of a threat.[9] Whatever the reason, the earliest human remains found in Europe were of a later species, *Homo heidelbergensis* (named after Heidelberg, in Germany, where the first remains were discovered).[10] *H. heidelbergensis* probably emerged around 600,000 years ago but quickly gave way, by about 400,000 years ago, to two other species with which we are familiar. In Europe, *H. heidelbergensis* gave rise to *Homo neanderthalensis*, the Neanderthals we have already met, but in Africa *H. heidelbergensis* gave rise to *Homo sapiens*, modern humans: us.

There is still debate about how *H. sapiens* came to colonise the world. A minority see *H. erectus* evolving into *H. sapiens* independently on each continent.[11] However, the majority see *H. sapiens* leaving Africa and beginning a huge migration that was to take them to Australia by 60,000 years ago, Europe by 40,000 years ago, and America by 15,000 years ago.[12] Although some interbreeding with existing *Homo* populations is possible, evidence from DNA analysis rules out any meaningful integration.[13] The first remains of *H. sapiens* in Europe (although not the oldest) were found at Cro-Magnon Caves in France. Cro-Magnon means 'big hole' in old French and it stuck as the name for all modern humans in Europe during the Palaeolithic. Mercifully, the name retained its French form and we have already seen the graves of some of these people in the previous chapter.

How *H. sapiens* ousted their close kin from around the world is still not fully understood. However, the reason that they did so is clear from the name: *Homo sapien* means 'wise human' and it was their brains that enabled them, or rather, us, to outcompete and, ultimately, outlast every other human species that had ever been before. But what is it about our brains that is so different from all the rest?

Of all the archaeologists who study the brain, Steve Mithen is perhaps the most compelling.[14] Keeping a flowing metaphor, he compares the development of the brain to a cathedral. At the very earliest stage, perhaps relating to the *Australopithecines*, there was only a central nave of generalised intelligence. This contained general purpose learning and decision making rules. It could be modified in the light of experience but behaviour was simple and learning painfully slow. During the next stage, separate chapels formed around the central nave; these were domains of specialised intelligence relating to social interaction, natural history, and technical accomplishment. Perhaps *H. habilis* had micro-domains but they are more evident in the later pre-modern humans. However, and it is a big qualification, there was no access between the chapels: each domain was independent from all the rest. This meant that a thought about tool making could not be linked to knowledge of natural history. Accordingly, although pre-modern humans made tools, they were never specific to any particular hunting strategy. If such a thought arose, it had to be processed in the central nave with the limited amount of general intelligence that was held there. That is why pre-modern humans sometimes seem very advanced (when they used their domains of intelligence) but then seem very basic (when they needed to join up the domains and could not do so). In fact, the largest domain at the time was for governing social intelligence, the ability to live in large, co-operative groups, and we have seen the success arising from this increased intelligence with the Neanderthals being able to take care of their sick and lame.

It was not until the rise of modern humans that the last stage was reached, the chapels started to develop doors to one other, and knowledge from each domain began to flow and combine in new and innovative ways: the cathedral was formed. Specialist tools were created by combining the domain of technical accomplishment with the domain of natural history, but that was not all. By combining the previously separate domains, something could now stand for something else. For example, a good food provider could be honoured (social intelligence) and compared to a fox (natural history intelligence). A fox may even become the totem of this person and perhaps this is why people of the time were buried with fox teeth. This is symbolic thought, making something stand for something else, and it made us who we are today.

There are many ideas as to what triggered this last stage, but most centre around small genetic mutations that allowed for brain development, especially in the direction of language.[15] Nursing mothers probably always burbled to their offspring as a way of bonding. This developed into common noises that stood for certain objects, tasks, and emotions, and that made sense to the wider community. This was the type of language available to humans prior to *H. sapiens* (and we have examined the language ability of Neanderthals, for example, in chapter 2). Genetic mutation in the brain allowed these noises to develop syntax and grammar until a sophisticated, symbolic language evolved where a number of words could be joined up and, depending on their combination, could stand for something.[16] Moreover, people did not necessarily need to have heard that combination of words previously to understand what they stood for. As language took on symbolic form, so other aspects of thought also took on symbolic form until something from one domain of intelligence could stand for something else in another domain of intelligence and the wall between them was breeched.

However, despite the importance of intelligence (and resulting language development) in the evolution of the mind, there is another element that sets modern humans apart: our consciousness. Our minds are not only different from earlier models by what they can do but also by what they can comprehend. Pre-modern humans were probably aware of things in the world but not of a past or a future, and certainly not of themselves as conscious beings. This is called 'primary consciousness'.[17] Modern humans, however, are aware of both past and future, as well as having an awareness of themselves as conscious beings. This is called 'higher-order consciousness'.[18] It is the ability to remember and to have an enhanced working memory that can hold several concepts simultaneously and work on them holistically that becomes crucial.[19] Moreover, consciousness does not just include the rational, waking mind, but also other states, such as sleep and trance (called altered states of consciousness). These altered states are as real and as important to our consciousness as any other element. However, although all higher-order mammals can enter altered states, only modern humans have the capacity to remember the experience, because only we have higher-order consciousness. Furthermore, because higher-order consciousness also gives us self-awareness, we can analyse, explain, and learn from our experiences in these alternative states of dream and trance.

While the industrialised world may have rejected trance experiences as something degenerate and to be avoided, in the non-industrialised world over 90 per cent of peoples have culturally patterned forms of altered states of consciousness.[20] For them, trance is not some strange unnatural 'trip' but something commonplace and, moreover, useful. From brain-imaging through EEG, it appears that trance causes a degree of instability in our mental processing that causes new connections to be made between neurons, the basic cells that make up the brain. The result can be realignment both of the understanding of the self (something that defines higher-order consciousness) and also of the world it inhabits.[21] Moreover, it is the frontal lobe of the brain that it stimulated during trance, and this is the area associated with working-memory (a vital part of the modern mind).[22]

Although pre-modern humans would not have remembered their experiences of trance, they almost certainly had them; staring into a fire throughout an evening may have been enough to trigger such a state.[23] Over time, this repeated experience of trance across countless generations may have allowed certain traits of thought and behaviour to become established (i.e. 'This is a good thing, I must keep doing it'). Although this in itself would not have directly caused the genetic mutation behind the evolution of the human mind, these traits could have set the conditions for a gradual genetic shift from primary to higher-order consciousness.[24] In effect, it was trance that made us human.

Trance is also good for problem solving.[25] We instinctively recall this when we 'sleep' on a problem, hoping that a solution will present itself overnight. If modern humans of the Palaeolithic regularly entered trance, then the edge that it would have given them in solving problems may help to explain why they out-competed the Neanderthals.[26] Again, it was trance that made us what we are. However, trance is not only about problem solving; it is also about journeying to an alternative realm. To return to sleeping, when we dream the world we inhabit is very different from our waking world but it is nevertheless very real to us, at least, while we are asleep. Once humans could start remembering their dreams, and had a language capable of communicating them to others, it is likely that the experiences they had while asleep began to form an important part of their world. This was coupled with an enhanced awareness of the self, and a consciousness of being conscious. It would not have been long, therefore, before people would have begun to wonder where someone went when they died. The answer, to them, might have been very apparent: since death resembles sleep, and the land of dreams was well known, it is likely that they thought that the dead, or at least their consciousness (here, read 'soul') went somewhere similar: the afterlife was born. This is why modern humans buried their dead with objects to take with them, whereas no other pre-modern human could ever have conceived of such a thing. That a similar realm could also be accessed in trance would have only compounded their belief that there was a different reality, an *otherworld*, that could be accessed through trance, through dreams, and through death.

At this point, it would be useful to understand what these people saw when they entered trance and journeyed to the otherworld and, fortuitously, we can do just that. Our brains are essentially the same as those humans that lived during the Palaeolithic; we can enter trance ourselves and experience something very similar to what they did. Although the actual detail might be culturally conditioned, the basic experience of trance is common to us all. It is time to see what this otherworld of the Palaeolithic looked like.

Chapter 5

JOURNEY TO THE OTHERWORLD

I was in a room with many other people. My eyes were covered and I lay wrapped in a blanket. Someone drummed over me, the repetitive beats thumping out a steady rhythm. I lay quite still, waiting to see what would happen. Before long, shapes appeared in the darkness before me and these quickly formed into a spiralling tunnel. I moved down it, feeling like I was being sucked along at great speed. There was a dim glow at its end and I knew that this was what I should aim for. Eventually I emerged. I stood at the edge of a vast landscape, filled with trees and rivers, lakes and mountains: I had entered the otherworld.

We have already seen how the brains of those who lived during the Palaeolithic were almost identical to our own, and, therefore, we can conduct research on the modern brain and then apply it to the past.[1] In this case, I was using my own. In our normal, waking consciousness, we are in what is called a 'beta state'. We can concentrate on what we are doing, be aware of the world around us, and also process other thoughts and anxieties. If we relax, perhaps by becoming engrossed in an activity or through light meditation, our brain waves slow and we enter an alpha state. If our brain waves slow still further, we enter a theta state, an altered state of consciousness.[2] This corresponds to either trance or, paradoxically, intense alertness.

There is a reason for this apparent paradox and it has to do with the way our brains manage our body.[3] The 'sympathetic' system of brain activity responds to either positive or negative stimuli; it creates arousal in the body through pleasure or pain. The 'parasympathetic' system looks after all the automatic processes, like eating, digesting, and sleep patterns. Since this system works best with no arousal, it tends towards quiescence, that is, complete calm and stillness. The two, therefore, usually work in opposition, regulating the way our bodies work. However, it is also possible to push either system to an extreme. In the case of the sympathetic system, hyper-arousal is associated with physical activities that totally overtake us so that we reach a state of flow, where everything but the activity itself is removed and we feel a rush of energy.

In the case of the parasympathetic system, hyper-quiescence is associated with sleep but also with deep meditative experiences, where the mind begins to empty and focus rests only on the experience itself. This can also occur with repetitive chanting or prayer. Beyond hyper-arousal or hyper-quiescence is a further state where one system, although usually kept quite separate, overflows into the other. This happens, for example, when we reach a point of hyper-arousal where the activity we are engaged in brings waves of peace and tranquillity, as if we have moved outside of our bodies and are experiencing complete and utter stillness. (This often happens immediately after sexual activity.) The sympathetic system has overflowed and the feelings we are getting are associated with the parasympathetic system. Conversely, when we reach a point of hyper-quiescence through meditation, we may suddenly feel an energy rush, as if we have left our bodies and have merged with a source of power beyond ourselves. The parasympathetic system has overflowed and the feelings we are getting are associated with the sympathetic system. In both cases, where one system overflows into another, we are left with an out-of-body experience that is at the heart of trance experience. When I was in trance, for example, I left my body behind to move down a tunnel or, at least, that is how it felt to me.

It was drumming that enabled me to enter trance. The regular beat of the drum slowed my brainwave pattern and caused hyper-quiescence. Eventually, this began to overflow and I felt the rush of energy and out-of-body experience that allowed me to move into the otherworld. However, there are many different ways of entering trance, some creating hyper-arousal, such as dancing, intense physical activity, or extreme emotional trauma (many car accident victims report leaving their bodies and observing events from a place of stillness), or hyper-quiescence, such as sensory deprivation, ritual chanting or prayer, and listening to a repetitive sound.[4] In all cases, brainwaves slow and trance, or an altered state of consciousness, will be achieved. Certain drugs provoke a comparable response, although they do so through a chemical stimulation of the brain. This inhibits the production of serotonin, responsible for transmitting stimulus from the body to the brain, and thereby causes hyper-quiescence.

The first aspect of trance is sometimes (but not always) the appearance of patterns before the eyes.[5] This is caused by what opthalomists call entoptic phenomena, since the patterns are created within the eye with no outside stimuli. The shapes themselves are called phosphenes.[6] These can be flecks, hashed lines, zigzags, and starbursts, and will be familiar to anyone who has experienced distorted vision through migraine, as the imagery is the same. Interestingly, these same images often crop up in the doodles of young children, suggesting that their production comes before, and is quite independent of, developed analytical thought.[7] The second aspect of trance is more universally experienced, as the phosphenes converge and a tunnel or vortex appears to open up. This is due to a spiralling stimulus within the brain cells that are activated at this time, giving the appearance of a tunnel.[8] Nevertheless, the compulsion to go down it is strong. After a while of travelling through the tunnel, there is a light at the end and, as this gets nearer, a landscape can often be perceived. Eventually, it is possible to step out of the tunnel and enter the landscape. Although many aspects will appear familiar, especially since there will be an initial blending of imagery from several sources, including the memory, there will also be an otherworldly quality to the sensation, as if the body has been left behind and a new world of experience has opened up.[9]

As I entered deeper into trance and began to orientate myself in this alternative realm, it was as if my body had grown. My limbs stretched and felt weightless. I realised that, without much effort, I could fly. I flew over trees of all colours of green until I reached a lake. Its water was still and the deepest turquoise. I flew down to it and dived beneath the surface. I could hear the water rushing in my ears and I swam through the water with as much ease as I had flown through the air.

My experience of trance is fairly typical of the range of sensations that can occur. The perceived changes of scale can be explained by phenomena known as macropsia and micropsia, which basically means seeing things much bigger or much smaller than they usually are.[10] It is a common experience in trance. Similarly, flying and the associated activity of swimming underwater are also common experiences.[11] Indeed, those in trance often report hearing the sound of flowing water.[12]

The elongation of my limbs and a feeling of weightlessness were the first signs that my self-identity was beginning to break down. When the sympathetic and parasympathetic systems overflow, we begin to lose track of our senses and any outside stimulus completely ceases. It is at this stage that the self begins to disintegrate. In some cultures, this can be interpreted as terrible violence inflicted on the body and there are stories of Siberian shamans who felt as if they were torn apart while in trance.[13] This sensation of violence may also be linked to the amygdala, a bundle of neurons within the brain responsible for an orientating response when someone moves in an exaggerated manner (such as Siberian shamans, who often drum themselves into a frenzy of movement). This can elucidate a fear response, which may heighten the expectation of violence or, alternatively, may produce feelings of religious awe.[14]

As I left the water, I became aware of a huge animal in front of me. I was a little nervous of its size but the animal spoke to me in a soothing voice. As I moved closer to listen to its words, I marvelled at the knowledge that it held; so much of what was said resonated with something inside of me. The more I observed this animal, the more I wondered what it must feel like to live in its skin, to stretch and to move in animal form. The more I thought about the animal, the more I could feel myself taking on its form. My hands became paws, my skin became fur, and my face lengthened into a snout. It was a blissful experience.

What I had come across is what shamans and, most likely, the people of the Palaeolithic, would have recognised as one of the spirits of the otherworld. In psychological terms, I had started to hallucinate. Although visual hallucinations are more common than auditory hallucinations, I both saw the animal and heard it talk.[15] Such hallucinations occur because of the overflow of the parasympathetic into the sympathetic system (or vice versa), allowing a seepage of brain activity from the preconscious into the conscious mind.[16] Moreover, there appears to be a certain predisposition for humans to hallucinate certain elements. 'Zoopsia', the hallucination of animals, is among the most common.[17]

Although the origin of the images we hallucinate lies in the preconscious part of the brain, this still does not explain how they arise. It has been suggested that we hold knowledge about things in discrete chunks of information. A phrase such as 'church wedding' or 'having breakfast' is understood all at once and on a myriad of levels, without us consciously thinking them all through.[18] Some chunks of information seem particularly prevalent across cultures, such as the wise teacher, the trickster, or the questing hero. Jung interpreted these as archetypes stemming from what he called a collective consciousness universal to us all.[19] He may be right, as there do appear to be such latent constructs within the brain.

The wise teacher, for instance, is found in myths and traditions from many societies and even in popular culture. This may be due to an aspect of trance whereby the brain starts to project a more advanced state of wisdom onto another individual.[20] This is part of the breaking down of the self and the relinquishing of responsibility and control to something outside the body. Coupled with zoopsia, it is not surprising that many shamanic traditions speak of guardian or power animals that aid and counsel those who journey to meet them in trance. I experienced the same on my journey and much of what was imparted made me think in ways that were new and unfamiliar, presumably because my mind was working in a different way to normal. However, it need not necessarily be an animal that becomes the wise teacher but it could also be another human, either living, dead, or entirely mythical. To the people of the Palaeolithic, the appearance of the dead while they were in trance would have probably been taken as clear proof that there was an afterlife and this was where people went when they died.[21] The existence of other 'spirits' within this realm would have confirmed that it was, indeed, a world apart.

As the awareness of self breaks down in trance, so there is a corresponding feeling of unity with the rest of the world. This can manifest as a sense of alignment with the universe as a whole (the experience of mystics) or, at a more local scale, the merging with whatever being or object is currently the point of focus. In my case, it was an animal and this is why I felt myself merging and then turning into an animal form. In many cultures, this is called *shapeshifting*: the ability to take on the form and characteristics of something else.[22]

When I returned from my journey to the otherworld, I was left disorientated and wondering which state was actually real: this reality or the one I had just left. Perhaps it depends on where we are when we pose the question? However, it seemed clear that what had happened was entirely natural and even necessary for me to know fully who I am. My brain, as does yours, allows for trance as part of our spectrum of consciousness; we have evolved that way.[23] We have seen how good trance is for solving problems (especially with the 'wise teacher' archetype to help us formulate our thoughts) and also for developing the capability of our brains through the formulation of new neural connections. This gives reason enough for the capacity to enter trance to be an important part of the human condition. However, regular experience of trance in the past may have helped people to recover better from illness and injury. There is evidence, for example, that journeying to the beat of the drum can improve the immune system,[24] and for those who were already ill, the reduction in stress caused by trance may have made recovery and survival a better prospect.[25] Moreover, as we have seen, there was also the considerable comfort of having a higher power to call upon and, psychologically, the benefit may have been considerable.[26] Over time, the feelings created by the disintegration of the self and the connection and merging with a power outside of the body may have given rise to thoughts of an ultimate authority beyond human existence and even beyond the world itself. It would not have been long before religion was born and a name given to this supreme being – God.

To those humans who lived during the Palaeolithic, trance would have both expanded and explained their world. It would have helped with problem solving, with understanding the behaviour and habits of animals, and would have provided proof that there was life after death. These relate to all three of the domains associated with the evolution of the human brain: technical accomplishment, natural history, and social interaction. The experience of trance was integral for the emergence of the modern human mind and may still be so today. Since that first journey to the otherworld, I have made many others. I find it adds something to my life that is difficult to achieve in any other way; perhaps people in the past felt the same?

There has been a lot of theory in this chapter but it is now time to leave it behind. Although we can have the same biological experience of trance as those who lived in the Palaeolithic, our lives are just too different for us to be able to see exactly what they saw. However, if we are prepared to travel deep into the earth, the otherworld of the Palaeolithic may be closer than we think. The tunnel is cramped, however, and there is only the guttering light of some burning grease to guide us. This may be an uncomfortable encounter.

Chapter 6

DEEP IN THE PAINTED CAVES

We follow a small group of people deep into a cave. It is almost totally black and we struggle to keep up with the bobbing torches ahead of us. We follow a small tunnel, which sometimes requires us to crawl on our hands and knees since the ceiling is so low. The earth is cold and it begins to seep into our bones. Eventually, the tunnel ends and we emerge into a large cavern. More torches are lit and the flames dance higher up the walls. The air is still, almost suffocating, and it claws at our lungs. We turn our gaze upwards and are met with an extraordinary sight. Covering the rough surface of the walls are paintings of deer, bison, and horses. They are in flight, their powerful legs kicked up, charging around the confines of the cave. The flickering light seems to bring out the detail in their design, each sinew and curve of their bodies etched in red or black paint. We feel intoxicated, dizzy from the circling maelstrom around us. We truly have entered the otherworld.

The images found in the caves of ancient Europe are among the most celebrated remains from our early past.[1] The earliest date from around 35,000 years ago and people were still painting the caves until the very end of the Ice Age, about 11,000 years ago. Despite lasting for almost 25,000 years, much of the painting was very similar throughout the period and whatever the motivation was for creating the images, it was certainly strong. Although most of the painted caves occur in small pockets of southern France and northern Spain, examples are also known from Italy, England, and Russia.

Unlike most art traditions, which go through several stages of development, cave art seems to have emerged fully formed in Palaeolithic Europe, as if springing up from nowhere.[2] However, the mental sophistication that led to the art (and that we surveyed in chapter 4) happened much earlier, probably before our species had moved out of Africa. In fact, at Blombos Cave, South Africa, excavators found small pieces of ochre engraved with images of hashed diagonal lines, dating to about 73,000 to 80,000 years ago.[3] If these patterns seem familiar, it is because they closely resemble the phosphenes that we met in the previous chapter. Whether these were the products of trance, or were merely the random doodles of our ancient forebears (rather like the phosphenes that crop up in the doodles of young children) is difficult to tell. Merlin Donald, Professor Emeritus at Queen's University, Ontario, believes them to be what he terms 'external symbolic storage', a device whereby parts of the mind can be stored on a portable medium for later recollection.[4] By the time modern humans had reached Europe, these simple geometric designs had exploded into the massive creative output of the painted caves.[5] Just what was it about being in Europe that led to such an outpouring?

Perhaps the Neanderthals provide the answer. As we have already seen, when modern people first moved into Europe, they had to share the continent, if only for a short time, with the Neanderthals. They must have quickly realised that the Neanderthals were more limited intellectually and that the ability of modern humans to conceptualise and create art set them apart. Perhaps this is why they started painting: a way of discriminating against the neighbours and demonstrating their inherent superiority: look at what we can do and you cannot.

Many of the images painted onto the cave walls also resemble phosphenes and it was these images in particular that led David Lewis-Williams and Thomas Dowson, two South African archaeologists, to propose a daring new theory as to why people created such art.

Such theories have changed over the years since cave art was first discovered towards the end of the nineteenth century. At first, it was thought to be art for art's sake, much like the creation of many modern pieces. However, ethnographic analogy showed that this was very unlikely to be the case: art was created for a reason. The next idea, inspired in part by ethnology, was totemism, where a certain animal came to symbolise a group of people and was revered accordingly. However, most of the caves contain multiple species and many of these overlap so it seemed unlikely that the caves were shrines either for a particular animal or for a particular group associated with that animal. Hunting magic was the next idea, with people believing that the animals painted on the cave walls could magically influence the actual animals that people hunted. However, in some caves, the animals depicted were not those that were hunted at all and so the idea fell short. In the late twentieth century, mathematical models were brought to bear on the cave art and complicated symbolism was developed that tried to predict where certain species of animal were painted. The art became a code understood by the people at the time, imparting messages about themselves and their world. This gained credence until new cave art was discovered that did not adhere to the expected pattern at all. We were back to the beginning, leaving the slate clean for a new idea: that the painted caves are full of images reflecting people's experiences in trance.

Before the mid-1980s, Lewis-Williams and Dowson were more used to studying rock art in their native South Africa. Many of the paintings seemed to them to have their origins in trance imagery and this was confirmed by speaking to the San Bushmen (the descendents of those who painted the rocks). By comparing the rock paintings to the practices of the San shamans, who regularly entered trance as part of their rituals, enough parallels were evident to convince the archaeologists that the art was, indeed, shamanic.[6]

When Lewis-Williams and Dowson turned their attention to the cave art in Europe, there were no indigenous people to whom they could ask for help, and so they concentrated on the imagery itself and compared it to the stages people pass through while in trance.[7] They had already identified phospehenes, the first images seen by those entering trance. These appeared on the cave walls in among the other images. Next, they identified images where people seemed to have been trying to make sense of the phosphenes and give them some semblance of recognisable form. This is the stage of trance where awareness of the senses begins to merge with the hallucinations of trance. Finally, they identified the more developed images of animals and, very occasionally, people, with the developed hallucinations seen while in trance. Animals, as we know, are the most common forms of hallucination. This gave a three-stage model of trance to explain the paintings on the cave walls but, although it has found favour with many specialists, there are also those who vehemently disagree with its conclusions.[8] As a result, Lewis-Williams and Dowson have accepted that not all of the three stages of trance need necessarily be present in the art.[9] Nevertheless, one of the main difficulties of accepting that cave art is linked to trance is the lack of context in which to place the tradition. In South Africa, the surviving San Bushmen were shamanic and so it seemed likely that the San Bushmen who painted the rocks were also shamanic. In the Palaeolithic of Europe, this is more difficult to ascertain. However, through a comprehensive review of all the evidence, such as that undertaken by this book, it can be seen that the painted caves did not arise as an independent practice of utilising trance but were rooted in a culture that was essentially shamanic in its outlook.

Of the images painted, most were of animals, especially large herbivores, and most were outlined in red or black, utilising red haematite and black manganese oxide. Although some images show minute details of animal behaviour, such as the lion hunt at Chauvet in France, where the males have joined in the hunt with the females as their prey is particularly large.[10] Similarly, in the Hall of the Bulls at Lascaux, also in France, the horses, aurochs (an extinct variety of large cattle), and stags are each depicted in the season corresponding to their mating.[11] Alternatively, other animals appear fantastical, even mythical, such as the so-called unicorn, also from the Hall of the Bulls, which does not seem to be any particular animal but possibly an amalgamation of many. This apparent contradiction between clarity and obscurity is exactly what is experienced in trance. Moreover, the positioning of the images, tumbled together with one animal often lying over another, is also indicative of trance experience.

Since the images would have been viewed under the flickering light of a burning torch or a grease lamp (and there is evidence for both within the caves), they may have appeared to come alive and gently undulate between this world and the world of the spirits. At Niaux, in France, a bison was painted to make maximum effect of this effervescent light.[12] This undulation between the worlds suggests that people considered the rock itself as a membrane through which the spirits could pass.[13] At Gabillou, in France, for example, the head of a horse has been painted so that it looks to have emerged from a hole by its neck,[14] and in other cases the animals are not fully formed, as if part of them has yet to emerge from the otherworld. At other times, where a rock formation resembles a particular form, the features have been emphasised with the subtle addition of painted lines. At Altamira in Spain, and at Vilhonneur in France, rock protuberances that resemble faces have had features added to accentuate the likeness.[15] Animals could also pass back into the rock and the numerous bones people wedged into cracks may have been an attempt to pierce this veil.[16]

If people saw the rock itself as a membrane between the worlds, then by scraping away a little of its surface, perhaps they thought that they might fleetingly make contact with this alien realm? At Cosquer, in France, there are many small scrapes on the clay walls where people have gouged out a little of the material. Since there is no trace of it within the caves, perhaps they took it home to their own private sanctuary.[17] Elsewhere, entire images were constructed by scraping away the surface of the cave with the fingers. By measuring the size of these indents or flutings, it is possible to discern that the artists were not always adults but, in some rare instances, small children.[18] Possibly this was where people brought their children for initiation into the mysteries of adulthood. Although the likely ages seem very young to us (two to five years old), the child burials at Sunghir show that these would not have been the only children so honoured. Men, women and children also left their handprints in many of the caves.[19] Perhaps this was another way of reaching behind the veil of the rock and physically touching the otherworld? Moreover, people made the prints by blowing paint over their hand as it was held flat against the wall. Covering both hand and rock with pigment may have created the impression of moving behind the veil and reaching out to the spirits.

Taking paint in the mouth, particularly magnesium oxide, may have led to poisoning and, eventually, to hallucinations.[20] Whether the animal images were painted while the artist was in trance or whether they were painted from memories of trance is difficult to ascertain. However, the positioning of the images seems designed to highlight the main aspects of trance, possibly for those who had not yet experienced its effects. Entering the cave is a direct analogy to passing through the tunnel in trance, and the emergence into an otherworld of animal images, all tumbled out in front of the viewer in a maelstrom of pulsating forms, provides an accurate portrayal of what the otherworld can be like. The effect of the guttering light, the sensory deprivation of being in the cave, and even the odd pocket of carbon dioxide gas, may have pushed people over the edge, so that they began to supplement the images on the wall with their own hallucinations until reality exploded around them and the spirits thundered free. These were no longer *images* of the spirits people were seeing, but the spirits themselves.[21] Even the sounds of trance were replicated in the caves, through the booming of bullroarers[22] to the sound of subterranean water roaring its way through the fissures in the rock. At Chauvet, the flow of water through a hole in the cave, and doubtless the deafening sound that it made, seems to have been marked with myriad images crowding around it.[23]

Beyond the hall of the animals is an even narrower tunnel. We move slowly along it, sometimes crawling, sometimes on our bellies through the mud. I feel your touch on my feet as you crawl behind me in the darkness. This must be a very remote section of the cave. Soon, we reach the very end of the tunnel and a small chamber; the air is particularly foul here and it makes our heads swim. The burning brand held by another visitor to this stale place gutters and we fear it may not last. Fortunately, it flares again and we see before us an image on the rock. It is a man, the only one we have seen painted in the cave. But, shockingly, his head is not that of a human but of a bird and he falls backwards before the image of a bison, itself speared so that its entrails cover the ground. In the suffocating confines of the cave, such an image is disturbing.

This image is from Lascaux and is in a particularly remote section of the cave noted for its accumulation of carbon dioxide gas, perhaps designed to affect the equanimity of its viewers.[24] Many of the human figures in other caves are also in remote locations and many of them also share the characteristic of being half-human and half-something else. In the image we saw, the figure was falling backwards, as if dead, and the disembowelling of the bison seemed to mirror this. In Cougnac in France, images of bird-headed humans are speared, again emphasising the theme of death.[25] However, perhaps it was not actual death that was represented but the death of the shaman to this world as he or she journeys to the otherworld? We have seen how shapeshifting is a common experience of trance, as is violence inflicted on the body. In the images deep within the caves, we seem to have both. The inaccessibility of the figures suggests that perhaps they were not meant to be viewed. Maybe the very act of painting the image was enough; releasing the spirit of the shaman to watch over and protect the cave and its visitors. These shadowy figures have many secrets and we are only now beginning to unravel them.

It is not just in the caves that shapeshifting shamans can be found in the Palaeolithic. At the same time that the images were painted on the cave walls, there was a corresponding explosion of sculptured art. Moreover, as we shall see, it also seemed to echo themes of shamanism and trance.

Chapter 7

BRINGING THE SPIRITS TO LIFE

Nicholas Conard, an American archaeologist working in Germany, is usually very calm when he digs. He was excavating a cave called Hohle Fels during 2003 when something, in his own words, 'got my heart pumping a bit'.[1] Conard can be forgiven, for he had just lifted out of the ground a 30,000-year-old ivory carving. A wonderful find in itself, but it was when he looked closely at the subject of the carving that his heart began to race: held in his hand was a figurine that he suspected was half-lion and half-human.[2] He knew that, potentially, here was the confirmation that people in the Palaeolithic were shamanic and that they regularly shapeshifted into animals while in trance. For this was not the only half-human half-lion figurine that had been found. At Hohlenstein-Stadel, another cave in Germany, a similar figurine had been discovered in 1939.[3] As Conard puts it: 'If there are two, there must have been hundreds of these things; they must have been part of daily life'.

With the figurine, Conard also found the head of a horse and a water bird, both in ivory. The bird was stretched out, as if in flight, and it was not lost on Conard that here was another find with potentially shamanic roots. Water birds are equally at home on the water, on the land, and in the air. Consequently, in crossing between these worlds, many shamanic people believe that they can also cross between this world and the otherworld.[4] The birds were seen as messengers of the spirits.

Southern Germany is particularly rich in figurines carved out of ivory and most come from the earliest occupation of Europe by modern humans, around 32,000 years ago.[5] Although many have finely carved bodies and heads, the limbs are often stumpy with no hooves or paws, as if the figurines are flying above the ground. However, if, like the water bird, these figurines represent the spirits of the otherworld, then perhaps an ability to fly was an integral element to their form. Moreover, as if to emphasise that these animals were indeed spirits, many of the figurines have geometric patterns engraved on their sides, which match the phosphenes that are seen in trance.[6] These were not ordinary animals that were depicted but, like the paintings on the cave walls, these were animal spirits.

The figurines were often worn smooth by the hands that had carried them, or were stained red by being tied onto clothing (ochre was used as a preservative for animal hide and rubbed off with use). Unlike the cave paintings, however, which were hidden away in dark recesses, these images were made to be seen and used in everyday life. Perhaps they were similar to Native American fetishes, carried for the power that was believed to emanate from them?[7] If so, then the type of animals represented may give some indication as to what sort of power was being sought. Most of the animals represented were large land mammals and many were predators rather than prey. Moreover, many of the animals assume aggressive or threatening stances, possibly as a prelude to attack.[8] A lion from Vogelherd, in Germany, has its ears cocked back in a threatening pose, and a bear from Geißenklösterle is in a similar position.[9] It seems that it was the strength and ferocity of these animals that people sought when they made and carried the figurines. However, a beautifully crafted stallion, also from Vogelherd, was not in an aggressive pose at all but rather was in a pose that seemed designed to impress the mares.[10] Whoever carried this figurine had very different aims in mind, but then, since Conard also found an 8in, 28,000-year-old dildo in his cave at Hohle Fels, perhaps Palaeolithic man felt a little under pressure.

The figurines we have considered so far were all carved from mammoth ivory; it was one of the few materials available for Palaeolithic people to work with. The skill demonstrated by the finished pieces is immense and it is estimated that the Vogelherd horse took around 40 hours to make.[11] However, despite this level of accomplishment, people of the Palaeolithic were not thought to make anything from clay. This was considered the preserve of the first farmers, who would not appear for another 20,000 years. However, at a site we have visited before, Dolní Věstonice in the Czech Republic, people were not only making figurines out of clay, but they were also manipulating them to create dramatic and, quite literally, explosive statements about their relationship with the spirits.

Unlike virtually any other settlement that existed at this time, Dolní Věstonice and the adjacent site of Pavlov were covered in over 10,000 clay pellets and fragments of pottery figurines.[12] When these fragments came from the living areas of the site, they were heavily worn, showing that they had been carried, dropped, and even walked over during their time; they were clearly used in everyday life. However, in a nearby structure, suggestively called the 'Shaman's Hut' by the original excavator, was a kiln and within this were over 2300 shattered fragments of clay figurines. Although the local clay was quite suitable for firing, these figurines had exploded and shattered when heat was applied.[13] Furthermore, the people were doing it deliberately; the normal process of firing pottery had been intentionally changed.[14] By making a clay figurine, letting it dry, and then re-wetting it just before firing, at the correct temperature the object will explode and shatter like a firecracker going off. It seems that it was this explosion that was of prime importance to the people and not the end product; just why were they doing such a thing?

When we looked at the cave paintings, we noted how the images seemed to float in and out of the rock as if the wall of the cave was a membrane between the worlds. One moment the animal spirit was visible, the next, it was gone. It is likely that the people of Dolní Věstonice shared a similar concept except that, for them, it was not a rock wall that provided the membrane to the otherworld, but fire. Burning something makes it disappear; even the flames themselves appear to flicker into nothing. By putting the figurines into the kiln and making them explode and shatter with the application of fire, perhaps people were passing them over to the otherworld? To shamanic peoples, what is broken in this world becomes entire in the otherworld and maybe similar ideas applied at Dolní Věstonice.[15] Whether people were returning spirits to the otherworld that had fulfilled their task, or whether the animal figurines were offerings to the spirits, is impossible to tell but it seems from the number of fragments found around the living areas of the site that this was both an individual and a community-based ritual. Whether there was a particular shaman who operated the kiln in the 'Shaman's Hut' and acted as the intermediary between the people and the spirits we will probably never know. Nevertheless, it is tempting to speculate that the possible shaman's grave at Brno, which we examined in chapter 3, was broadly contemporary with the exploding figurines at Dolní Věstonice and was located only a short distance away.

One of the very few entire figurines from Dolní Věstonice is an exquisitely carved figurine of a woman. Although it is difficult to define what art and aesthetics meant to people who lived so long ago, it is hard not to conclude that whoever created this piece did so with an artist's eye.[16] Careful examination of the figurine shows a fingerprint on the back. It comes from an 11-year-old child, who was unlikely to have been its maker but was perhaps an impressed observer. The Věstonice Venus[17] has all the usual features of Palaeolithic female figurines: wide hips, a sagging belly, pendulous breasts, and emphasised buttocks. The facial features were hardly defined at all, with mere slits to resemble eyes and the extremities of the arms and legs omitted altogether. It seems that the artist wanted to emphasise only certain aspects of womanhood, and most of these seem connected to pregnancy. Another female figurine, this time from the Laussel rock shelter in France (and reminding us that not all rock art was confined to the caves but was also painted and etched in rock shelters), was engraved as if she were emerging from the rock itself, which, to the people of the time, she probably was.[18] She holds her left hand across her distended belly, but in her right she grasps a bison horn at shoulder height. The horn has 13 incised lines across it, which, for a tradition seemingly obsessed with the fertility of women, corresponds to the menstrual cycle of an entire year. Finally, as if to confirm that these images are, indeed, pregnant, the Monpazier Venus, also from France, has all the usual signs of pregnancy as well as a hugely dilated vulva, as if the woman depicted was just about to give birth.[19]

The wide distribution of these figurines across Europe hints at hugely significant ideas. That each figurine is carved slightly differently with seemingly no standard form, suggests that it was not what was carved that was important but rather the ideas behind it, and these seem to have centred on pregnancy. Indeed, at Gagarino in Russia, there is a partly sunken hut with 10 niches set around the circumference of the wall. In each niche was a Venus figurine, leading some to speculate that this was a birthing chamber.[20] However, this is not the only site in Russia where female figurines were given such prominence. At Kostenki, the partly subterranean dwellings were formed into a rough oval of about 20m by 30m, with a line of 10 large fireplaces running down the middle. Around these fireplaces, people had dug an enormous number of pits. Most of these were filled with flint tools, ivory implements (decorated with tell-tale geometric engravings), and female figurines.[21] One pit in particular had an entire figurine leaning against the side wall and facing the central line of fireplaces. It had been left with three chunks of bone (the usual fuel for fires), decorated ivory objects, and over 20 flint tools (an enormous investment of time); these are items we might expect to find in a grave, not a pit. Furthermore, the top of the pit had been sealed with the shoulder bone of a mammoth, replicating houses built for people, which were also covered with mammoth bones. This was not just a pit, but a fully functioning house for the figurine that resided within it. These were not just inconsequential playthings that were made and discarded with little thought, but were hugely important and significant to the people who lived at this time. Given their clear association with pregnancy and procreation, perhaps they represented the separate lineages of the group – an important consideration when determining potential breeding partners in insular communities. Perhaps they even came to represent the ancestral mother to whom all in the lineage were descended? If, like the other images of animals and people we have seen, the figurines came to embody the actual spirit of the lineage, the ancestral mother herself, then it would explain why they were treated with such care and respect.

Another Russian site, Avdeevo, was laid out in a very similar style to Kostenki: a pit contained two figurines that interlocked with each other, one facing upwards and one facing downwards.[22] Given what we know of shamanic journeying, we recognise that, to journey to the otherworlds, people can go up, and fly into the sky, or they can go down, into the earth. Perhaps these figurines were designed to symbolise both? Moreover, the Lespugue Venus, from France, was carved so that it can be viewed either way up with the buttocks and breasts interchangeable. It is a work of supreme skill but it could also show the alternate directions that a shaman can travel to get to the otherworlds. A number of female figurines from the Grimaldi caves in Italy were also paired, but the double is grotesque and was carved so that it appears to emerge from the body of the first.[23] Perhaps these figurines were representations of shapeshifting shamans, their spirit body or soul emerging in its partially formed animal identity? It brings us back to the carved animal forms with which we began this chapter. If people could be animals and animals could be spirits, there was a marked fluidity to life and form, where the otherworld was close and its inhabitants could be encountered almost anywhere. This was a very different way of thinking about the world.

In addition to the carvings people tied onto their clothes, a number of others were pierced or had small holes in their designs to allow for a hanging loop. These were among the first items of jewellery that people wore. However, like all things in the past, these pendants stood for more than is immediately obvious. To people in the Palaeolithic, what you wore was most certainly who you were.

Chapter 8

BEAUTIFUL BODIES

To make a pendant from the tooth of a fox, you first need to catch your animal. Then, after possibly removing its skin for later use, you can cut away the tooth. It is a very bloody process. Once it is extracted, either you can bore a hole through it with a piece of flint, or you can file a groove around the top that will hold a string. Finally, you need to polish it. If you want more than four canine teeth in your necklace, you need more foxes. The boy from Sunghir, who we saw prior to his burial, had 250 teeth in a belt around his waist. That was a lot of teeth and would have required at least 63 foxes to provide them all. The girl, on the other hand, had no teeth in her grave. Perhaps fox teeth were the preserve of males (the man buried above the children also had a few fox teeth in his grave). The fox was an animal whose tenacity at hunting and scavenging in these frozen lands would have been much admired. By collecting its teeth, perhaps people hoped that some of its skill might rub off on them, or perhaps they thought that by carrying a tooth, the spirit of the fox might even join them as they set out to find food?

Teeth were a popular ornament in the Palaeolithic and were usually taken from animals that hunt, such as foxes, wolves, and bears, and not from species that were considered prey.[1] This makes it more likely that they were indeed considered an aid to hunting. (Deer teeth were worn in central Europe and around the Mediterranean, but deer were not eaten in great numbers until later in the Palaeolithic.)[2] Exceptionally, human teeth were also pierced for suspension, such as at Brassempouy in France. The excavators have suggested that this was part of a mortuary practice that did not involve burial,[3] but perhaps it was, rather, a way of the living keeping the spirit (and the power) of a dead individual close, in the same way that people carried the teeth of animals for similar purposes. The teeth were used in a metonymical way, where part of something stands for the whole – in this case, the whole person or animal and all of the attributes that were associated with it.

Teeth were a convenient part of the animal to use for decoration but they may have had other significance, such as being the part of an animal that enables it to kill and devour its food. Teeth also have an aesthetic appeal and look good as their shiny enamel surface catches the light. Perhaps people liked this effect or maybe the brilliance of the surface also carried its own meaning. Ivory, a material used for the majority of ornaments, also had a shiny surface but, as Clive Gamble, an expert on this period, notes, it needs polishing to bring out its brilliance. Certain modern-day hunter-gatherers equate brilliance with spiritual power and Gamble suggests that perhaps the people of the Palaeolithic did the same.[4] It is also interesting to note that the polishing medium used to make ivory shine was ochre, the red earth pigment that covered the dead. If brilliance was a source of power, and ochre revealed this brilliance, then maybe this was another reason that it was spread over the dead: it brought forth their power.

Other materials used to make ornaments included mother of pearl, lignite (a type of coal), and soapstone. With ivory and enamel, they share a visual but also a tactile similarity that, with the eyes closed, would have been difficult to tell apart.[5] These materials were probably chosen because of this tactile quality and suggest that those who wore the finished items frequently handled them. Perhaps touching or holding a tooth or an ivory bead was a means of releasing the power that it contained? The importance of how an object felt seems to have been so significant that at La Souquette, in France, shells (which were often used to make ornaments in their own right) were replicated in ivory, perhaps bringing the power of two separate realms together in one piece.[6]

Some of the earliest ornaments made by humans were fashioned from shells and are found in Africa, particularly at Blombos Cave, familiar to us as the place where the engraved ochre pieces were discovered.[7] Until 2006, these were considered to be the oldest ornaments made anywhere in the world at around 75,000 years old. However, several shell beads have recently been discovered at Skhul, in Israel, that may be over 100,000 years old, pushing back the dawn of what might be considered 'art' by at least another 25,000 years.[8] Shells retained their significance over thousands of years, and at Balzi Rossi, in Italy, they were worn from when the site was first occupied, 36,000 years ago, to when it was abandoned, some 27,000 years later, despite almost every other element of the site undergoing significant change.[9] The power of shells must have been particularly strong to be so persistent. A wide variety of shells were pierced and tied onto clothing or strung for hanging. However, rarer shells seem to have been preferred and most were of similar sizes to the beads made by people further inland; it is almost as if there was a certain size of ornament that was universally preferred.[10]

Away from the coast, shells were far rarer, with only 72 having been recorded from inland areas.[11] Interestingly, the nearest French occupation sites to Balzi Rossi have similar varieties, suggesting a likely source for the shells, whereas those further away got their supply from another source.[12] In fact, shells were carried over huge distances, with Mediterranean shells turning up on sites in central Europe some 700km away.[13] It is doubtful that one person would have made this trip independently and so the shells would have been traded from settlement to settlement until their final destination was reached. These remarkable trade networks are something that we will explore further in the next chapter.

Shells were clearly valued at great distances from the sea (and we have already seen how some were even copied in ivory), but what did they represent to the people who owned them? Alien objects often bring with them alien ideas, as the item itself develops a history and biography of its own.[14] Perhaps the shells held ideas of far-away places; of contacts and relations rarely seen, and of something people inland were likely never to have seen: the sea. Worn on clothing or around the neck, the ornament would have much to say about the person who wore it (and the patterns of wear suggest that ornaments were worn for lengthy periods). Over time, object and person merged and ideas about one were also assigned to the other, the object slowly releasing the power that it held.[15]

We have seen how ornaments could be made from a variety of raw materials but often these were exotic to the locations in which the beads were used. The people at Balzi Rossi preferred shells that were rare and it seems that such scarcity added value to any ornament. Perhaps this is why, at Kostenki in Russia (the site where female figures were placed in pits), ornaments were created from sea coral and a fossil sea urchin; their scarcity must have made them extremely valuable.[16] Randall White, an expert on Palaeolithic ornaments, goes further and suggests that these scarce, tactile, and often shiny materials carried a spiritual value to the people who wore them. If they were indeed sources of power, then this is no more than we would expect. However, if we want to find the ultimate source of this spiritual power then we need to wait until the end of the Palaeolithic, when bead production had reached a stage where designs could be engraved upon the surface. From a deer-tooth necklace from Saint-Germain-la-Riviere in France, to pendants and bracelets from Mezin in Russia, ornaments were engraved with geometric designs, continuing a tradition that originated with the phosphenes of trance.[17] If these items were full of spiritual power, then such power originated in the otherworld, the realm people went to in trance. The teeth, the beads, even the human remains that all form part of the ornaments worn by people at the time, were drawing power from the otherworld and the spirit of the person or animal represented. We have seen in the previous chapter how a select few carried carved statues of animals or even of people for similar reasons. Perhaps beads were the mass-market equivalent: a connection with the otherworld and its spiritual power that could be worn and called upon by everyone.

Ornaments were a source of spiritual power but they also communicated that power to others. Wearing a fox tooth brought forth the power of the fox but it also showed others that you claimed that power and were, presumably, a good food pro-vider as a result. Ornaments allowed people to say things about themselves that were not readily identifiable in any other way. We *know* that the children from Sunghir were important because of the ornaments that they wore; without them, they would probably never have made it into this book. Moreover, such meanings could be stand-ardised – fox teeth possibly signified being a good food provider – but they could do much more besides.[18] The quantity worn would reinforce the message, a way of shouting through ornamentation, and the scarcity, and therefore cost, of an item (and doubtless the implied worth of the person wearing it) could be easily identified

(Palaeolithic 'bling', perhaps). Furthermore, beads, their meanings, and the spiritual power that they held, were easily transferable from person to person.

Beads had a common language that was immediately understood by those who saw them. They might have been a source of spiritual power but it was a power that was readily advertised to others, particularly those who were intimate enough to come close to the wearer, and thereby see the bead, but were clearly not intimate enough to know the information anyway.[19] Several beads worn together may even have imparted several discrete areas of information, such as the source of spiritual power, skills held, ancestral lineage, and to which group the person belonged. Some have extended the latter to propose several large regional groupings of people, all identified by a particular ornament design, although others dismiss such ideas.[20] Whatever the truth (and the evidence is perhaps too insubstantial for a conclusion), it is clear that people were organising themselves into larger and larger networks of contact and exchange. If shells could travel 700km then clearly people were interacting with each other over huge distances. Although family groups were still probably small and close-knit, the Palaeolithic worldwide web was beginning to form.

Chapter 9

MAKING FRIENDS

We are sitting around a small fire, which, despite its size, keeps the chill of the approaching night out of our bones. The other members of this small community talk quietly among themselves; some are working fast upon some small carving they hold since the light will shortly disappear. Just then, there is a shout, followed by another. There is a murmur of alarm in the group and several of the young ones rise to their feet. Four strangers walk purposefully towards us. The disquiet of alarm soon gives way to laughing and calling and it becomes apparent that these are not strangers at all but are traders who visit the group once or twice a year. This time they are joined by a boy, who looks furtively around the group, his eyes finally alighting on a girl a little younger than himself. The strangers carry a small bag and soon their wares are laid out before the fire. They carry shells. They talk animatedly with much gesture and it is clear that they are telling the story of how they came upon such treasures. Perhaps they visited the coast themselves or perhaps they knew of others who had; it is hard to understand. You point to the other side of the fire where the boy has engaged the girl in a stilted conversation. He keeps fingering a small bead he wears around his neck. It is a wolf's tooth and she seems impressed. Perhaps the boy will join the group and they will wed?

Modern humans first entered Europe around 40,000 years ago but, to begin with, they left scant trace of their presence. It was only 35,000 years ago, or perhaps a little later, that they began to paint the walls of the caves and fashion the ivory carvings that still enchant us today. Trade and exchange, such as we witnessed in the camp, came later still, perhaps around 33,000 years ago, when there was a marked increase in the circulation of raw materials. It was not that people were unable to develop these aspects earlier; they just had other concerns on their mind.

The route that humans took on their great migration out of Africa was probably through the Near East and then into Europe, via the Balkans. The enormity of this undertaking is difficult to imagine today, when even the surfaces of distant planets are mapped in detail. These people could have had no idea of what lay ahead; it must have been like the crew on Columbus' first voyage across the Atlantic, wondering if they were going to fall off the edge of the world. The motivation for such migration remains a mystery. It used to be thought that the population in existing territories got too large for the resources available and people were forced to move in order to survive[1] but this does not accord with the evidence and has been rejected in recent years. Rather than factors that *push* people forward, the focus is now on factors that *pull* them onward.[2] However, it is still not entirely clear what these factors were. Perhaps it was to follow prey, or to find better materials for making tools, or perhaps it was an innate, instinctual desire? Anyone with young children knows their propensity to wander; the urge to look around just one more corner is sometimes irresistible. Similarly, behind the most significant of human endeavours has been our urge to explore and discover new places: it even took us to the moon. Possibly, this drive to explore came from peoples' experience of trance and the benefits of journeying to the otherworld. When I experienced trance, the otherworld was a landscape that had no end, where I could walk through forests and across plains that seemed eternal. The urge to know what was just out of sight was often too hard to resist. If people in the past felt the same when they journeyed to the otherworld then perhaps it gave them the strength to travel to the far ends of *this* world? Their minds had already taken them to places that their bodies would follow.

The first people entering Europe probably did so with a sense of purpose, hopping along the coast or using rivers to penetrate the interior.[3] Rivers would have been particularly easy to travel along when they froze during the Ice Age winter, and the existence of the earliest settlements on either side of the Danube seems to bear this out.[4] Although raw materials appear to travel over large distances during this early stage, it is likely that these pioneer groups were carrying things with them rather than forming exchange networks. It is even possible that particularly useful raw materials were cached as a forward-thinking insurance strategy if retreat became necessary.[5]

Even though people might have felt an innate drive to cast out into the unknown, it is difficult to envisage how they would have thought about such an endeavour. It is unlikely, for instance, that they would have comprehended space in the same way that we do. To us, space is somewhere 'out there', areas we have never visited and find hard to conceptualise beyond a vague feeling of otherness. Once we get to know somewhere, an area no longer becomes space but, rather, becomes a series of inter-linked places: locations with which we are familiar. We overlay places onto the emptiness of space. However, this attitude owes a great deal to our modern stance of separation: us and them, inside and outside, place and space.[6] In the past, people probably formed their sense of space at the same time that they overlaid it with a series of places.[7] This is not to say that they had no conception of the vastness that lay before them, but that this vastness was a continually formed concept; their existence on the land came only with knowing what was around them. If we adopt an approach taken by anthropologist Tim Ingold, we see that early people did not attach meanings to space as we might, but that they gathered those meanings from the places in which they found themselves.[8] Eventually, people found their own place in the world and began to settle, not entirely in one location, as we do, but in a bounded area with sites and landmarks that were familiar to them.

Clive Gamble calls these places 'locales', a series of sites that were familiar to the groups that lived there.[9] A locale need not be substantial; a single event may have been enough for a place to be significant.[10] Gatherings of people, however, especially in camps and at ritual sites such as the painted caves, would have become the most familiar locales. These locales were linked by 'rhythms', networks of paths and tracks that people followed to get from one locale to another. Rhythm is a good word as it implies that there is an element of time in their formation. This may be self-evident, such as the time it took to walk along them, but may also relate to the activities that were undertaken at each locale. For example, if one locale was good for finding flint, another was good for finding wood to make spears, and a third was the temporary camp where everything was brought together, there was a temporal link among all three sites. Moreover, there was a rhythm to the interval that a person would move from one to the other. Gamble calls these 'operational sequences' and suggests that, in their entirety, they formed a 'taskscape' – a network of separate tasks that overlay the land. Another element that may add to the rhythms of the land was the migration routes taken by animals and the best spots in which to hunt them. Taken together, they formulated the way in which people would have thought about their world.

There is, however, a further aspect to the landscape that would have been of huge importance to Palaeolithic people but is now completely lost to us: the myths and stories that people would have told about the land. We can, perhaps, get a small impression of what these may have been like when we listen to people like the Australian Aborigines and their description of the 'Dreamtime', where the songlines of ancient beings brought the world and all its features into being.[11] Although we might not know the stories that Palaeolithic people told, it does seem that they singled out and celebrated places and items that created some form of boundary. Indeed, almost everything given significance during the Palaeolithic had an element of liminality: caves being boundaries into the earth, seashells originating on the interface of land and sea, teeth being neither inside nor outside of the body, ochre changing from earth to pigment, and ivory whose surface needed to be polished to uncover its brilliance. This preoccupation with liminality seems to be another innate aspect of the human mind and may, again, relate to experience of trance and leaving this world to cross the boundary to another. On the walls of the decorated caves, where the spirits appeared to pass from one world to the other, and in the images of shapeshifting shamans that lay deep within the earth, this fixation reached its apogee.

As people began to settle and form the locales that we might call home, the rhythms of their world began to increase. Clearly, the raw materials that the first people brought with them to these places would not have lasted, but perhaps the memory of them, and the desire for some more, lingered. It would not have taken long before a message was passed from locale to locale and from group to group until someone, somewhere, thought to collect what was plentiful to him or her, such as seashells, and to exchange them with someone who lived too far away to gather their own. Exchanged from community to community, or, possibly carried longer distances by itinerant bands, shells were to travel inland for some 700km. The rhythms had developed a faster tempo.

Like the concept of space, the concept of exchange (what we would call trade), was probably also very different in the past. Rather than a modern transaction, which finishes as soon as trade is concluded, early exchanges probably had an ongoing relationship of reciprocity that became an integral part to the process. An exchange within traditional Maori society, for example, had its own spirit, called 'Hau', that adhered to the item exchanged but always found its way back to the original owner of the item.[12] In this way, a web of reciprocity was built that gave Maori society its strength and stability. If we envisage something similar for the Palaeolithic, it is clear that procuring raw materials was only a small part of what exchange was about. It is particularly telling that it seemed to increase significantly just as the climate started to deteriorate and people needed to rely on each other more. Indeed, around 18,000 years ago, when the glaciers of the final Ice Age reached their maximum extent, exchange and the networks that it formed seem to have been at their height.[13]

However, it was not just the living that people could call upon in times of need but also the spirits of the dead. Although we think of people relinquishing their role in society when they die, in the Palaeolithic it was likely that the dead still played an important part in people's lives. The items we have seen buried with the dead formed the terminus of their own rhythm through the landscape and were in themselves a form of exchange: gifts to the dead in return for their continuing aid for the living. The proliferation of geometric imagery at this time, and its potential connection to the phosphenes of trance, suggests that the denizens of the otherworld were perhaps being called upon with increasing frequency.[14] Even the dwellings people lived in, erected in some regions from interlocked mammoth bones, formed their own geometric patterns, and this was reflected in the designs painted on other bones, such as the mammoth skull found in one of the huts at Mezirich in Ukraine.[15] It seems that the imagery of the otherworld was everywhere.

The rhythms of the landscape, the tasks carried out there, and the items that were exchanged among otherwise separate communities, kept the Palaeolithic world turning. It was a time when people, although living extremely insular lives (at least by our standards), also felt connected both to the external world around them but also to the otherworld that they could reach through trance. From this distance, it almost appears peaceful.

It is now night and the exchange has been concluded. Five shells for 15 fox teeth and as much meat as the traders will need to make the five-day journey to the next settlement. The fox teeth will be kept until they return again to the coastal region; they are much rarer there and will likely fetch more valuable goods in exchange. You settle down to sleep but, just as you close your eyes, I jab you in the ribs and point to the place where the boy and girl had spoken earlier. They now lie under the same fur and it is clear that the talking has finished. It has been settled: the boy will stay with the group and become the girl's partner. He looked strong and the wolf tooth he wore attested to his bravery in hunting. Everyone understood this; he would be a good addition to the group. You smile at me knowingly and then turn to sleep. This night, even we feel as if we belong.

PART TWO

THE COMING
OF THE FORESTS:
THE MESOLITHIC

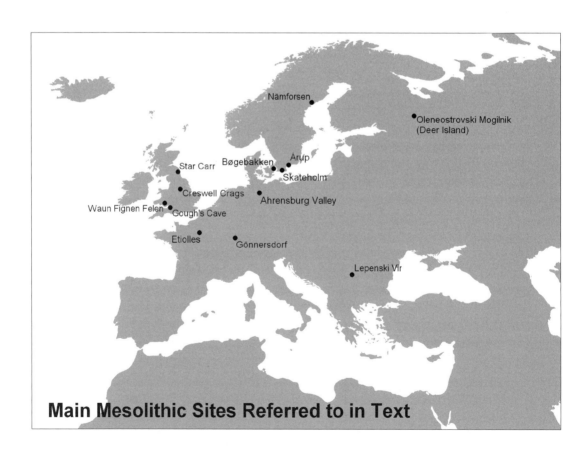

Main Mesolithic Sites Referred to in Text

Chapter 10

THE VALLEYS OF DEATH

We are cold, wet, and, quite literally, starving. We have not eaten for three days and even then, our last meal was of a frozen and half-devoured hare left behind by a predator that had already eaten its fill. It was my suggestion that we should move north, to see the land that is emerging as the ice slowly withdraws. But there is little to see; the landscape is wide, flat and almost featureless, except for the deep valleys and scars left by the ice. Vegetation, what there is of it, hugs the ground; there are no trees here. We desperately need food but all we see are hares, and these are but small flashes of silver in a grey landscape. We have neither the means nor the knowledge to catch them.

Although we do not know it, we have actually journeyed to the land that will one day be southern England, just to the south of the Bristol Channel. Of course, neither of these places exist at this point in time, about 12,000 BC, since much of the water in the world is still held in the vast glacial sheet that covers much of northern Britain and Scandinavia. The English Channel, the Bristol Channel, and all but a thin slice of the Irish Sea are still dry land and, without knowing it, we have walked from France straight across into England. It is almost the last time that this will be possible until a tunnel is completed in another 14,000 years.

At the height of the last glaciation, around 18,000 years ago, people moved south to survive; most of the sites we explored in previous chapters were abandoned to the ice. It was only as the ice receded, around 15,000 years ago, that people began to move north again. Initially, grass and shrubs reclaimed the barren lands, which, in turn, attracted herds of horses and reindeer to graze it. People soon followed and moved inexorably northwards at an average rate of about 1km a year.[1] At 14,000 BC, they arrived in northern France and at 12,700 BC they reached Britain. However, these first people did not come to stay; they were pioneers in this frozen land and probably retreated south each winter to avoid the savage cold.

We reach a narrow, steep ravine and you point to a small cave in its side. It will give us shelter from the biting wind and we may even find timber with which to light a fire. We head down across the broken scree of the slope. Nearing the cave, you stop suddenly and gesture to me. We listen intently and hear voices from just inside the interior. They are human voices; we are not alone in this land. As we move further towards the shelter and our eyes get accustomed to its gloom, you point out what I have also noticed: they have food. We crawl closer, hoping to steal a little of what they have. The group is now quiet, intent on cutting meat from a bone. One man holds a sharp flint and is sawing to release something from the item he holds. I look more closely and my blood chills. In his hands is a head, a human head, and the man is attempting to saw away the tongue at its root. I hope that you have not seen it, but your bulging eyes show that you have. We reel backwards, desperate to get far away from this cave, to breathe pure air again. That night though, as we lie cold and hungry, we both think about the tongue and how it would have filled our bellies. The rules of this land are harsh.

Although it is not clear whether the travellers we saw, at a place called Gough's Cave in southern England,[2] actually killed the dead bodies they had with them, the cut marks on the bones are unequivocal signs that they butchered and presumably ate the flesh; some even shows signs of having been roasted.[3] It seems that, although we have seen how people revered the dead and their spirits, in such harsh conditions practical considerations won out. However, there is also evidence that people had other sources of food, as horse and deer bones were mixed in with those of the humans. If they had an alternative, just why were they consuming their dead? Perhaps it was desperation, but perhaps it was for more ritualistic reasons? These were barren places and maybe eating those who had not survived was a means of ensuring that part of their bodies (and maybe their spirits) would return to the homeland further south and not remain in this desolate land, particularly as it appears that the survivors did not intend to remain long. From the horse bones, people had taken sinews to use as thread, probably to repair their clothes. They would need them, for it seems that, before returning home, this band had plans to move yet further north, to Creswell Crags in north-west England.

Although there was a good mixture of bones from the caves at Creswell, there were no human bones and the bones from horse and deer were likely dragged in by carnivores.[4] Rather as we had wanted to do, the people here caught arctic hares and survived on them, albeit sometimes eating them raw. However, despite surviving on hare, people clearly had other animals on their minds, since they engraved and, in a single instance, painted, images of animals on the cave walls.[5] The art was only discovered in 2003 and caused a sensation, as it was the first to be found in Britain. Although it stemmed from the same tradition as the great painted caves of France and Spain (and the last of these caves probably only slightly predates the images at Creswell, if at all), it is clearly nowhere near as dramatic, nor are the images as numerous.[6] It seems that the art was the result of a small band of pioneers putting their unique mark on the rock walls. Perhaps the images were involved in some sort of ritual at the cave, perhaps they were merely a way of marking a human presence in a land that must have appeared empty and, at times, truly terrible.[7]

Why people wanted to explore these barren wastes is not immediately obvious. Perhaps it was due to the same instinct that first took humans out of Africa so many years ago, an instinct honed by the corresponding exploration of the otherworld and of the denizens that lived there. Maybe trance experiences also gave the people at Gough's Cave the strength to eat their own kind – believing that you can meet the spirits of the dead in the otherworld would certainly have put a different complexion on consuming their flesh. These people were true pioneers and they left behind a life that could have been so much easier, for, a little further south, animals were so abundant that at certain times of the year people could catch and kill them in huge numbers.

About the same time that intrepid groups of pioneers were exploring the more northerly reaches of the land, and living on a meagre diet of arctic hare, others were engaging in a very different type of hunting. At Meiendorf in northern Germany, the Ahrensburg Valley formed a bottleneck as the land squeezed tightly between two lakes. This was also the migration route for thousands of reindeer, passing through the valley to reach the frozen lands of Scandinavia.[8] This was an opportunity that people could not resist and the deer were killed in huge numbers, leaving behind the remains of thousands of bones. The ground would have been slick with blood by the time the migrating deer had passed. As the deer were travelling between the lakes, people probably drove them into the water and, as the animals were floundering to escape, let fly with their deadly spears.[9] The hunters gave even more power to their arsenal by using a spear-thrower to increase velocity.[10] Experiments have shown that spears thrown in this manner can penetrate the flesh of a reindeer by 32cm; since people were aiming at the hearts of the animals, this was guaranteed to be fatal.[11] However, to affect such penetration, the spear needs to be tipped with good quality flint (experiments with antler points penetrated flesh to only 15cm). Fortunately, there were ready supplies nearby – this land appears to have held all that an early hunter might need.

At Etiolles in northern France, for example, flint blocks were brought to be knapped into tools, including the spear points used to hunt reindeer.[12] Through careful analysis of the heaps of chippings left by each knapper as he or she sat around a central fire, it is possible to discern a pattern. The best knappers were those who sat closest to the fire (no doubt a perk reflecting their skills), whereas apprentices and those whose quality of work was not first rate were, quite literally, out in the cold, and sat around the perimeter of the fireside group.[13] It is an unusually intimate picture of life in the past.

Many of the spear-throwers of this time were decorated with finely engraved images of prey animals – likely those that the spears were designed to kill. However, the animals are not shown in a state of panic or distress but are calm and serene, perhaps reflecting the respect that the hunters had for their prey.[14] It is also possible that the images reflect the spirit of the animals, their carving being an act of appeasement for the violence that was to follow. Calling on the spirits of prey animals in this way might also help to explain another site in these lands, at Gönnersdorf, in western Germany.

It is night and we have joined a community before a large fire. It is a larger group than we have come across before, at least two deep around the flames, and the people seem relaxed and well fed. It is the time of the migration and we have already come across piles of bones as we made our way into the camp. You stopped to eat a piece of venison and I had not the heart to tell you that it was probably horse. There is a commotion by the fire and a group of women emerge from the gloom; one carries a baby strapped to her back. They start to dance before the throng, a slow sinuous movement that affects awe in those who watch. Clearly, the movements the women make are part of a planned choreography as they circle around in a clockwise direction, but it is beyond our understanding. Each woman holds a piece of slate and, as they catch the light of the fire, we can just make out some engravings on their surface. One is a horse, another might be a deer, and another almost certainly represents the dancing women themselves; there is even an image of the woman with the baby on her back. The women display the panels to the people assembled around the fire and there is excitement as the designs come close to those at the front. A few go to touch the images but think better of it and resist. We cannot understand what we are seeing but we can admire the beauty of it nonetheless. Then, just as suddenly as they appeared, the dancers are gone.[15]

The schist plaques from Gönnersdorf make up the largest collection of images from central Europe at this time. Animals make up the most abundant images with horse being a favourite subject, perhaps reflecting its position as the main food resource for the people who lived there.[16] However, mammoths were also commonly depicted and these were extremely rare in the area, if not absent altogether.[17] Among the most celebrated engravings are those of the women, numbering just over 400, including several carrying babies on their backs.[18] However, unlike the animals, which were depicted in fine detail, the women were extremely schematic with most missing heads and feet; this must have been a deliberate choice.

We have come across such schematic women before, in the Grimaldi caves, where carvings of women from an earlier period were perhaps shamans shapeshifting into their spirit form. The women engraved at Gönnersdorf may depict something similar: their lack of heads and feet showing the breaking-down of the physical body. These schematic images are mirrored at La Roche, in France, where the engravings on the walls of the rock shelter were almost exact replicas of the Gönnersdorf women,[19] and also at Wilczyce, in Poland, where similar designs were chipped from flint.[20] Whatever this imagery represents, it had extensive currency, both geographically and through time, and perhaps it was only the belief that people had in their shamans and the otherworld that could have had such widespread following. Moreover, the images of the women at Gönnersdorf appear to have been blocked in with hashed lines, reflecting the explosion of geometric imagery at this time.

The communities that found a living at the edge of the ice lasted, at most, 3000 years. A little after 11,000 BC, the climate crashed once again and the region was plunged back into arctic conditions. The horse population was decimated and the people of Gönnersdorf, having lost their main prey species, abandoned their homes and fled south. Some sought refuge in the Ahrensberg Valley; at Stellmoor, there are plenty of reindeer bones that attest to the presence of humans. However, rather than using a spear-thrower, these hunters had found a new way of killing deer: using a bow and arrow.[21] They had a little over 1200 years to hone their skills until the land warmed again and people could spread northwards once more. What they found was an entirely new landscape that would consign old hunting methods to oblivion and usher in the reign of the arrow. The Mesolithic had begun.

Chapter 11

DANCE OF THE DEER

After Gönnersdorf, we are at another performance, this time in the far north. The wind is fresh but not biting, as if it is finally losing its memory of the ice. We stand not far from a small lake, its surface reflecting the fire that forms the centre of the roughly assembled camp. There are about half a dozen of us, all tightly packed and tense. Some are staring intently, their eyes fixed on the darkness beyond the fire. All of a sudden, there is a slight movement, and then another, and I feel a chill down my spine. You must have noticed as your form huddles against my back, pressing in closer to the group. Then, the others drop into a crouch and move away from the fire in a slow deliberate stoop. We do the same, although our movements are nowhere near as fluid. With a bellow, a shape crashes out of the darkness and rears up at the people arrayed before it. It is a deer, its antlers slashing through the air with a murderous sound. There is another bellow and another deer, then another, and another. We are surrounded. It is then that we see the bodies of the deer, but these are human bodies. These are not animals but humans, wearing the skull and antlers of the deer as a mask. But their movements and their energy is beyond human; the dancers have left their bodies far behind and have shapeshifted into their prey. These people are now deer.

As the ice withdrew from northern Europe, a little after 10,000 BC, it left behind a bruised landscape that had been scraped clear of all vegetation. However, it was not long before the plants began to return. Blown north on the breeze, the underbrush came first, rapidly followed by trees.[1] Initially, birch, pine, and hazel proliferated in the warm, dry climate, with oak, elm, and alder following after 6000 BC, when the weather turned wetter. The new conditions were hard for the large animals of the tundra and mammoths and woolly rhinos rapidly went extinct. Other animals, such as reindeer and elk moved north, where they remain today. However, the forests were ideal homes for other deer species, the red and roe, and also for wild boar, which surged out of their Ice Age refuges in southern Europe. People soon followed and the site of the deer dance, Star Carr in northern Britain, is one of the earliest Mesolithic sites that archaeologists have found.[2]

As the deer-masked dancers career about the fire, those who are crouched around us slowly creep forward, stopping dead if one of the dancers looks towards them. When they are as close as they dare go, we see them lift a bow from where it was tied to their back. Setting an imaginary arrow, they fire at the deer and then follow up their kill with whoops and wails. The deer dancers take their final steps before crashing to the ground, their bodies writhing in the throes of death. One lands not far from where we remain crouched and we can see the dancer's eyes, rolled back so that only the whites show. The hunters stop and let the dancers complete their homage to the spirits of the deer. Perhaps the dance will bring more prey to the lakeside tomorrow?

The days of hunting deer in their thousands, such as we witnessed in the Ahrensburg Valley, have gone. Deer became more solitary during the Mesolithic and, hidden in the trees, required a new technique to catch them: stalking. The hunters we joined at the deer dance played their part by stalking the dancing deer before drawing their bows and loosing an arrow. We have briefly come across arrows before, at Stellmoor in Germany, on the cusp of the change from Palaeolithic to Mesolithic lifeways, but now they are the hunting weapon of choice. At Lilla Loshult, in Sweden, two complete arrows were recovered from a peat bog, revealing how they were made.[3] A straight shaft had a small flint point secured with resin at one end, with a notch for the string cut at the other. An additional flint barb was then inserted on the side of the arrow, so that, when fired, the arrow would remain in the prey and not fall out.[4] The small flints are called 'microliths' (literally, 'little stones'), and became the main tool of the time, used not only in hunting equipment but also for all sorts of household activities.[5]

At Star Carr, in addition to stalking the prey, there is also evidence that people burnt the reeds around the water's edge, perhaps to encourage new shoots that would attract the deer and leave them vulnerable to ambush.[6] The efficacy of such ambush was probably improved by the wearing of deer costumes, people becoming the proverbial wolf in sheep's clothing. When the site was first excavated in the late 1940s, several deer skulls, with antlers attached, were found in a ditch along with butchered bones and abandoned tools. Two eyeholes bored into the front of the skull suggested that they may have been worn as masks, perhaps with the pelt of the deer hanging down the back.[7] Whether these were used as a hunting disguise or had a more ritualistic purpose, such as shapeshifting,[8] is a subject still debated by archaeologists.[9] However, in reality, there is no reason why the deer masks could not have been used for both functions.

Dividing the sacred from the profane is a modern construct that had no bearing in the past. What we have found in our journey through the Palaeolithic, and now into the Mesolithic, is that there was little division between this world and the otherworld, and that spirits inhabited and influenced every aspect of people's lives. Everyday life was ritual and ritual was everyday life.

To early hunting communities, reciprocity was of great importance. Peter Jordan, drawing from his time living and working among the Khanty of Siberia, shows that many northern communities of hunters believe that by showing proper respect to the animal that they have killed, the Master of the Animals will look kindly upon them and send more game to take its place.[10] Moreover, the animals themselves are believed to give themselves willingly to the hunter, safe in the knowledge that their remains will be respected and treated with care.[11] It is likely that such attitudes also prevailed in the Mesolithic. For example, among the remains at Star Carr were 191 barbed points (a hunting weapon resembling a small harpoon), all but two of which were made from deer antler. Although these points were made at Star Carr, they were then used elsewhere, before being brought back to the site to be deposited.[12] Given that some of these points may have even been fashioned from the tines of the red deer masks, it appears that people were returning to the site what they believed belonged to the site, perhaps as a sign of respect to the spirits of the deer that they killed. Similarly, all the masks were also left behind, as if their use was proscribed to this single location.

People also left other items at Star Carr, including beads and axes. Since these could have been readily reused and are extremely rare or absent on other Mesolithic sites in the region, it is likely that these were also left deliberately. While they may have also been gifts to the spirits, there is another reason why they may have been discarded. At Årup, in Sweden, a flint-knapping location revealed a number of almost perfect microliths that had been used only once and then thrown onto the chippings pile. There seems to be no reason to throw away these points and the excavators have suggested that the flints may have been polluted in some way, perhaps by missing their target.[13] However, rather than being abandoned where they fell, they were gathered up, brought back to the settlement and mixed with the chippings from new flint points. Again, a resource from the natural world had briefly entered the world of humans before returning once again to its natural state. Clearly, there was a spiritual aspect to working stone.[14]

This was not the only time flint was so treated at Årup. Two nodules of exceptional quality (and corresponding worth) and a worked point were left in a river next to the site. These were not lost accidentally but probably marked a place that was of particular significance to the people who lived there. As if to confirm this, overlooking the flint deposits was a post hole, which the excavators think may have held a totem pole.[15]

Rivers themselves were probably a hugely symbolic part of the landscape. Not only were they the main routes of communication but they may have also been seen as a veil between the worlds. The flint placed in the river at Årup may have been a gift to the spirits that was passed through the membrane of the water and directly into their world. In a similar vein, Jordan notes that many modern-day hunters of the north believe that the dead travel downstream to reach the afterlife.[16] Again, the route of access is via a river.

Tracks through the forest were probably also of symbolic significance. Tim Ingold, who we met in chapter 9, comments that the world of the forest hunters was probably limited to a single dimension: sites (zero-dimension) linked by tracks (first dimension). The second dimension, the surface of the earth, was unknown to them because of the existence of the trees masking an open view. Moving along the tracks and forming taskscapes introduced a third dimension, time, but it is clear that, through omitting the second dimension, their way of thinking about the world would have been very different from our own. The trees themselves would have been hugely significant to people and there was likely a spiritual interaction between tree and human that has left no physical trace.[17] We can perhaps imagine people measuring their own progress through life with that of a tree, perhaps carving images on its trunk, and even singling it out for use as a totem pole. Jordan notes that carving trees is an important ritual for modern-day hunter–gatherers, and there is a growing recognition in anthropological research that trees are a means through which people think about their world.[18]

The passing of the seasons was probably linked to the annual cycle of deciduous trees, with the buds, leaves, and fruit forming key means of orientating the time of year. The nuances of such natural progression, as seen and understood by people who lived in such an intimate relationship with the trees, are beyond our understanding. Similarly, the soundscape they would have noticed is not something we would recognise, much less understand, especially since our modern world is filled with so much artificial disturbance. The hours of daylight and, perhaps more importantly to a hunting community, the hours of darkness, and the corresponding phases of the moon, would have also been important cycles through which people would orientate their activities. For those who lived in coastal communities, the cycle of the tides was probably more significant than that of the sun.[19] The taskscape of these people had a cyclicity based on the natural world.

We have already seen how people probably saw their relationship with the natural world as one of reciprocity, where prey would only give itself to be killed providing its remains were then treated with respect. As people in the Mesolithic gathered as well as hunted their food, it is likely that such attitudes also extended to other food resources and perhaps the trees were propitiated in return for their bounty. However, these people were not conservationists and, as we saw in the Ahrensburg Valley, where food was available, people would readily glut on it. On Colonsay in Scotland, for example, hazel trees likely declined because of the quantity of nuts that people gathered, and at Culverwell in England, the same happened to shellfish through over-gathering.[20] However, such local depletions could easily be countered by a mobile population and people simply moved on to somewhere new.

Despite this mobility, some locations were returned to, as if they had become special, maybe even sacred, places. (But would a sacred place have differed from any other place?) Star Carr, for example, was abandoned for a while before being returned to, and the ritualistic behaviour at the site continued in the same way as before.[21] Another place that may have been returned to over time is Waun Fignen Felen in Wales, a palaeo-lake that I regularly walk to from my home.[22] Climbing high in the Black Mountain, I follow a route up a steep valley that was likely followed by the Mesolithic hunters themselves. Due to the topography of the ground, there is cover almost all the way to the lakeside (which is now a large expanse of bog). It is easy to slip back through the millennia and imagine what it must have been like to stalk the water birds that were the likely prey: noticing the movement of the air so that it did not betray my presence; using the tilt of the sun to act as a foil for my final approach and aiming my imaginary arrow just in front of the bird to account for its impulse to fly. Of course, I would have also have had to honour the bird had I caught it and treated its remains with care and reverence. Hunting, like everything else in the Mesolithic, was a deeply spiritual activity.

During my imaginary hunt, I was trying to think as a bird might, accounting for all the cues that might betray an alien presence and cause it to flee. Perhaps, if I was a Mesolithic hunter, I would have entered trance and shapeshifted into the form of a waterbird? All the better to understand and honour my prey. This was likely what the hunters were doing at Star Carr, where their preferred quarry was the red deer. Shapeshifting may have been as important to hunting as fashioning an arrow or loosing a bow. However, it was not only deer that people transformed into, it was also fish, and they did this at a site almost as far away from Star Carr as it is possible to get in Europe, on the bank of the Danube in Serbia.

Chapter 12

HALF-HUMAN,
HALF-FISH

It was a race. Not one that Dragoslav Srejović of the Belgrade Archaeological Institute wanted, but the rising waters of the Danube gave him no choice – the site had to be saved. It was in 1960 that the dams were placed across the river and, while they would supply hydro-electricity to Romania and Yugoslavia,[1] the two countries that bordered its banks, it was accepted that the river terraces, and all the archaeology that they contained, would be destroyed. There was no time to lose. Romanian teams scoured the left bank and Yugoslav teams scoured the right. It was not until 1965 that Srejović dug his spade into the site of Lepenski Vir, named for a large whirlpool just off shore. Neolithic pottery had been uncovered five years previously and Srejović thought a few test-pits would enable him to record anything relevant. What he found was to exceed his wildest expectations. Lepenski Vir turned out to be one of the most important Mesolithic sites in Europe and it ushered in an entirely new view of the past. Sadly, the rising waters could not be abated and, after several seasons of work, and with the river lapping at its edges, the entire site was cut away from the earth and dragged almost 30m uphill, where it now forms the centrepiece of the regional museum. Srejović had saved Lepenski Vir for the world.

Before people moved to the riverside in the Iron Gates region (named for the towering gorge that squeezes the river to a narrow defile before it slows and widens again), they lived in rock shelters and caves, where they had been since the passing of the ice.[2] It is not known exactly when people decided to leave their caves (perhaps around 7600 BC) but it is clear from the images that they used to decorate their bone tools that it was very much on their minds. Initially, they engraved their tools with parallel zigzag lines, a common motif at the end of the Palaeolithic. However, this slowly gave way to cross-hatching and net-like designs.[3] Both are extremely similar to the phosphenes seen in trance and this may account for their origin. In chapter 5, however, we saw how people's existing predisposition will affect how they interpret what they see, since there is an initial merging of trance imagery and memory. In this case, people first chose to emphasise the zigzag phosphene but, as their focus altered, they changed this to the crosshatch phosphene, presumably because it resembled a net. It seems clear that people had fishing on their minds and it was not long before they moved to the riverbank and put these thoughts into action.

The style of dwelling that people built along the shore of the Danube has been accurately reconstructed from the remains that were left behind. To build a typical structure, people first dug a trapezoid platform into the bank and made a small wall of crushed stone around it. Then they hammered in posts to hold a tent-like cover and made a fan-shaped stone threshold at the entrance. Inside, people constructed a hearth of stone blocks and, curiously, surrounded it with slabs set in a shape resembling an inverted 'A'. Over the floor, they spread a mix of red limestone plaster. To the rear of the hearth, people built stone altars and, next to the altars, placed stone sculptures.[4] We shall be hearing more about these later.

Both altars and sculptures had engravings, including the familiar net pattern but also meanders and fishbone designs. It seems that this was a people obsessed with fishing. Items within the structures included clubs, which may have been for stunning caught fish. Certainly, one had a fish engraved upon it and others had the familiar fish imagery.[5] In one dwelling, a club was accompanied by two flutes, which hints that the act of catching fish involved more than merely killing.

The focus on fishing seems to extend to fish predators from the animal kingdom and, in particular, the white-tailed sea eagle.[6] The bones from this bird form a disproportionately large part of the sample from the site and perhaps these were amulets, carried by people to bring them success with their own fishing expeditions. However, despite the all-consuming concern with fishing, it seems that, as a part of people's diet, fish were relatively unimportant. The beluga migration (the largest concentration of fish) occurred for only a few short months in the summer; for the rest of the year, and particularly in the winter, people hunted deer in the surrounding woodland. However, when the deer moved to higher pasture in the summer, people did not follow them, but remained at the river, catching fish, and coping as best as they could.[7] The lure of the water was just too great. This reluctance to stray from the river even caused occasional malnutrition in their children, but still they refused to move.[8]

It was not only malnutrition that affected children but also other serious, sometimes fatal, ailments. At the rear of many of the dwellings at Lepenski Vir, newborn children lay under the floor, placed there as the structure was being built.[9] It was first thought that these were sacrifices: newborns killed and buried under dwellings in order to mark the construction of the house. However, a study of foetal and newborn burials at nearby Vlasac reveals that these children, rather than being pitiful victims, were actually treated with care and attention.[10] In several of these burials, the infant was placed on its deceased mother (or, in the case of foetuses, remained in the womb) but all were covered in red ochre, the pigment that has always been associated with the dead. Some newborn bones are even covered in fish teeth, which may have been pierced and tied onto a blanket. Given the obsession with fish in this community, this must have been a hugely significant and valuable gift.[11]

Rather than seeing the burial of newborn children as a stage in the construction of the dwelling, perhaps the construction of the dwelling only took place *because* of the death of the child? In effect, the dwelling represents and is connected to the brief life of the newborn. Certainly, upon abandonment, assorted adult bones were buried or left in the dwelling (sometimes accompanied by antlers as some sort of 'closing' ritual) and these are presumed to have been taken from cemeteries to the rear of the settlement.[12] If newborn bones equated to the beginning (birth) of the dwelling then it seems natural that old bones would have equated to its end (death). Between these two extremes, the bodies and bones of adults, presumably soon after they had died, were also buried in the dwelling.[13] It seems that the lifecycle of the dwelling was closely linked to the lifecycle of human beings.

Above some of these adult burials were placed the sculptures that we briefly touched upon earlier. These (sometimes massive) boulders were engraved with fish imagery and the most notable also had heads (and exceptionally bodies) carved with features that were a cross between human and fish.[14] While the down-turned mouth and goggle-eyes were representative of a fish, the placement of the eyes on the front of the head and the addition of a nose were representative of a human. These sculptures depict the act of shapeshifting, in this case, human to fish.[15] It is likely that the fish depicted was a beluga, not only because these were the fish most often caught as they migrated upstream during the summer, but also because of a distinctive characteristic of the fish. Beluga are known to be quite passive when caught, as if they are giving themselves freely to the hunter. We have already seen how such a view accorded with many modern hunter-gatherers, as the prey was believed to offer itself willingly to the hunter. Here, the fish were positively acquiescing with such beliefs.[16]

In addition to those inside the dwellings, other burials occurred outside and in-between the structures, mostly of men but occasionally of women.[17] These were aligned so that their bodies lay parallel to the river, with their heads facing downstream. This alignment on the river was repeated with the burials in the cemeteries and also in the arrangement of the settlement itself, which originally formed two parts: upstream and downstream. The symmetry between these two areas was preserved until the central area began to be filled in during a later stage of the site. However, even then, a degree of symmetry was maintained through matching burial types and the items left in the grave, upstream and downstream.[18] Again, it seems that it was the river that was the overwhelming presence in people's lives, but just why should this be so?

We have already noted the importance of water and of rivers to people who lived in the Palaeolithic and also to modern hunter-gatherers. Moreover, we saw in the previous chapter how groups living in the north of the continent believed that the souls of the dead travelled downstream to reach the afterlife. While the people living in the Iron Gorge during the Mesolithic were far removed from these groups in both time and space, if they also experienced trance states (and the engraved imagery and shapeshifting human-fish would suggest that they did) the effects would have been the same, including the sensation of swimming or floating and the sound of rushing water in the ears. Coupled with the possibility that people still spoke of the river as the portal into the world that they inhabited (the first inhabitants likely travelling up the waterway), the river took on an importance that lured people towards it and would not let them go.

The run of the beluga upstream in the summer and (even if only figuratively) downstream thereafter, may have been interpreted as the fish crossing and re-crossing the portal to the otherworld. In effect, these were not fish anymore but spirits. Furthermore, these animals readily gave themselves to humans; they made clear their willingness to enter the realm of the humans and, presumably, to lend them their aid. The annual run of the fish was now far more important symbolically than it ever had been economically, and the imagery around the site seems to support this. Over time, people, especially those with particular aptitude (the shamans), shapeshifted into the fish and joined them on their journeys to the otherworld. Perhaps these individuals even led the dead on the route to the afterlife, and this was why the dead were aligned facing downstream: the route they had to take in death. When the fish returned in the summer, they brought with them the promise of life and perhaps, at this time, a new dwelling was constructed? This dwelling was dedicated to and contained the life-spark of a newly born infant and there is evidence that their tiny bodies were kept and stored for just such an occasion.[19]

The theme of this life-spark is continued through the colour red – the colour of the ochre pigment spread over the newborns and foetuses in the cemeteries. The floors of the dwellings were red, the rock for the altars and the sculptures was red, tools, including fish clubs, and even the sculptures themselves were stained with ochre. The colour red, symbolising the ambiguity of life in death, was everywhere.

The dwellings at Lepenski Vir were so soaked in imagery that some believe that the site was not for living in at all, but was a sacred centre for rituals connected to the river, or even a resting place for the dead and the spirits.[20] However, from what we have seen of the Palaeolithic, and now of the Mesolithic, such a division would have made little sense to people who lived at the time. The dead, the spirits, and the rituals concerning the river would have been just another part of everyday existence.

The belief that water was a gateway to the afterlife has been a recurring theme in our travels through the Mesolithic. Although not as obsessed with rivers and fish as the people of Lepenski Vir (who else would be?), the communities that lived in the north found their own way of incorporating rivers, and the animals that lived around them, into life and, of course, into death.

Chapter 13

THE ISLE OF THE DEAD

I could not see the island from the shore; but as we sailed across the grey expanse of Lake Inare, deep in the taiga forest of Finnish Lapland, it soon revealed itself. Shaped like the carapace of a turtle and covered with trees, it was unmistakable. This was Ukonsaari, a place sacred to the indigenous people of the region, the Sámi. As the boat drew nearer still, I could just make out a small, shallow cave in its side. It was within the cave that, in 1873, a young archaeology graduate called Arthur Evans undertook a swift and completely unauthorised excavation, finding layers of bone, mostly from bear and reindeer, and a small silver earring. Outside the cave were reindeer antlers, which Evans later learnt were set in a circle as part of a ritual to make offerings to Ukon, the thunder god.[1] This was a sacrificial site, probably used around 1000 AD to 1350 AD, although retaining something of its mystical aura, even into modern times.[2] A question remained, however: why did the Sámi choose such an isolated and inaccessible place for their rituals; surely there was somewhere nearer?

It was not just the Sámi who considered islands sacred, especially those that appear to rear out of the water, just as Ukonsaari does, or those that are covered with trees. Peter Jordan, whose work we have looked at before, notes that the Khanty, a people who also dwelt within the taiga forest, often located their sacred sites on raised ground. This makes sense, as it is one of the few natural forms that would be evident through the trees. Moreover, heavily-wooded islands, located within the myriad of lakes that criss-cross the land, are considered to be especially sacred.[3] Perhaps similar beliefs lie behind the location of one of the largest cemeteries of the Mesolithic at Oleneostrovski Mogilnik, a heavily-wooded island in Lake Onega, Russia. Oleneostrovski Mogilnik means Deer Island, and for our convenience, perhaps this is the name we should adopt here.

Deer Island was excavated by Nina Gurina of the State Institute for the History and Material Culture of Stalinist Russia.[4] She dug from 1936 until 1938, when she was forced to stop. Of all the reasons ever given for ceasing archaeological work, hers is the most compelling – Russia was planning to invade Finland and her site lay directly on the route. As a result, she excavated only 170 burials of the estimated total of 500 but what she found in these burials was incredible. The cemetery was probably used for only four, possibly six, generations between 6700 BC and 6000 BC. People likely chose the island for the same reasons that the Sámi and the Khanty also chose islands for their sacred places, because it stood out in the landscape as a place apart, a place of the otherworld.

Many people were buried with teeth at Deer Island, probably strung into neck-laces since they were perforated, but only three species were represented: bear, beaver, and elk. The appearance of bear is easy to explain; ethnology would suggest that these animals were considered special across almost their entire range, even being consid-ered the master of all the animals that live there. The Sámi, for example, afforded the bear such status that hunting it involved complicated ritual, both before and after the hunt, and the remains were given a burial no different to human dead.[5] Beaver teeth, which are usually found with female burials, come from an animal that would have been primarily hunted for its fur. However, the beaver was also probably considered a special creature since it lives above ground during the summer but then retreats under the water through the winter. Animals that live simultaneously in two worlds, as we have seen before, were often given particular significance. Moreover, the beaver was another animal that was docile and easy to hunt and may have been seen as acquiescing to people's beliefs about the world where prey gave itself willingly to the hunter. Elk would have been an important food source for the people, especially in the winter when waterfowl and fish would migrate elsewhere, but this does not entirely explain why their teeth were selected to lie with the dead; there were plenty of other prey species that were not chosen. People even made staffs topped with a carving of an elk's head and four of these have been found with burials at Deer Island. To understand the meaning of these, however, we have to temporarily leave Deer Island and move some distance away.

Nämforsen lies on the River Ångerman, in Sweden, where three islands contain images carved by the people of the late Mesolithic, several thousand years after the people were buried at Deer Island.[6] However, the images seem to mirror elements of the Deer Island burials, including the elk staffs. At Nämforsen, the staffs were held aloft by people sailing in boats, formed from dug-out trees. The Khanty use such boats as coffins[7] and it may be that the boats at Nämforsen also contained the dead. Moreover, the boats had no oars, presumably because the journey to the afterlife was thought to have been made with a different sort of propulsion.[8] Even the location of the art, in the midst of the last major rapids on the river before it joins the immen-sity of the sea, is highly charged with symbolism of the journey to the afterlife. The figures holding the staffs are perhaps the shamans, journeying with the dead into the otherworld and ensuring their safe passage to the afterlife. Moreover, shamans in the region still carry a 'turu' or shaman's stick, which denotes their power.[9] The graves at Deer Island in which the elk staffs were found possibly held those who also helped the dead in their passage to the afterlife. These were perhaps the shamans, who would watch over the community of the dead as surely as they once might have watched over the community of the living.

Other unusual burials at Deer Island include several men who were buried upright in the grave. This was a rare form of burial but its occurrence at several other sites suggests that its symbolism was readily understood over a wide area. At Skateholm II in Sweden, for example, the upright burial of a man, coupled with a particularly elaborate headdress, has led some to believe that he may have been a shaman.[10] There are other examples from places far away from Poland, but in all cases, upright burial is matched by other elements that also mark the occupant of the grave as special.[11] At Deer Island, these burials were reversed so that, instead of facing east, as all the other burials do, they faced west. Marek Zvelebil, the leading expert on hunter-gatherers in the region, suggests that those orientated to the east (the majority of the burials), faced the direction of the upperworld and of the afterlife. Conversely, the upright burials faced the direction of the lowerworld, where they would journey to seek out their ancestral guides and spirit helpers.[12] Clearly, despite being deceased, these people were still thought able to function in the otherworld. As if to emphasise their role in crossing boundaries, beaver teeth were added to the graves, which were usually reserved for the graves of women. Perhaps they emphasised the skill the shamans had in crossing all boundaries – between the genders as much as between the worlds.

In addition to elk, snake effigies were also found at Deer Island. Snakes have had a mixed reception over the years, moving from revered icons to the incarnation of evil, but it is likely that their natural habits marked them out as special during the Mesolithic. People would have noticed how the snake retreated into the ground for the winter, before emerging, seemingly reborn, in the spring. Analogies relating to death and rebirth often form the focus of traditional societies and may even mirror the journey of the shaman passing out of this world and into the other.[13] The snake also sheds its skin regularly in order to grow, and the transformation from an imperfect to a perfect state may have led people to associate the snake with healing. The effigies of snakes in the grave may therefore have moved seamlessly from providing healing to the sick to providing guidance to the dead. It is interesting that beaver teeth also have associations with healing.[14]

In addition to snakes, antlers may also have been associated with death and rebirth. Antlers grow anew on a deer every year. They start soft, covered in velvet, and grow rapidly until their full size is reached. Then, after passing through a bloody stage as the velvet is torn away, they become hard and brittle. Finally, they are shed and return to the earth where, unless gathered, they will rot. The analogy with a human life is startling. In life, humans are soft, but in death our bones are hard and brittle. Transforming from one state to the other can often be painful and bloody, with the flesh eventually falling away from the bone like velvet peels from an antler. Antlers stood for human life and death but also, since they grew back in the spring, the possibility of eternal rebirth.[15] At Ukonsaari, Evans found a clear differentiation between antler and bone, as if they represented different categories of object to the Sámi. Certainly, antler can be found in graves of the Mesolithic but, like its use at Lepenski Vir, where they seemed to form part of the 'closing' ritual surrounding the house, their use in graves seems designed to frame the body and, perhaps, to put it into a symbolic context that was recognised by the graveside mourners: the closure of life.[16]

Antlers may have also related to the seasonal cycle and it is interesting that, despite antler being shed in the winter months, they were often collected and deposited into shallow water that would have likely been frozen until the spring.[17] This suggests that antlers were gathered and retained throughout the winter before being deposited into the water when it thawed. The same was likely true of human bodies buried in places such as Deer Island. Since the ground would have been frozen through the winter, any corpses would have had to be kept until the thaw in the spring. This may explain why some of the burials were truncated, as if certain body parts had fallen off along the way.[18] It also provides another example of how antlers in the Mesolithic could have stood for, and represented, human life.

Water birds were another recurring image at Deer Island and were also engraved on the rocks along the shore to the lake. Of all the water birds depicted, it was swans that were most abundant.[19] Perhaps it was the migratory nature of the swan that was considered important, just like the beluga at Lepenski Vir. It could have been the brilliance of its feathers against the steel-grey of the lake. Or maybe it was just the sheer majesty of the bird. Whatever the reason, swans seem to have held a deeply significant place in the minds of those who lived at this time and were almost certainly seen as messengers of the otherworld.

This becomes apparent at another cemetery at Bøgebakken, on the island of Sjælland in Denmark.[20] Like the graves on Deer Island, analysis of the items buried with the bodies shows that the items declined with age and were totally absent with children. This was a society where status had to be earned. However, these rules applied to all burials except one. A baby boy had been given a large flint blade, an object he may have rightfully earned for himself, had he lived. Why he was honoured in this way is unclear but this was not the only special feature of his grave. The tiny body had been placed and encircled by the wing of a swan. What better means could there have been to ensure swift passage to the afterlife? Why he was considered so special is something we may never know, but the evidence from Deer Island would suggest that items that had a ritual or sacred element in the grave were not proscribed by age. Perhaps this boy was considered sacred in some way, through being born wrapped in a cowl or disfigured in a manner that was meaningful. His status may have even rubbed off onto his poor mother, who, at about 18 years of age, was consigned to the same grave. Lovingly wrapped in a dress decorated with perforated teeth, and with her head resting on a rolled cape, it is difficult not to share the grief of those who had buried her and her newborn son.

There is one final element to the cemetery of Deer Island that we have yet to explore: the fact that it was an island, surrounded by water. Some have interpreted this as a means of stopping the dead from walking,[21] but perhaps it was exactly the opposite, and the water was the medium through which they walked to the afterlife. We have seen how the experience of water in trance often leads to it being seen as a gateway to the otherworld. It may be telling, therefore, that most of the cemeteries of the Mesolithic were situated close to water.[22] Indeed, at Nämforsen, the site with engravings of people passing to the afterlife in boats, there are also footprints, as if to show people the way they must go.

We have looked at a great number of human graves and the array of objects that were placed with the bodies. Sometimes, these have been the remains of animals, particularly their teeth but also their antlers and bones. In all cases, however, it was the animal that joined the human; these were the graves of people. In some places, this was reversed and it was animals that were buried as if they were human. For a people who regularly shapeshifted into animals, it appears that, this time, it was the animals that were shapeshifting into humans.

Chapter 14

TAMING THE WOLF: A DOG'S LIFE

We watch as the girl embraces the limp form of her dog. Her tears fall on its shaggy pelt and we can see her shoulders heave with sobs. About her stand others who also seem to be moved at the dog's death. We all stand a short way from the settlement, in an area where the ground has been pockmarked with pits; this is a cemetery, a cemetery, it seems, that is as much for dogs as it is for people. The dog is gently lowered into its prepared grave. Several items are placed beside it, including three flint blades and a decorated hammer made from an antler. You look at me with some disbelief, why would a dog need these things? Finally, the girl takes a bowl and blows a thin coating of red ochre over the body of the dog, and a man places an antler to rest on its back. He then speaks a few low words over the body before standing stiffly. Perhaps this is the dog's master and the girl's father? At a sign, the grave is filled with fresh earth and the small group disperses. Only the girl and her father remain, watching until the pit is full and the earth smoothed flat. Then, they also turn and head back to the settlement, back to the land of the living.

This scene, or one very much like it, was played out at Skateholm in southern Sweden. We have briefly come across this place before, as it was the burial site of the man with the elaborate headdress who was placed in the ground in an upright position. It seems that his was not the only unusual burial within the community.

Skateholm is one of the largest Mesolithic settlements in northern Europe and was occupied for several hundred years around 5000 BC.[1] Although there is no direct evidence for the dwellings people lived in, presumably because they were too makeshift for their remains to have survived, there are plenty of other indications that people lived here, including a large cemetery. In fact, the cemetery was actually divided into three discrete areas. As Skateholm lies within a lagoon, and the seawater continued to rise throughout the time the site was occupied, successive cemeteries became inundated and new bodies had to be buried somewhere else. However, for the excavators, this gave a clear indication as to how burial rites changed over time and, as we shall see, is extremely revealing about the way people treated their dogs.

At first sight, Skateholm appears to have been a paradise for those living in the Mesolithic. The inhabitants had the sea on one side and the forest on the other and could feast on the produce of both. Analysis of the bone remains from the site, showing what people likely ate, reveals an incredible 87 different species. This was a community where obtaining a varied diet was clearly not a problem. However, these bones also show something else. Careful analysis of the age of the animals when they were hunted, especially young pigs (whose age is easy to ascertain from their remains), and the migration patterns of others, shows that they were all killed in the winter months.[2] Despite the apparent abundance, it is clear that people were forced or perhaps felt the need to disperse in the summer, perhaps to the interior forest or further along the coast. Perhaps the cemetery served to claim territorial rights to the site when the living were absent; a form of supernatural guardianship ensuring that no other group could claim what was rightfully theirs.[3]

However, despite the communal cemetery, it seems that the community at Skateholm was anything other than a cohesive group. Several of the bodies show trauma that was less likely related to hunting injuries and more likely to be the result of brawls and violence.[4] Perhaps this was why people dispersed in the summer: to cool the tensions that had built up over the winter months. Moreover, the cemetery itself shows no uniformity to the burials, as if people were doing what they wanted to do rather than following the rules of the community. Since we have already seen the importance of community rituals in maintaining group solidarity (and thereby allowing people to call upon others when things got bad), it is clear that what was happening at Skateholm was a breakdown of Mesolithic society. The reason for such a breakdown will become apparent as we continue our journey through the past. For now, however, the disintegrating relationships between people may have allowed new and different bonds to form, not between two people but between a person and a dog. People had found their new best friend.

People had previously lived with wolves for thousands, perhaps even hundreds of thousands of years. Even as early hominins turned to a meat diet and started to scavenge at kill sites, they would have been aware of other predators, some working alone but others, such as the wolves, working as a unit. Perhaps something of the wolf took hold of the early hominin mind and they began to emulate some of the hunting strategies that they saw, or maybe this, like so much else, was beyond the capacity of their partially evolved brains. There are some who think we may have even co-evolved with the wolf, so that our weaknesses became the wolf's strengths and vice versa, but this would have required a level of intimacy and co-operation that may have been impossible for all but modern humans to achieve.[5] However, as humans became skilled hunters and took larger game in greater numbers, perhaps some wolves became camp-followers and, just occasionally, there may have been a degree of interaction between human and wolf that began to break down the boundaries between the two species.

It was not until the last Ice Age was in retreat that there is evidence for the existence of dogs; a single jawbone was found in a human grave at Oberkassel in Germany, dating to about 13,000 years ago.[6] However, even accepting the experts' view that the bone is definitely from a dog and not a wolf, it tells us nothing about the relationship between people and dogs at this time. For that, we have to wait another 2000 years, when an elderly woman was buried in Israel with a puppy of several months old.[7] As if to demonstrate that the animal had definitely moved from wolf to dog, the woman was arranged in the grave with her hand resting upon the dog's flank. Is this the first sign of the affection we still hold for dogs?

It is possible that dogs were first integrated into the human world not because of what they could do for people (that came later) but, rather, because of what they represented. They appeared to acquiesce with the beliefs people held about the world, where animals gave themselves willingly to humans, just like the beluga at Lepenski Vir. The initial appearance of dogs in graves may even suggest that they were seen as guides to the afterlife. If dogs could cross the divide between animal and human, then perhaps they could also cross the divide between the worlds. Interestingly, in many ancient religions, dogs still retain the role of gatekeepers to the afterlife.

It was probably not until the late Mesolithic, when people first settled in permanent or semi-permanent villages, that the behaviours we associate with dogs began to appear. It is likely that the camp-following wolves started to rely more on human settlements, eating food waste and human excrement and perhaps this was a role that people appreciated.[8] Over time, those animals would breed with others who were also choosing to live among the humans until, slowly, the village wolves became the village dogs. In effect, the dog domesticated itself. Evidence for modern hunter-gather villages where semi-tame dogs roam, shows that these animals do not necessarily form packs but tend to organise themselves into groups of no more than three which then adopt a particular dwelling as their own.[9] In the Mesolithic, perhaps this was the time that people began to interact with dogs on an individual basis and began the relationships with which we are now so familiar.

For a hunting community, dogs were undoubtedly useful. Although shellfish and plant foods were tremendously important during the Mesolithic, people still hunted game where they could. Moreover, since the forests had claimed the land, hunting strategies had changed. Pits and traps were certainly used, and even snares for small creatures, but animals like red deer needed to be found and, if they were mortally wounded in a hunt but still capable of flight, they also needed to be tracked.[10] Enter the dog. It would not have been long before a partnership was formed.[11]

In the earliest cemetery at Skateholm, dogs were sometimes buried in the same grave as people.[12] These were likely animals that were sacrificed – a clear indication that people wanted to take their dogs with them to the afterlife. However, some dogs were afforded their own grave and, as we witnessed at the start of this chapter, they were given items that would usually be the preserve of a hunter. But then, perhaps this is exactly what these dogs were considered to be, and accordingly they were buried as such. The human graves, like those we saw at Deer Island and Bøgebakken in the previous chapter, show that wealth accumulated to the young and fit, and status had to be earned, probably in the hunt. The dogs were no different, they provided food from the hunt and they were honoured accordingly. Moreover, this was a time before any other animal had been domesticated and the cognitive boundary between humans and animals was still fluid enough to be breached: human into animal and, now, animal into human. It was a very different way of seeing the world and is almost diametrically opposed to everything we think about animals. However, as for the little girl we saw mourning the dog, it was unlikely that she had ever experienced a hunt. She probably saw the dog as her pet, just as most of us do with our dogs today.

The dog burials at Skateholm were not unique. Other burials are known from Polderweg in the Netherlands,[13] Vlasac near Lepenski Vir in Serbia,[14] and at Popovo in Russia, where, in addition to graves containing dogs, a human was buried with a necklace made from dog teeth.[15] It seems that, across a very wide area, there was a blurring of boundaries between humans and dogs that allowed dogs to cross over into our world and, seemingly, to appropriate the status of a hunter.[16] Whether they were still considered animals or had actually become humans is perhaps something the people of the time would not have thought about, such was the fluidity between the two. However, this was not to last, as a later cemetery at Skateholm makes clear in a subtle but unmistakeable form.

Although dogs were still afforded their own burial in the later cemetery at Skateholm, there are signs that perhaps their status relative to humans was beginning to change. Of the 65 graves, eight contain dogs but these were grouped together, as if there was an area for canines that was separate from that for humans. Dogs and humans appear to have now been considered different and discrete. This has far wider ramifications than just the division of humans and dogs, however, and suggests that people were beginning to classify and divide their world in new ways.[17] Previously, there was little division in people's minds between what we might think of as nature and culture; there was merely a continuum that encompassed and included all aspects of their world. Although people utilised resources from the natural world, this was done with reciprocity at its core and was, accordingly, in balance with the natural order and cycles of nature. Animals could become people just as easily as people could become animals, because both were merely parts of the same whole. The later cemetery at Skateholm shows that these beliefs were beginning to break down. Dogs had moved from being equal to humans in the hunt to being subservient to their masters. Perhaps, as their usefulness increased, their worth actually diminished?

We still retain something of this contradiction in our own relationship with dogs. They can be our closest companions but are also the source of our cruellest insults.

A bitch can be both our best friend and our worst enemy. The same attitude prevailed for all the animals that humans eventually domesticated. Calling someone a pig or a cow is insulting and comparing him or her to a chicken or a sheep is unkind. Domestication brings animals close but, in so doing, it also repels us. Domestication, of course, is one of the hallmarks of agriculture and a completely new way of living. As we shall see, it was both to enthral and to repel the Mesolithic communities of Europe in equal measure.

Chapter 15

STRANGERS
AT THE GATE

We have been walking for two days and you look at me imploringly; I can read your thoughts as they mirror mine – when are we going to stop? Ahead, our companions follow the snaking paths of the forest creatures; they never seem to cut even a branch unless there is no alternative. Last night, a trail revealed fresh spoor and, after loosing the dogs, we had boar for dinner. A welcome feast, even if we did have to leave some of the meat for the spirits of the forest. The woman leading the party stops abruptly and makes a sign for us to do the same. Although she cannot see through the trees, she has heard something. Instantly, we are alert and our companions seem to merge with the forest, their progress now silent. Sadly, we cannot do the same as we struggle to keep up. Eventually, we reach a clearing, the tree stumps at the edge still showing the signs of the axe that felled them. Within the clearing, people mill about and it is apparent that they are building something. There are gasps from our group as we watch them raise a post and set it in the ground; it is so tall it is as if they are replanting the trees themselves. It is clear that these people are making a dwelling, but it is massive, not like anything we have seen until now. Then, a man walks close to us and there are more gasps: he is leading an auroch on a rope. Except this beast does not resemble the mighty auroch of the forest but is smaller and quite docile. Our companions look at each other and make signs – this is good, we must know more. A young man is selected and pushed to the edge of the trees. He is reluctant to take on the responsibility but it is clear that he has been chosen to speak to the strangers. At the last moment, some meat and a fur blanket are thrust into his hands – he is to offer them as presents. As he moves forward on unsteady legs, we look at each other and know that, for our small group of hunters, life is about to change, forever.

The strangers we were observing were among some of the earliest farmers in Europe. This new way of living spread from Greece and the Balkans into central Europe from around 7000 BC.[1] The move from a hunter-gatherer lifestyle to farming is perhaps the most momentous change human beings ever made. It led to population expansion, wealth accumulation, monuments, cities, civilisation, and, eventually, us. It is no wonder that people embraced the change as they did. Except that, for the people who made the change, all of this was completely unknowable; they had no idea of the ramifications of the decision they were making.

The move to agriculture is often called a revolution – a term first coined by Gordon Childe in the 1920s – and it captures something of the immensity of its importance.[2] However, a revolution implies that people knowingly and quite deliberately overturned the past and ushered in the new, but there is no evidence that they did this. The decision to move to farming was likely taken in a series of small increments, each change that was adopted led on to the next. Over time, and perhaps without fully realising it, people had moved from being hunter-gatherers to being farmers. Moreover, in terms of the changes people had made to this point, the move to farming occurred very rapidly. Within 1000 years, agriculture had been adopted throughout most of central Europe with only the west and north yet to make the change.[3] It was an incredible shift and must have been motivated by an overwhelming belief that it was the right thing to do.

Since the Mesolithic people of central Europe did not have a complete knowledge of farming when they first encountered it (although they had probably heard stories from visiting traders), we will limit ourselves in this chapter to seeing it from their side only. The tale of the farmers will be one that will be told later. This means that we cannot conclude that Mesolithic people did anything because of what it might lead to, as they would not have shared our hindsight. Whatever attracted them to farming had to be understood on their own terms.

Farming itself originated in the Near East and it was likely to have been brought to Europe by people who colonised parts of Greece and, possibly, the Balkans.[4] The reason that they moved to Europe was probably the same as migrants anywhere: economic opportunity. They desired more land to practise their lifestyle and south-eastern Europe had that in abundance. They probably brought all that they needed with them, including their livestock and seeds for their crops. The question for the rest of Europe, therefore, is not why agriculture was introduced but, rather, why it spread.

In addition to livestock and crops, the farmers also brought polished stone tools, particularly axes, pottery, and more substantial houses that were lived in all year round. These elements were once believed to be so indicative of agriculture that they became known as the 'Neolithic package' and, where all five occurred together, excavators knew they had found a farming rather than a hunter-gatherer community.[5] More recently, however, the association among the individual elements of the package has broken down, and it is now recognised that some farmers adopted agriculture without pottery and some hunter-gatherers adopted pottery without agriculture. The Neolithic package, rather than being fixed and universal, was more likely to have been a set of resources, some material but others symbolic, that were adopted and adapted by people in different ways.[6] However, it is clear that whatever else farming offered people, it had to fit into their existing way of seeing the world.

Farming is often seen as a complete break with the past, with the adoption of both a completely different way of life and a completely different set of beliefs.[7]

However, this seems counter-intuitive; if people were to adopt agriculture, it was probably because it gave them advantages within their own society and way of living. People were more likely to adopt something new if it enhanced something that they were already doing, rather than completely rupturing it. It is with this in mind that we follow our young hunter as he goes to meet the farmers for the first time.

The first thing that he would have noticed would have been the domesticated cattle and other animals, probably sheep and pigs. Apart from dogs, it was unlikely that he would have ever seen a tame animal before and, yet, the idea may not have seemed quite as outlandish to him as we might suppose. From the Palaeolithic onwards, we have seen how people developed relationships with animals that went beyond hunter and prey. The half-human half-animal statuettes from the Palaeolithic, the deer dancers at Star Carr, the fishers at Lepenski Vir; in each case, the barrier between human and animal was fluid and malleable. People did not divide themselves from animals in the same way that we do and, for some, this was taken to a literal conclusion as they shapeshifted into animal form. Moreover, when hunting, animals were thought to acquiesce to the hunter's wishes and allow themselves to be caught. The beluga at Lepenski Vir gave themselves to the hunters, the beavers at Deer Island put up little resistance, and dogs positively wanted to join human society.

We have also seen at Star Carr how animal parts were fashioned into tools, moving into the world of humans, before being returned to their point of origin and absorbed back into the natural world. The crossing of boundaries went both ways: human to animal but also animal to human. The graves of the dogs at Skateholm were perhaps the culmination of such views. Domestication was not something that would have been rejected by hunter-gatherers and our young hunter likely saw the cows, pigs and sheep as fitting into his own beliefs about the world.[8]

The hunter-gatherer prerogative for sharing is often opposed to the farmers' aim of accumulation. However, there is no reason that our hunter, upon seeing the surplus stock and crops produced by the farmers, would not have immediately thought of sharing it with his community. Just because agriculture *could* lead to the accumulation of surplus (and, through that, wealth), does not mean that this was what the hunter-gatherers had in mind when they first adopted it. More likely is that they saw new ways of sharing and strengthening existing ties of reciprocity with other communities. Perhaps this is the reason that, once one community had adopted farming, the others followed close behind; they had to match the new level of gifts that were offered to them.

Due to their ethic of sharing, hunter-gatherers are often viewed as egalitarian and any status that accrued to an individual was bestowed by the community. Such status was always earned. However, for farming communities, status could be bought through amassing wealth. Moreover, such status, when gained, could also be hereditary so that unproven youngsters inherited the status of their parents. Even if this was explained to our young hunter, it is likely that he thought of status only in relation to his own beliefs. If he could provide food for his family, and still give some to others, his status would rise. Moreover, if he took as a symbol of that status something exotic from the world of the farmers, such as a pot or a polished axe, his standing would be enhanced yet further. When we examined the cemeteries of the Mesolithic in chapter 13, we saw how status was earned, and that the richest graves were those of young men, presumably because they were the best food providers. However, we also noticed how this apportionment of wealth did not apply to ritual items, which seemed to be associated with certain individuals regardless of age. Since the items taken from the farmers would have been exotic and would not have had any pre-existing symbolism attached to them, it is very likely that they would have been considered ritual items and, as such, were outside the usual rules of hierarchy. This is perhaps why, in south-west France, hunter-gatherer communities adopted pottery and decorated their vessels with the horns of cattle, sheep, and goats; the images were outside their everyday world and were therefore considered special, possibly even of the otherworld of the farmers.[9] The more of these symbols an individual could claim, the higher their status may have been, regardless of any other aspect of their lives. Perhaps these thoughts entered the mind of our young hunter as he exchanged some pots for the items he carried? It would not have been long before the notions of accumulation espoused by the farmers began to make sense to his Mesolithic outlook.

We have seen in earlier chapters how certain items were deliberately deposited during the Mesolithic at places that were meaningful, such as into water. There is even the hint that these places were marked in some way, perhaps by raising a totem pole. Indeed, new research from northern France suggests that the tradition of erecting standing stones, even those that were worked smooth, started in the Mesolithic, perhaps as a development from what we have already observed.[10] Later farming communities may be renowned for constructing huge monuments but the ideas first arose from a Mesolithic mindset.[11] It is possible that our hunter even viewed the act of forming the forest clearing itself in monumental terms, in much the same way that high ground or islands were considered sacred. Opening up the forest by forming a clearing not only created a totally new environment but also allowed the world to be seen in a different way, without the trees blocking the view.[12] If our hunter had ventured into any of the houses, he would have noticed the dense array of posts holding up the beams of the roof. Perhaps he thought of this as bringing the forest inside, closer to people: another way of domesticating the wild?

If our young hunter had been told that the farmers 'owned' the land upon which they built their houses and the fields in which they grew their crops, he may not have immediately understood. However, it is likely that, at this stage of farming development, ownership was more akin to the territorial rights with which our young hunter would have been familiar. Ownership, as we understand it, may not have evolved until agriculture was intensified during the middle Bronze Age when the land required long-term investment. The Mesolithic community at Skateholm certainly asserted rights over their lagoon islands, and they buried their dead there as part of these claims (something the farmers were to replicate in time), so our young hunter would have probably understood the exclusive right for a community to use an area. In any case, such musings would have been unlikely to have held him back in trying out some of the techniques he was seeing.

The basis of agriculture, with its delayed return while crops grow and animals mature, is often opposed to the Mesolithic ethic of instant gratification: if you were hungry then you hunted and you ate. However, this emphasises only the practicalities of a hunting lifestyle and ignores people's wider beliefs. We have already seen how animals that migrate, such as the beluga at Lepenski Vir, or the swans at Bøgebakken, can become imbued with significance that goes far beyond their economic value. Similarly, animals that hibernate in the earth, such as bears and snakes, or in water, such as beavers, are also considered special and their parts or effigies lie with the dead as if they can accompany their souls to the afterlife. If our young farmer was told about how crops were planted into the soil and then tended through the winter before they emerged in the spring, he would have undoubtedly been familiar with the practicalities of what he was being told.[13] However, he would have also situated this into his own views about the cyclicity of the natural world and the rhythms of the seasons, where a period of fallow was followed by a period of abundance. The Mesolithic people may have lived in harmony with nature but all farming asked of them was to extend this to new areas: crops and domesticated animals. Beliefs that separated humans from the natural world (although showing incipient stages of development with the segregation of dog burials in the later cemeteries at Skateholm) would develop over time. To the hunter, however, accepting the values behind agriculture would not have been difficult.

As our young hunter returns to us, he is bursting with news to tell. He immediately hands round the pots that he has been given and also some of the seeds that spill out of one. When everyone gets a fair share, we turn and head back through the forest. Despite the silence that was imposed on our way to the farmers, it seems that now all everyone wants to do is to talk. Although we cannot make out the words, it is clear that what the young man had to say has caused much excitement. Perhaps people might plant the seeds that they hold, or perhaps they might return to the farmers to trade for some cattle or for the secret of how to make pots. It is clear that the people of this community are now on their way to becoming farmers themselves and, as we quietly slip away to continue our own journey, we wonder if all transitions to agriculture will go as peacefully. It is not long before that illusion is shattered.

Chapter 16

CATASTROPHE

The man swaggers a little as he walks past us. It is clear that he thinks he is somebody impor-
tant. In his hands he holds the bow and arrow that we have become familiar with, but he also
holds a beautifully polished axe that seems to catch the sun in its depths. The man holds the axe
proudly, hoping that people will notice that he is carrying it. Just then, another man approaches.
He is angry and gesticulates to the man with the axe. Behind him is a boy who keeps his eyes
lowered. I shrug but you point back towards the hut the man with the axe has just come from.
Within the doorway stands a girl, slightly younger than the boy and obviously distressed.
Behind her, we can just make out a pile of what looks like grain. This must have come from the
farmers and we wonder if she even knows how to use it. The argument has got heated, with the
father of the boy gesturing towards his son and then pointing at the girl. The man with the axe
shakes his head. I glance towards you and it is clear that you are thinking the same thing – this
is a broken engagement. The man with the axe points south, towards the land of the farmers. It
seems clear that this is where his daughter is headed. As he turns, the father of the boy lunges
and strikes his adversary on his head. The man with the axe does not fall but he looks enraged.
He pushes the other man sharply and fists start to fly. If it was not for the other inhabitants
rushing to break up the fight, it is clear that one of the men could have been severely hurt, even
killed. Both men walk away slowly, scowling at each other. This feud will be hard to forget.

When we looked at the spread of farming across Europe, we noticed how many
of the Mesolithic communities in central Europe converted readily, and we saw
the frontier between farmer and hunter moving rapidly north and west.[1] However,
when it reached northern Poland and Germany, probably by 5000 BC, it stopped.
The people of the Baltic, and Britain and Ireland beyond, resolutely refused to
change their lifestyle to farming.[2] Perhaps this was because their hunter-gatherer
lifestyle gave them all that they required and they had no need for the novelties of
farming, after all, unlike much of central Europe, they had the sea to provide for
them as well as the land.[3] These Mesolithic communities held out for almost 1000
years, but with the farmers just a few hundred kilometres away, the resulting stress
must have been enormous.

However, although we might view the last remaining Mesolithic communities as *refusing* to switch to agriculture, it is very unlikely that they would have shared this view. We know that they did eventually convert, but it would not have felt like a foregone conclusion to those who lived at the time. We never ask why the farmers refused to convert back again but only because we know that they did not and, therefore, we assume that they never considered it. For the hunter-gatherers, life probably went on much as before; agriculture was not seen as an unfulfilled destiny but, rather, as a new source of objects and ideas that could be integrated into their existing worldview.

When we followed the young hunter to meet the farmers in the previous chapter, he did not go with any thought of converting his community to farming but he was sufficiently excited by what he saw that this was the eventual result. The people of the Baltic would have met similar farmers but they were more selective in what they chose to take from them. We know that trade took place, with the hunter-gatherers exchanging furs, amber, and produce of the forest in return for pottery, polished stone axes, possibly some animals and even a little grain.[4] We saw some of these items in the settlement that we visited at the start of this chapter. As we noted in the previous chapter, however, since these items were new and exotic, they cut across the usual symbolic categories of objects, and immediately became imbued with a different power. The man we saw swaggering around the village with his traded axe thought he was somebody special for wearing it. It did not matter that perhaps he was not the best hunter, or did not offer the wisest opinions during meetings, or even that all his other skills were considered poor; the axe did not stand for any of these things and by wearing it he could say something completely new about himself. The fact that the axe was clearly exotic may have even given it a supernatural quality, as if it had originated in the otherworld itself.

The introduction of a completely new symbolic code into an existing and well-established system invariably causes tension. How do the new items compare to the old, and will everyone understand and, more importantly, respect the new objects as special? It was clear from the encounter that we witnessed that the axe did not impress the father of the boy and he obviously felt that existing obligations should come before any arrangement made with the farmers. The community we met in the previous chapter passed through these agonies far more quickly, as they converted to farming wholesale; they rapidly moved from being hunter-gatherers to being farmers and therefore the new objects and ideas were not divorced from their context for long. Their initial compulsion to acquire these objects may have been the same as the Mesolithic people of the Baltic, but the result was very different.

The farmers probably met the hunter-gatherers along the border between their two domains, in forest clearings. Perhaps this was neutral territory or maybe it was just the most convenient place to meet.[5] I got an indication of what such a place might have felt like when I visited the Sámi winter market at Jokkmokk in Swedish Lapland, which occurs every February. Originally, this was the place where the reindeer-herding Sámi met the agriculturalists of the south and, over many years, a town formed around the trade. Today, the market is an important cultural event with thousands of people forcing their way into town but, owing to the deep snow and freezing temperatures, it still retains something of its frontier past. Settlements also grew around the trading posts in the Mesolithic and we can trace several farming villages that probably owe their origins to trade with the hunter-gatherers. Some, such as Esbeck in northern Germany, and Darion in eastern Belgium, were surrounded by ditches, and these may have been for defending the sites against restless natives. However, the ditches were possibly too shallow to be defensive and come late in the sequence of contact rather than at the beginning, when tensions might be expected to have been at their worst.[6] Although there are signs of violence within Mesolithic communities, and several bodies at Skateholm reveal serious injuries, this aggression seems to have been contained within the community itself and did not seem to spill over into aggression towards the farmers.[7]

Perhaps similar antagonisms explain one of the most gruesome finds of the Mesolithic. At the cave of Ofnet, in Germany, 33 people, mostly women and children, were decapitated and their heads arranged in two shallow pits. Moreover, death was not necessarily quick or clean, with some remains showing the results of several heavy blows with an axe. This was clearly a massacre but, from the remains, it is impossible to determine who carried it out.[8] After their grizzly deaths, the people (or, at least, their heads) were buried in the usual Mesolithic fashion and decorated with shells, some from as far away as the Mediterranean, and pierced teeth, before being covered with ochre. Did those who carried out the massacre honour the bodies in this way, perhaps to pacify their spirits, or was it another group of survivors, who cleaned up after the assailants had gone? Whatever the reason, it is a reminder that the items that we have been associating with peaceful trade could just as easily be as a result of war, either taken as booty or offered as tribute.[9]

It was not just objects and stock that moved between the hunter-gatherers and the farmers but, as we witnessed at the start of the chapter, also marriage partners. It is only recently that technology has allowed us to establish where a person was born and grew up. At Lepenski Vir, for example, bone-chemistry analysis on three bodies within the cemetery shows that they had a farming diet, full of protein from grazing animals. Analysis of all the other bodies shows that, conversely, they got more of their protein from fish, probably at the time of the beluga migration. Were these three born and raised farmers, who moved into the fishing community upon marriage? Or was the movement the other way around and they married away from the fishing community in which they were born, returning only when dead to be buried at their ancestral home?[10] There are fewer questions surrounding the influx of hunter-gatherers into the first farming communities in south-west Germany. Utilising similar chemical analysis of bone remains, it is apparent that many of the females in the cemeteries came from regions inhabited by hunter-gatherers.[11] Moreover, since they appear to have moved following adolescence, it seems likely that they married into the farming community. Interestingly, like the bodies at Lepenski Vir, who may have returned to their ancestral homelands upon death, these women were buried differently to the local farmers, perhaps preserving something of their unique heritage.

Historically, it was usually women who moved to new groups while the men remained behind, and from the evidence we have examined, it appears that this was also the case in the Mesolithic.[12] Such migration could seriously affect existing communities and may amount to as much as 15 per cent of the female population, all taken from women eligible to marry.[13] Research on modern hunter-gatherers in Africa shows that the abandoned men utilise two strategies to increase their relative standing and thereby attract a mate: either they hunt more or they become farmers themselves.[14] In the interim, they may try to acquire more and more objects from the farmers and flaunt them within their communities. If this also happened in the Mesolithic, such untrammelled demand for farming objects would have been seriously inflationary and it is likely that the hunter-gatherers could not have produced enough furs, or found enough amber to exchange for the items they desired. Moreover, where once pottery and axes had been exotic, over time they became more common and their value as special items probably diminished. Perhaps some of the men even started to work for the farmers, tending crops and herding livestock, further eroding the hunter-gatherer way of life.[15]

Throughout the time of transition for the Baltic hunter-gatherers, the climate warmed and, eerily reminiscent of the risk we face today, the sea levels rose.[16] We have already seen the effects this had on communities like Skateholm, where occupation had to be continuously moved as the sea inundated more of the land. The rising sea would have submerged some lagoons completely, while others may have been cut off through changes in sand accumulation. Either way, the Mesolithic communities that relied upon them would have faced ruin.[17] Ironically, the rise in temperature may have been good news for the farmers, as it would have increased the growing season and made previously unproductive land suitable for cultivation. Perhaps the Mesolithic communities realised what was happening, although, of course, they would not have known the reasons behind it. Maybe they thought that the spirits had abandoned them and it was now the farmers who attracted supernatural aid.

The situation could not continue and, around 4000 BC, the pressure on the hunter-gatherer communities of the Baltic became too great and they converted to farming. As in central Europe, when farming was adopted by indigenous hunter-gatherers, the transition was incredibly rapid: mere hundreds of years after 1000 spent in stand-off.[18] Britain and Ireland followed (after a similar period of stand-off) until almost the entire continent had adopted this new way of life.[19]

We have seen the Neanderthals erased from European history, and now we have seen the same fate befall the hunter-gatherers. The scene is now set for the development of new societies that will slowly lead to our own. However, before looking at them, we need to go back – back to the time when the first farmers came. We need to hear the story from their side.

PART THREE

FARMING THE LAND:
THE NEOLITHIC

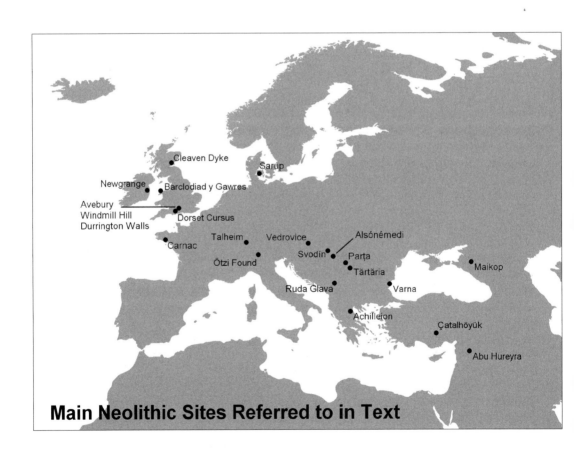

Main Neolithic Sites Referred to in Text

Chapter 17

A TOUGH LIFE

Andrew Moore may not have thought about Dragoslav Srejović, the excavator of Lepenski Vir, as the waters covered his own site, but it is likely that he shared the same feeling of despair for the loss coupled with elation for what he had found. Moore, a Professor of Archaeology at the Rochester Institute of Technology, spent two seasons digging at Abu Hureyra, in Syria, and the next 25 years in the laboratory examining what he had recovered.[1] The newly constructed reservoir of Lake Assad took the rest.

Farming originated at Abu Hureyra – this is where it all began. In reality, of course, there were probably a number of different sites where people made the tentative shift to agriculture at around 11,000 BC, all located in the fertile crescent of the Near East, but this is the site that contains an unbroken record of the change. The people at Abu Hureyra began as hunter-gatherers, collecting wild plants and killing gazelle and wild sheep for meat. After a period of climatic cooling, the wild plants were no longer as abundant, so people focused more on small-seeded grasses. Despite requiring more processing, these grasses allowed people to remain at the site. As the climate deteriorated further, people began to concentrate on rye, a grass that could withstand the colder temperatures. They began to clear the ground of other vegetation and grow rye instead. As their dependency on rye grew (and they needed to remain close to the settlement to tend it), they stopped hunting gazelle and shifted their attention to sheep.[2] These animals could be herded, corralled, and, eventually, domesticated into the animals whose descendents we still farm today. The people at Abu Hureyra had moved from being hunter-gatherers to being farmers and the most significant event in human history had begun.

Farming was not an easy path to take. People now worked longer hours, endured risks of catastrophic crop failure, and both humans and animals suffered from new diseases through their close interaction. Hunters did not become farmers because it was an easier way to live; if that were the only motivation, then we would all still catch our breakfast in the woods.

More and more communities in the Near East converted to farming until, a little after 7000 BC, some people moved offshore to colonise the islands of Cyprus and

Crete and from there, sailed to mainland Greece.[3] Perhaps productive land in the
Near East had run out and people were forced to move because of population pressure, or perhaps there was something else that drew them across the water to discover
new worlds. We have already seen the human urge to explore in previous chapters
and maybe the first pioneering farmers came to Europe for the same reason. It is even
possible that, like their Mesolithic forebears, they considered islands to be special and
this was another motivation to make the initial move across the Mediterranean.[4]

Cultivated crops and domesticated animals were certainly brought to Europe from
the Near East (they did not occur naturally here) but thereafter the picture becomes
less clear. While some see waves of colonisers forging into lands otherwise devoid of
human presence,[5] others think that the absence of Mesolithic people in Greece and
the Balkans is illusory and that the change to farming, when it came, was driven by
the conversion of indigenous people to this new way of life.[6] The reality is probably
somewhere between the two and Ruth Tringham, an expert on the subject, calls it a
mosaic process of transformation: some colonisation, some conversion, and, certainly
around Lepenski Vir, some rejection.[7]

We have already seen why farming might have appealed to the existing hunter-
gatherer population when we followed the experience of a young hunter as he first
met the farmers. Everything he saw he interpreted according to his own beliefs
about the world. Moreover, his community adopted farming because it enhanced
their existing way of life, rather than because it replaced it. In some respects, this initial adoption was not the most significant change that hunter-gatherers made in their
conversion to farming. That came later, when their new lifestyle allowed them to
develop new ways of thinking about the world (and, as we shall discover, the opportunity to express these thoughts as monuments).

Achilleion is an early farming site in Greece and, when it was first occupied shortly
after 6500 BC, people built flimsy shelters, half-dug into the ground.[8] These temporary structures were probably not that different to the dwellings that people had lived
in when they were still hunter-gatherers. However, over time, these dwellings were
replaced with more substantial, timber-framed buildings that may have been among
the first permanent houses in Europe.[9] All of a sudden, people had a new medium
through which to define themselves and their existence and it appears that they readily utilised it.

What made a good place to live for farming people was very different to that
favoured by Mesolithic people. The suitability of soil for cultivation and the avail-
ability of open pasture were far more important than stands of wild plants, or places
where animals could be approached unseen. In fact, wild animals were probably now
seen as pests: deer could trample crops as easily as wolves could take young livestock.
Similarly, it would not have been long before certain wild plants were called invasive
weeds. Farmers would have looked at their reality very differently: rather than seeking their livelihood in the dense forests, they would have appropriated and contained
most of what they required in the open spaces around their houses. This was a world
within a world and, in the main, it was one created and maintained by humans.

Houses agglomerated into groups and farming communities sprang up. In some cases, boundaries were constructed to surround the villages and, immediately, a contrast was made between those who could pass over the boundary and enter the village ('us') and those who were kept on the other side ('them').[10] Moreover, some sites were rebuilt over many generations, the new houses being constructed on the remains of the old until huge mounds were formed, called 'tells', further defining the village as a place set apart. The height of the mound would also display the age of the village and be a store of memories reaching far back in time. Anyone who lived there would be constantly reminded of the site's permanence in the land and of his or her own place within it.

As villages distinguished people within the landscape, so houses distinguished people within the village. However, some went further still and started to divide their houses into separate areas, each dedicated to separate tasks. At Slatina in Bulgaria, a remarkably well-preserved house was carefully divided into sleeping and living areas with specific places reserved for different tasks.[11] In other houses, these distinct activity areas were divided into rooms and virtually all the tasks that were formerly conducted outside were brought within the house; people's world had just got smaller still.[12]

In effect, people's lives were represented by the houses in which they lived; their past, future, and present were contained within the house so that the life of a house became closely associated with the life of a person. We saw a similar attitude to deer antlers during the Mesolithic, where the stages of human life may have been mirrored by the growth of an antler. However, like all things that came from the natural world, antlers were eventually abandoned and returned to nature. Houses were different; they were created by humans and, to keep the same symmetry at their end, they must be destroyed by humans, and this is exactly what appears to have happened. Many houses were deliberately burnt (perhaps when the head of the household died), with people taking pains to ensure that the conflagration was sufficient to completely level the house.[13] In some cases, the charred remains were incorporated into the daub walls of the house constructed in place of the burnt structure, perhaps emphasising the rebirth of the dwelling and the family that lived inside it.[14]

Fire itself is an ambiguous medium, since it is both an essential part of everyday life for heating and cooking, but is also the cause of terrible destruction. Perhaps this contrast formed a metaphor for the ambiguity of farming itself where people care for animals that they will later kill? Maybe people even felt that their own lives were poised between similar forces: friend and foe; life and death; order and chaos. Fire also emphasised the link between humans (and their animals) and houses, since both generate heat internally: the body through being alive, and the house through the hearth that was contained within it. Only one other entity generates such heat, and that is the sun. It may be significant, therefore, that later villages are ordered around the cardinal directions, alignments that can only have been taken from the rising and setting of the sun.[15]

Pottery was another medium through which people expressed themselves and designs show that different regions decorated their pots in a manner that was unique to them.[16] Moreover, the vessels people made were not used in the preparation of food (it is likely people retained their old hunter–gatherer methods for this) but were for display and special purposes, maybe even for the consumption of drugs.[17] Pottery was certainly considered special and this may have been because of its creation through fire. Again, that which destroys also creates.

It was not only pots that were fashioned from clay but also figurines, often of women, although there are plenty of examples where the sex cannot be determined. Like the figurines we saw during the Palaeolithic, those of the Neolithic also emphasise sexual organs, although now through decoration rather than exaggeration. Interestingly, there seems to be two broad divisions of figurines. Those that are found in the permanent tell settlements of Greece were often doing something, as if the concern to differentiate areas of activity in the houses was reflected in the models people made. What people *did* was perhaps the means through which they defined themselves. Conversely, the figurines in the more ephemeral sites, which show little signs of permanent occupation, were more generic, as if just being human was all people had the capacity to express. It is on these sites that people also made animal figurines, particularly cattle, and perhaps these served to define opposing categories of existence: people against animals.[18] The figurines, possibly through performances, were used to tell the story about who people thought they were and their ideas about the world they inhabited.[19]

The emphasis on female figurines may imply that women had an enhanced status during this time but the burial evidence seems to contradict this. While initial burials were, perhaps predictably, confined to the settlement areas (along with all other aspects of people's lives), they were mostly simple and the graves contained little of value.[20] However, after around 5500 BC, cemeteries arose and the dead were buried in their own place. The very richest graves were those of the men, with women and children having very few items placed in the grave with them; clearly the status of women appears to be below that of men. At Varna, on the Black Sea coast, figures of cattle were cut from gold plate, giving an indication of how wealth was measured in these societies.[21] Intriguingly, also at Varna, as in many other cemeteries of this time, 27 per cent of burials were cenotaphs, that is, empty graves, and yet they were among some of the richest in the cemetery. While it may be that people died in such a manner that their bodies could not be recovered, it may also be that these graves belonged to people who existed only in the mind.

The figurines that are contemporary with the graves at Varna are more highly decorated, and spirals were one of the most prevalent designs.[22] Perhaps this echoes the tunnel to the otherworld and shows that these figurines represent ancestors from the afterlife, even those distant relatives who first brought farming to the area. These figurines may represent the same people that were honoured through the cenotaphs in the cemeteries: actual graves that people could go to and tell the story of their origins and their existence. It would not have been literally true but it would have certainly reflected the world that people had created for themselves.

An increasing awareness of the role of the ancestors is a theme that reoccurs throughout the Neolithic. By giving people a past, the ancestral dead also gave people a future. This seems to have been particularly important as farming spread out from the Balkans and moved into the forests of central Europe. Although many of the new farmers may have been descendents of indigenous hunter–gatherers, this was not the story they told about themselves. Like those who created the cenotaphs at Varna, the first farmers of central Europe also invented their past and they lived with the effects of this lie every day of their lives.

Chapter 18

MAKING PLACES OUT OF SPACES

We have been walking through the forest for days, seeing nothing but trees, brambles, and fallen logs. At night, we hear the wolves howl and other animals go crashing through the under-growth. By day, we hear and see nothing; it seems that the entire world is just one large wood. Then, quite suddenly, we emerge into a clearing. Crude stumps show that this is no natural clearing and the neat rows of crops confirm this. We have finally reached a human settlement, one of maybe thousands spread throughout the primeval forest. At the centre of the clearing are the houses and it takes us some time to walk over to them. They are huge, each a great hulking structure, well over 20m long, with roofs of thatch. The walls are covered in rough plaster and we walk along the long side of one, trying to find a way in. Rounding the corner, we find a door set in the short end of the house. You point out that the door to every house is arranged in this way and that they all face the same direction, towards the south-east. Passing over the threshold of the house, we enter its confines. Even within, the house feels huge, and we walk unsteadily through the huge timber posts that support the roof; in a way, it is not unlike our walk through the forest. Suddenly, we hear voices at the far end and we freeze. Fortunately, the house is so big, we are unlikely to have been spotted and so we carefully retrace our steps to the door.

Although we did not know it, we could have entered any settlement site through-out central Europe and come across much the same house style and layout. They belonged to the first farming groups that colonised the loess soils of the lowlands from around 5600 BC. The speed that such settlements sprang up is striking, with an area from Hungary to the German Rhineland (a distance of about 650km), being covered in 300 years. Whether these settlements were founded by farmers moving away from the Balkans, and effectively colonising new areas, or whether they were founded by indigenous hunter-gatherers, converting to an agricultural lifestyle, is still debated.[1] Perhaps the answer lies somewhere between the two extremes, and pioneer colonisers from the Balkans arrived first, slowly converting the indigenous hunter-gatherers to their way of life. The rapidity in which this new lifestyle was adopted is testament to its attractiveness to the indigenous societies and we have already examined why this might have been so in chapter 15.

These new societies are known as *Linearbandkeramik*, a German word describing the way in which people decorated their pottery, using curved lines, engraved when the clay was still wet. Mercifully, the word is usually shortened to LBK. Since the first farmers would have settled different areas to those occupied by hunter-gatherers, the good soils of the lowland being more attractive than the lakes, wetlands, or thick forests where game was abundant,[2] their first task would have been to hack a clearing out of the forest. This would have been essential, both to clear land for cultivation and grazing, but also to source suitable trees with which to build their enormous houses. The forest would have comprised mainly oak and people needed over 100 middle-age trees to make a single house; that meant clearing 4 hectares of woodland.[3] Within the resulting clearing, they grew a variety of crops and also grazed their livestock, predominantly cattle. Some settlements, such as Ulm-Eggingen in Germany, had fenced areas next to the houses, presumably to keep the cattle off the crops.[4]

As we saw for ourselves, the houses were massive; some up to 30m long and 6-7m wide.[5] Their form can be reconstructed from the holes left by the posts holding up the roof. Many houses appear to have been divided into two or even three separate sections and it was thought that this allowed for a granary in the section nearest the door, a living area in the middle section, and a byre for livestock at the far end[6]. However, this would have meant that every time cattle were taken in or out of the byre, they effectively traipsed through both the central living area and the granary; not an arrangement to enhance domestic bliss. It is far more probable that the different sections relate to different building stages, which may or may not have been occupied at the same time.[7] The houses were generally spaced at least 10m from each other,[8] and with the possibility of small fields or gardens attached to each house, they would have given the impression of being quite independent from one another. Perhaps this was deliberate and served to emphasise one of the key themes we noticed emerging in the first farming communities in Greece: defining individual identity.

Identity comes from not only from who a person is but also from where they have come from: their ancestral lineage. Some houses had child burials placed near to the structure, perhaps to mark its creation.[9] We have already seen how houses in the Balkans were symbolically connected to human lives and the same may be true for dwellings in the LBK. It is revealing that many houses were abandoned long before it was necessary, and while some were burnt, many were left to rot naturally while a replacement house was constructed nearby.[10] Perhaps this happened on the death of the head of the household, and there certainly were adult burials around the settlement that may be the remains of these people. The house was likely linked to the birth and death of these presumably significant people, with other individuals being defined through living in and being associated with it. At Zauschwitz, in Germany, however, another theme was introduced, as a child buried in a pit was covered with the burnt debris of a house.[11] The death of the old house was presumably juxtaposed with the birth of the new to form an unbroken cycle of rebirth and renewal. Perhaps this also explains why some of the human bones on LBK sites show signs of can-nibalism: people were ritually absorbing the identity of those who had gone before.[12]

It seems that identity and permanence were twin themes that were played out within these settlements. Every day, people would wake in their massive houses, knowing that their ancestors were buried close by. They would feel connected to the place and, through their everyday actions, would join their lives to those who had gone before. It is interesting that many sites have large pits, either down the side of the houses (where clay was dug out for the walls), or located near activity areas. These were slowly filled over 25 years or more, perhaps as part of organised events such as feasts, and would have been a store of memories about the past in much the same way as tells may have been in Greece.[13] However, the past speaks differently to each individual and some stories would have been too important to leave to the vagaries of individual interpretation. If identity arises from the past as much as it does from the present, people's origins would have been particularly significant. If asked, every person in an LBK settlement would answer quite definitively where they had come from – and they would all be lying.

When we walked through our LBK village, we noticed that all the houses and, accordingly, all their doorways, faced towards the south-east. There was some variation across the geographical spread of these settlements but, within each, the orientation is unwavering. Richard Bradley, from the University of Reading, has traced the orientation of each settlement across their entire range and has found that each points to the direction from which farming spread to the area.[14] If LBK people stated that, this is where *we* come from, they would be wrong. What they meant was this is where our *lifestyle* comes from. To them, however, there may have been little difference, so intertwined was their identity with the lifestyle. It was not only houses that were aligned to this direction; the bodies buried in the cemeteries also faced the same way.[15] Perhaps it was spoken about as being a mythical place of origin, a loca-tion from where the world began and to which all could expect to return on death? Interestingly, there was an active trade in spondylus shells at the time, and these were traded along the same route as that taken by the spread of farming. The shells were clearly considered extremely special and were likely indicators of status. Perhaps they were even thought to have an otherworldly nature, their exoticness linked in people's minds to their mythical place of origin.

Some people, however, were not buried facing the prevailing direction and, in fact, were orientated to the opposite. Revealingly, isotopic evidence shows that these people were not local to the area but had been born and raised in the surrounding highlands. Since most were female, it is likely that they were marriage partners from the surviving hunter-gatherer populations.[16] Clearly, they never forgot their roots and, upon death, refused (or were refused) entry to the mythical lands of the farmers.

The movement of women into the farming communities suggests that it was men who owned the houses and livestock and remained in close proximity to them throughout their lives. Intriguingly, within a mass grave at Talheim in Germany (comprising 34 individuals who all met violent deaths), one distinct group appears to have been a nuclear family of a man, woman, two children and an older grandparent.[17] Such an arrangement often occurs in male dominated societies where inheritance is deliberately limited by having only one marriage partner.[18] Where wealth is held as livestock, there will always be something to bequeath (the house, of course, may have been ritually abandoned). The need for marriage partners and the lively trade in spondylus shells and other raw materials belies the seeming independence of each settlement and each house within it. People would have needed one another, however much they avoided admitting the fact. Nevertheless, acquiring such things may not always have been peaceful.

To benefit from agriculture, unlike hunting, it is necessary to wait; crops must grow and animals must mature. However, rather than find such patience, there is always the option of stealing the supplies of others and, as LBK communities became established throughout the region, this is what seemed to happen with increasing frequency.[19] Turning again to the mass grave at Talheim, another distinct group comprised males and children. The striking absence of women suggests that they were kidnapped by the assailants (presumably for marriage), while the remainder of the population were massacred. The killing blows were inflicted by an adze, a tool otherwise used for cultivation. Adzes are often recovered from graves, especially, although not exclusively, from male graves, and this hints that they may have held special significance, perhaps indicating status.[20] People were very particular in selecting the stone with which to make the adzes and material was quarried (and presumably traded) from as far as 200km away.[21] Like the spondylus shells, it is likely that the adze had something of the otherworld about it. Perhaps this is what made it an ideal killing tool: an object of the otherworld providing passage to the afterlife. In any event, it is unlikely that the victims would have appreciated the symbolism.

Although the adze was a cultivation tool, and its use as a status symbol was surely connected to this role, wealth was probably held in livestock. Unlike the Balkans, where sheep were the dominant animals, cattle were now preferred, which, although reflecting the different ecological zones of the two regions, also reveals something about the society that kept them. Cattle are large animals and, when one was slaughtered, its meat was likely too much for one family to consume alone (so much for independence). There is evidence that feasts occurred in the spaces between the houses (presumably communal areas and thereby unconnected with any single household) and that the ritual nature of these occasions was signified by the part of the animal that was eaten. Since only bones from the head and neck were found in the pits at these locations, either the rest of the meat was consumed elsewhere or it was not consumed at all, with the greater part of the beast being deposited outside the settlement.[22] It is striking that many traditional farming societies consider the sacrifice of a cow as the greatest offering they can make to the spirits. Not only is the animal itself slaughtered but so is the time and effort spent raising it and all the feed it has consumed over its life. Sacrifice does not always preclude eating the animal after its death but such consumption may be ritually curtailed, as it appears to have been during the LBK period.

Cattle retained their significance throughout the Neolithic and, in many cases, they appear better to think with than to eat. Unlike dogs, which appeared to cross the divide between humans and animals during the Mesolithic, cattle always seemed to be quite rigidly divided from humans. However, such rigidity reveals a serious ambiguity. Unlike hunting, where hunter and prey are clearly defined, agriculture required the long-term care of a creature whose sole purpose was to be slaughtered and eaten. Cattle seemed to embody this ambiguity. They were domesticated: a group in-between humans and animals and, as we have seen throughout our journey so far, such liminality was always considered significant. People of the Neolithic shared their lives with cattle and, as we shall see shortly, they also took them to the afterlife.

Chapter 19

ANIMAL RELATIONS

It is drizzling slightly and we stamp impatiently to be in from the cold and wet. It is a long walk back to the houses, and the welcome heat of the fires within, and we are anxious to be gone from this desolate place. It seems like an age since the inexplicably enormous grave before us was dug and the two dead bodies, a woman and a man, were laid within it. You were quite touched by the care taken to bring the heads of the dead together: the woman lying on her right side facing the man lying on his left side. Their similar ages suggest they might have been a couple. We also admired the fine pottery vessels laid around them and the copper bead given to the woman, the first time we have come across such metal. However, since that flurry of excitement – nothing. Some people have wandered off and some are now so engrossed in conversation that they are no longer bothering to keep their voices low. Eventually, we hear a noise and some sort of order prevails. A woman approaches with what I think are two cows, until you nudge me and point out that the smaller one of the pair is a male. Their handler puts some fodder on the ground and, as they bend their necks to eat, they are simultaneously struck and have their throats slit. This happens so fast that before we are aware of the bellow of protest, the beasts are dead and have rolled into the grave. Now we understand why the grave needed to be so big: this couple were taking two of their stock with them to the otherworld. However, the cattle are not left where they fell but are now hauled into the same arrangement as the people in the grave: the cow lying on its right side and the heifer lying on its left side. This is clearly of great importance as people spend a lot of time and effort getting it right.

The burial we witnessed was at Alsónémedi in Hungary.[1] It dates to 3500 BC and clearly demonstrates the increasing importance that people were attributing to their stock. Since the cattle were placed in the grave whole and had not been butchered first, perhaps they were intended to be the progenitors of a new herd in the afterlife. However, the care taken to arrange the animals to match the positions of the people suggests a closer connection between human and animal that went beyond simple economics. We have already seen how some animals, such as dogs in the Mesolithic, managed to bridge the gap and enter the world of humans as equals. At Alsónémedi, it is as if the cattle almost but not quite achieved the same feat.

The reason that cattle seemed to be treated differently during the Neolithic can perhaps be traced back to a time before their first domestication, when their wild ancestors, aurochs, roamed across much of Eurasia. Aurochs were huge, powerful beasts, 2m tall and weighing around 1000 kg, with lethal horns rising in a shallow arc from their heads.[2] Although they were widely distributed, DNA analysis shows that aurochs were first domesticated in the Near East and that, allowing for a little interbreeding with wild populations along the way, all modern cattle stem from this region.[3] Aurochs have been admired by people since they were first painted on the walls of the Palaeolithic caves. Hunting such a beast would have been a risky undertaking and it is likely that the animal became a symbol for tremendous power. For the shamans of the time, it might have proved simply irresistible to shapeshift into its form and to take something of this power for themselves. Aurochs were likely the largest animal they ever saw and perhaps there was significant prestige to be had in working with such a beast.[4]

The settlements at this time start to be ornamented with horns that resemble those of the auroch. Skulls and horns were built into the structure of houses at Mureybet in the Levant, for example, hinting perhaps at the emergence of a cult surrounding these animals.[5] This reaches its apogee at the Turkish settlement of Çatalhöyük where entire rooms were dominated by the skulls and horns of aurochs, emerging from the walls and surrounding low platforms, as if to provide a fixed point where due reverence could be shown to this mighty beast.[6] There were many aurochs in the vicinity of Çatalhöyük and this may be what induced people to stay in this area and develop a new subsistence base, farming, to allow them to remain. Effectively, it was the presence of the aurochs and people's need to be close to this symbol of power that led to agriculture being introduced and developed in the region.[7] However, the prevalence of auroch remains within the settlement shows that they must have been frequently hunted, primarily to obtain the skull and horns needed for decoration and, presumably, for associated rituals. Over time, such exploitation of the auroch herds may have induced people to try to manage the animals and there may have been a general progression of herding, corralling, and tending that eventually would have led to domestication. While some animals were certainly eaten, perhaps as part of the ritual surrounding their sacrifice, it was sheep and goats that provided most of the meat for the inhabitants. Aurochs, it seems, retained their special significance even after they were tamed.

Cattle remained special when they were brought into Europe with the first colonising farmers and structures resembling those at Çatalhöyük can be found in the Balkans. At Parţa, in Romania, for example, a notably large building had a raised platform surrounded by cattle skulls.[8] Upon the platform were two linked figurines, each over a metre high. One appears to have had a human head and the other an animal head, perhaps even that of an ox, betraying the ambiguity that such animals had at this time. Like the dogs of the Mesolithic, cattle seemed to occupy a position between animal and human, their importance as spirit animals outweighing their economic importance as a source of food. The inner part of the building at Parţa contained more animal heads and seemed to have been divided symmetrically into four parts. Like many special buildings at this time, it ended its life in flames. The division of the building at Parţa into four has resonance with a burial at Tărtăria, also in Romania, where a body, often identified as a shaman, lay with numerous figurines, a spondylus shell bracelet, and three clay tablets.[9] Each of these tablets had designs on their surface, one neatly divided into four by a cross with images in each quarter (perhaps mirroring the structure at Parţa), and another with a stylised human behind an ox. While some have seen this as a scene of early ploughing, the elongation of the human's limbs and curve of the back suggests that it may, in fact, be another representation of shapeshifting, the image showing both the transforming shaman and the final form of the ox.

The special status held by cattle continued as farming spread into central Europe and we have seen in the previous chapter how LBK populations feasted only on selected cuts of the animals that they slaughtered. Moreover, such feasting was communal and took place between rather than inside the houses. As at other sites, sheep and goat were eaten normally and it is clear that cattle were differentiated as special and extraordinary. It is notable, however, that pigs were treated in a manner that was similar to cattle and may have been eaten as part of communal feasts rather than as everyday meals.[10] Like domesticated cattle, but unlike sheep and goats, pigs would have had a wild equivalent in the forests surrounding the settlements (wild boar), and this may have enhanced the status of their respective domestic species as animals that defied categorisation. If any interbreeding occurred between wild and domestic populations, either through deliberate or accidental mingling, their ability to cross between the worlds (an essential trait of anything considered to be imbued with spiritual power) would have been confirmed. Revealingly, where wild aurochs were hunted and killed, their meat was now consumed in a manner equivalent to sheep and goats and no special ceremony seemed to attach to it. Clearly, the special status of domesticated cattle did not extend to their wild brethren. It was their ability to straddle both wild and domestic worlds that appears to have been held in such esteem – something an auroch could not do.

Owing to their ability to reproduce and replace their dead, the herds of cattle kept by Neolithic farmers would have been a constant and unchanging feature of the landscape.[11] It is possible that people drew on this symbolism in their own quest for identity and permanence. Perhaps the herd of cattle even started to represent the community that they belonged to, with each individual or family group closely identified with particular cattle? Perhaps this is why the couple at Alsónémedi that we saw buried at the start of this chapter were accompanied in the grave by their cattle and why the arrangement of the animals mirrored that of the people? The cow and heifer were so closely identified with their respective owners that it may have been inconceivable to separate the group, even in death.

There are many other burials of cattle in the period after 3500 BC, some accompanying humans in the grave and some buried independently.[12] However, it seems apparent that, unlike dogs during the Mesolithic (which had individual graves and a suite of objects to match those given to people), cattle were not being buried as if they were human. Maybe they were intended to serve the deceased in the afterlife (many animals were buried in pairs, suggesting a role as draught animals), or perhaps they had their own role to fulfil, rather like the half-human half-fish shamans at Lepenski Vir. However, although these cattle were not buried as humans, there is evidence from Britain that some cattle could be buried in place of humans.

Cattle were associated with many of the monumental structures that became a fea-ture of the British Neolithic.[13] However, it is where their remains are found in tomb chambers that their role as 'substitute people' becomes most apparent. In many cases, the dead cattle received the same treatment as people, their remains being burnt, dis-membered, or left whole depending on what happened to their human equivalents.[14] Perhaps, like the burial at Alsónémedi, certain individuals were so identified with their animals that one could represent the other in burial or pseudo-burial situations? It may even have been that an animal was slaughtered and placed in the tomb at the initiation of a new shaman; the death of the animal representing the symbolic death of the initiate. Certainly, the image at Tărtăria hints at a connection between the two that draws on the liminal position that each occupy within their respective groups. Perhaps such an occasion was marked by feasting and it is striking that many pig remains, the other animal that appears to have been singled out for special treatment during the Neolithic, were often found littering the area immediately surrounding the tombs.

In one particular tomb at Beckhampton Road, in southern England, the excavator found no burial but three ox skulls where the body should have been.[15] He surmises that one of these may have comprised the head and hide of the beast, perhaps suspended on a post to retain something of its original form. Even if the meat was otherwise con-sumed, the hide of an ox would still have had significant value and may have even played a part in the burial ceremony. We can, possibly, imagine the shaman wrapped in such a hide and shapeshifting into the beast itself. Intriguingly, head and hide offerings were arranged in a similar manner by Mongolian peoples as offerings to their ancestors.[16] If the same was true in the Neolithic, it provides another reason why these animals may have been placed in the tombs, the last resting place of those that had gone before.

Cattle and, to a lesser extent, pigs, were considered special during the Neolithic because of their ambiguity, touching categories of wild, domestic, food resource, and symbol but without being totally subsumed within any of them. They were perhaps considered not entirely of this world, even of having something of the oth-erworld about them. Cattle crossed the boundaries that were becoming evident in the Neolithic and they were esteemed for doing so. Another boundary that seemed to arise from Neolithic beliefs was the division of certain places by enclosing them inside a bank or ditch. While those around the villages may have been defensive, and we have come across some of these on the interface between farming and hunter-gatherer communities, others seemed to do no more than seal off an area and define it as a place apart. Over time, these places grew in importance until they became a world in themselves; places where, it seems, almost anything was possible.

Chapter 20

ENCLOSING THE WORLD

Sharing food with others seems to be a universal human trait. All across the world, people demonstrate their hospitality and warmth to others through offering food. The same was true for the past, and we have seen how the first farmers of central Europe slaughtered a cow and brought their community together to feast on its meat. This communal feasting took place between the enormous houses, as if those occasions stood in contrast to the appearance of isolation and independence of each household. Since we know that such independence was far more symbolic than real (people needed others for trade, marriage partners, and probably also for help with the day-to-day tasks of life), perhaps the feasts were their way of saying: yes, we may be independent but we also still need each other. These were occasions when the everyday world was ruptured and other realities came to the fore.

It was not long before the areas between the houses were marked off through digging ditches and forming banks around them.[1] Perhaps this was to define the area in which communal feasts were to take place or perhaps it was to mark those that had already occurred. Certainly, at Langweiler 8 and 9 in Germany, the enclosures were formed just before the settlements were divided into smaller units.[2] Perhaps these enclosures were designed to remind people of the importance of community as opposed to individuality; a way of defining the true reality of people's dependence on others when most other symbolism seemed to suggest the opposite? This is why the enclosures were constructed just before the settlements split into smaller units: it was to reinforce the importance of community and the strength of the bonds that existed between rapidly diverging family groups. Moreover, people were defining their community by what they did together, in this case, eating, and this seems to echo the earlier figurines from the Balkans, where people defined themselves not by who they were but by what they did. Actions, it would seem, spoke louder than words.

As the LBK developed into the *Stichbandkeramik* (meaning 'stroke-ornamented pottery', and named for the new pottery style that was decorated with small stroke-like depressions; it is usually abbreviated to SBK), enclosures continued to be built.

Many of these appear to serve a small group of houses, perhaps continuing as places of communal gathering.[3] Since some of these enclosures now comprised more than one circuit of ditch and bank, while others had elaborate entrance causeways, even their construction would have brought the community together in order to pool their labour for the project. It seems that there was now more formality given to these places and at Svodín and Bučany, both in Slovakia, the four entrance causeways cut the circular enclosure ditch into four equal quarters.[4] We have come across the division of space into quarters before and it always seems to symbolise somewhere special and not quite of this world. The causeways at Svodín and Bučany were aligned to the rising and setting of the sun at the solstices (something that appears to be repeated at equivalent sites in Germany), and perhaps people came together at these times and watched as the rising or setting sun seemed to enter their enclosure and bathe them in its light. Such a shared occasion would have enhanced the solidarity among those who witnessed it. This was their place and people would have felt as if they belonged there.

After about 4000 BC, enclosures proliferated until they appeared in most parts of Europe. There does not seem to have been any unified form or layout, however, and there was wide variety in size, shape, number of circuits, and entrance elaboration; some were even surrounded by fenced palisades or were sub-divided into discrete areas.[5] However, although some might have been suitable as defensive barricades or as livestock corrals, there is little evidence that this is how they were used. Rather, they appear to have continued the traditions of feasting and other special activities that were the main features of earlier enclosures. However, unlike objects that can move from place to place, earthworks were fixed in one location and, in order to have gained such widespread distribution, it must have been the ideas behind their construction that spread and induced people to emulate what they had heard.[6]

As people constructed enclosures in greater numbers, it seems that the enormity of their houses began to diminish until they became slight and ephemeral.[7] Moreover, the enclosures themselves moved away from the houses until they occupied marginal, perhaps even liminal, locations in relation to other, everyday activities.[8] If enclosures originated to mediate between the seeming independence of the massive long-houses as opposed to the importance of communal activities, it now appears that the latter is paramount, at the cost and almost complete denial of individual households. The individual had been subsumed by the community. Intriguingly, this attitude seems to mirror parallel changes in the treatment of the dead, where individuality was slowly subsumed by an overreaching concept of the ancestor, and this is a theme that we will be exploring in the next chapter.

As before, however, the shift from individuality to community is subtle and perhaps more symbolic than real. At Sarup, in Denmark, for example, the enclosure seems to replicate the arrangement of the settlement with ditch segments and possibly even separate palisaded areas corresponding to each household or family group.[9] Although it is the community that is emphasised and celebrated within these enclosures, there seems to have been an acknowledgement of the place held by individual households within it. Perhaps this explains why many enclosures in north-west Europe were formed by numerous small segments of ditches on either side of entrance causeways; each segment and, perhaps, each causeway symbolising individual households or groups that made up the community as a whole. However, if this was the case, the items left in the ditches seem to have followed another pattern, where every item appears to have had a specific and predetermined location where it could be deposited. Again, the ambiguity of the enclosure and the tension between individual and community finds its form in the activities that were carried out there. Moreover, the deposited remains suggest that these activities were many and varied. However, rather than confine ourselves to the remains alone, perhaps we should go and take a look for ourselves.

It is dawn at midsummer and the dew is rising in little wisps of mist from the small woodland clearing in which we find ourselves. We follow a band of people across the top of the hill towards a large flat area just off the summit. As we get closer, people stop, barely containing their rising excitement. Looking down at the ground, we notice for the first time a large ditch before us, curving off in either direction to form a circle around the hill. Within this ditch is another, and then another, except that each ditch is not a continuous circle but has been dug in small sections, so that from above it must resemble a dashed line. The crowd parts as three women approach. They are chanting some words that seem to be a sort of opening ceremony. At last, we are allowed to cross the ditch and enter the circle itself. Some of the people stop here and immediately begin to unpack items such as half-finished axes and antler pieces. While some set to work crafting tools, others approach and try to barter for the finished items. As we watch two old women haggle with a young man over some worked flint tools, you point out a small group, seemingly burying a child in one of the outer ditches. They proceed with their task solemnly, almost oblivious to the raucous activities going on around them. I wonder if the girl digging the grave is the child's mother. Later that day, the three women we saw earlier return with two cattle. Remembering my past difficulty with sexing cattle, you inform me that they are both male. They are driven right into the central circle and quickly killed, using a method very similar to that which we have seen before. The meat is swiftly butchered and split into separate portions. It looks like we will fill our bellies handsomely tonight. However, just before we join the queue for some meat, you notice the heads of the cattle being placed in the ditch, right next to the entrance causeways. The similarity with the burial of the infant makes us pause. But it is too late to think about such things, especially when there is so much meat on offer.

We were at the causewayed enclosure at Windmill Hill in southern England, which dates to around 3500 BC, and, although a spectacular example, contains many of the elements that underlie the thoughts and ideas encapsulated in these sites.[10] At one level, the enclosure and the activities that occurred there became a physical manifestation of these thoughts, a three-dimensional representation of what was inside the Neolithic mind.

Windmill Hill had three concentric ditches, one inside the other. The outer ditch contained entire animal carcasses or substantial parts of animals, especially from pigs and goats. It also contained fragments from stone axes and unworked antler, and also two infant burials, one of which we witnessed ourselves. It seems that this ditch contained everything that had not yet fully entered the world of humans: artefacts were unworked or incomplete; animals were in their natural form; and even the human burials were of young, perhaps unsocialised children, who had not yet assumed their place in society. The middle ditch also contained animal parts, but this time from cattle and dogs, animals that we know had a far more intimate relationship with people.[11] Similarly, the items left in this ditch had been worked and had clearly been in close association with people for a lot longer than those items in the outer ditch. It seems that there was a progression towards increasing intimacy with people that was reflected in the items that were deposited within the ditches. Finally, the inner ditch contained fully butchered animal parts as well as flint knives, perhaps used in the butchering process itself. The animals in the outer ditch have now turned into portions of meat suitable for human consumption. Perhaps this is the most intimate relationship that can exist between people and animals, with the butchered meat being completely subsumed and absorbed into the person who consumes it? It is undoubtedly significant that feasting seems to be particularly prevalent at many enclosures. It seems that the ditches at Windmill Hill represent a move towards intimacy and absorption into the world of humans. By entering the enclosure and walking towards its centre, people embodied what they wanted to say about themselves: we may be individuals but it is through belonging to a community that we are able to survive. The enclosure becomes a microcosm of Neolithic society: all their beliefs about the world contained within a few concentric ditches.

The site of the enclosure at Windmill Hill was not selected at random but rather covered an area of earlier activity that included animal and plant processing, feasting, flint working, and human burial. Many of these tasks were continued when the ditches were dug, although they were now separated and formalised into a more regular pattern. However, the enclosure was not designed to be the equivalent of a map that could be understood and read in its entirety, but rather was a bounding of specific actions and activities through which people marked their presence at the site. The items left in the ditches created a lasting presence of those activities and enabled people to mark their interaction with a place that was theirs. The biography of object, site, and person merged to create a palimpsest of time where each individual element referenced the entirety of the others. It was a way that people represented their lives in a single moment of time.

The intimacy with the world of humans that we observed at Windmill Hill was represented through a process of transformation, whereby an unaltered item became more and more processed until it was completely subsumed into the realm of humans. This transformational character of the site mirrors its liminal position at the margins of inhabited land. We have already noted that enclosures may have been viewed as places outside usual time and space, rather like the otherworld of the shaman. The tantalising evidence of opium at Etton enclosure in eastern England, and the more widespread occurrence of henbane, hint that perhaps these were even sites where trance journeys took place.[12] Themes of transformation take many forms within the enclosures, such as unworked to worked, animal to meat, life to death. Even the crossing of the threshold would have been its own transformation, leaving behind everyday concerns for an alternative reality where the entire world was condensed into a small, bounded area. Again, comparisons with the otherworld of the shamans are hard to ignore.[13]

The transformation represented at enclosures that seems most pregnant with meaning was the death and burial of humans. Enclosures were not necessarily burial sites but places where the dead could be processed, their remains entering the symbolic world that was represented there. This mirrors the wider treatment of the dead, whereby individuals might die, but it did not necessarily mean that they left the realm of the living. This was a time in which the dead walked.

Chapter 21

TOMBS OF REBIRTH

The man had survived the blow to his head and had even survived the cure for the resulting pain – boring a small hole into his skull and snapping away some of the bone – but it was to no avail. He was likely in discomfort until the day he died and was lain in a small grave at Vedrovice in the Czech Republic.[1] One of the excavators of the site, Paul Pettit from Sheffield University, thinks the position of his hands in the grave, seemingly clutching at his head, mirrors the pain he suffered in life.[2] The settlement at Vedrovice was one of the uniform LBK villages that we met in chapter 18, with its cemetery for the dead set a little away from the houses. This was where the man lay buried. However, this seeming division between areas for the living and those for the dead is deceptive and there are many burials that were made in the settlement itself, seemingly connected with the construction and abandonment of the massive long-houses. We saw in chapter 18 how these houses were often abandoned before they really needed to be and then left to rot and disintegrate while another house was constructed nearby. This probably occurred on the death of the head of the household, the house being so intimately linked to an individual that when one dies so the other must follow. The surviving family members presumably moved to a new house with a new head.

Over time, the abandoned houses would have collapsed and decayed to become grassy mounds between the occupied houses of the village. It is certain that people would have remembered that the mound had once been a house and they would have likely thought about the family that had lived there. In people's minds, the mound may have taken on the role of a memorial or cenotaph to the old household in the same way that a grave would have fulfilled the same role for an individual.[3] The dead did not occupy the old house mound but they would have certainly been associated with it.

These mounds increased in significance until their locations became so charged with power that, instead of leaving abandoned houses to rot, they were cleared away and the new house was positioned directly over the top of the old. Perhaps this was an attempt to appropriate something of the power that would have otherwise accrued with the formation of the mound: a way for the living to claim something from the dead. However, this left a problem, since the old house would not develop into a mound and there was no place that the memory and, in people's minds, perhaps even the spirits of the household, could go. The solution was to construct mounds that were dedicated entirely to the dead; seemingly replicating the house form and shape in every detail to achieve an artificial reproduction of an abandoned house mound.[4] This probably started in Poland, where the last long-houses overlap with the first artificial mounds.[5] Moreover, rather than leaving these mounds as empty cenotaphs, people now buried their dead beneath them so that the mound became a barrow: an enormous grave to match the enormous house the person might have once lived in. However, as the massive houses fell from fashion and the Neolithic moved into what is called the *Trichterbecherkultur* (characterised by the funnel-necked beaker pottery style dating to after 4500 BC, and generally shortened to TRB), the long-barrows remained and became a feature of the landscape that was to last, in various forms, for another 1500 years.

Although the presence of these long-barrows may have defined the territory of the group, it seems unlikely that this was their prime purpose. Good land was hardly scarce and regular movements among various locations in the course of a year may have established claims better than the existence of the barrows, regardless of any perceived supernatural guardianship the dead might evoke. However, the mounds may have represented a more intimate territory: that of home and a sense of eternal belonging.[6] We have seen in previous chapters that people might have returned to their homeland upon death and this was even given mythical form with the early farmers all being buried facing east. Here, home was far more immediate and memories of the long-houses and the corresponding shape of the barrow could only have reinforced such feelings.

Some of the long-barrows were arranged to match the layout of associated settlements, as if they began to form entire villages for the dead. In some cases, these cemeteries were even placed over abandoned settlements with the barrow exactly matching the ground plan of a house.[7] However, there was another widespread tendency to situate the long-barrow cemeteries near to sources of water, either on dry 'islands' in otherwise waterlogged locations, or next to rivers and springs.[8] This probably has its origins in trance experience and the impression of floating or of hearing running water when passing from one world to the next, which, in people's minds, the dead would have needed to do if they were to reach the afterlife. We have already noted that water was seen as a gateway to the otherworld during earlier periods and the same beliefs seem to have been prevalent in the TRB. As if to emphasise the connection further, some long-barrows were constructed from water-derived deposits, such as silt from rivers or bogs.[9] Clearly, if the dead could not get to water, then water would be brought to them.

Once the dead were sealed under the mound of earth that covered them, they were no longer accessible and their remains would have been beyond the reach of the living forever. Although the exact form varies, there is often a small chamber or cist beneath the mound in which the remains would have been placed. However, the covering of these remains was likely to have been the last act of a long sequence of interaction with

the dead, and there are structures around many long-barrows that hint of rituals or ceremonies either before or, more likely, after a body was placed in the cist.[10] Perhaps, until
the body was finally covered, it was not even considered properly dead?

For many traditional people, death has two stages: leaving the world of the living, followed by joining the world of the dead.[11] Between these stages, the spirits of the dead
are thought to stay close to the living and, if such a view prevailed in the Neolithic, this
may explain why burial places had so much activity that went beyond mere disposal
of the corpse. In effect, while they remained between the worlds, the dead became a
resource that could be approached and, perhaps by undertaking trance journeys, even
spoken to as if they were still alive. There are signs that certain bones were retained and
even passed around by the living before being deposited in the grave and perhaps this
indicates that it was not always necessary to retain the entire body in order to keep the
spirit of the deceased close.[12] When the tomb was finally covered, this was probably the
point at which the dead were thought to start their journey to the afterlife, travelling
via the water source that they lay close to (even if it was only the memory of water held
in the soil piled above them). Finally, the mound was covered with turf, possibly replacing the skin lost by the bones before they were finally laid to rest. The occurrence of
cattle hides in and around similar graves perhaps served a similar role.

As time progressed, people seemed to want more and more access to the dead until
the sealed long-barrows were replaced with tombs that remained open and accessible. At first sight, this appears to be a major shift in focus. However, if earlier remains
had been retained and handled by the living, before being sealed in under the long-
barrow, then all the new style of tomb introduced was a more formalised setting in
which the processing of the dead could be carried out. It is likely that entire corpses
were placed in the entrance passageways or even left outside of the tomb, where they
would putrefy and rot. When the remains started to fall apart, certain bones might be
removed and used for ceremonies in which the dead spirit may have been contacted.
As the bones hardened and lost all resemblance of flesh, some were returned to the
tomb to be sorted and stacked with matching bones that already lay in the far depths
of the chamber.[13] The deceased would only now pass to the afterlife and enter the
realm of the dead. The individual had, perhaps, become an ancestor.

Although these tombs were concentrated in north-west Europe, they have many
and varied forms and a similar assortment of names.[14] The existence of a chamber at
the heart of the tomb, accessed by a length of passage, seems to be one of the more
common features, however, and the term 'chambered tomb' will be used here to refer
to all varieties.

Although the interiors of these chambered tombs were sometimes spacious, they
were presumably crowded with bones, and the passageways leading to them were
often small and cramped. Moreover, the space was probably highly charged with the
presence of the dead and may have been considered dangerous, even taboo. It is likely
that only a certain few had the necessary ability to enter the tomb and remain among
the dead. These were the people who regularly moved between this world and the
otherworld as part of their vocation: the shamans of the community.

We stand before the entrance to a large tomb. The stones that form the threshold are massive and provide an eerie presence in the flickering torchlight. The body of the dead woman lies just before us and, sitting over her, is an old man with long greasy hair and, from what we can tell, no teeth. It has been a while since the shaman, for this is what the old man is, ingested the drugs and he is beginning to sway, his chant getting louder. Just then, some younger men to his right start drumming, pounding their hands onto skins, pulled taught over wide-brimmed pots. The shaman gets up slowly and moves into the tomb. There is a gasp; he is now entering the otherworld of the spirits. He emerges almost immediately, his arms filled with bones, some with bits of flesh still hanging off them, and he jabbers incoherently at the small group of mourners about us. The drums continue to pound and we start to feel light-headed ourselves. The entrance to the tomb seems to take on enormous proportions and we know that to enter its confines means never to return. Suddenly, the shaman grasps the corpse of the woman and drags it roughly into the tomb. We can just see him scatter the remains of half-rotted bodies to make enough room. He then disappears from sight, swallowed completely by the darkness within. It will be some time before he emerges and we wait, in awe of his powers.

If the shamans were to interact with the spirits of the dead (and even to survive what must have been the hellish experience of being among so many rotting bodies), they needed to shift their consciousness into trance and, besides taking drugs, drumming may have been one way of achieving this. In fact, it seems that some of the tombs heightened the sound of the drum to achieve the exact frequency required to facilitate trance.[15] In some Welsh and Irish tombs, there are engraved patterns which have been matched to the phosphenes seen in trances induced by psilocybin mushrooms.[16] Perhaps this was the drug taken by the shaman we saw. Some of these images seem to mark significant stages of the journey into the tomb, perhaps determining places where the spirits needed to be placated.[17] Even the form of the tomb itself, with a passageway leading to the realm of the spirits, closely matches trance journeys to the otherworld and the shared imagery would have been readily understood as referencing both experiences. However, the very earliest tombs had no passage and even some of the phosphenes engraved within the chambered tombs were later additions, suggesting that these monuments were not *initially* designed to replicate the experience of trance. Rather, tombs seem to have been the catalyst for such experiences (the sound effects would have heightened the sensation), which led to them being developed to better reflect the association between the two.[18]

Not all carvings within tombs mirror the phosphenes of trance; those in Orkney, for example, bear far more resemblance to the designs found in nearby houses.[19] Perhaps this symbolised the merging of life and death, something the shaman might have thought about as he or she entered the tomb. In Sweden, the imagery may have been replaced altogether with textured and patterned stone.[20] Clearly, there was no single way that such tombs should be read and it is likely that they relied on a shared experience and understanding that was meaningful to the specific communities that used them. At Gavrinis in France, for example, the stones of the passageway are covered in phosphenes, which converge around paired axes.[21] We have already seen how such objects may have been status symbols at the time and perhaps this reveals something about the inhabitants of the tomb.

At some tombs, there is tantalising evidence of the sort of thing shamans might have done when they entered the chamber. At Barclodiad y Gawres in Wales, for example, a stew made from the remains of fish, amphibians, a grass snake, and small mammals was boiled and then poured over the smouldering remains of a fire, before being covered with small stones and shells.[22] Although the full import of this event can probably never be known, it is striking how the animals chosen for the stew mirror the realms of water and earth. Moreover, the amphibians and snake are equally at home in both worlds. Perhaps the stew referenced the ability of the shaman to move between comparable worlds and was therefore a highly symbolic offering to make to the dead?[23]

When the dead had served their community for as long as they were required, they were returned to the tomb to join the serried ranks of the ancestors. The bones now lost their individual identities and it appears that they may have even been sorted into matching groups, each with its own distinct place within the tomb.[24] For the dead spirit, this was probably the time when it was thought to make the final journey to the afterlife, leaving contact with the world of the living behind. However, in long-barrows, such a journey was achieved via rivers or other sources of water near to the tomb. In the case of chambered tombs, water played a less important role and the dead needed to find another way of undertaking their journey.

At a very small number of tombs, the way to the afterlife may have been guided by the rising sun, shining down the entrance passageway and illuminating the chamber itself. Such tombs were generally aligned so that this happened on a significant day, such as the solstices or equinoxes, and this is the case at Newgrange in Ireland. On the midwinter solstice, the rising sun shone through a slot above the entrance, constructed so that the beam could be angled correctly to reach all the way to the inner chamber.[25] It was a sight few would have witnessed (and those outside the tomb may have had to form a clear route for the sun's rays to penetrate), but perhaps it was never meant to be seen by the living. When the sun reached the chamber, it hit a small section of wall, low down on the right-hand side. Engraved on the wall were three joined spirals and these flared brightly under the glare of the sun. Perhaps this was the sign that the dead spirits were believed to be waiting for: the illumination of the spiral that symbolised access between the worlds. This may have been the day when the sun was at its weakest (itself perhaps a liminal time), but from this point onwards it would strengthen and grow until it reached its apogee of power at midsummer. Perhaps the journey of the dead spirits into the afterlife of the ancestors was believed to take on similar proportions: a rebirth and fluorescence in another realm.

The journey to the afterlife was of immense magnitude and, apart from those shamans brave enough to follow, it was the exclusive preserve of the dead. But, if the dead had their ceremonial journeys at this time, then so too did the living and, once again, these were marked by monuments.

Chapter 22

A WALK TOWARDS DEATH

We move forward, crammed between many bodies. There is nothing to mark the route we are walking but the shamans leading us seem to know the way instinctively. At places, we pause and people point out certain features in the landscape, their gaze carefully avoiding the mounds of the dead. We walk further and people are silent now, focused only on what lies ahead: the powerful glow of the setting sun. It is midwinter and there is little warmth left in its rays. I see you shiver and pull your cloak more tightly around your shoulders. As we reach the top of a small rise, people push forward slightly, packing us even closer together; the slanting light forming halos around the forms of those before us. Slowly, the sun sinks and we notice that it now lies just above a large burial mound. As it sinks further still, it seems to enter the mound and, finally, be extinguished within it. As the last rays of light are taken from us, there is a collective exhalation of breath. The sun has joined the dead and now lies in the otherworld; we stand on the brink of the longest night of the year. All of a sudden, it feels even colder.

The route we were walking lies in southern England and was defined by a bank and ditch that runs along its entire 10km length. However, on our journey along its course we saw no trace of either; we were there before the earthworks were constructed. Rather than defining the path that people should take, the bank and ditch may have enclosed an area where people were now forbidden to go, sealing forever a passage through the land.[1]

When we looked at enclosures in chapter 20, we saw how they originated in LBK settlements in central Europe before spreading north and west to give rise to the causewayed enclosure we visited at Windmill Hill. Although this was an English monument, the ideas behind it arose somewhere else. The same was also true of the bank and ditches that defined the routes across the land, except that these did not arise in the south, in central Europe, but in the north, in Scotland.

Recent excavations have uncovered several massive structures in Scotland, which, on account of their enormous dimensions, have been interpreted as communal halls.[2]

Although it is not clear what activities went on at these halls, most gatherings seem to have involved food, and perhaps they were places for marking special events in the life of the community: births, marriages, and deaths.[3] As these halls developed, they became larger and larger until it is unlikely that they could have been roofed.[4] From our vantage, the halls now turned into something else, but to those using them, they may have been no different at all, just larger and now open to the elements. It seems that several of these structures were deliberately burnt down and replaced in exactly the same spot. Holm Farm, for example, may have been destroyed and rebuilt on three occasions – no mean feat for a structure that was 70m long.[5] When we came across the deliberate destruction of a structure previously, such as houses, it seemed to have occurred on the death of the head of the household. The same might be true of the Scottish structures, except that the head was perhaps that of the community.

While some unroofed halls were clearly rebuilt, there were others that were not replaced. We can only guess at why this was; perhaps the community disintegrated, or perhaps a different place was found for gatherings? However, rather than merely being burnt and abandoned, it seems that some were surrounded by a bank and ditch.[6] Since there was no means of crossing this boundary (unlike the enclosures in chapter 20, where causeways made entry easy), access was possibly forbidden, and the site dedicated to the memory or even the spirit of the community that used to use it.[7] Like the long-barrows, these sites had now become places of the dead.

This was not the only similarity between these structures, however. Many long-barrows began with a post-built timber arrangement that was presumably connected with the burial, perhaps as a mortuary house.[8] This formed the focus for the subsequent raising of the barrow in the same way that the post-built timber structures in Scotland formed the basis of the subsequent enclosures, except that one was a gathering place for the dead whereas the other had been a gathering place for the living. Even the shape of mound and enclosure were similar: long and rectangular and often (but not always) with rounded ends.

Since size seems to have mattered to those living in the Neolithic, people lost little time in making these new features as enormous as possible. They even extended existing long-barrows with ditches and banks that reached incredible proportions. At Cleaven Dyke in Scotland, for example, a low bank with ditches on either side appears to abut and thereby extend an existing long-barrow by 2km.[9] Intriguingly, the bank stretched towards the south-east, the direction of the sunrise at the winter solstice, although, because of the surrounding landscape, the sun was not visible from within the earthwork as it rose.[10] Any alignment was, therefore, purely symbolic. However, the bank was constructed in segments, as if each stage was marking the stages in a progression towards the direction of the sunrise. Since the point of origin was a grave, perhaps the route was not for the living at all but for the dead; actually seeing the sun would therefore have been irrelevant. Although a much later monument, we have seen how the sun entering the Newgrange burial chamber may have been a means through which the spirits of the dead were thought to reach the afterlife. Newgrange and Cleaven Dyke may have arisen entirely independently, but they both emerged from similar beliefs and a shared experience of the world (perhaps ultimately derived from trance journeys) and therefore such similarities of purpose may be more than just coincidental.

It is difficult to classify exactly what Cleaven Dyke was, as it seems to fall outside the standard definitions of other monuments. Like much of the Neolithic, people seemed to experiment with ideas and try different things at different times. For the people that built it, however, it was a route across the landscape, not for the living to follow, but for the dead. Cleaven Dyke was defined through use and not through form. The ditches, while providing the soil to form the adjacent bank, also prevented access to the interior and even the bank itself may be less of a platform for walking upon and more of a cover, protecting the route that ran underneath it.

The idea of sealing a pathway through the land spread south into England and Wales (and, to a lesser extent, into Ireland) and, although elongated banks were constructed, it was those routes that were enclosed between bank and ditch that formed the most impressive monuments. Curiously, these are known as 'cursus' monuments, since the first antiquarians to study them thought that they resembled the chariot-racing circuits from the classical world.[11] They were wrong, of course, but the name stuck.

The lack of any remains in the ditches surrounding the cursus monuments seems to confirm that these were not places in which people gathered after they were built.[12] We have already seen that at places such as causewayed enclosures, depositing items in the ditches was an integral part of what the place was all about, but this was not so at the cursus monuments. These were locations where people were not meant to go. However, this does not discount people ever having walked these routes, only that they would have done so *before* they were enclosed. Landscape archaeologist Chris Tilley, for example, provides a memorable narrative of what it is like (and, presumably, what it might have been like) to walk the Dorset Cursus in southern England, part of which we followed ourselves at the beginning of this chapter.[13] They were likely to have been recognised as special, perhaps even sacred, routes and it is possible that they even pre-date the construction of some of the long-barrows themselves, so that the burials were situated in a landscape already bubbling over with significance. Perhaps these paths were even used as part of the funerary procession, for taking the body to the grave. However, once they were enclosed, the foot-traffic would have stopped and they would have become the preserve of the dead and of the spirits as they travelled along them to reach the afterlife.

If these were indeed routes for the spirits, then we would expect there to have been a means through which they could have reached the afterlife. We have seen how Cleaven Dyke was orientated to the rising sun and how the Dorset Cursus was aligned to its setting on the same day.[14] These probably represented the means of reaching the afterlife at these locations. However, just as solar alignments were rarely found in the later chambered tombs, so they were also rare for the cursus monuments. Far more common was that other well-worn route to the afterlife: water.

Cursus monuments seem to be closely associated with rivers throughout their range and in many instances the alignment of the cursus mirrors that of the river so that the natural flow of movement appears to be downstream.[15] We have already seen how people may have believed that this direction led to the afterlife, and perhaps the cursus monuments were positioned to take advantage of this. At Rudston, in northern England, four separate cursus monuments even appear to converge on a right-angled bend of one of the very rare rivers that run across the chalkland.[16] It is as if the departing spirits might be thought to have needed guidance when negotiating this abrupt change in direction.

Although cursus monuments are an entirely British and possibly Irish phenomenon, there are other structures in northern France that follow similar principles. At Carnac, in Brittany, some 2700 standing stones were arranged in rough lines over a 3km route across the land.[17] Structurally, these might seem closer in form to the Scottish post-built timber structures since there was nothing physically stopping people from walking among them, but perhaps there were other taboos that prevented this. Of the four main sections that make up the alignment, all but one were orientated north-east to south-west. Moreover, the visual experience of following the alignment would suggest that movement was in a westerly direction[18] and it appears that even the sequence of erection of the stones followed this route.[19] Perhaps, like the Dorset Cursus, this was so that the setting sun at the midwinter solstice would shine along the route, although, if this was the aim, the alignment was only approximate at best. More likely is that the rows of stones formed a route that merged existing monuments into a path that was followed, perhaps by the living, or, more likely, by the dead. Two long-barrows were incorporated into the stone arrangement itself, with their alignment being respected by the stones. In one instance, a standing stone associated with a long-barrow was reused in its same location as part of the new alignment.[20] Clearly, the stones were meant to enhance rather than replace the existing features and focus of the landscape. At the western terminal of the alignment, the stones became more massive, as if emphasising that the climax to the journey was near, but then it all gets rather messy and complicated with stones seemingly erected all over the place.[21] What appears to happen is that two parallel rows of stones end at a circular stone enclosure, but these have been added to subsequently with further parallel rows that appear to miss the enclosure entirely. Nevertheless, perhaps this was actually the aim of the builders, that the enclosure was only to be entered by a select few, perhaps only by the dead spirits themselves, and that anyone else following the route would take one of the different paths and end their journey next to, but not inside, the structure.

Although the stone alignments at Carnac followed a linear route across the land, it is perhaps fitting that they ended at a circular enclosure. A straight line entering a circle seems to mirror one of the most common forms of rock carvings at this time, which comprised shallow circular impressions, sometimes ringed by other engraved circles, and sometimes cut to the centre with a line.[22] Perhaps this visually represented the route to the afterlife and the similar journeys that the shamans undertook to the otherworld. If so, then the arrangement at Carnac emerged from a similar mindset and, as seems typical of the people of the Neolithic, gave form to their ideas on a monumental scale. The causewayed enclosures we saw in the previous chapter also took the form of a circle and this was to be the preferred shape for the next group of monuments to emerge as the Neolithic progressed: the henges and the mysterious circles of stone.

Chapter 23

CIRCLES OF STONE

It is some time before dawn and, despite being midsummer's day, the chill in the air still seems to find its way inside our woollen cloaks. We shiver to keep warm. It was my idea to climb the bank, a huge circular feature that rises to twice our height and surrounds the village before us. Fortunately, there are two entrances, north and south, where the enclosure is broken and we climbed up one of these ends to avoid the massive ditch that lies just inside the bank. The ditch is so deep that it still has the winter rains in its base; we might be cold but at least we are not wet. The village is not like any we have seen before. The houses are decrepit and needing repair; some appear to have decayed entirely. Nevertheless, this does not seem to concern any of the people we see milling around – they have far more important things on their minds. We have also been making our preparations: gathering small offerings that we will leave for the spirits. Just then, people start to make their way towards a large round structure by the southern entrance; the first ceremony of the day is about to start and we must hurry down if we are to join it in time.

The massive bank on which we were standing was part of a henge monument, generally dating to the period after 3000 BC, and identified by the unusual arrangement of an internal ditch surrounded by an external bank. Generally, defensive enclosures were the other way around.[1] Although excavations at the henge we visited, Durrington Walls in southern England, are ongoing, it appears that the bank and ditch came after the village, even covering some of the houses.[2] This was probably why the place looked so decrepit when we were there – it had already been abandoned. The earthworks may have been intended to seal-in earlier activities, rather as we saw the cursus monuments seal routes across the land in chapter 22. If so, then ours may have been one of the last gatherings to take place there. Although there are a number of henge monuments spread across southern England, to find their origins we have to look again to the north and west, in Scotland and Ireland.

The last of the chambered tombs that we looked at in chapter 21 were not rectangular but round, with the covering mound forming a huge inverted bowl over the burial. Although some were aligned to the rising sun, very few people would have ever witnessed the event since the available space was so limited. While people might have been told about what happened inside the tomb they may have felt detached from the ritual itself and craved more involvement. It was a fair plea and it seems that their demands were met by constructing viewing platforms to encircle the tombs, the pit from which the earth was dug forming a ditch mirroring the shape of the bank.[3] However, these platforms would not have been much use if the main rituals still went on inside the tomb, as people would still not have been able to see them. Accordingly, by making the enclosure an oval rather than a circle, a wider space was left outside the entrance and this presumably now formed the focus for activities at the tomb.[4] At Newgrange, the tomb with the engravings in Ireland, some of these images were now placed around the outside of the tomb where people would have been able to view them easily.[5] Moreover, several of the enclosure ditches had bits of human bone and flint tools placed into them, exactly the sort of things that would have previously been deposited in the tomb.[6] However, it is important to distinguish exactly what people were observing and, presumably, taking part in, from their platforms. It seems clear that people could not have been witnessing the final journey of the dead, when their bones joined the hoard of ancestral remains at the back of the tomb and their spirits departed to the afterlife, as this could only occur inside the tomb. More likely is that people were marking the initial death of a member of their community; the time when an individual left the company of the living but their spirit stayed close and became a resource that people could call upon and approach. The enclosure surrounding an excarnation platform (where the bodies would have been placed to rot immediately after death) at Balfarg Riding School in Scotland, seems to underline the point.[7]

Eventually, these enclosures completely overshadowed the tomb. The activities that now took place became more and more divorced from their original context until the existence of the tomb was no longer considered necessary and the bank and ditch could be positioned anywhere. The henge monument was born. The lack of a tomb at the centre of the enclosure meant that people could now move down from their viewing platforms and enter the interior space itself, but it is likely that this was still considered a very sacred area and there may have been many taboos limiting behaviour. These were places associated with transition and the items found within the ditches match those that we saw within causewayed enclosures (the earlier monuments that also seemed focused on transition). Even the few actual burials found within henges all seem to be children and, where an adult was found at Avebury, she was of diminutive height.[8] Perhaps, like those children buried at causewayed enclosures, these were individuals who had not yet made the transition to complete individuality and therefore reflected the wider ideas behind these sites as liminal, in-between places. There is even a new type of pottery that seems to be especially associated with henges. Called 'grooved ware', because of the way that the surface decoration was formed, the designs reflect those engraved within the chambered tombs of Scotland and Ireland, some of which seemed placed to aid the journey of the dead.[9]

Only a few of the designs on the grooved ware pottery seems to match the phos-phenes of trance (which formed the basis for one corpus of designs in the chambered tombs), and the shape that seems to have been especially chosen is the spiral. We have seen how this design mirrors the tunnel seen in trance and, although still not a common motif, pottery with spirals seems to concentrate around the entrances to henges. Perhaps this was to emphasise that moving across the threshold was to make an individual transition, from this world to another, and from ordinary time to a more sacred time, such as the time of the sunrise on midsummer's day?

Moving down from our vantage point on the bank, we follow the thin line of people to a par-tially covered wooden structure. Entering this, we are confronted with masses of upright posts, set in ever decreasing circles. Fabric screens stretched across them seem to determine the route we must walk. I gesture to you to go first and we join the line of spiralling people. Our minds drift and we feel ourselves getting dizzy, as near the centre of the circle there is a fire billowing smoke. We quickly drop our offerings at the base of one of the posts: some remains from last night's pig-roast, and a few flint tools. When we finally reach the centre, there is a man sitting by the flames, wearing a necklace of bones. He chants softly and seems unaware that so many people are passing before him. We look closer at the necklace and realise that it is made up of human jawbones. We shudder and hurry on; the sun will soon rise and we have a lot more we need to do before it does.

Just inside the southern entrance to the henge at Durrington Walls was a structure comprising a number of wooden posts set within roughly concentric circles. There was another similar structure just outside the eastern bank, appropriately called Woodhenge.[10] These timber circles are part of a long tradition of monuments that seem intimately bound to henges. Some of the chambered tombs in Scotland and Ireland were not only encircled by a bank and ditch but also on occasions by a circle of wooden or stone uprights. At Maeshowe, the tomb in Orkney where the burial chamber followed the same arrangement as the houses, four standing stones within the central space are so similar to those at the stone circle within the henge at Stenness, that they may have had the same origins.[11] It seems that anyone explor-ing one structure would immediately think of its associations with the others and how, together, they tell the story of human existence. Life in the houses, death in the tombs, and the transition between them within the henges and circles of stone.

At some sites, wooden circles precede those of stone and it has been suggested that this might reflect a change from being places frequented by the living to becoming places devoted to the dead.[12] Certainly, in contrast to stone circles, the objects recov-ered from timber circles suggest that they were well used, although, as with other sites, there seemed to be a specific pattern determining where particular items could be left. At Woodhenge, for example, pig remains were placed near the outer posts but cattle remains were left closer to the centre.[13] We have seen this arrangement before at the long-barrows and at causewayed enclosures, where it seemed to mark increas-ing intimacy with humans. Perhaps at the timber circles, it symbolised the fact that the transition celebrated within the monument was nearing completion. A similar arrangement occurred at Mount Pleasant henge, also in southern England, where the transition from pig to cattle remains was matched by the pottery: undecorated in the outer ditch and decorated in the interior.[14] It seems that both timber circles and henges encompassed similar ideas.

However, many of the timber circles seem designed to be walked;[15] people were not only made to think about these ideas but were required to act them out, and the offerings we made when we walked our circle included us in this process. As we noticed, there may have even been partitions or screens to direct the route that people took, making them take a circuitous path around the uprights before they were allowed to reach the centre. Even at those circles comprising a single ring of posts, people may still have followed a circuitous route around and through each upright before finally entering the interior. Doing so may have induced a light trance, and walking comparable mazes and labyrinths has long been recognised as providing out-of-body experiences. The Sámi of Lapland, a historically shamanic people, constructed a labyrinth at Mortensnes, along the Varanger Fjord in northern Norway, comprising 14 concentric stone rings centred on a large raised slab.[16] The burial of animal remains within the structure adhere to their own pattern, but the location of the labyrinth, between the settlement area and the burial area, suggests that it may have had a role in the transition of individuals from life to death (other labyrinths adjacent to burial sites are also known). Perhaps walking the labyrinth induced the trance necessary for the shamans of the community to oversee the process, providing a vantage that straddled the worlds and enabled them to interact not only with the living but also with the dead. We have walked our own timber labyrinth and we are now prepared for the last stage of our journey – into the realm of death itself.

Leaving the circle and still feeling the effects of walking its route and the pungent smoke from the fire, we are handed small bowls full of burnt bones – those of the community who have died since the ceremony took place last year. It seems everyone holds a similar bowl and we follow the snaking line out of the village enclosure and along a short track to a river. Some have already climbed aboard one of the small craft that await us and we take our place in one of the last to leave. We have not gone far before the drums start and people begin to scatter the burnt bones into the river. We do the same and watch as they briefly settle on the surface before being pulled into the watery depths. Silently, we wish whoever these remains represent a safe passage to the afterlife. Lost in thought, we are startled when the boat pulls into the shore and we join another procession, silently making its way along an avenue defined by a low bank on either side. We walk some distance across a shallow valley before the aim of our journey suddenly becomes clear. Rising out of the land is a circle of stones, the resting place of the spirits. We have just reached a huge flat stone marking its entrance when we feel a slight prickling on our necks: the sun has started to rise and it slowly enters the circle, as it has been designed to do, exactly where our avenue joins it.

Mike Parker Pearson, head of the Stonehenge Riverside Project since its inception in 2003, has been exploring the links between Durrington Walls and Stonehenge, the stone circle that we have just visited.[17] Despite its name, Stonehenge is not a henge and Parker Pearson thinks it may have even begun as a burial cemetery, perhaps for the community that first brought the bluestones to the site from Wales.[18] The stone arrangement, in all its myriad forms across the years, never lost this association with the dead, and formed a contrast to the huge henge at Durrington Walls. This was the place where people seasonally gathered at the solstices to feast and remember their dead, and, on the morning of the solstice itself, to journey via the river and avenue to visit the stones themselves. Perhaps, before leaving, they would walk the maze of timber posts to bid a personal farewell to the departed, scattering ashes over the river as they travelled to the stones? Once at the stones, people would watch the sunrise, its first rays following the same avenue that they had just traversed, before the light entered the circle and illuminated the stones at its heart. If this was indeed a place for the dead, then the rising sun revealed the route to the afterlife.[19] However, this was a route reserved only for a special few; the majority of the dead had to make do with the river, making their own way to the afterlife along its length. It is perhaps significant that the direction and flow of the water mirrors the direction of the first rays of the rising sun at the summer solstice; perhaps this is why Stonehenge was built where it was.

As we found ourselves, the avenue leading to the stones seems to hide all sight of them until the last moment, as if heightening the tension of the journey. Another avenue near to Stonehenge, leading to the stone circle at Avebury, does similar and massive stones at the southern entrance seem designed to block the view still further.[20] The stones at Avebury form their own pattern, a huge outer ring containing two inner rings until these, in turn, give way to smaller features, the northern circle enclosing an open chamber rather like those contained in the long-barrows surrounding the site.[21] Nearby, Silbury Hill may have drawn its inspiration from the corbelled burial chambers that were a feature of the lands to the north and west, another occasion where a structure hidden away has been turned inside-out and displayed to the masses. Overshadowed by Silbury Hill were several fenced enclosures that, like Durrington Walls, may have been gathering places for solstice celebrations.[22] There was even a wooden labyrinth at the beginning of the avenue leading to the stone circle[23] and a river connecting the two (although, compared to Stonehenge, the flow is reversed). It seems that the rituals we witnessed at Stonehenge had currency elsewhere.

Even the bluestones that formed part of the Stonehenge circle may have had properties that were considered special. Examining the place from where they were quarried, Tim Darvill, an archaeologist with a special affinity with Stonehenge, and Geoff Wainwright, the original excavator of Durrington Walls, found that the place was riddled with springs reputed to have healing properties. Surmising that this quality may have rubbed off on the stones themselves, the pair suggest that this might have been why they were so sought after and why people clearly went to such extraordinary efforts to move them to Stonehenge[24]. Was the stone circle therefore a temple of healing rather than a place for the dead? It does not seem possible that it could have been both. However, this presupposes that people in the Neolithic would have followed our neat division between life and death and, as we have seen, there is little evidence that they did so. Stonehenge was less a domain for the dead but more a place of final transition for the dead to reach the afterlife. Illness in the past may itself have been thought of as a similar transition; either a person recovered and became well again, or else they worsened and died. Perhaps it was the bluestones that decided which it would be and Stonehenge would either claim the afflicted body or set it free?

In time, Stonehenge attracted a new band of people who buried some of their dead in fabulously rich graves around its perimeter. It was as if they were keen to associate with the famous stone circle but did not want to encroach too closely into its territory. However, before meeting these people, we will first visit others who also commanded wealth of staggering grandeur. To do so we need to leave Britain and travel far across the continent until we reach its most easterly reaches: the grasslands of the steppes.

Chapter 24

GOLD ON THE STEPPE

The last time we travelled so far to the east was during the time of the ice, when people built shelters out of mammoth bones and buried small model figurines in their own miniature houses. Since then, the Mesolithic has come and gone, people first hunting the herds of horses that roamed the plains following the retreat of the ice, and then shifting to the massive auroch when the herds diminished. Agriculture, when it came, was sufficiently developed that it is likely that it was introduced whole-sale by farmers moving into and colonising the area.[1]

The first recognisable Neolithic group in the region are the Cucuteni-Tripol'ye people and the name neatly encapsulates their geographical spread: from Cucuteni in Romania to Tripol'ye in Ukraine.[2] They emerged some time around 4750 BC and, like the pioneering agricultural communities of central Europe, they are also known for their substantial settlements. The houses were rectangular, perhaps 20-30m long and 6-10m wide, with an upper storey for living and workrooms and a possible byre for animals underneath.[3] Each house was almost identical to its neighbour and betrayed no difference that might suggest different social classes within the village. However, although some settlements could be massive, others were much smaller and perhaps there was an unequal relationship between them. Like other Neolithic houses, many had burials beneath their floors and it is likely that, as in other parts of Europe, this marked both the birth of the house and also closely linked its life to that of its human occupants.[4] As we might expect, the house was burnt upon abandonment.

At many Ukrainian settlements, the houses were arranged in a ring and joined together to form an impenetrable barrier to the outside. Although at first sight this may appear to have been a defensive precaution, it was more likely to provide a suit-able area to corral their livestock. Over time, as houses were abandoned and rebuilt, the ring of dwellings expanded until, at some sites, such as Tal'janki in Ukraine, the settlement covered 400 hectares. That was enough to support 15,000 people; these were not so much villages as small towns and were the equal of many of the incipient city-states that emerged in the Near East almost a millennium later.[5]

Like many other Neolithic sites in south-east Europe, female figurines were abundant and the grains of wheat and barley incorporated into their fabric suggests that they were associated with the growing of cereals, perhaps by associating female fertility with that of the crops.[6] However, as the massive corrals demonstrate, it was livestock that was the driving force behind these communities and, in particular, cattle. From the broadly contemporary cemetery at Varna on the Black Sea coast, we have seen how people cut out images of cattle from sheets of gold and attached them to their clothing, perhaps celebrating the source of their great wealth. The same was likely true for those communities of the Cucuteni-Tripol'ye people, although here wealth led to larger and larger settlements (and presumably herds of cattle) rather than to precious metals and fabulously rich graves. Sadly, these trappings never arrived, because by around 3500 BC the massive settlements had all but gone. Although many houses were destroyed, perhaps suggesting some degree of inter-community strife, it is likely that environmental changes and, in particular, a prolonged drought, sounded the louder death knell.[7] There are some signs that people might have moved to more favourable locations, especially since they probably had carts and draught oxen to make the journey easier. Although there is no direct evidence for such transport, the occurrence of model wheels in some of the graves suggests that people understood the technology required.[8] It is also likely that, owing to the drought, people turned away from arable farming and concentrated on pastoral herding, moving their animals whenever grazing became scarce.[9] It was an existence strangely prescient of the nomadic lifestyle that was to dominate the steppe into modern times.

To the east of Ukraine, where Russia is squeezed between the Black and Caspian seas until it gives way to Georgia, the Neolithic followed a similar pattern of increasing dependence on domesticated plant and animal varieties, permanent houses (forming tells across the flatlands), and the development of decorated pottery. It was all very unremarkable. Until, that is, about 3500 BC, when everything changed and the area between the seas became one of the richest regions of its time. The reason was quite straightforward: they had discovered how to work metal.[10]

Copper had already been mined in Bulgaria for almost 1500 years, but it was not until mining galleries were opened at Rudna Glava, in Serbia, that the metal became widely available and was distributed in ever-increasing networks of trade.[11] We will return for a closer look at these mines in the next chapter but, for now, the collapse of the Cucuteni-Tripol'ye communities, and the subsequent population movements that it generated, may have induced people to join these trade networks. Perhaps they offered some of their cattle in return for supplies of metal? However, it was not just copper that people obtained but also the skills that allowed them to work it. The region became a centre for metalworking and perhaps formed a link between the metal producing west and the nomadic herders of the east. It made them rich beyond their wildest expectations and they were able to decorate their graves (the usual depository for vast wealth at this time) in sumptuous style. Perhaps we should go and take a look for ourselves.

The inner sanctum of the tomb is almost complete and people are preparing to cover it with a mound of earth that will reach over 10m into the sky. Although the chamber will be completely sealed, at least until archaeologists open it up in another 4000 years or so, you notice a small entrance in the side that has yet to be filled and, checking that we are unobserved, we slip silently inside. We find ourselves in the main burial chamber, a room lined with wooden walls and a stone floor. In the centre is the body of a man, dressed in fine robes and covered in red ochre. Above him is a canopy, held up by poles of gold and silver, the fine cloth decorated with gold animal plaques, mostly lions and bulls. Towards the base of these poles, you point out exquisitely detailed models of bulls, the shaft passing through them as if they are holding up the canopy themselves. Looking closer, we gasp when we realise that they have been modelled from gold. You also point out several objects placed upon and around the body: gold diadems, a necklace of gold and turquoise, and, close by, a headdress of gold wire. We shake our heads in disbelief at such riches. Along the wall are storage vessels filled with liquid, presumably alcoholic – we dare not try it to find out. You count each vessel: there are 17, two of gold and the rest of silver. Walking over to the body, we look at the tools placed around it, including a few flint arrowheads and a curved copper blade. They look almost trifling in comparison with all the gold and silver. Adjacent to the main chamber are two smaller rooms. In one is a man and in the other a woman. Since they have only a few possessions and nothing like the wealth contained in the main grave, we grimly conclude that these must be servants, executed in order that they can continue to serve their master in the afterlife. It casts an oppressive pall over the spectacular sight.

The grave we visited was excavated in 1897 near to the small town of Maikop in Russia, which gives its name not only to the spectacular burial but also to the community from which it arose.[12] The golden bulls that held up the canopy are among some of the most celebrated remains from the past and show that, at heart, these communities still considered themselves herders. The flint tools also seem out of place in such a sumptuous grave and might be another indication that the sudden influx of wealth had not yet led to technological advances beyond the sphere of metalworking. Alternatively, it may be that they were placed in the grave as an acknowledgement of the past and of the origins of the community.[13]

Few were buried in such fabulous graves, and the evidence for insubstantial houses, with only few items within them, shows that the majority of people led very different lives. Herding seems to have been the predominant way of life, perhaps hinting that the Maikop people had their roots in the break-up of the Cucuteni-Tripol'ye communities to the north.[14] Wagons would have made travelling between pastures easier and it is notable that they appear in several of the rich graves of the time. Clearly owning a wagon was a mark of success and those that had them were loathed to give them up, even on death.

From about 3000 BC, the burial practices of the Maikop people spread widely and gave rise to the pit-grave tradition, so named because the grave was dug into the earth and then lined with heavy wooden beams. Over this, earth or stone was piled, forming a mound or, in local terminology, a 'kurgan'. Sometimes, the kurgan was topped by a stone figure, possibly representing the spirit of the deceased, although, at a kurgan in Usatovo, in Ukraine, one was topped by a carving of a bull's head.[15] Again, the imagery of cattle is pervasive and probably shows that wealth was still represented through ownership of a large herd. Whereas the objects buried within the kurgans demonstrate that people could obtain fine items from as far away as the Aegean, it seems that it was still cattle that lay at the heart of these communities.

Some kurgans could reach enormous proportions with mounds reaching 20m high and 100m across. The very largest from Azerbaijan may have taken 48,000 worker-days to construct, an overwhelming investment of labour. Some kurgans in Georgia have stone-lined pathways linking them and we can perhaps imagine people progressing from grave to grave and thinking about the ancestry of their community as revealed by its leaders.[16] On a rather more sombre note, the practice of sacrificing retainers to accompany their master or mistress in death appears to continue. It seems that the elite of the community held sway over its members.

This seems to be particularly evident on a silver goblet from a kurgan near Yerevan in Armenia. Rows of images show the leader of the community at a banquet, feasting on the delicacies laid before him and with his warriors standing on either side. Weapons and scenes of war fill the remainder of the goblet's surface, including a pile of decapitated heads and the bodies they once belonged to.[17] War probably took the form of occasional cattle raiding, but it is clear how the elite of the community now believed themselves to be. Another goblet, from a kurgan at Trialeti in Georgia, and dating to a slightly later period, seems to show a different side of life.[18] It has two bands, the lower showing a procession of deer, and the upper showing a procession of people, heading in the opposite direction, but with the heads of wolves. We are used to recognising shapeshifting by now; could this be what the design represents? Their destination is a figure seated by an altar and next to a tree. Could this be the shaman overseeing the ritual? The tree is persuasive as many Siberian shamans speak of reaching the otherworld via a tree: the *axis-mundi* connecting the realms.[19] Was the seated figure teaching the techniques of shamanism to a group of initiates: how to shapeshift and how to journey to the otherworld via a tree? It may be more than coincidence that a cylinder seal buried in a kurgan at Krasnogvardeisckoe also carried a design of a tree.[20]

The other cult image that seems prevalent at this time relates to the horse. So-called horse-head sceptres, although rare, were widely distributed and comprised rough representations of horses' heads carved in stone. Some seem so schematic, however, that without more definitive comparisons, it would be difficult to know that they represented horses at all.[21] At Botai in Kzakhstan, horses were buried with humans, the remains from 14 forming an arc along one side of the human graves.[22] People also engraved horse bones with patterns resembling female dress, perhaps to emphasise the closeness that existed between human and animal.[23] Elsewhere, at Khvalynsk in Ukraine, horse hides were buried with head and feet attached; we have seen similar in the long-barrows of north-west Europe, where we surmised that they may have been worn as part of the burial ritual. At other nearby cemeteries, bone plaques had been carved in the shape of horses, pierced holes showing where they might have been strung for wearing as talismans.[24] Since it seems likely that horses were not domesticated and ridden until a later period,[25] we need to find other reasons for such an affinity with a wild creature.

When we studied the domestication of cattle, we saw how, initially, their wild ancestors, aurochs, were revered creatures and perhaps became the animals into which shamans chose to shapeshift. The horses on the steppe may have played a similar role. Besides being majestic and powerful runners, horses lived in groups not dissimilar to the human societies at the time: a paramount stallion guarding his community from interference by outsiders. If these animals did have a role in shamanic ritual then perhaps the pelts were used in shapeshifting rituals where the shaman would assume the form of the horse? Maybe the horse-head sceptres show different stages of this transformation and this is why they were so schematic. People may have worn carvings of the horse around their necks but, in time, they would have wanted closer contact. The horse seems to have followed a similar trajectory to the auroch: first, hunted for food, secondly, revered for its spirit, and, finally, domesticated to take its place besides humans.

The people of the steppe already had a propensity to move to different pastures with their herds of cattle, so the domestication of the horse would offer them true mobility. When it came, it was a momentous event that would eventually lead to the warriors of Genghis Khan and the sacking of much of Europe. All that is many millennia away, but the signs of what was to come started here, in the Neolithic, with the reverence that was shown to the horse.

When we return to the steppes in the Iron Age, nomadic peoples will dominate the region and their entire way of life will revolve around the horse. For now, we will return to the west and see how the introduction of metal began to shape the communities that would eventually herald the start of the Bronze Age. It was not always an easy time, however, and first we must join in the last desperate flight of a man who became extremely famous indeed in the latter part of the twentieth century AD.

Chapter 25

MURDER!

Erika and Helmut Simon usually liked to complete their mountain excursions in a single day; they were experienced climbers and knew what they could comfortably manage. On Wednesday 18 September 1991, therefore, they knew that after being held up while crossing a glacier, and then still pressing on to climb the peak that was their aim for the day, they would have to spend the night on the hill. That was no problem as there was a refuge nearby. The next morning dawned bright and, like any other climbers, Erika and Helmut found the conditions irresistible and decided to bag another peak. It was on their return to pick up their rucksacks from the hut that it happened. Erika saw it first: a brown smudge in the snow, which, as they came closer, took the form of a man. For mountaineers, death is always a possibility, so the find, gruesome as it was, did not unduly surprise them and they tried to prise the remains out of the ice with their axes. What they had no way of knowing is that the body, christened 'Ötzi' for the region in which he was found, had been dead for 5300 years. He was the oldest frozen mummy in the world.[1]

Dressed for travelling, Ötzi wore leather trousers, a deerskin coat, and a cape fashioned from woven grass. His shoes were finely made with bearskin soles and stuffed with grass as a precaution against the cold. His cap was pieced together from odd bits of fur but it would have been warm. He also carried a backpack, an unfinished bow and arrows, some tools (including a fire-lighting kit) and a copper-headed axe. He was, perhaps, as old as 45 when he died, a grand age for a man at this time. What he was doing so high in the mountains remains a mystery but the circumstances surrounding his death are slowly being pieced together by an international team of experts who are bringing to life the sorry tale from almost five millennia ago.

We follow a small band of four young men across the foothills of the mountains. We cannot understand what they say to each other but their manner suggests that this is no pleasant stroll. One carries a bow, with a quiver of arrows strapped to his back, and another has a knife. They seem to know where they are going. We have difficulty keeping up with them and lose the direction they took. Fortunately, we have now reached the snowline and you point out footprints that we can follow. As we round a rocky spur, the four men have now met another, an older man, who seems to be barring their way. The four men shout and the scene turns menacing. I fear for the older man, who seems to be losing his grip on the authority he has over his younger brethren. From the way he holds his hand, we can see that it has been recently dressed but the blood from the gash betrays itself as a foreboding red stain. There is a scuffle and the old man is pushed hard. He retaliates and blows are exchanged. He tries to seize his most vocal opponent but the group is too strong for him. Unable to defend himself further, he turns to run but the four go after him, raining more blows about his body. Finally, they let him go and the old man climbs higher into the mountain. The young men shout after him but make no attempt to follow. We are startled, therefore, when the man with the bow fires an arrow after the old man, hitting him just below the shoulder and making him stumble. We have seen enough hunting by now to realise that this is a killer strike. The man who loosed the arrow runs quickly through the snow; they are almost at the top of the pass when he catches the old man and sends him spinning with a sharp blow to the head. The old man falls heavily, his assailant roughly turning him and pulling out the arrow from his back. It has snapped, the point still embedded in flesh, but the young man takes it anyway, carefully returning it to his quiver. He then turns, and, shouting at his companions, they all return towards us. If we had not scrambled behind a rock when the trouble started, we might have been seen. We wait until the group are out of earshot and then approach the old man. He is clearly dying but seems to be trying to grasp something nearby. You notice an axe, just out of reach, the glow of the metal blade is quite mesmerising in the slanting light. Perhaps this is the symbol of the authority the old man has now lost. You reach for it but, just as you have it to hand to the man, it is clear that he has died. We walk away; there is nothing more we can do and the darkening skies show that a storm might be forming. As we reach another small outcrop of rock, you leave the axe behind, propped against the same stone where archaeologists will find it some 5000 years later. It will become one of the greatest treasures of the Neolithic, so perhaps it is a good thing that you did.

Ötzi came from the southern side of the Alps and was born and raised in the folded valleys of the foothills. We can be reasonably certain about this as the chemical analysis of his teeth and bones, as well as the microscopic bits of stone in his gut (originating from the stone tools used to prepare his food), leave a geological signature that can be precisely located.[2] He probably left a settlement in the Val Venosta, in Italy, on that fateful morning of his flight into the mountains. As we have seen, he was dressed for the hills and carried much of what he would have needed to make an extended stay comfortable, that is, provided he did not venture too high. In addition to his tools, which included a beautifully made flint knife, he also carried several pieces of birch fungus strung onto a leather thong.[3] An analysis of Ötzi's colon shows that he suffered from whipworm and the fungus, being antibiotic and also a mild laxative, may have soothed the discomfort that he suffered.[4] It is an indication of natural medicine that is seldom found but must have been very common in the past. One of the main roles of the historical shamans was to look after the physical health of their communities and it seems that Ötzi was possibly afforded the same care. This might also explain why he had small lines tattooed onto his lower back, behind his knee, and on his ankle.[5] Owing to his age, and the likely physical exertions during his life, Ötzi may have suffered from arthritis. Perhaps the tattoos were a way of countering the pain in the same way that Chinese acupuncture focuses attention on certain locations on the body to heal a myriad of complaints. He had also suffered from sporadic episodes of disease within the last few months of his life; Ötzi was clearly getting old and perhaps this was why he was singled out to die.

Ötzi carried something we have not yet seen outside of Eastern Europe: copper. The axe that his hands seemed to be seeking when he died was made from this new material, marking him out as a wealthy man and, maybe, even a leader. Further to the south, at Remedello in the Po Valley, similar axes accompany people to the grave, but in Ötzi's community they were not so common.[6] If he did hold a position of authority, Ötzi's deteriorating health gave others the chance that they needed to seize power. The discontent had clearly festered, as there are signs that Ötzi had suffered a cut to his hand a few days before his death.[7] The nicks on the edge of his axe-blade may have been as a result of this altercation, although we shall never know whether he was using it as a weapon or as a symbol for his diminishing status. It seems likely that similar threats forced him to make that fateful journey into the mountains, the differing accumulations of pollen in his gut showing that he had recently descended from the mountains, perhaps to visit his village, before heading high again.[8] Eventually, he followed a pass up into the mountains where he was hit by an arrow, expertly aimed so that it cut an artery causing him to suffer hemorrhagic shock and so bleed to death.[9] Before he died, however, the arrow was removed, perhaps to mask the telltale mark of his assailant (assuming that arrows were identifiable to an individual) and he may also have been struck on the head.[10] An ignominious end for an ageing man. Whoever killed him, and there may have been more than one involved, left Ötzi's belongings and his axe where they lay. Again, this may have been a precaution to avoid later detection but possibly the items were just too special and too closely bound to Ötzi that their removal could not be countenanced. Enough harm had been done that day.

Ötzi was clearly trying to evade his assailants on the day that he died. However, it is not immediately clear why he took to the high mountains, as they can be dangerous and unpredictable. I was once caught in a blizzard myself at roughly the same height at which Ötzi was discovered. It was a frightening experience and, despite being well equipped, our small group suddenly felt very vulnerable. What could possibly have lured Ötzi to such a place? In a roundabout way, the answer is contained in his axe and in the metal from which it was made.

Dotted about these Alpine valleys during the Neolithic were stelae, upright blocks of stone carved in the shape of humans, sometimes making a family group with mother, father, and children. The largest stelae were covered in carved objects, most of which comprised axes and knives. The designs match the axe carried by Ötzi and also those from the cemetery at Remedello, showing that these were images of items made from copper.[11] It seems that this was important to emphasise: copper was what someone carried if he or she wanted to impress. Although copper had been known in the Near East for some 2000 years previously, it had only reached south-east Europe sometime after 5000 BC. Fortunately, people then found that they had their own copper seams, and mines were dug in Bulgaria and Serbia. This enabled a steady supply of copper and the nascent metalworking artisans soon outstripped their Near Eastern neighbours in both sophistication and refinement.[12] It took until 4000 BC for copper working to reach the Alpine region and the people who buried their dead at Remedello were among the first to master the art.[13]

The offerings left in mines such as Rudna Glava in Serbia, where pottery vessels and, presumably, their contents, were left near the face, suggest that mining was seen as an interaction with the spirits of the earth, which had to be placated with offerings before the ore could be extracted.[14] Perhaps the mine itself was seen as a portal to the otherworld, like the painted caves of the Palaeolithic (the similar interpretations drawn from a common experience of trance)? The metal was special because it had something of the otherworld attached to it and was instantly as such. This happened with other materials, such as chert (a light-coloured flint), which was painstaking extracted from mines at Heinheim, in Germany, despite other flint being easier to reach.[15] Similarly, people sought dark-coloured flint from deep mines in eastern England despite lighter coloured varieties existing on the surface.[16] In both cases, the inaccessible material was instantly recognisable. It seems that it was the symbolism of the mine that was important to people and its connection to the otherworld and the spirits that resided there (the same spirits that were appeased by the miners who took the raw material). In Grimes Graves, a flint mine in eastern England, grooved ware pottery was left in the shafts, along with discarded flint axes, which had clearly been broken through use.[17] Perhaps this was a faint echo of the tradition we observed during the Mesolithic, where whatever originated from the natural world had to be returned there at its end; again, ideas that may have independently arisen from a shared experience of trance. Peter Topping, an expert on prehistoric mining, suggests that the miners themselves would have had a propensity to experience trance while working in the dark confines of the mine. There are even small clusters of charcoal in some shafts where hallucinogenic plants may have been burned to heighten the experience further.[18]

Richard Bradley has coined the phrase 'pieces of places' to describe objects made from these special sources, but he does not necessarily limit these to the products of mines.[19] In addition to sources under the ground, those high in the hills also seemed to have had something special attached to them. An international project has sourced the origins of the beautiful jade axes that were an important status symbol in the Neolithic in Brittany (the carvings of axes we noted in the tomb of Gavrinis were copies of those made from jade). Researchers traced the stone to the mountains of the Italian Alps, where the quarries were located in inaccessible and remote locations on just two peaks.[20] By collecting the jade from these remote and sometimes danger-ous places, the axes retained something of the otherworld about them. As we have seen, the otherworld was also a remote and sometimes dangerous place reached only by a few intrepid explorers. On a more local scale, at the stone quarries in north-west

England, people deliberately took stone only from the most vertiginous and inaccessible ledges.[21] Other, more easily sourced material was ignored.

Clearly, portals to the otherworld could be found either under the ground or high on a mountain. This was where the veil between the worlds grew thin and the spirits moved close. Some of the stelae that were dotted about the hills were on routes leading to the high passes. Perhaps these were the guardians of the route, ancestral spirits offering safe passage into the realm that they now inhabited. Stone slabs set before the statues, with traces of fire and flint scatters, suggest that offerings accompanied entreaties for safety.[22] Ötzi may have even done this himself. If he held a position of status, and his axe implies that he did, he may even have led some of the ceremonies, providing the link between the living and the dead. He would have known that the spirits resided in the mountains and perhaps this is why his last desperate flight took him to their realm; looking for their help in his last desperate gamble for life. The spirits were silent and Ötzi died where he fell. However, perhaps through fear of offending the spirits of the mountains, his attackers sought to cover their tracks and they left the copper axe where it lay, just out of reach from its struggling owner. Maybe Ötzi's last thought was for his axe and the need to feel its power one last time.

In the heart of the Neolithic Alps, the new overthrew the old. It was to become a common theme that we will return to in the next chapter. Copper spread from the Alpine region to reach central Europe and, from there, almost all the way to its fringes. Its spread was matched by a novel pottery style: decorated beakers. However, before we meet the people who ushered in these innovations, we must first consider the fate of Helmut Simon, the man who found Ötzi. In October 2004, his dead body was recovered from the ice where it had been trapped since he died, just like Ötzi, so many years before. It immediately gave rise to talk of a mummy's curse, as such deaths are inclined to do, and it is strange that a man so entwined with Ötzi during his life, now holds a similar distinction through his death. It is perhaps as well that the next people we will meet on our journey will be so drunk they have left such troubles far behind them. If we grab a beaker ourselves, perhaps we can still join them.

Chapter 26

A DRINKING PARTY

It is late afternoon and most of the people we sit with are either asleep or retching noisily in the bushes. They have been drinking for most of the day. We tried some of the alcohol earlier, when a man left his beaker unattended while he went to relieve himself. Nobody else touched it; clearly it was his alone. The liquid was sweet and did not seem particularly potent, but then we have not drunk the same quantity as those around us. Some men lie with their arms draped around equally inebriated women; others sprawl on their backs, snoring loudly. We move among them, avoiding the flailing arms that reach for just one more cup, more out of bravado than any real desire to drink any more. The men are all dressed similarly, and have a flat stone set in a leather band around their wrist. You point to it questioningly and I mime an archer firing an arrow, and how the leather protects the wrist from the recoil of the string. There are a few bows lying by their owners' sides with quivers of arrows, although most appear unsullied by any real use. However, it is the drinking beakers that really catch our eyes. You lift one free from the arms of its comatose owner, a risky thing to do given how protective these people seem to be over them. The top of the vessel flares out and all over the surface are designs made up from geometric shapes pressed into the clay. The man whose beaker we hold stirs and you quickly slip it back. There will be more than a few headaches when this lot wakes up.

The Beaker people, named for their distinctive pottery vessels, one of which we admired at the drinking party, seemed to take over widespread pockets of Europe at around 2500 BC. While they may not have been a wave of colonising migrants (an explanation that has fallen from favour in recent times), there are signs that they were a very mobile people. Analysis of the chemical signatures in the teeth and bones of beaker graves in central Europe has revealed that a significant number grew up somewhere other than the place where they were buried. Exactly where is impossible to pinpoint, but it is clear that individuals moved around during their lives.[1] The extent of such journeys was dramatically revealed when a rich Beaker burial was discovered near to Stonehenge in 2002 and christened the 'Amesbury Archer', to describe both his location and a number of the objects found in his grave.[2] Using similar analysis to that undertaken on the central European burials (where chemical signatures in teeth

were compared to those in drinking water), it was discovered that he originated far
to the south, only a little short of the Alps. His journey must have been incredible
and, if those who lived near to Stonehenge had understood his language, he must
have had amazing tales to tell.

The way of life that he represented, the Beaker tradition, spread across Europe not
only because people like him carried the word (and what an impressive figure he
must have cut in the communities he passed through), but also because something
about it was clearly very attractive. From what we have seen so far, its main tenants
seemed to rest upon mobility, weaponry (either for hunting or for war), and drinking.
However, there was another aspect associated with the Beaker lifestyle: metalworking.
The Amesbury Archer, for example, was buried with some of the first metalworking
items ever brought to Britain. Individually, these attributes were not necessary new
and some can be found in the Corded Ware tradition that preceded, and possibly ran
parallel to, the introduction of Beakers into north-west Europe.[3] The Corded Ware
people (named, with little originality, after their pottery style) were essentially pastoral
communities, their livelihood centred on cattle, and it is likely that the Beaker people
followed a similar approach. Certainly, the impressive count of over 40 cattle and an
additional 145 cattle skulls in a single Beaker grave in Irthlingborough, central England,
shows they had the means to rustle up a good feast when the occasion demanded.[4]

It is intriguing that the way of life held dear by the Beaker people is very close to
the mobile, war-fixated, drinking, and feasting metalworking bands we came across
in the eastern steppes. Even the burial ritual was similar, with some central European
graves comprising pits lined with wooden logs and covered by a mound of earth.[5]
While it might be tempting to see the Beaker tradition emerging from the steppes,
the evidence would suggest that Beaker pottery originated in Iberia, with a separate,
slightly later emergence centred on southern Germany.[6] While it may be speculative
to link the two, it is curious that when farming spread from south-east Europe during
the start of the Neolithic, it travelled inland along major river highways to southern
Germany (the LBK farming groups we came across in chapter 18), and, quite separately, along the Mediterranean coast to reach Spain and Portugal (the Cardinal Ware
people, named, naturally, after their pottery). If the Beaker tradition did spread from
south-east Europe, then it seems to have followed the same route and arrived in
the same regions. However, in the south there is little evidence that people paused
on their way to Spain; it was only once there that they appeared to have settled
and developed their distinctive lifestyle. The existence of a nascent copper-working
industry in the south-east of the peninsula may have been the lure that enticed them
to stay.[7] Although the Beaker people did not introduce metalworking into Spain,
their distinctive pottery was soon associated with it and it may be that they took over
production, perhaps feeling that, coming from a land steeped in working copper, this
was their due.[8] Through maintaining links with their homeland, and with the groups
that subsequently moved into central Europe, the almost simultaneous emergence of
a tradition in two disparate areas of Europe, while seemingly originating from a third,
is perhaps now explained.

From Spain, the Beaker people appear to have moved again, via Portugal and up the Atlantic coast to Ireland.[9] They appear to have taken their metalworking skills with them, for soon after they arrived in Ireland, the first copper mine opened at Ross Island.[10] Certainly, the gold lunulae (an open collar worn around the neck) that were made at this time have designs etched onto their surface that match the Beaker pottery.[11] From here, the Beaker tradition may have spread into Britain, taking the knowledge of metalworking with it, to meet and merge with other migrants arriving from the continent. However, the particular significance of the journey from Ireland will be something we will return to at the end of the chapter.

The Beaker people themselves are best known from their graves, where a set of fluid ideas seemed to determine the position of the body within the ground and also the type of objects that could be left with it. In southern Germany, for example, the corpse was placed in a foetal position, men with their heads to the north, women with their heads to the south, and all facing east.[12] Similar arrangements are found across Europe. Within the grave, there seems to have been a narrow range of items that could be left with the body.[13] For the men, these included a dagger (preferably made from copper), a stone wristguard (probably the decorative element of a leather sheath[14]), flint arrowheads, boar tusks (shaped remarkably like a bow, which is what they might have represented), tools relating to metalworking or to the care and production of archery equipment,[15] and, very rarely, items of gold or amber. Women had a rawer deal and were buried with bone buttons, copper awls, and, exceptionally, with gold jewellery. Both sexes also took a beaker to the grave, the ubiquitous symbol of their identity. Indeed, this seems to be what the graves were all about: identity. The objects were included for the story they told. For the men, these revolved around hunting or warfare (the archery equipment could have represented either or both), metalworking, and the care or production of archery equipment. Again, we see old themes surface, as individuals were not being remembered particularly for who they were, but more for what they did.

The beaker, the pervasive sign of belonging, speaks of drinking, of sharing, and of community. These were not just items for the grave but were actually used, and excavation of the scanty remains of Beaker villages reveals not only the standard drinking beaker (ranging from 0.5 to 2 litres capacity) but also enormous serving beakers that held up to 20 litres of liquid.[16] Some vessels were made especially for burial, however, and there are indications that the designs on the surface may have been altered accordingly.[17] Clearly, the rituals surrounding drinking must have had a significance that extended into the grave. Although the patterns engraved onto the sides of the pots were geometric, these do not necessarily reflect the phosphenes seen in trance (though they might draw from a similar design canon) and, in any event, alcohol does not induce the same sort of trance as hallucinogenic drugs. However, in a very few pots, residues of the hallucinogenic compound from henbane have been discovered, suggesting that drugs may have, exceptionally, been part of the drinking ritual.[18] Moreover, these would have induced trance. Perhaps it was only the leaders of the ritual, the shamans perhaps, that took the drug, while the rest of the community drank alcohol. This would have given people a similar experience to the shaman (but far safer and easier to control) and may have given authenticity to the otherworldly visions the shaman later retold. People were not going to the otherworld themselves, but had an experience that must have felt very similar.

However, if people were kidding themselves when they drank, they were also kidding themselves when they buried their dead. For all the martial image people carried to the grave, recent research in southern France shows that violence actually diminished when Beaker traditions arrived.[19] Moreover, some of the men buried with archery equipment were so disabled that their bow drawing days must have been long past.[20] The graves depicted not how people actually were, but how, in their minds, they craved to be; each item referenced a certain activity with which people wanted to be identified. It was not even necessary to have a complete set of anything, a single item would do. However, since all the Beaker graves seemed to hark towards a common ideal (presumably with a full range of items from the available repertoire – the Amesbury Archer came close), suggests something more. Perhaps people were not actually being buried as themselves (that is, how they actually were in life) but as ideal, almost mythological, figures, that encompassed each aspect of Beaker life: hunting or warfare, metalworking, craftwork, and, of course, drinking.[21] Perhaps the very wealthy graves, like the Amesbury Archer, were even imagined as a putative founder of the community, a mythical ancestor from whom all were descended?[22] It is tempting to recall that a common experience of trance is the sensation of a higher power, often embodied in human form. Could this be what the shamans experienced when they drank the drugged beer and could it also be what was represented in the graves? It was a heady and persuasive lifestyle that these people followed.

If the burials did represent transmuted founders (and it is likely that only the richest and most complete burials held this status), then others would have presumably wanted to be buried near to them. This appears to have been the case, with additional burials clustering around rich graves or being buried at a higher position within the same mound. Moreover, there seems to have been a predetermined order as to where these additional burials could be placed, as if people were setting out the lineage of the community.[23] Since this genealogy was based on ideas of descent rather than reality, it may explain why some child graves contain a range of adult burial items that they could not possibly have used.[24] They were buried as their destiny determined they would have become (transforming, perhaps, into one of the many representations of the putative founder) and not as how they actually were.

The Beaker tradition spread to most parts of Europe, although it only dominated in small enclaves. Other traditions, such as the Corded Ware people, often existed alongside. It was probably a mix of both traditions that found its way to Britain around 2500 BC. To begin with, Beaker burials seemed to stay away from the great henge monuments that pockmarked the land, preferring instead to associate with older and likely disused monuments from the remote past. Perhaps they did not wish to upset the balance of power (their warrior image was reserved for the grave) or perhaps they were awed by what they found? Either way, it took some time before the Beaker people commandeered the henges and the stone circles they contained, burying their dead within their confines, and leaving their telltale pottery at the sites.[25] They may have even been responsible for the change from wooden circles to stone circles, which, as we saw in chapter 23, may have signified a symbolic shift from these sites being places of the living to becoming places of the dead – a change made more appropriate since this was now where the Beaker people buried their deceased. It is likely that existing populations converted to the new lifestyle, perhaps lured by the stories the Beaker people told, or by the special items they carried, particularly those made from copper. Without analysis of their descent, however, it is not possible to tell whether individual graves contained converted locals or Beaker incomers.

Near to the Amesbury Archer were other burials, such as a family of male adults and younger children (the bones revealed shared characteristics suggesting that they were related).[26] They were not all buried at once but corpses were kept and interred with the eldest man when he finally died (again, we may be seeing something of a putative founder figure). Analysis shows that the family came originally from the mountains of the west, perhaps from the very place where the Stonehenge bluestones originated in the Preseli hills.[27] Since it was at this time that the stones were moved, could this family have been involved in their transportation? If they were, then the prominence of their grave suggests that their role was considered to have been an important one. However, their actual journey may have been one that was regularly taken by their Beaker kin. The route to the copper mines in Ireland would have passed the bluestone outcrops of Preseli – visible landmarks rising in pinnacles above the mist of the sea. Could this scene have been the inspiration for Stonehenge, forming a monument that drew together all aspects of the Beaker lifestyle? If so, then it is no wonder that someone as important as the Amesbury Archer travelled so far to see it.[28]

The movement of metal and the associated technology for its working was beginning to coalesce Europe into a vast trading network. However, unlike in modern times, most journeys were probably undertaken by sea, with the Atlantic façade forming an important route. People are likely to have passed through Cornish waters and they may have even broken their journey in one of the many coves that crenulate the coast. Perhaps it was while breaking such a journey that the treasure of the peninsula was discovered: tin. An ordinary metal today but, to those in the past, it was revolutionary. Tin mixed with copper gave bronze – a new age was about to begin.

PART FOUR

WARRIORS AND HOMESTEADS: THE BRONZE AGE

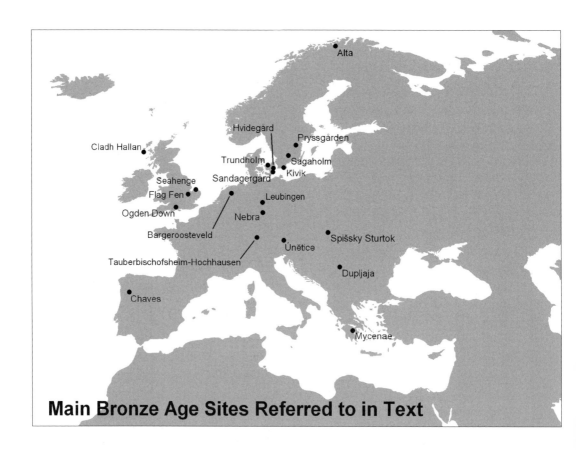

Main Bronze Age Sites Referred to in Text

Chapter 27

VOYAGES TO THE OTHERWORLD

We have been standing for hours; our legs are so numb with inactivity that we kick our heels together to draw life back into them. Before us, the dead man is being laid out within a specially made wooden hut. Nobody is allowed to enter it except for those attending to the funeral. Next to him is laid a girl, a trace of blood betraying her recent demise. You look enquiringly at me and I know what you are thinking: a sacrifice to accompany the man to the afterlife. Both the man and the girl are finely dressed and are smothered in jewellery. The man has a heavy armlet of gold and the earlobes of the girl are distended to fit around her immense earrings. Looking at her clothes, we see that they have been pinned with gold. She may have had a short existence in this world but she goes to the other dressed as a princess. The funeral attendants then bring daggers and lay them around the couple, followed by halberds, a type of axe that seems common here. You nudge me and I follow your eye. The last attendant is bringing what looks like metalworking equipment, chisels, and a miniature anvil. Possibly this man was a metalworker, but, in all his finery, he looks more like a chief. When the last items are squeezed into the hut, people turn to the pile of earth they will use to cover it. It will be a massive task and, when we return the next day, it is still not complete. Just how high do they intend this barrow to be?

In fact, the barrow of the Leubingen grave, in Germany, ended up at over 8.5m tall.[1] That is almost as high as a house today. It was built by the Aunjetitz people, who had emerged from the earlier Beaker communities and spread themselves across southern Germany and into the Czech lands. Here, they are known as the Únětice people, named after a large cemetery just outside Prague. They arose at around 2300 BC, although the Leubingen barrow we saw constructed was not built until around 1900 BC. The grave was actually one of a pair that were discovered in 1906 when workers were building a railway to a modern copper mine. Whether or not they appreciated the coincidence at the time, it was copper that brought the region its wealth in pre-history and, although the man in the grave might have resembled a chief, we were right to think that some of the items buried with him were metalworking tools. All

across this area, rich burials held similar items.[2] Perhaps these were chiefs pretend-
ing to be metalworkers or perhaps they actually were the metalworkers; after all, we
have already seen the status that can accrue from an involvement with this seemingly magical process. However, there is another possibility: that the person in the
grave was a chief who controlled the production and trade in metal items. The area
inhabited by the Aunjetitz people lay on the main trade route between the lands to
the north and south and it is likely that control of this trade enabled a few individuals
to become fabulously wealthy. Some of this wealth was undoubtedly used to develop
local copper extraction from the deposits that seam the mountain valleys, and so
wealth begot even greater wealth.[3] However, it was only a tiny few who commanded
sufficient riches to enable a burial like the one we witnessed. Most graves had no
timber interior, no covering mound, and only modest items left within them.[4] In
fact, far more items were buried in hoards than were ever left in graves.[5] The hoards,
however, pose their own problem: were they votive offerings to the spirits, or were
they a hidden source of metal awaiting retrieval? The existence of metalworking
items in some of the hoards may suggest the latter. However, since the control of the
metalworking process was considered so important (it was represented in the graves
of the chiefs, after all), perhaps these are precisely the items that would have formed
the most prestigious gifts to offer to the spirits.

We have already seen how people at the end of the Neolithic, such as the Amesbury
Archer, travelled long distances and presumably took valuable items along with them
to trade for food and lodging. With all this travelling, it would not have been long
before trade routes developed (one of which provided the Aunjetitz communities
with the source of their wealth). Initially, the most intensive routes were focused on
the supply of items from the Near East and Egypt, and it was the Minoan civilisation
of Crete that first took advantage of the trade. When many of their cities collapsed in
around 1500 BC, their role passed to the Mycenaean civilisation of mainland Greece.[6]
The Mycenaeans still speak to us through the pages of Homer's epic tales of war
and conquest, and it would appear that these people saw themselves as the warrior
elite of the Mediterranean. How realistic this was is difficult to say, but their greatest
strength probably lay in organising trade: the Mycenaeans were go-betweens without compare.

The Mycenaeans were not alone in portraying themselves as a warrior society
and we have already seen how Beaker communities drew on similar themes of war,
metalworking, and drinking to define themselves. This approach probably originated
in the Steppe regions, and it may be more than coincidental that the chiefs of the
Aunjetitz people were buried under barrows that mimic the kurgans further east. In
fact, burial under a barrow, at least for the elite of society, became widespread after
1600 BC, giving rise to the Tumulus tradition.[7] Metal was still tremendously important to people and metalworking tools are still found in some barrows, suggesting that
the process remained the preserve of the elite.[8] As with the earlier Aunjetitz people,
women were also afforded rich burials and many wore fine jewellery to the grave.
The proliferation of spiral decoration, and its association with the portal between the

worlds, hints that perhaps such jewellery was produced with the grave in mind and there certainly seem to have been rules as to how it should be arrayed.[9]

Despite the rise of the Tumulus tradition in central and Western Europe, the main centre of metalworking seems to shift east to the Carpathian region. Here, however, there were very few rich graves since most metal items of value were buried in hoards, presumably as gifts to the spirits, since it seems unlikely that so much would have been hidden and then forgotten about. At one settlement, Spišsky Sturtok in Slovakia, for example, 20 separate hoards of metalwork were excavated: a considerable investment to consign to the ground.[10] However, perhaps this was the way the elite showed off their status: rather than being buried with their wealth, they gave lavish gifts to the spirits with their community present to witness the event (and, no doubt, looking suitably impressed). The hoards at Spišsky Sturtok would suggest that such occasions took place close to the settlements and the introduction of chariots at around this time (another imitation of traditions further east) may have provided a startling means by which the donor and gift arrived at their moment of triumph.[11]

However, although the settlements of the Carpathian region were certainly the locations for hoards, it is less clear whether they also contained the homes of ordinary people. Many were fortified and may have been the preserve of a chief and an entourage of craftworkers, rather than containing houses for large groups of people.[12] Produce also appears to have been stored within the walls and, presumably, it was the chief's role to redistribute it accordingly. It is intriguing that it was ultimately the impact of metal that led to this arrangement as almost exactly the same seems to have happened in south-east Spain, another metal producing region, albeit considerably poorer.

We have already seen how the incipient copper working of this region was taken over and developed by the Beaker people at the end of the Neolithic. By the Bronze Age, the grip of just a few significant people on the industry had tightened to the extent that ordinary people probably saw very little metal in their everyday lives. This was a Bronze Age for the elite of society only.[13] These high-status individuals seem to have followed the same ploy to demonstrate their importance as those in the Carpathians. They built fortified settlements, controlled the storage and redistribution of resources, and kept craftworking, including the bronze industry, under tight control.[14] Moreover, just like the Carpathian elite, they did not bury the dead under prominent barrows but chose to keep them close, under the floors of their houses, although admittedly accompanied by lavish items fashioned from metal.[15] However, unlike the Carpathian region, south-east Spain lay at the very edge of the European trade routes. Their metalworking was not as advanced as that further east and it is likely that metal items were always scarce; this was a society living on scraps.[16] In addition to this, when their main trading partners of the Atlantic seaboard were drawn into alternative networks running out from central Europe, the elite of Spain crumbled and fortified settlements and rich burials disappeared.[17] For the ordinary people, however, little appears to have changed; they may even have had a better chance of getting their hands on a metal object – such were the vagaries of fate.

We have already seen how the sea route up the Atlantic coast enabled the earlier Beaker people to settle in Ireland and establish copper mines at Ross Island. It is curious, therefore, that except for a number of burials inserted into the mound covering the Neolithic tomb at Tara, there is very little evidence of an elite emerging at the start of the Bronze Age.[18] Perhaps, as in other regions where elite graves were scarce, people demonstrated their status and importance through offering gifts to the spirits and the recent discovery of many fine gold items that were not associated with a corresponding burial would appear to support this.[19] A little further south, however, where Brittany thrusts itself firmly into the Atlantic, there were many barrow burials, with some containing items made from gold, amber, and jet.[20] Of particular note is a gold box from la Motta, an amber plaque from Saint-Fiacre, and a jet necklace piece from Kerguévarec. Although gold had a long history of being prized as a valuable metal, amber and jet were more recent must-haves. The properties of both are strangely similar, and when rubbed by fur or textile, they give off an electrical charge. This may have been why they were so sought after, as such supposed supernatural effects may have been associated with the spirits.[21] The jet necklace piece from Kerguévarec deserves particular attention as it almost certainly originated in Britain, where several rich burials of the Wessex people contained similar items.[22]

There were other similarities between the graves of Brittany and those of Britain, such as their loose alignment to the sunrise and sunset at the solstices, which suggests that both followed a set of common beliefs in their form.[23] However, in terms of the items placed within the grave, there were notable disparities, showing that such traditions diverged widely on points of detail. It is only through their shared use of precious items – particularly gold, amber, and jet – that the two traditions converge again.[24] While it seems clear that these items were crossing the channel, in the absence of widespread movement of less valuable items, it is difficult to envisage how such a trade could have supported itself. That is unless there was no trade as such but, rather, isolated journeys undertaken solely to source and obtain these valuable items. Anthropologist Mary Helms has shown how people in some traditional societies seek out exotic and unusual objects as a means of acquiring status within their own communities. The ownership of such an item not only shows that a person has journeyed to a far-off place – somewhere she likens to an otherworld – but also that some of its supernatural power might have adhered to the individual upon their return.[25] We have seen similar beliefs ourselves, with the acquisition of shells and teeth of the Palaeolithic, and the jade axes of the Neolithic, except that these items were probably exchanged through many intermediaries before they reached their final destination. In the Bronze Age, people were going to get the things themselves and it was the journey that was as important as the item they acquired. Moreover, such a journey needed to be an extraordinary feat in itself if it was to mark out those who embarked upon it as special. Perhaps this was why most involved crossing the sea?

By now, we are used to the symbolism of water and how, owing to the common experience of trance, it was often associated with crossing to the otherworld. If the exotic items that were being acquired in the Bronze Age were thought to originate in the otherworld, then crossing an expanse of water would have been a highly symbolic means of reaching them. The boat building technology of the time was certainly up to the task.[26] Moreover, the star disc found at Nebra, in Germany, made by the Aunjetitz people, shows that people had begun to take an interest in celestial movements, which would have been an important navigational aid. Although, owing to the landlocked location where the disc was found, perhaps this was more symbolic than real: a means of displaying control over the routes across the earth and even to the otherworld itself.[27]

From around 1700 BC, metal finally flowed into Scandinavia and perhaps the inhabitants of the region also made voyages to far-off places to obtain it. The proliferation of boat imagery engraved on the rocks certainly hints at an obsession with travel.[28] At Kivik, in Sweden, carved panels lined the grave and may have depicted an actual journey across the sea and over land, far to the south.[29] The carvings of horses, boats, even a whale, hint at the adventures of travel, and the carving of a chariot suggests that the final destination may have been the Carpathian region, where we have seen that such transport existed. There is also a strange depiction of a person, perhaps dancing, leading a procession of mysterious forms that seem more animal than human. Could this be the crew of the boat, shapeshifting into animal form, as a journey to the otherworld may have required them to do? It seems appropriate that all of the engraved slabs at Kivik faced into the grave, as if the occupant wanted a reminder of this epic voyage for all eternity.

From 1300 BC, another change swept across Europe and the great barrows of earth and their fabulous contents were balanced by a more modest tradition. There were still those who could command great riches, of course, and we shall be meeting these people later on our travels. First, however, we must join a small community where the death of a respected elder has caused much sadness. Arriving in the midst of mourning, we can do little but watch as the events of the day unfold.

Chapter 28

FIELDS OF THE DEAD

There is a sombre mood over the settlement this morning. People speak little and keep their eyes lowered as they go about their chores. Leaving the small, rectangular dwelling where we spent the night, we find ourselves opposite the house of mourning, the former home of the elder of the community. He died at a good age and has been dressed and laid out in his house one last time. People enter to say a last farewell and we wait patiently until every member of the village has taken their turn. It is late morning before the last person leaves and the man is brought out, carried high on the shoulders of four of his kinsmen. People gather to watch, and to follow his last journey to the burial ground. We look for where the earth has been dug to receive his body, but there is nothing. Nor are there any barrows to show where existing burials lie. Instead, they take the body to a great pile of kindling and set it on top. A woman comes forward and, speaking loudly and with passion, delivers a eulogy praising the deeds of the dead man. Some in the crowd sob but many just watch silently. Suddenly, three young people come forward with blazing torches. They touch the kindling and the flames begin their slow ascent to claim the body. The people seem content to watch the body burn and some have even brought food and drink to share, but we walk some distance away. Modern sensibilities are sometimes a real disadvantage in the past. When we return, the fire has burnt almost to nothing and people are picking over the embers, collecting what we realise must be the remains of the man. The people place these in a pottery urn. When it is reasonably full, the woman who delivered the eulogy takes it to a small pit and, kneeling in the damp grass, quickly places something in the urn. You are better placed to see what it is and tell me later that it looked like a small figure of a bird. The woman then covers the urn with a cloth and places everything in the pit. The soil is backfilled and stamped almost flat. Looking around, we can now see that the field we stand in contains many small mounds and presumably a similar number of urns and cremated remains beneath them. We follow the people back to their settlement, and they immediately busy themselves with their neglected tasks. How quickly life follows death.

From about 1300 BC, a new burial tradition swept across Europe that was so compelling that people adopted it over vast areas. Essentially, it comprised cremation followed by burial in a pit, with the remains often being placed in an urn. The existence of several burials gathered into small cemeteries provides the name for these communities: the Urnfield people. At first sight, the new burial practices appear so different from previous traditions that they were once thought to herald the arrival of a completely new people.[1] Such explanations have fallen out of favour in recent times and, in any case, the change is not necessarily as marked as it might appear.

Throughout the early Bronze Age, the elite of communities had been buried under large barrows with an assortment of valuable items and, although the size of some of the barrows might have diminished in the Urnfield period, they were still widespread. Clearly, at the top, nothing much changed. However, for the ordinary people, who never really had a burial tradition before now, things changed enormously as they now developed their own customs. Moreover, these were complementary rather than in opposition to the elite barrow tradition. In fact, the absence of mounds within the cemeteries may have been a quite deliberate signal to the elite that the new burial practice was not meant to challenge them or their existing symbolism in any way. With regards to the barrow, if size was important, the ordinary people were content with a flat grave with very little to mark its existence.

Since the urnfields were the graves of ordinary people, we should not expect them to contain the riches that we are used to seeing with the burials of chiefs. In fact, weapons, the must-have items for the elite, were in very short supply. Analysis of cemeteries in southern Germany, for example, shows that there may have only been a single person in each community who owned a sword at any one time.[2] Perhaps these were the village leaders and ownership of a sword symbolised their role as protectors of the group; it is hard to see otherwise how a single weapon would have had much practical use if real fighting were necessary. Since the individuals with swords often form the focus of small groups within the cemetery, it is tempting to see their role continuing into death. Despite the existence of the odd sword or, especially in later periods, other fancy items, the urnfields give the impression of uniform and egalitarian communities.

However, as we have seen, there were still rich graves and, in the main, these were removed from the urnfields, as if the elite wanted to separate themselves from the common people.[3] Many of these graves contain weapons and armour, although often an odd assortment of each, suggesting that their occupants either did not own the full repertoire of battledress or that the people who buried them chose not to consign it all to the grave. It is telling that the burials closest to the bronze producing areas contained the most weapons and armour; wealth, it seems, was still founded on the control of metal.[4] Where weapons were not prevalent, their place seems to have been taken with sets of metal cups, servers, and strainers that were probably used for drinking. Whereas the Beaker people made do with a solitary drinking cup, these people seemed a lot more serious in their habits. Moreover, the existence of so much paraphernalia suggests that the whole process may have been highly ritualised, with the liquid being strained and served in precisely the right way. Clearly, this was terribly significant because it was often the entire drinking set that people took with them to the grave and not just a few odd pieces. However, although people obtained entire sets, as custom required them to do, it is clear that not everyone knew how to use them. At Kostraede in Denmark, for example, a sieving bucket for straining the alcohol was merely lined with resin and used as any other container.[5] Perhaps the owners thought that they had been palmed off with faulty goods?

It is likely that drinking and feasting were a large part of the funeral rites attending rich burials. The drinking sets placed within the grave may have even seen service in toasting the deceased one last time. These may have been rowdy affairs but it is likely that they were impressive too. The prevalence of vehicle imagery within graves (something we shall examine later), and the occasional inclusion of wheels with the burial, suggests that the deceased were sometimes carried to the funeral on the back of a carriage.[6] It must have made for an impressive send off. For the ordinary people, carriages were probably unknown, but there is every likelihood that the funeral ritual would have been just as memorable. In fact, since the graves themselves left little sign of their presence (perhaps, as we have seen, to avoid challenging the elite), the funeral ritual became the last occasion in which the deceased had an opportunity to make their mark. The focus shifted from the lingering presence of a grave to the fleeting occurrence of a funeral. These needed to be impressive, and perhaps this was why people burnt the body before burial. Psychologists show that people have a far higher chance of remembering events if they are dramatic, in which case even small details can be recalled with startling accuracy.[7] Moreover, these memories retain their emotional import and, unlike most recollections, are extremely resistant to change.[8] Watching a body burn must have been dramatic, even for communities that faced the realities of death far more regularly than we do, and perhaps it was the impression of the burning that stayed with people and meant that details about the deceased would be remembered. However, although the Urnfield people adopted cremation almost exclusively, they were not the first to burn their dead.

During earlier periods, when bodies were generally placed whole into the earth, cremation seems to have been something people experimented with. Even as far back as the Aunjetitz period, a grave at Jessnitz in Germany contained a body which had been placed inside a coffin and then burnt.[9] This mirrors many of the later coffins from Denmark, which frequently held cremations, despite being made to fit an entire body.[10] This mix of traditions may reflect a reluctance to change customs wholesale and people tried a tentative mixture of the old and the new. Alternatively, it may show that what to us seems like a very radical change (from entire burial to cremation), was actually not considered that different at all, more a variation on a theme.

We have already seen how, during the Neolithic, death was viewed as a two-stage process: leaving the realm of the living before joining that of the dead. The first stage was represented by the putrefaction of the flesh and the second when the bones were placed with others in the chambers of the tombs. Even in the single graves of Beaker times, there was a period of display, where the body was arranged and decorated with the standard burial repertoire (and almost certainly viewed by the community), before being covered and confined to the earth. The body did not rot between the

first and second stages of death, but they were still observed nonetheless. With cremation, the first stage is more sudden and dramatic but it still represents the departure of
the dead from the realm of the living. The collection of the charred remains and their
burial in the communal cemetery represented the second stage: entry into the realm
of the dead. Cremation adhered to existing beliefs about death and may not have
been seen as that different. Moreover, during the Neolithic, fire was often used to
mark the death of a house, or the sealing of a monument; it already held connotations
of ending and transformation. Its new role in marking the transition of a human individual from life to death may have felt quite natural. Indeed, fire may have played a
part in the barrow burials of the Wessex people, where one recently analysed wealthy
barrow reveals three episodes of burning on top of the mound. If this was repeated at
other barrows, we can perhaps imagine the skyline lit by beacons of fire, marking the
passing of the deceased and, perhaps, guiding their route to the afterlife.[11]

Within the urnfields, family groups may have been buried together and analysis of
a large cemetery at Vollmarshausen, in Germany, shows six discrete burial areas, each
with slight variations in burial practice that may betray family traditions.[12] Similarly,
at Gremeinlebarn, in Austria, three larger groupings may relate to different communities, with individual families contained within them.[13] Perhaps descendents would
visit the urnfield and trace out the route of their descent, remembering the past (or
even making it up) from the barely perceptible contours that covered the ground.

When we witnessed the burial of the man in the community we visited at the
beginning of the chapter, you thought that you saw the woman place a small figure
of a bird in the urn before she placed it in the burial pit. You were probably right,
as birds were a common symbol associated with Urnfield burials. We have already
come across similar attitudes during the Mesolithic, especially at Bøgebakken,
where a young boy was laid on the wing of a swan. We reasoned that perhaps the
role of the bird was to protect the infant's spirit and to guide it to the afterlife. The
same was probably true for the bird symbols left with the urnfield graves; such amulets are especially found with child burials.[14] Maybe this was the last thing that the
grieving parents could ever do for their child. Snakes were other creatures we came
across in the Mesolithic, when models were left with burials on Deer Island. Like
birds, images of snakes also make an appearance in urnfield graves. It is not cred-
ible that people should have remembered such ancient traditions across thousands
of years and the convergence of beliefs may, therefore, be due to a shared experience of trance and the consequent interpretation of the world that resulted from it.
Traditional shamanic communities also see birds as 'psychopomps' to the afterlife
(literally meaning 'guiding the spirit'). Among the Ob-Ugrians of Siberia, for example, birds were tattooed onto the bodies of the dying so that they could guide the
spirit of the deceased to the afterlife.[15] The Sámi of Lapland also consider water birds
to be conduits to the afterlife and small carvings of birds adorned graves in Finland
well into modern times.[16]

Bird imagery was also apparent in the rich barrows of the Urnfield period, showing that belief in the ability of birds to psychopomp the spirit was shared across

all strata of society. However, given their preoccupation with drinking, the occupants of these graves came up with a neat ploy to ensure that their imbibing was not necessarily curtailed upon death. Model carriages often adorned these graves comprising four-wheeled chassis holding huge vessels, presumably with a requisite supply of drink.[17] To ensure that it reached the afterlife without mishap, model birds were portrayed around the vessel, sometimes in great numbers. Perhaps these people thought that, if the birds were headed to the afterlife anyway, they might as well bring some alcohol along with them? No horses or other means of traction were attached to these carriages and it is likely that the birds were expected to move the vehicle on their own. Indeed, at Dupljaja in Serbia, to the east of the main Urnfield tradition, a terracotta model of a carriage is fashioned so that three ducks would have pulled it forward.[18] Driving the carriage is a figure that seems to have a human body but the head of a duck. Could this be another representation of an individual shapeshifting into animal form in order to cross the divide between the worlds? The numerous spirals marked upon the cloak of the figure suggest that it might be.

Accessing alternative realities, be it the otherworld of the shaman or the afterlife of the dead, seems to have been an overriding concern to people of the Bronze Age. We have already seen many of the myriad means through which people got there and, yet, there are plenty of others. Engraved on the rocks to the far north of Europe are images so detailed that they almost become a roadmap to the otherworld: this is where it is and this is how you get there. I visited these rocks myself at the end of a very long summer, and what I found there was astonishing.

Chapter 29

BETWEEN HEAVEN AND EARTH AT THE PAINTED ROCKS

My own visit to the land of the midnight sun was during early autumn, so that night was slowly creeping back into ascendancy. I was far north of the Arctic Circle at Alta in Norway, one of the finest rock-carving sites in the world.[1] As I walked down to the images, which are found all around the shoreline of a small bay, I was immediately struck at how appropriate it was that they occurred on the boundary between land, sea, and sky. For many shamanic people, the otherworld is divided into three: the upperworld, middleworld, and lowerworld.[2] Although these three realms are usually accessed by a shaman in trance, they also have parallels in this reality where the sky equates to the upperworld, the earth to the middleworld, and below the earth or underwater to the lowerworld.[3] The rocks on the shore were probably recognised as a location where all three worlds came together; possibly even as a place where transition among them was possible.[4] The lowering of sea levels during the Bronze Age and the exposure of much new ground perhaps heightened the belief that the shore provided access to different realms.[5] This natural phenomenon was observable over the span of a single lifetime and must have been a powerful metaphor, confirming much of what people believed about their reality.

At first, the images I saw at Alta were of domestic scenes: hunting elk, corralling reindeer, and catching fish. A predatory bear also put in the odd appearance and one panel seemed to show a hunt at its lair. However, among these images were others that seemed to denote rituals or magical practices, and I was quickly reminded that the people who created the carvings did not separate ritual and domestic life as we do. Hunting a bear, for example, was both sacred and profane. This became particularly pertinent when I viewed the many images of boats. Some were clearly being used in fishing expeditions, or as platforms for hunting, whereas others seemed to have a very different role altogether. Of these, the most curious were those depicted upside down.

The otherworld is often seen as a mirror image to this world, so that what is dead in this world is alive in the other, and what is broken here becomes whole over there. Similarly, things upside down in this world are the right way up in the otherworld. These beliefs formed part of the historical Sámi cosmology, whose ancestors engraved the rocks in the first place.[6] The upside-down boats at Alta may, therefore, have been travelling between the worlds.

When we examined the painted caves of the Palaeolithic, we noticed how people seemed to treat the rock itself as if it were a membrane between the worlds, and the same seems to have been true of the later artists in Scandinavia. Boats were not only depicted upside down but also moving in and out of the rock. Moreover, the level of detail of the carved boats, and also the depth of the carving itself, all contributed to the effect that certain images disappeared into the rock and then reappeared elsewhere.[7] In a similar manner, other boat images seem to have been deliberately placed near rivers, where they would be flooded and covered during the spring spate.[8] Perhaps this was another means through which the boats were believed to journey to the otherworlds? Elsewhere, features in the rock itself were incorporated into designs, so that a fissure of quartz, where it appears next to boat carvings, seems to stand for the sea, and keel-shaped hollows form the centrepiece to a larger arrangement.[9] John Coles, an expert on the rock carvings of the region, has even observed how the slanting light of dawn and dusk highlights individual images before making them disappear again into gloom. The prevalence of carvings arranged to take advantage of such effects suggests that it was deliberate.[10] A lot of trouble was taken to emphasise the passage of boats to and from the otherworld.

Back at Alta, I noticed that a number of boats seemed to be filled with dancers, some holding things that vaguely looked like mushrooms. Further south, in Denmark, bronze metalwork, particularly razors, also carried designs showing mushrooms in boats.[11] These images are much clearer and the mushroom can be identified as fly agaric (*Amanita muscaria*), the archetypal red-and-white toadstool that grows in the birch woods of the region.[12] The alkaloids contained within fly agaric will rapidly induce trance if ingested (an effect which can, apparently, be heightened if a person is prepared to drink their urine thereafter). Historical studies show that shamans in the region readily did this in order to fuel their journeys to the otherworld.[13] Interestingly, one of the symptoms of taking fly agaric is excessive movement. Could this explain why people in the boats at Alta appeared to be dancing: allowing the drug they had taken to course through their bodies?

If such boats were thought to journey to the otherworld, then they would have also provided a means through which the dead could reach the afterlife. During earlier periods, people were buried in coffins fashioned from hollowed-out oak trees.[14] Since boats were almost certainly made in exactly the same way, the dead were effectively buried in boats – a fitting symbol given people's beliefs. This use of boat imagery continues even after coffins were no longer used, with some graves being surrounded by stones arranged to resemble the keel of a boat.[15] Some burial cairns even have images of boats placed beneath or around them. Significantly, some of these, such as at Hjortekrog in Sweden, contained no crew, as if the boat were for the sole (and soul) use of the occupant of the tomb. Those at Rogaland, in Norway, had even been turned upside down.[16]

The route to the afterlife was also represented through the position of the designs on the rock outcrops. Where these overlooked the sea, burial cairns were located on the high ground behind them. Footprints engraved onto the rock surface were placed as if left by individuals walking from the cairns to the sea. Given what we know about water being the route to the afterlife, this is the path we would expect the dead to take. Furthermore, in a line crossed by the footprints are boat images, as if the dead picked up their transport on the way to the water.[17] There are also small hollows pecked along the top of some of the outcrops. These so-called cup marks were a regular feature during the Neolithic, when they were associated, first with ceremonial monuments, and then with tombs. The circular scoop they form in the rock may have been a representation of the tunnel that gave access to the otherworld (passing through the membrane of the rock) and, in places, this seems to have been emphasised with spirals surrounding the hollow or with a line leading to its centre, as if indicating the route to be travelled.[18] Their occurrence on the path of the dead, and often in association with boat images, was perhaps more than coincidental.[19]

In his survey of one of the largest rock-carving sites in Sweden, John Coles found that many of the boats engraved on the rocks sailed in a south-easterly or north-westerly bearing.[20] We have come across these directions before since they correspond with the rising of the sun at the winter solstice and its setting at the summer solstice. This not only divides the year into two but the resulting halves also equate to the period in which the sun grows in intensity, and the period in which it wanes. This observance of the cycle of the sun also occurs on the Danish razors that we looked at earlier. Flemming Kaul, an archaeologist who has exhaustively surveyed these razors, has pieced together a cosmological scheme that only becomes apparent when a number of examples are placed together. Essentially, the sun is carried across the sky in a boat, with prows resembling a horse. In the day, it moves from east to west across the sky and, at night, it moves from west to east through the lowerworld, which, as we might expect, seems to equate to the sea, owing to the appearance of fish.[21] Kaul's ideas are also apparent in the sun horse of Trundholm, also found in Denmark, where a horse seems to be pulling the disc of the sun.[22] A bright side on the right of the disc represents the day, and a dark side on its left represents the night, so that the horse appears to pull the disc in a clockwise direction, just like the razors. Since some of the boats on the razors have prows that resemble birds as much as horses, Kaul believes that all three images may have shared a similar significance in aiding the daily journey of the sun through this world and into the otherworld.[23] We have already seen birds perform a similar role in the central European urnfields.

Since most of the razors were left in graves, it is likely that they were owned and used by a single individual. Perhaps these were initiatory gifts associated with a boy's first shave, the ritual cutting of a girl's hair, or even scarification marks given to each[24] when the wider mysteries of the world were first revealed to them. The fact that a single razor only showed a small part of the overall scheme was, perhaps, a reflection of the small but significant role the individual would play in his or her own community. Unlike their owners, however, the razors would never be burnt on the funeral pyre,[25] and perhaps the unsullied image of the boat still served the purpose of ferrying the soul of the deceased on its journey to the afterlife.

At Sagaholm in Sweden, there is barrow with an outer ring of slabs, of which 15 of the remaining 45 have carvings, mostly of ships, sledges, and animals, which are probably horses or deer.[26] What distinguishes this barrow from the Kivik structure that we saw in chapter 27 is that the carvings, although covered, faced away from the burial and were, presumably, viewed by the mourners rather than the deceased. The omission of the sun on any of the panels is initially puzzling (its presence might be expected to complete the scene),[27] unless the barrow itself was intended to represent the sun. If so, then perhaps people believed that its occupant had merged with the sun and joined it on its journey to the otherworld. Could such an overtly symbolic burial have even belonged to a shaman, the expert on these journeys, with the slabs placed as a visible reminder to the community of the power that the individual once held?

Some of the figures on the boats I saw at Alta had drums and may have also been shamans. I was reminded of the classic image of Siberian shamans, and indeed the Sámi shamans, who had once lived in the area, beating their drums and journeying to the otherworld. I also recalled my own journeys to this realm and how they had been initiated by the drum. Intriguingly, the historical Sámi sometimes referred to their drums as boats – vessels that carried them to the otherworld – an echo, perhaps, of very ancient beliefs.[28]

Since the images on the drums were almost identical to those carved on the rocks, they may have served similar roles.[29] The drums in the north of Lapland, for example, were often divided by three horizontal lines, reflecting the division of the cosmos into the upperworld, middleworld, and lowerworld. Those in the south tend to be divided according to the four directions, with the centre portrayed as a stylised sun.[30] In both cases, the drum provides a map to the otherworld,[31] and it is possible that some of the images on the rocks did the same. Certainly, within the grave at Kivik, the images seem to merge real and mythical journeys and the location of the panels, facing into the tomb, may have been useful to a wandering spirit after death. One of the figures I observed at Alta was flying over a boat with arms outstretched – a shaman, perhaps, on his or her way to the otherworld? The design was carved on a rock that sloped upwards, with images of feet helpfully pointing out the direction of travel. Walking upwards, I passed the flying shaman again; this was definitely the route to take. When I reached the top of the rock, I was rewarded with a spectacular view of the fjord, all the way beyond the headland and out to sea. Was this the route to the otherworld that real shamans took? If so, then the images provided a neat map of how to get there.

Sámi drums were also used for divination, a copper and iron hoop jumping across their surface and alighting on images provided a prophetic narrative.[32] The flow of water across rock carvings may have provided a similar basis for foretelling the future, highlighting features in a pattern that may (or may not) have been random. Certainly, the existence of burning and of broken pottery around carved rocks at Hornnes, in Norway, suggests that some sort of ritual took place there.[33] Moreover, at Kotojärvi in Finland the bones of elk and, perhaps tellingly, water birds, were scattered beneath the images.[34] Were these remains from actual shamanic journeys? If so, then at Pyhänpää, also in Finland, Antti Lahelma, an expert on the rock art of the area, believes that he has found an image of such a shaman in flight, merging with his or her helper spirit in the form of an elk and carried to the otherworld in a boat.[35]

Although shamans used drums and psychotropic mushrooms to free their spirit and access the otherworld, it was the cremation pyre that served an equivalent role for the dead. However, when we considered the razors that accompanied people to the grave, these had not been burnt, as if there were different rules pertaining to metal objects. This seems to reflect more widespread beliefs that bronze items were regarded as having an existence quite independent of their human owners. In fact, rather than viewing them as inanimate objects that were made, used, and discarded by humans, they actually seem to have been treated as being alive and having a consciousness in their own right. Some were even known to pacify angry bears.

Chapter 30

THE MAGICAL METAL

For the Inuit people of Greenland who lived around 100 years ago, killing a polar bear meant facing many dangers. The weather could be fickle, the ice treacherous, and the bear itself was a fearsome adversary. It took a brave hunter to bring down a bear with a spear. People believed, with some justification, that the bear would be angry with them for taking its life and, unless appeased, its spirit would stay to cause trouble within the community.[1] Fortunately, there was a way out. Bears were said to like metal items. Therefore, when the skin of the bear was stretched and dried next to the settlement, people gave it metal objects that it might appreciate. After a number of days, the bear's soul departed, but it did not go alone. As the bear's soul left, it took with it the souls of the metal items that were left beside it, so they might be used and enjoyed in the afterlife. Since the bear had been honoured, or perhaps bribed, it would depart happily and would not stay to cause trouble for the people. What is notable about this custom is not so much that animals were thought to be alive and have souls (that does not require too great a conceptual leap), but that the same applied to metal objects. For the historical Inuit people of Greenland, metal items were also thought to be alive and have souls of their own.

In our modern, industrialised world, the division between what is alive and what is not is so fundamental to our way of thinking that might call it common sense: something innate within all human thought.[2] However, for a large part of the non-industrialised world, this is not the case and the division between living and non-living is not recognised. This is called 'animism', the belief that all things are alive and have souls that are equivalent to those of humans.[3] (Of course, it is ironic that the assumption that a human has a soul has no more basis in fact than the tenets of animism, and, yet, we might readily accept the former while completely dismissing the latter.) For the animist Inuit, for example, they believed that everything was alive and had a soul that survived them after death – including humans, polar bears, *and* metal objects. The people of the Bronze Age, who were probably far closer to the Inuit way of thinking than they were to ours, probably believed the same.

We have already seen, for example, how mining was a hugely symbolic act for people in the past. In addition to mineralogical requirements, existing features such as monuments and burials, or even the landscape itself, may have determined the locations of mines. Promontories, hills, and river sources were all particularly favoured.[4] Since metal was believed to originate in the otherworld, perhaps it was important to select such liminal locations for the mines – places where the veil between the worlds was thin and it might easily be brought across the portal. People may have also wondered how the metal came to be in the earth in the first place and reasoned that, like any other living being, it gestated in embryonic form, in this case, as ore.

However, if the time the metal spent in the earth was a period of gestation, then the process of smelting was the moment that it was born. Such imagery is prevalent in many traditional African societies where people give smelting furnaces female properties, sometimes even decorating them with breasts and the cicatrisation marks worn by childbearing women. The taboos surrounding the invariably male smelters were also those that applied when their wives were pregnant. This metal is not made; it is quite literally given life and is born.[5] While such imagery is overt and unambiguous in traditional Africa, there is growing acceptance that people in the European past probably shared similar beliefs and that the magical aspect of metal production was of equal importance to the technological process.[6] If people saw smelting as equivalent to the metal being born, they probably also thought of it as the time when the soul of the object being made would cross from the otherworld. If so, then we might expect metalworking to take place in liminal locations where the veil between the worlds was thin and such passage was easily accomplished.

In general, metalworking took place at the boundary to the settled area, which, although a clear liminal zone, also made good practical sense as it kept a highly flammable activity away from the wooden houses.[7] Other boundary locations, however, were more figurative. Many metalworking sites were located close to water and in Ireland the process took place on crannogs, artificial islands set within a lake.[8] Again, proximity to water may have had practical advantages but we also know that people saw water as a portal to the otherworlds. These were not necessarily purely utilitarian locations. Metalworking also took place close to burial sites, such as at Burderop Down and Dainton, both in southern England.[9] These places could have served no practical purpose but were certainly ripe with symbolism. At Sandagergård in Denmark, a curious walled structure contained cremations and also metalworking debris, as if the departing human souls may have met those of the metal items that were newly arriving.[10] At the entrance to the structure were plaques engraved with stylised hands, held as if warning of the dangerous events that were taking place inside.

In traditional societies, it was the shaman who would often oversee these dangerous events and mediate the passage of souls between the worlds. This may be why shamanism and metalworking are often connected, to the extent that among some Siberian peoples, shamans are believed to be formed on the metalworker's anvil by special smith-spirits.[11] The Bronze Age metalworkers were probably also seen as midwives to the soul rather than craftworkers, with their trade steeped in mystery, magic, and the supernatural.

Following a human birth, many traditional societies have taboos surrounding the disposal of the umbilical cord and placenta, items that are highly charged with the imagery of delivery and of the newborn itself.[12] The equivalent for the birth of a metal item is, perhaps, its mould: the clay casing that held the molten metal as it solidified and provided the object with its form. In many cases, these moulds do seem to have been treated in ways that mark them out as special and having importance in their own right.[13] In Ireland, for example, sword moulds have been recovered from what the excavators believe was a purpose-built ritual pool, designed so that precious objects could be left there, presumably as offerings to the spirits.[14] Sometimes the moulds in a certain region bear no relation to the metal items found there, as if the mould and the object that came from it needed to be kept apart. In northern France, for example, a particular axe type is absent despite there being abundant moulds from its production.[15] Similarly, another type of axe is prolific in South Wales, despite there being no corresponding moulds to go with it.[16] Clearly, the mould and the finished items were being kept apart.

If an item is born rather than made, then presumably it will also have a life of its own. Increasingly, anthropological research is showing how traditional people treat their objects as having an existence separate from human influence. For example, the Kwakwaka'wakw artists on the Pacific north-west coast of Canada produce elaborate masks for their ceremonies. These masks are sacred and can only be used for this single purpose. However, identical masks are also made for selling to tourists. There is absolutely no difference between these masks and those made for the ceremonies except for how they will be used. Yet the masks made for tourists are called fakes.[17] It is how the mask will live its life that will determine whether it is a ceremonial mask or a fake, therefore, and not how it was made. The same seems true for Bronze Age metalwork.

Instead of the life of a metal artefact being largely dictated by the actions of people, it may be that certain artefacts determined the way that people behaved and acted in their presence. Weapons, for example, and especially swords, seem to have been treated with particular reverence. Although north and west Europe made use of its own supplies of copper ore at the beginning of the Bronze Age, by its end, almost all swords were made from ore that originated far to the south, in the central European mines we looked at in chapter 27.[18] Either finished swords were being imported from these regions or copies were made locally using foreign ore and adopting foreign designs. It seems that it was the exotic nature of the swords that was of particular importance to people, and the further a sword was thought to have travelled, the more status it accrued. As we have already seen, trade and long-distance contacts were especially important during this time and possibly something of the adventurous life lived by the sword was thought to rub off onto those who wielded it. Everyday tools, however, gave no such status to their owners, and could be made from whatever metal was available, utilising purely local designs and styles.[19] There was no comparison between owning a sword and owning a tool.

Some of the swords from northern Europe were either extremely ornate or far too large to be used sensibly.[20] Possibly these were particularly special and were made solely for display or even just for offering to the spirits (many were left in water). It is as if the sword, like the Kwakwaka'wakw masks, already had a destiny before it began its life journey. Perhaps some swords even became famous in their own right and it is curious how many of the myths from the past revolve around a noteworthy sword.[21]

What lives must eventually die, the soul departing this world and moving to the afterlife. Metal items were no different. Many of the swords in north and west Europe have been found in rivers or other wet places.[22] Although placing things into water was not new in this area, it dramatically increased during the Bronze Age, largely at the expense of grave deposits.[23] In central Europe, however, where the swords (or the metal from which they were made) originated, this was not the case and swords continued to be placed in graves.[24] It seems that the rules changed with the distance travelled by the swords. When they were local, they were placed into graves, but when they were exotic, they were placed into water.

Wielding a big impressive sword was probably all about display; they indicated to others just how impressive their owners were (or at least how impressive they believed themselves to be). Being buried with a sword therefore made sense; not only did the individual get to show off their sword one last time, but they were also able to take it to the afterlife. Why, therefore, would anyone consign his or her most treasured possession to a river? Maybe they felt that they had little choice.

We have seen many instances in the past where rivers were treated as portals to the otherworld; the same seems to be the case here. Placing the sword into a river may have been a way of ensuring that its soul would reach the afterlife. The needs of the sword clearly outweighed any desire from its owner to take it to the grave, again suggesting that swords had lives (and deaths) quite independent of human inter-vention. Moreover, it seems that the death of a sword was something marked by groups of people, perhaps equivalent to the mourning rituals associated with human deaths. At Flag Fen in eastern England, for example, people constructed a wooden platform stretched across an open expanse of water, and stood on it when dropping their swords into the water below.[25] There is even the suggestion that the walkway was divided into separate rooms, each perhaps linked with a community group and affording some privacy for what might have been an emotional event.[26]

We had not expected so many people to join us, squeezed tightly onto the small platform above the smooth expanse of water that gently laps beneath us. Some fight to get to the front but we stay back from the edge; it is too cold today to risk a dunking. The jostling stops when the woman arrives. She carries a sword before her and we marvel at its beauty: its surface is the colour of the sun. The woman speaks some words to the group, which invoke both laughter and sorrow. People seem visibly moved. Then, with a scream, the woman brings the sword crashing to the ground. As it hits a stone, which, we realise, must have been placed there for the purpose, there is a flash of sparks and the sword snaps cleanly into three. There is a howl from the crowd and a lament. The sword is dead. The woman gathers each piece and we move back slightly as people come forward to touch them one last time. Then, crouching low, the woman drops them silently into the water. We watch them fall until the ripples subside and the water becomes smooth once more, reflecting only the troubled faces of the group.

Swords were not only placed into water, many of them were also broken before-hand.[27] This was no easy matter. As we saw, it took considerable force to snap a sword; clearly this was an important part of the process. In the previous chapter, we saw how things in the otherworld are opposite to how they are in this world. For the swords, that meant that if they were broken in this world, they would become whole again in the other. Analysis has shown that breaking the sword seemed to have been a violent and intense event; these were not calm, rational acts but reached frenzied, almost ecstatic, levels of violence.[28] Perhaps this invoked something of the battles that the swords may have witnessed: a final eulogy for their life. For the weapons themselves, it must have been as if their lives were flashing before them.

Finally, and in a strange inversion of the usual burial ritual, human bones were also occasionally dropped into the water, perhaps to accompany the swords on their journey to the afterlife. In the River Thames in England, and also in later periods the River Meuse in the Netherlands, human remains were broken up and the head and limbs thrown into the water.[29] This seems to mirror the treatment of the swords, as if it was the metal object that determined what happened to the people rather than the people that determined what happened to the metal object.

Perhaps joining a sword on its journey to the afterlife was reserved for the lowli-est members of the community, or perhaps this was a prestigious and sought-after role? Certainly, owning a sword was not only a sign of prestige but was also inti-mately bound with the way individuals thought about themselves. In some instances, wielding a sword could be a means to immortality, as some people seemed intent on fashioning their own legend. The time of champions had begun.

Chapter 31

MYTHICAL WARS AND BEAUTIFUL MEN

The two warriors stand about 10 paces from each other. Both men are in the prime of life: broad, muscular, and beautifully groomed with small neat beards and oiled hair caught back in an elaborate plait. Those they command stand on either side, equally handsome and well turned out. Some carry armour to their respective chiefs: bronze body plates, horned helmets, and finely worked shields of engraved bronze. Two women then enter the arena. Both are beautiful, with hair fashioned into elaborate styles and their necks, arms, and ankles weighed down with fine gold jewellery. These are so cumbersome that their movements are restricted and they appear to glide in tiny steps rather than to walk towards the men. When each stands before a warrior, they proffer a sword, polished so finely that their reflections stare back at them in the metal. The men grasp at the blades, each longer than a man's arm at full stretch: these are the swords of champions. The women withdraw and the warriors bow, conferring respect to their worthy opponent. The confrontation has begun. Except that it probably would not last for long. Even if the men could move in their heavy armour and helmets, or wield their enormous swords, the bronze shields that they held would probably shatter upon first impact and be entirely useless as protection. This was not reality; this was the sort of Bronze Age that Homer wrote about when he retold the stories of the Trojan War. It was an image capturing the heroism of battle and it was an image that was particularly pervasive throughout Europe at this time: this is how people wanted to be.

The focus on aggression, drinking, and hospitality that had been steadily growing throughout the Bronze Age had now reached its height. Warriors could ride in chariots, live in forts, and carry weapons so ornate that they still rank among some of the finest examples of the metalworker's art. Carrying arms, especially a sword, became the ultimate status symbol.

It was only with the Bronze Age that weapons moved from being designed to kill animals to being designed to kill humans. We have already seen that some earlier weapons were used to kill people but this was never their primary purpose. The weapons of the Bronze Age had no other function. Even the sword had evolved from a utilitarian knife; first becoming a dagger, then a rapier, before longer and thicker sword blades were developed by the late Bronze Age. This likely reflected the changing fighting styles, with the sword giving more options at close quarters. Whereas a knife or rapier could only be thrust at an enemy, a sword could additionally be brought down in a slashing movement, increasing the chances of maiming or killing an opponent.[1] The thrust of the rapier was taken over by the spear, which also provided a far longer reach. Tellingly, however, spears were never ornamented like swords and they do not appear to have been revered in the same way; clearly close combat was where glory was to be found.[2]

Defensive armour also developed, perhaps as a result of the diaspora of metalworking artisans from the Mediterranean following the decline of Mycenae.[3] Warriors now wore helmets, breastplates, and greaves (shin guards) on the body, and carried a shield to parry the blows of their opponent. Many of these shields were decorated in similar ways, with circles centred around a raised boss and cut by a notch. Examples of this design have been found across Europe so it must have been very significant to people.[4] At first sight, it recalls the cup marks that we saw in chapter 29, which, although concave rather than convex like the shield boss, could be surrounded by circles and cut through with a line leading to the centre. It was suggested that this might reflect the tunnel to the otherworld, with the line indicating the route to get there. The shield designs may have drawn on the same imagery, with an implied threat when displayed to an enemy: fight me and this is where you will end up. It is striking that a lot of early weapons and armour also had spiral designs, perhaps for similar reasons.[5]

Some of the arms and armour produced were far too ornate to be used effectively. We saw in the previous chapter how some swords were too elaborate or long to ever have been wielded, but it seems that a large number of swords were also too fragile to be used in anything other than the lightest skirmish. These were swords with solid rather than flanged hilts, that is, the handle was made from bronze and riveted onto the sword separately, instead of the blade and hilt being cast together with flanges allowing for a grip of wood or bone to be attached. These solid-hilted swords, while fine for thrusting, tended to snap alarmingly if used to slash at an enemy. Those who carried a solid-hilted sword (rather than a flange-hilted version) were probably carrying it for display rather than with any real intention of using it. The light wear on the edges of excavated examples bears this out.[6] In addition to swords, metal armour was also more for display than for real fighting; two helmets found at Viksø in Denmark even had elaborate horns.[7] A famous experiment in the 1960s, when two archaeologists arrayed themselves with bronze armour and then hacked away at each other with swords, showed that most examples were likely to shatter on impact.[8] The bronze shields, breastplates, and even the helmets were for showing off and it is likely that real warriors limited their attire to leather armour and carried a wooden shield. Some of these have been recovered from the bogs of northern Europe, where such organic items have been preserved, but, if people were as militarily minded as they made out, there must once have been many more.

Right: A model created by
the Anthropological Institute
at the University of Zurich
showing how a Neanderthal
child may have appeared. It is
based on remains discovered
in Portugal in 1926 by
Dorothy Garrod, the first
female professor at Cambridge
University, holding the
position of Disney Professor of
Archaeology.

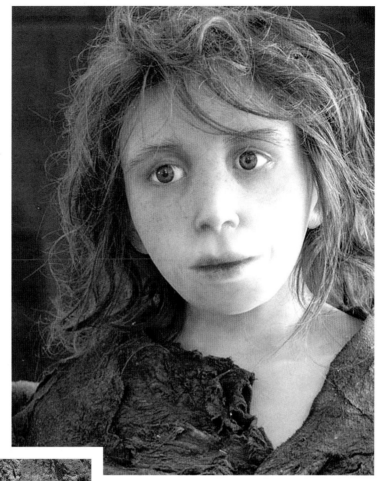

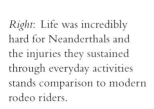

Left: The entrance to Shanidar cave, where Rose and Ralph
Solecki found several Neanderthal burials between 1953
and 1960, including one that at first appeared to contain a
bouquet of flowers.

Right: Life was incredibly
hard for Neanderthals and
the injuries they sustained
through everyday activities
stands comparison to modern
rodeo riders.

Above: Painting the walls of the caves from a reconstruction at Dan y Ogof in Wales.

Right: A 28cm-high statue of a human with the head of a lion carved from mammoth ivory and found at Hohlenstein-Stadel in Germany. Could this be a portrayal of a shaman shapeshifting into animal form?

Below: A scene painted in a separate chamber in the caves at Lascaux in southern France showing a bird-headed human falling backwards, perhaps in a trance, before a disembowelled bison. The bird-headed staff may have been part of the ritual regalia used by the individual portrayed.

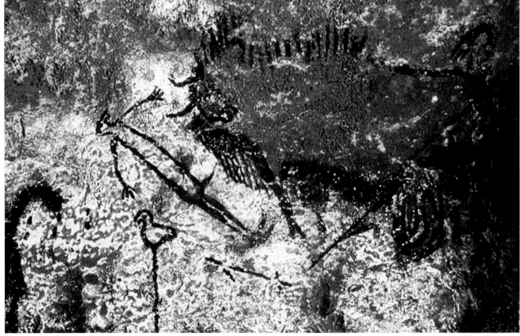

Left: Cheddar Gorge, in southern England, where hunters at the very end of the Ice Age took refuge in a cave and may have killed and eaten other humans.

Below: A carving from Lepenski Vir, in Serbia, showing a human-fish hybrid. These may have represented the dead, as they shapeshifted into fish and ensured that the beluga returned during their summer migration past the settlement.

Below: A reconstruction of how the Mesolithic settlement of Lepenski Vir may have appeared on the banks of the Danube. Whether it was occupied year round, or only used seasonally, perhaps for the return of the beluga in the summer, is still uncertain.

Above: The site of a Mesolithic hunting camp by the side of a vanished lake at Waun Fignen Felen in the Black Mountain of Wales. The hunters may have burnt the reeds around the lakeside to attract deer to the regenerating shoots.

Right: Tools and waste chippings of black flint left by the Mesolithic hunters. The tools are called microliths, which means 'tiny stones'.

Left: All that remains of the Mesolithic lake is a large black peat bog that covers the base of a small hollow in the hills. The pool in the foreground is still known locally as Pwll y Cig, meaning 'The Flesh Pool', perhaps echoing some distant memory of the hunters who used to visit here.

Above: The Bush Barrow, south of Stonehenge, where a male burial was accompanied by fabulously rich funeral gifts, including a gold lozenge with a hexagonal design engraved on its surface. Three daggers and an axe were also laid with the deceased and these mirror the same arrangement carved onto one of the uprights at Stonehenge, directly facing the burial. The carvings may have been a reminder of the exceptional individual under the adjacent mound.

Left: The Amesbury Archer, a rich beaker burial also located close to Stonehenge. Analysis of the chemical signatures in the man's teeth show that he originated in central southern Europe. Some of the items in his grave related to metalworking and he may have been one of the first bronzeworkers to visit the area. He also carried an injury to his left knee and his incredible journey may have been, in part, a quest for healing.

Below: Stonehenge from the south.

Above: The entrance to Tinkinswood tomb in the Vale of Glamorgan with the long barrow mound behind it.

Left: A reconstructed long house from Cockley Cley Museum in Norfolk that seems to mirror the arrangement of the long barrows.

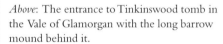

Right: A reconstructed roundhouse from St Fagans National History Museum in Wales that seems to mirror the round barrows below.

Left: A round barrow cemetery in Dorset showing how the barrows cluster together as if they were houses for the dead.

Above: View of Barclodiad y Gawres tomb on Anglesey. The right inset shows the inner chamber where a stew made from the remains of various small animals was made. The left inset shows one of the decorated stones.

Left: Gavrinis tomb in Brittany.

Right: A decorated stone from Gavrinis showing the tunnel imagery that lined the passageway leading into the chamber.

Above: Machrie Moor on Arran in Scotland. The stone circle was originally erected in wood before the posts were removed, the ground ploughed, and stone pillars put in their place.

Right: Templewood stone circle in Scotland. At the centre of the circle is a grave cist, linking the monument with death, a familiar theme for many stone circles.

Left: Part of the stone alignment at Carnac in Brittany, where some 2700 stones were arranged in rough lines over a 3km route across the land.

Clockwise from above
A boat carved into the rock during the Bronze Age at
Alta in Norway. Some of the people in the boat are
drumming, perhaps indicating that this is a spirit boat on
its way to the otherworld.

The shaman's spirit has now left its body and flies above
the boat towards the otherworld.

Footprints on the rock show the shaman's spirit which
direction it should take and it can be seen flying upwards
on the top left of the rock.

The rock the shaman ascends is orientated towards a gap
in the surrounding landscape.

Passing through the gap the shaman's spirit now reaches
water, a traditional entrance to the otherworld.

Right: Reconstruction of Bronze Age metalworking. The crushed ore is placed within the smelting furnace and heated to a little over 1000°C until the copper melts. The huge bellows provide the air required to reach these temperatures.

Left: Bronze Age metalworkers would have watched the colour and texture of the smelted metal to determine when it was ready to remove from the furnace and pour.

Right: The molten copper is poured into moulds, which, in the Bronze Age, would have been made from two pieces of clay bound together.

Below left: Once the molten metal has cooled, the mould is split and the item removed.

Below right: The completed item, which now requires finishing.

Above: Cremation was the main death rite for much of prehistory. Here, the body and its attendant offerings sits on top of a pyre of stacked wood. The fire is fierce, fed by the fat that drips from the burning body.

Left: After 45 minutes, the body has burnt and the pyre considerably reduced.

Below: After two hours, the pyre has virtually extinguished and the charred bone may be gathered together for burial.

Left: The Sun Horse from Trundholm in Denmark. The image of the horse pulling the sun was a familiar theme in the Bronze Age and may have induced people to follow its path.

Right: When ingested, Fly Agaric mushrooms induce trance and create sensations of the soul leaving the body. Images of the mushroom were engraved onto razors, which also seem to incorporate the theme of the sun horse above.

Below: A burnt mound from the Black Mountain in Wales. Within an enclosed space, the steam generated by putting hot rocks into water would also have been sufficient to induce trance.

Above: The ramparts at Maiden Castle hillfort, in Dorset. They were so wide and deep that it is unlikely that they could have been successfully defended, suggesting that their real role may have been for display.

Above: The interior of Danebury hillfort, in Hampshire. The houses would have squeezed against the walls allowing the central area to be used for grain storage in granaries and silos.

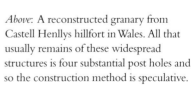

Above: A reconstructed granary from Castell Henllys hillfort in Wales. All that usually remains of these widespread structures is four substantial post holes and so the construction method is speculative.

Left: The outline of the shrine from Maiden Castle. These appear to have provided a focus for ceremonies and rituals within the hillforts and small offerings were often left buried around them.

Above: The cauldron found in a bog at Gundestrup in Denmark. The scenes on the internal panels show an antlered human surrounded by animals and a large figure inserting armed warriors into a cauldron.

Right: Lindow Man, ritually killed during the Iron Age and placed in a bog where his remains survived.

Below: A coin of the Iceni tribe showing a stylised horse and a circular sunburst above it. The meaning of the image may be connected to that of the earlier sun horse from Trundholm.

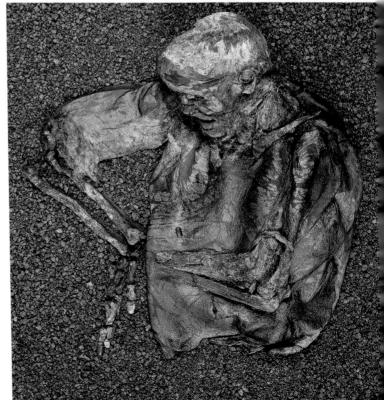

Above: Reconstruction of an Iron Age roundhouse from St Fagans National History Museum in Wales. Notice the smoke escaping through the thatched roof.

Left: Life inside the roundhouse would have been dark and smoky.

Right: A fire would have been constantly tended to provide heat, light, and a place to cook.

Left: Yellow Top promontory fort on Gower, South Wales. Sealing off such spurs of coastal land was common throughout the coastal regions of southern Wales, south-west England and Brittany.

Below right: Tre'r Ceiri hillfort on the Llyn Peninsula in North Wales. This was one of the most densely occupied hillforts with over 150 house remains still visible. Up to 400 people may have lived here at the fort's greatest extent. Unlike the hillforts of the lowlands, where the boundaries comprised banks and ditches, Tre'r Ceiri is surrounded by two stone walls.

Below: Dun Beag broch on the island of Skye in Scotland. The walls still stand to almost 5m but would have originally been much higher. Such tower houses were once common along the western seaboard of Scotland and the adjacent islands.

Just how often these warriors saw real battle, however, is a moot point. The imagery was presumably based on genuine experiences; the development of killing weapons could not have happened without their being refined through use. Certainly, analysis of many of the swords shows that they had been used in actual combat (probably to parry the blows of another sword) and some had been re-sharpened as a result.[9] However, there is very little evidence of widespread injury as a result of battle (even accepting that most bodies were cremated) and, as we have seen, swords were the almost exclusive preserve of the elite. If battles were being fought in the Bronze Age, it seems that only a certain few took part in them.

The rock engravings of Scandinavia that we explored in chapter 29 show many battle scenes. However, most of these involve just two, or occasionally three, individuals and some even take place on the deck of a boat.[10] Since a lot of the imagery seems true to life, with weapons portrayed and used correctly, perhaps this is, indeed, how people fought. Instead of massed ranks of warriors fighting large-scale wars, perhaps disputes were settled by two opposing champions, each representing their respective communities? The prevalence of wheeled carts in central European graves, and the images of similar vehicles engraved on the rocks,[11] suggest that these champions arrived at their battles in some style, even if that did not quite measure up to the Mycenaean chariots from where the custom probably derived.[12] Perhaps the champions even paraded their bronze armour and oversized weapons before combat and our reconstruction at the start of the chapter was not so far-fetched after all. Certainly, some individuals (mainly men) seemed to define themselves through the weapons that they carried and, in some of the Scandinavian rock images, there are oversized figures where the length of their weapon is matched only by the length of the suitably erect penis.[13] These were 'big men' in every sense.

In the far north-west of Spain and Portugal, people shaped standing stones roughly like a body and engraved various types of weapons upon them. On one of these, from Chaves, the figure has an erect penis, again associating battle with manhood.[14] Other standing stones were also engraved with weaponry, although the shape of the stone made no attempt to reflect a body. It is almost as if the person had become superfluous and all that mattered were the weapons.[15] Moreover, these statues were erected in places where the weapons depicted were probably only rarely encountered. It is as if people tried to display their prowess without actually owning the proper means to do so.[16] Other depictions show a single large weapon with smaller examples grouped around it, perhaps representing the champion and his accompanying entourage.[17] However, once again, it is only the weapons that were portrayed and not the individuals that presumably carried them. The pre-eminence afforded to weapons may reflect their status as independent entities that lived a life associated with, but not determined by, people. Within the rock engravings, it seems that weapons could speak for themselves.

We have already seen how much of the metalwork in north and west Europe was consigned to rivers and bogs, whereas in central Europe it was buried with the dead. Additional items within the graves mirror other status symbols, primarily drinking and feasting. In addition to the beverage vessels and cauldrons we have seen before, cooking utensils were also consigned to the ground, particularly meat hooks and spits.[18] Again, images of water birds adorn these implements, perhaps to ease their crossing between the worlds. Clearly, people were expecting to entertain in the afterlife, perhaps with the equivalent of a Bronze Age all-you-can-drink barbecue. However, there were also other objects that seem to mirror the preoccupations of the time: toilet items, particularly combs, tweezers, razors, mirrors, and awls. Moreover, these were dominant in male rather than female graves. Clearly, these men wanted to look their best when they entered the afterlife. But then, if these were the champions that Homer wrote about, why not?

Homer's Troy was not necessarily the Troy of archaeology, but the Troy of legend. What the combatants seemed to desire above all was to be remembered and talked about after their death. This was a society where drinking and hospitality were the touchstones for behaviour and it is almost inconceivable that these occasions would not have involved storytelling. The champions of the time wanted to be remembered forever, and to achieve that, they needed to become legends. The beautiful warrior, perhaps laid out on a wagon, surrounded with enough drinking and feasting equipment to guarantee a rapturous welcome on the other side and, perhaps most importantly, with those items that guaranteed his vitality would never fade nor his looks ever tarnish. These men were making themselves the stuff of myth.[19] Even the women fashioned their hair into fantastic arrangements, and were arrayed with so much jewellery that it may have restricted their movement.[20] The reconstruction at the start of this chapter is looking less like myth and more like reality.

Of course, a warrior needed a castle, or at least a settlement with a degree of fortification around it, and these proliferate at this time. In central Europe, hillforts emerge in areas where there had been very little prior defensive enclosure.[21] Moreover, these fortifications were certainly built to repel attack, as Velim Skalka in the Czech Republic, starkly illustrates, when its defences were burnt and many arrows were let fly at its defenders.[22] This was no battle of champions but large-scale and, if the associated burials represent the combatants, potentially deadly conflict. The Urnfield villages were also protected by solid boundaries. Some, such as the Wasserburg fortified island in Germany, took a novel approach, surrounding the island with a fence and building towers to guard its perimeter.[23] Such settlements seemed to reflect the bellicosity of the time.

However, in the Bronze Age there was much that was worth fighting over. The vast accumulations of bronze, presumably kept at the settlements before being deposited elsewhere, must have been a tempting target for raiders and thieves. It may have even been a point of honour to obtain the weapons of another through fair means or foul. Indeed, many of the first Urnfield sites to be fortified lay on trade routes and perhaps these were refuges where traders could safely spend the night.[24] Other sites may have been centres of metal production, and at Spišsky Sturtok (the site in Slovakia that had numerous metalwork hoards), it should perhaps not surprise us that stone walls surrounded the central part of the settlement from an early stage.[25] Similarly, in Spain, where metal weapons seemed to be more important than the warriors themselves, we have already seen in chapter 27 how metalworking and the fortification of settlements seemed to go hand-in-hand. The development of silver technology may have given this an added impetus.[26]

In eastern and southern England, ring works, which comprised a circular enclosure ditch with a large central roundhouse, emerge in the late Bronze Age.[27] It is difficult to assess whether these were the residences of warriors or halls for communal gatherings (and there is no reason why they could not have been both), but, as in other regions, several seem to also have been metalworking sites. At Springfield Lyons, for example, sword moulds were recovered from both entrances to the site,[28] and at Mucking North Ring, knife moulds were found in the boundary ditch.[29] (It is curious that both of these locations are boundaries, reflecting the liminal locations for metalworking and mould deposition that we observed in the previous chapter.) It may be significant that these sites appear in regions with sizable deposits of metalwork and also where the first large-scale division of the land into regular fields took place.[30] In addition to the control and protection of metal, it seems that if these were the residences of the warrior elite, they now had something else to protect: land.

The late Bronze Age may have been the era of the beautiful and glorious warrior but it was likely the more mundane aspects of life that most concerned the ordinary people. Shelter, food, and a place to bury the dead were probably foremost in their thoughts. However, it seems that even here, things were not always as straightforward as they first appear and people went to extraordinary lengths to link all three and to make sure that their world was just as they believed it should be.

Chapter 32

FACING THE SUNRISE

Late last night, we crept into an empty house somewhere in southern Britain. It seemed strange at first since it was round rather than the rectangular shape we are familiar with. It is also a lot smaller. You spotted the tiny hamlet first, nestled into the side of a hill and betrayed only by the faint glow of a fire. The midwinter frost was beginning to coat the trees with its glitter and we were glad to find shelter for at least part of the darkness. Waking this morning, the air is frigid as it drifts straight through the open doorway and into my face. Since you spotted the house first, you got to sleep on the side furthest from the door. As we begin to make sense of our surroundings, we notice that the sun is rising from the other side of the shallow valley. In the space of a few heartbeats, the first rays have raced across the ground and we are assailed by its brightness. The sun is perfectly framed by the doorway to the house, almost as if it had been planned that way. Blinking, we stand up and move outside; maybe we might find something to eat in the fields next to the settlement.

Although we could not have known it, the positioning of the doorway to face the morning sun at midwinter was deliberate, and was repeated across many settlements throughout southern Britain. Joanna Brück, an expert on this period of the Bronze Age, found that 58 per cent of houses had doorways facing south-east, with another 20 per cent facing south.[1] On Dartmoor, which has a number of well-preserved houses with stone foundations, most of the doorways also face south-east, with the second most popular direction being south-west.[2] Furthermore, these orientations appear to ignore prevailing wind directions or attempts to maximise the light entering the house during the day, concentrating instead on lining up the doorway with the sunrise at the midwinter solstice or, in the case of some of the houses in Dartmoor, the midwinter solstice sunset.[3] We have seen similar alignments before, in the stone circles and burial monuments of the Neolithic, when it was suggested that the rays of the sun at these significant times indicated the path that the dead needed to follow to reach the afterlife. In the Bronze Age, however, the rays of the sun enter houses, ostensibly the places of the living rather than the dead. Nevertheless, while this might have been true when the houses were occupied, the next chapter will show that, upon abandonment, they changed to become places of the dead. Perhaps the houses were actually built with this dual purpose in mind; the rising sun at the midwinter solstice a reminder to people that their time was transitory and that only the dead were a permanent presence in the landscape.

As we know, on the continent people built rectangular houses, perhaps because they had a lengthy history of using this design and it held memories of longevity and permanence. Perhaps they were trying to negate the same thoughts about the impermanence of life that their contemporaries were wrestling with in Britain? The houses certainly shared a similar alignment, with the majority of the rectangular long-houses having a short end facing to the south-east.[4] Many of these were divided internally between a living space in one half of the house and a cattle byre in the other.[5] There seems to have been little reason for the cattle to be brought inside, however, and it may have had more to do with displaying wealth and prestige rather than any real farming need (in fact, there are even advantages to keeping the cattle outside all year round).[6] Since cattle also got smaller at this time, presumably through manipulated breeding, it may have allowed people to keep more animals on the same amount of land, thereby increasing their herd (and available animals to flaunt).[7] In the large majority of these houses, the cattle byre was located on the eastern side, meaning that for those houses aligned to the south-east, it was the cattle byre that received the first rays of the midwinter sunrise.[8] It seems unlikely that this was to provide a path to the afterlife for the dead cattle and so it must have drawn on other themes associated with the sunrise at the solstice.

The rising sun at the midwinter solstice comes at the darkest part of the year and, from that day forward, the days lengthen and the sun increases in strength. For the cattle in the byres, these symbols of renewal and rebirth may have related to their fertility and the anticipated birth of calves in the spring (some cows were probably noticeably pregnant). Perhaps the confinement of the animals over the winter was a way of passing them into the dark otherworld travelled by the sun, with the belief that, like the sun, they would emerge with renewed vigour in the spring? Since each cow was likely to have been pregnant only two or three times in her life, this would have been a hugely significant event. Furthermore, if the cattle were so entwined with the cycle of the sun, other aspects of the agricultural year may have been just as involved.

As we leave the roundhouse and reach the fields, we have to climb over a small stone wall. This is the boundary of the cultivated land. Similar walls are repeated all the way along the valley, forming a patchwork of small fields, possibly belonging to different individuals or families. We climb on top of the wall and take in the view along its length. All the other walls follow a course parallel to this wall, with short cross walls to delineate the ends of the fields. Following its length, we both squint, as we now have the sun full in our faces. Then it hits us: like the door to the roundhouse, all the fields are also aligned to the rising sun. This cannot be a coincidence.

The fields we observed have been given the unfortunate misnomer 'Celtic Fields', which they certainly are not. Most have been firmly dated to the middle part of the

Bronze Age and are mainly found in those countries bordering the North Sea and English Channel.[9] The preferred archaeological term for these fields is 'coaxial', since most adhere to a common alignment, and as we have already found out for ourselves, this seems to follow the alignment of the houses. However, since these fields were rectangular, their boundaries would have formed two orientations, at right angles to each other. Although the majority of fields fit into a south-east to north-west and south-west to north-east grid, the primary alignment (the one taken by the longest side of the fields) varies from place to place. In the Netherlands, most of the fields had their longest boundaries aligned to the south-east[10] and this was also the case in Dartmoor in southern England.[11] However, in the rest of southern England,[12] and also in Denmark,[13] the south-west alignment was predominant. Despite this difference, the standard grid was always respected when laying out the fields. People did not deviate from this grid even when the fields crossed a river valley, which would have made ploughing very awkward, or if it meant that some of the fields would have been in shadow.[14] Perhaps people felt that arranging their fields to face the rising sun at the midwinter or midsummer solstices, and the symbolic bestowal of fertility that this might have provided made up for any practical drawbacks?

We have already seen how many earlier burial sites were aligned to the rising sun and how the rays of the sun may have symbolised the route of the dead to the afterlife. This may be why the newly laid-out fields respected many of the older barrows and, rather than flattening the mound or digging through it, the fields either avoided the site altogether or incorporated it into their boundaries. The same cannot always be said for some of the houses set among the fields, which are so randomly placed and so insubstantial that they may not have formed part of the overall design.[15] These may have been the makeshift homes of the labourers that created the fields, while the designers lived elsewhere, at the edge of the system.[16] Moreover, if the fields systems were imposed from outside, then it provides another reason why the alignment to the sunrise was so overriding.

In chapter 29, we saw how Bronze Age razors carried images of the passage of the sun through the sky, a theme that seemed to resonate across much of northern Europe at this time. However, owning a razor was also a mark of status and we saw in the previous chapter how they are often found in the graves of people who were likely to have been very important within their communities. It seems that the journey of the sun was something that the elite readily identified with and it came to define their place in the world. If the field systems were imposed from outside the local area, then it is likely that it was the same people involved. The arrangement of the fields became a way for the elite to display their status and influence and their connection to the journey of the sun. The people working the fields would have had no difficulty in accepting this, after all, the symbolism was hardly new and it also introduced other themes, such as fertility and renewal. For the elite, it was a way of putting their mark on the landscape: this is who we are and this is what we stand for. It is unlikely, however, that their power went as far as coercing people to arrange their houses to face in the same direction (but if it did, perhaps the exceptions were a subtle form of rebellion) but people possibly aped the elite of their own accord, as a form of Bronze Age social climbing. Over time, it is likely that the association with the elite was forgotten and people continued the tradition for the same reason that customs are retained anywhere: because it had always been done that way.

This aping of the elite may also be found in the burial sites. At the start of the Bronze Age in the Netherlands, certain people, presumably those of high status, were buried under a mound. To begin with, the majority of bodies were orientated north to south but this changed, as the Bronze Age progressed, to south-east to north-west, matching the alignment of the contemporary fields and houses. Other people, pre-sumably of lesser status, were buried in and around the same barrow but they did not follow any particular alignment; this was clearly the preserve of only a special few.[17] Following the move to cremation, urnfields developed and these often centred on a long mound.[18] Most of these contained a central uncremated body, presumably that of a high-status individual equivalent to those buried under a barrow in earlier times.[19] At this stage, much of the prestigious metalwork was being placed into rivers and so these burials had very few items accompanying them in the grave. However, what they did have were razors, tweezers, and awls, the same show-off objects that signified high-status individuals throughout much of Europe.[20] Moreover, the align-ment of the body, and thereby the long mound, was mostly towards the south-east.[21] Regular cremation burials clustered around these long mounds, perhaps because people wanted to be close to the esteemed individual they knew lay within them.

In southern England, people may have gone a stage further. High-status individu-als were still buried under their own mounds, although since bodies were usually cremated, it is not possible to determine their orientation. However, some of these barrows had a ditch encircling them, and where there was a causeway left uncut to provide access to the mound, these faced south-east.[22] At Ogden Down, something similar happened when a Neolithic barrow was encircled in the Bronze Age by a ring of posts and an avenue, again facing south-east.[23] Perhaps this barrow had always attracted attention and, through surrounding it in this manner, people embraced it within their own beliefs? Where later burials cluster around these primary barrows, they tend to favour the south-eastern quadrant, again aping the symbolism used by the elite but also drawing upon the time-worn importance attributed to the sun and the route to the afterlife.[24]

If these burial sites were necessarily fixed in the landscape, the same was not true of the houses and we shall see in the next chapter how these were abandoned and rebuilt somewhere new every generation or so. People may have worked the fields but it does not seem that they had any particular claim over them. It may have been the elite that owned the fields, the same group of people who may have once deter-mined their form. However, despite the emergence of fortified settlements and the circulation of prestigious weaponry, it is unlikely that any single group could have maintained ownership of such extensive areas, or commanded the obedience of people to work them. There is no evidence that certain individuals were sustained through the labour of others, as might arise in such a feudal system (although the hillforts, which have their origins at this time, do seem to have become storage centres by the Iron Age). Even those afforded high status in the urnfields may have been household heads rather than previously absent rulers; after all, image was as important as substance in the Bronze Age. However, if the people did not own the fields, and there was no landowning elite, then who did own them?

Towards the end of the Bronze Age, the land was again divided, this time into much larger parcels, and these new divisions seemed to ride roughshod over the existing fields.[25] Only existing barrows were respected, and in some cases, even incorporated into these new divisions so that the boundaries appear to arise from (or lead to) selected burial mounds.[26] This was also the case when the fields were originally laid out; only the dead seemed to generate such universal respect. Could this be because they were actually believed to be the owners of the land? The dead were the only permanent entities in the transient world of the Bronze Age: they alone were unmoved and unchanging. If they did own the land, then it was in good hands, until, that is, the living wanted it back.

Chapter 33

HOUSE OF THE SPIRITS

We return from another cremation. We are getting used to seeing bodies burn although it is always slightly disconcerting to watch as the flames first touch and then blacken human flesh. We even helped collect some of the charred bones, placing them in the waiting urn. Since the burning, the small family has been busy collecting together their belongings, as if they are making ready to leave. The woman we watched burn had been the family's head and this responsibility now lies with her eldest son. We follow him as he checks on preparations, chiding the slow and praising the hard working. He looks a good sort. Just as people are finally ready to go, he turns back to the house in which his mother had lived; in his hands he carries a small earthen pot, almost identical to the one in which his mother's remains now lie. When he reaches the house, he smashes the pot on the floor, spreading its remains liberally over the surface. From his pocket, he takes some flint chips and he also spreads these across the floor. Finally, he lifts a bronze spearhead from where it was attached to his belt. I hear you gasp. This is a valuable piece indeed. Speaking a few words over the newly polished spearhead, he leaves it in the centre of the house. Then, turning abruptly and without looking back, he walks swiftly to where his family awaits him. Later that day, when we reach the burial site that the family use, we notice a repeat of the earlier ceremony. Once the urn is placed in the ground, the young man drops a few pieces of broken pot around it and then a few pieces of flint chips. We realise that he had kept these from this morning, when he had spread the rest over the house floor. The family look pleased with what he has done and they turn to move off once more. The rest of the day will be spent looking for a new home.

About midway through the Bronze Age, around 1500 BC, people started building sturdy houses. This was a change from earlier times, when (apart from the huge LBK houses) settlements tended to be more ephemeral and lightly built. This was probably because people did not stay in one place for very long, usually spending the year following the herds, collecting wild foods, and perhaps intermittently tending small patches of cultivated ground.[1] By the middle Bronze Age, this all changed and houses became more substantial (and probably more comfortable as a result). This mirrored other, wider changes that we have already seen, such as the laying out of regular fields and the burial of the dead in cemeteries. It seems that identification with particular places and increasing permanence were the touchstones for this time. It is strange, therefore, that these substantial houses were abandoned every generation or so and that people moved on to build new houses in other locations.

Research by Joanna Brück has shown that only 7 per cent of middle Bronze Age houses in southern England were ever used beyond a generation or so, and the remainder were abandoned.[2] The same was true for continental houses, which are known as wandering farmsteads because of their propensity to shift locations.[3] The regularity of abandonment suggests that it probably occurred on the death of the head of the household. We have already seen in the Neolithic how people could be intimately bound to their houses so that, when one dies, so must the other.[4] It is even possible that some middle Bronze Age houses were symbolically killed either through burning, dismantling, or even by driving a spear into the floor, as happened at Penhale Moor in south-west England.[5] Others, however, were treated differently and seem to have become surrogate barrows: burial chambers without the body. Despite their intimate bonds with the house, the owner was generally burnt and presumably buried in the cremation cemeteries that were often located a short distance from the settlement.[6] We have already seen how barrows tend to be associated with high-status individuals and perhaps the surrogate barrow was a means of recognising the status of the deceased as head of the household. However, since the body was removed and treated like anyone else, there may have been tensions arising over the relative hierarchy of people within these communities.

We have already seen how the entrances of many of these houses faced south-east and this may have been incorporated into their design precisely because people knew that they would, one day, become places of the dead. To emphasise the new role of the house as a barrow, certain items were spread over the floor, particularly broken pottery and flint chips. Both were also scattered in and around the urn cemeteries, drawing a clear parallel between the two.[7] Small items of bronze were occasionally left on the floor of the house and these were mirrored by the very rare examples left with burials.[8] Mostly, the items were tools, broken jewellery, or spears, suggesting that people may have occasionally been called upon to fight, perhaps by the warrior champions we met in chapter 31. Occasionally, human and animal bones were brought into the houses, although people may have collected these while they still lived there, hinting at earlier rituals connected with death.[9] Furthermore, the animal bones were definitely not food residue. At South Lodge, for example, half a cow was buried under the floor, and parts must have been sticking above the surface when the place was still inhabited.[10]

The change from house to burial place was matched elsewhere, and in south-west England (where both tended to be built of the available stone), after houses were abandoned, they were covered with stone so that they resembled cairns.[11] One, at Callestick, was even circled with quartz stones, just like some burial places.[12] In Denmark, barrows were built over the top of abandoned houses.[13] At Trappendal and Hyllerup, for example, the outline of the barrow exactly covered that of the house so that the central burial was just inside the door.[14] This may have been significant, since, at Handewitt, the barrow did not exactly match the outline of the house, but this ensured that the central grave, again, lay just inside the door.[15] It seems that, as with the English examples, it was important that death actually entered the house.

Many of the continental long-houses lack preserved floor surfaces, which hinders the reconstruction of abandonment ceremonies. However, certain items were often buried into the floors, called foundation deposits because it is assumed that they were left as the house was built. At Pryssgården, in Sweden, however, it is possible to differentiate between those items left when the house was constructed and those left at its end.[16] What is particularly interesting is that the items chosen were identical: axes, pottery, bones, and pieces of quernstones. Like the south-east alignments that were arranged when the houses were first built (and all the houses at Pryssgården face south-east), the foundation deposits may have been anticipating the end of the house, when it became a place of the dead. Perhaps this also explains why people brought human bones into their houses or buried dead animals under the floors: their homes were only theirs for a short time before being returned to the dead, and people were acknowledging this.

Most of the foundation deposits buried at Pryssgården were placed near the hearth, perhaps the central symbol of the home, and it is curious that at Barnhouse in Scotland, when the houses were abandoned, the hearths were removed and placed into the new dwellings. This matches other sites, where parts of the old house were incorporated into the new.[17] Perhaps the foundation deposits were actually part of the same group of items that were also placed into the preceding house when it was abandoned. Again, death was being brought into the house and incorporated into the new life that would exist there.

This sequence brings a new theme into the houses: rebirth. We have seen how people may have believed that the sun was reborn at the midwinter solstice and that something of this event was incorporated into the houses and burial sites through their south-east alignment. This was also mirrored in the orientation of the fields, in part, perhaps, because the agricultural cycle itself was positively bursting with images of death and rebirth.[18] Maybe this is why items associated with agriculture, and particularly crop cultivation, were also left in abandoned houses. These may have been places of death but they were also shot through with images of rebirth.

Grain itself is perhaps the most striking deposit and, in order for it to be preserved, it was burnt first. This may have been accidental, of course, but the 40kg of grain, from two separate pits at Black Patch in southern England, was no accident, especially as the grain had been burnt elsewhere and then placed into the pit.[19] The burning of the seed, while essential for preservation, may have also mirrored the cremation ritual and formed an association between cooking food and 'cooking' the dead.[20] At Bestwall in southern England, for example, a heap of burnt stone covering an abandoned house may have been used for cooking food.[21]

An intention to symbolise rebirth may have determined the choice of animal and human remains that were brought into the settlements. Within southern England, a foetus was placed in a pond at Cock Hill (presumably upon abandonment); at Poundbury, an infant was placed in a ditch; at Crab Farm there was a pregnant cow and a sheep with two lambs; at Dean Bottom, a newborn calf; and at South Lodge, an immature cow.[22] It may have been that each being young or newborn symbolised the hope of rebirth after death.

In other cases, rebirth seems to have been a continuum, with people playing their own part in the regenerative process. For the cut grain to become food, for example (thereby bringing life out of death), it first needed to be ground on a quern and perhaps the act of grinding itself became a symbol of this transformation.[23] This may be why querns were smashed and scattered over the floor of abandoned houses: introducing an image of rebirth at the transition of the house from life to death.[24]

Ploughing was another transformational activity, this time at the commencement of cultivation. In the early Bronze Age, the ground beneath barrows may have been ploughed before construction, and at Machrie Moor stone circle in Scotland, the ground was ploughed before the wooden circle was reconstructed in stone.[25] At Lusehøj in Denmark, one of the richest graves of its time was mounded over abandoned houses but, before work commenced, the ground was first ploughed.[26] In every case, ploughing marked a transformation from life to death. Clearing the fields of stones was another task before cultivation and these were often mounded up into cairns that so closely resemble the burial cairns that, without excavation, it is often impossible to tell the difference between the two.[27] Perhaps this was intentional and was another means of marking the cycle of life, death, and rebirth?

Waste from the houses also found its way onto fields, presumably to maintain their fertility and, perhaps predictably, human bones were added to the mix.[28] Although this may have been unintentional, the burial of bodies into chalk quarries at New Buildings in southern England was not.[29] Chalk was likely mined as fertiliser for the fields and the appearance of bodies buried at the quarries again illustrates the theme of rebirth stemming from death.

It seems that death had to be introduced into anything that led to life. Houses, fields, crops, manure, and fertiliser all provided for life and, yet, each was saturated with images of death. Perhaps people believed that there *must* be death for there to be life? Rather like the Mesolithic hunters who believed that the animals they killed had to be reborn if there was to be a continuing supply of game, perhaps Bronze Age people thought that life was limited, and for there to be new life, it had to be matched equally by death.[30] To return to the abandonment of the houses, perhaps this was also bound into the beliefs about regeneration: if a new household was to arise, then the old, and everything associated with it, must die. Similarly, the land, which had provided for the people for a generation or more, must also be allowed to wither and be returned to the dead.

As we have seen, the dead were the only fixed feature in the landscape and it is likely that they were seen not only as the guardians of the land but also as its owners.[31] This was probably why field divisions respected the burial sites. In earlier times, when people moved around throughout the year, land was probably used communally; nobody owned it and it could be safely left in the care of the dead. By the middle Bronze Age, however, people began to work smaller areas and used manure or fertiliser to enhance fertility. There was a long-term investment in the land and, rather than handing it back to the dead, it would have made more sense for it to be inherited by living descendents. Perhaps this was what the symbols of rebirth in the house really stood for, a plea to the dead to release their grip on the land and allow the living to remain: rebirth out of death.

At some places, people tried to hedge their bets and only move a short distance away.[32] What first appear to be villages were actually a series of houses that were rebuilt close to one another. Black Patch in southern England is an example where two houses were replaced by two others very close by.[33] Whether the people who did this were also trying to cheat the dead out of their rightful ownership of the land is a distinct possibility, especially since the two abandoned houses contained the largest number of bronze items left in any abandoned house, and each had a pit with 20kg of burnt grain inside. If the living were trying to cheat the dead, they certainly attempted to make up for it in other ways.

Although the dead were an enduring presence throughout prehistory, it was only now that they had become an encumbrance to the living. The living wanted the land; to return it to the dead, as tradition decreed, was a waste of years of investment. There was clearly a conflict arising between the needs of the living and the demands of the dead. For their very survival, this was a battle people could not afford to lose.

Chapter 34

EYE TO EYE
WITH A MUMMY

When a person dies, the muscles stiffen, contorting the face and pulling the limbs into grotesque angles. Cells die and release enzymes that begin to break down the fats and tissues, puffing up flesh and turning it first green, then purple, and lastly, a shiny black. It then starts to get unpleasant. Bacteria from the gut eat the body from the inside and maggots eat it from the outside. Both use a similar technique: liquefying the flesh while belching out a foul gas behind them. The body swells to three times its size before splitting open, oozing its putrefied contents. This is also when the skin sloughs off and the eyeballs fall out of their sockets. It is not pretty. To stop the decay, the destroying enzymes need abating, and modern undertakers achieve this through a cocktail of chemicals.[1] In certain parts of the world, particularly in very dry climates, bodies were preserved naturally. Over time, people added their own expertise to these natural processes and certain individuals were mummified, their dried bodies preserved forever.[2] Mummies are found across the world in places such as South America, Egypt, Siberia, and, now, even in Scotland.

It is dark before the family comes together in the small, circular house. We sit at the back, propped against the rough daub of the walls, and as far way from the smoke of the fire as we can get. There is a hush in the room, as if people dare not break the atmosphere by speaking. We watch as a new piece of wood is added to the fire, the sparks leaping towards the thatch of the roof until they finally extinguish into the blackness. Presently, the door of the hut opens and two men bring in a bundle, wrapped tightly in coarse cloth. There is a low murmuring from the people sitting around the fire, almost as if they are chanting prayers. The bundle is set before the fire and then turned to face the room. We stiffen as we realise what it is. The bundle covers a dry and wizened mummy, the old, cracked face still visible through a gap in the cloth. The skin is like leather and its legs are pulled tightly into the body. People are now cooing at the mummy and a platter of food is laid before it. The two men sit close behind their charge, stopping it from toppling onto its back. Some reach forward to touch the mummy, others even stroking its face. They speak to it intently, pausing now and again, as if waiting for the mummy to speak back.

Cladh Hallan, the village with the mummy, is on South Uist in the far north of Scotland. The village comprised four roundhouses sunk into the soft sands of the shore. In the most northerly house were two mummies, a man and a woman, each tightly bound, as if they had been kept wrapped in a shroud.[3] They were likely to have been mummified, either through being smoked over a slow fire or by being buried in a peat bog for several months. The acids in the peat would inhibit the actions of the enzymes that would otherwise rot the body.[4] Skin will discolour due to the tannins in the water, but it is preserved in almost pristine condition. The mummies at Cladh Hallan were probably kept for centuries before being buried under the floor.

In the conflict between the living and the dead, keeping preserved bodies may have been a means of controlling their influence. If the dead wanted the return of the land, mummifying the newly deceased may have been a way of trapping their spirits and negating their demands. Tellingly, at Cladh Hallan, people occupied the same site for many generations. People may have believed that the mummified dead could speak and still voice their opinions to the living. If so, then people made sure that they were told only what they wanted to hear. The male mummy at Cladh Hallan was not a single individual but three: the body of one, the skull from another, and the jaw from a third. Perhaps the skull and body were from important people whose opinions carried weight, but the jaw, the speaking part of the body, came from an individual who was more compliant to the wishes of the living. Weasel words seemingly spoken by an influential figure.

Removing, or in this case, replacing, a person's jaw may have been a way of stopping them from sounding their opinion; the voice of the dead was, quite literally, taken away. Of the skulls retrieved from the River Thames, for example, less than 5 per cent had jawbones.[5] The same is true for skulls retrieved from wet places in Ireland.[6] Even allowing for the natural disintegration of the remains, the lack of jawbones is striking. Elsewhere, it seems that the jaw was separated from the rest of the skull. At Runnymede, a settlement on the Thames, for example, a skull was placed in a pit by the entrance with two jawbones nearby.[7]

Gagging the dead had a long history and may have begun as soon as people started to settle and cultivate the land. Around Stonehenge, for example, the early Bronze Age people, who, as we know, likely led a partly nomadic existence, built massive barrows full of prestigious and valuable items. As some of these people began to remain in one place and plant crops, they continued building barrows but made them smaller and less conspicuous, and left fewer items inside them.[8] It seems that with the introduction of settled farming, people began a long process of marginalising the dead, reducing their influence and, over time, negating their demands. The move to cremation and the development of urnfields further reduced the visibility of the dead, giving them less and less room in what was becoming the landscape of the living.

Through marginalising the dead, people probably lost some of the respect that they once held for their deceased brethren. Certainly, removing the jawbone from a corpse is not a friendly act. However, there were also other signs that the living were taking less care over the dead. In Sweden, for example, people initially washed the bones they collected from the funeral pyre, making sure each was clean before burial. By the end of the Bronze Age, however, this had changed and the remains were now placed straight into the ground; even bits of the pyre found their way into the mix.[9] In the urnfields of the Netherlands, broken or damaged urns seemed to suffice for some burials,[10] and, across the region, only token amounts of bone were collected from the funeral pyre and buried.[11] This may have been more expedient but it is striking how the primary burials in cemeteries (those, presumably, of greatest importance) had the most remains collected from the pyre. Clearly, the decision was based upon respect.[12]

If people were openly disrespecting the dead in this manner, it was a dangerous strategy. Far better, perhaps, to contain their influence. The inhabitants of Pryssgården, for example (the village in Sweden that we explored in the previous chapter), buried their dead on an island.[13] However, only a few individuals were buried and, even then, not all bodies were complete; the majority were probably cremated. Next to the cemetery was a small building, orientated, as we might expect, to the south-east. The building was open to this side and overlooked a semicircle of stone slabs and three huge hearths. Could this have been where the bodies were burnt? The cup marks engraved onto the slabs (perhaps showing the route to the afterlife) and the piles of burnt stone suggest that it was. The building may have been a place where death rituals were enacted and its central hearth and adjacent altar may have played a role in the preparation of the corpse. Not surprisingly, metalworking debris was also found on the island.

Similar buildings were built in other parts of Sweden, all situated next to burials.[14] Perhaps, in addition to being structures for preparing the body, these were also places where people could go and speak to the dead – keeping their demands in check. Sculptor's Cave in Scotland may have served a similar purpose, since the severed skulls of several individuals appear to have been kept in the interior, possibly even hanging from the walls.[15] The copious metal items, animal remains, and pottery across the floor shows that people brought gifts as well as their demands when they visited these remains.[16] Another skull may have been hung in a hazel copse, at Poulton-le-Fylde in northern England, on the boundary between the productive lowlands and the unproductive highlands.[17] Tellingly, the skull was without its jawbone. Here was another head that had lost its voice.

While some remains were isolated on islands, placed in caves, or hung from trees, most were buried in the urnfields that dot the landscape. Since controlling the dead seemed to be important to people, it is likely that the arrangement of burials within the cemetery was not random but was carefully arranged to reflect the information that people wanted the dead to impart. From the late Bronze Age, for example, continental long-houses almost halved in size.[18] Given that populations remained stable, the smaller houses suggest that families were breaking down into smaller units. Dividing the land among these smaller units presumably depended on an individual's line of descent. This may have been why the dead remained a presence in the landscape; to remove them completely would have been to remove the genealogical evidence people needed to back up their new-found claims over the land.[19] Of course, some of these genealogies could have been made up, and in northern Germany there were many burials at this time that were placed into far older

Neolithic tombs.[20] Perhaps people sought to draw their lineage from a presence that, as far as they were concerned, had always been there. At Pokedown and Latch Farm, both in southern England, the lack of remains in some of the urns may have filled any gaps in the story.[21]

If people needed the dead to support their newly emerging claims over the land, it may explain why some of the bones that did not reach the cemeteries appear within the settlements. Again, it was skulls that were most prevalent.[22] While some of these might have been displayed, as they were in Sculptor's Cave, others were kept closer still and amulets made from skulls have been found at Reading Business Park and also at Ivinghoe Beacon, both in southern England.[23] Many of the skulls were left in enclosure earthworks or in pits dug at entrances to the settlement.[24] These boundary locations match the other places that bones were left: caves, rivers, and even the hazel copse, itself on a boundary between productive and unproductive land. By placing the remains in these liminal locations, however, were people helping the soul of the deceased find its way to the afterlife, or was it the opposite, actually making the dead more accessible for the living to reach and control?

The gradual erasure of the presence of the dead seems to be matched with an increasing focus on the identity of the living. In chapter 31, we saw how certain people were laid out at funerals in all their finery, with the body carefully prepared to retain the vestiges of living beauty. It was the individual and their life (real or imagined) that was celebrated, and not, as in earlier times, their passing to join the realm of the dead. Similarly, some people were even buried in urns with faces moulded on their sides.[25] Whether or not these were accurate images, it was clearly the identity of the living person that was emphasised and not the contents of the urn.

Elsewhere, the living tried to make themselves more visible by enclosing their settlements. In the middle Bronze Age, these were often tentative, as if people recognised that, until now, it had been the dead with the enduring presence in the landscape and not the living. At Rams Hill, Crab Farm, and South Lodge, all in southern England, ditches were dug and then filled in shortly thereafter.[26] Clearly, people were trying to assert their existence, but perhaps their nerve had failed them. It was only during the late Bronze Age that settlement enclosure became widespread.[27]

From the mummies of Cladh Hallan to the skulls and bones collected at the settlements, the aim seems to have been to contain and control the dead in order to force them to relinquish their rights to the land. Dissenting views were silenced, perhaps by removing the jaws of the cadavers, while others, like the rearranged mummy at Cladh Hallan, were allowed to be heard. However, not just anyone could speak to the dead; this was a role for the shamans, who could pass through the portal between the worlds and approach the deceased on their own terms. With the enormity of the task before them, we might expect an explosion of activity at places where such crossings were possible. Since this was a time of conflict, we might also expect these places to be on neutral territory, at places that belonged neither to the realm of the living nor to that of the dead.

Chapter 35

PORTALS TO ANOTHER WORLD

Having shrugged off most of our clothes, we crawl through the low doorway into a small cramped chamber. It is too dark to make out the form of the walls but it is clear that any gaps have been plugged with animal hides. Some have obviously not been cleaned very thoroughly and in the confined space the smell makes us gag. As we crawl across the bare earth, we are careful not to bump into the water trough that takes up the middle of the space. We huddle near the back and wait while the others crawl in; there is an old woman, two men, and a girl. They arrange themselves around the trough and the old woman starts to chant. Almost immediately a wooden paddle is thrust through the doorway with several glowing rocks on its end. We noticed a small fire being lit as we entered the tent and now we know its purpose. The rocks are dropped into the trough and more and more follow until the water starts to boil. The flap of skin covering the entrance is then swung shut. It is now as black as night. Waves of hot steam begin to billow against our faces and we draw the thick, hot air into our lungs. More hot stones are added to the trough whenever the boiling subsides until the atmosphere becomes almost unbearable. Still, the old woman continues her slow, lilting wail. We are now fighting for every breath and can feel the stifling air pressing down on our bodies. You lie flat, hoping to take comfort from the cool of the earth. Our heads pound, and still the wailing sound continues. More hot stones are added to the water and we feel as if we might pass out from the heat. Then, quite suddenly, I feel a calmness descend. Shapes form in the darkness, and then a tunnel. I know it is the entrance to the otherworld and I wonder if you see it too.

Anyone familiar with the Native American sweat lodge might think this is what we have just experienced, since an almost identical practice forms an important part of many Native spiritual traditions, such as the Lakota 'inipi'.[1] However, the sweat lodge we visited did not exist in America but in Europe during the late Bronze Age.

Piles of burnt stones, often associated with a small trough and makeshift structure, were widespread across much of Europe at this time, often occurring next to flowing water. Hot stones were probably added to water in the trough and experiments have shown that this will rapidly cause it to boil.[2] At first it was assumed that people used the boiling water to cook joints of meat, and where burnt mounds occur on settlement sites, or where they have food residue around them, this may have been what they were used for.[3] Many of the central European burnt mounds, for example, have copious remains from feasting in their vicinity and cooking seems a likely explanation for their existence.[4] However, whether the boiled meat was then consumed or, as some researchers believe, buried as an offering, is not so clear.[5] It may have been that different methods of cooking were associated with different spheres of activity. We have seen in chapter 31 how roasting spits were prevalent in many graves and it may be that, in certain regions, roast meat was acceptable for consumption whereas boiled meat was suitable only for votive offerings. The Sámi had similar traditions relating to the meat from bears, which, in deference to the animal, could only be boiled and never roasted.[6]

At many burnt mound sites, however, there is a dearth of food remains and, although the technology was identical, the water was clearly being used for something very different. Boiling water produces copious amounts of stream and, if trapped within the small structures that appear next to the mounds of burnt stone, would form a rudimentary sauna.[7] While it may be that people in the Bronze Age had high standards of personal hygiene, the remote locations of many of these sites makes another explanation more likely. Lengthy exposure to steam (coupled with the resulting abnormal body temperatures) causes a simultaneous discharge of both the sympathetic and parasympathetic systems of the brain, which, as we saw in chapter 5, is sufficient to induce trance.[8] The Nenet shamans of Siberia use precisely this method to access the otherworld and it is likely that people in the Bronze Age were doing the same.[9]

Since this was a time when the living were in conflict with the dead over the ownership of the land, many journeys were probably undertaken to this end and the prevalence of burnt mounds at this time (they are found in far fewer numbers during other periods) may reflect the gravity of the situation. In Ireland, many burnt mounds were located close to burial cemeteries,[10] as if people were taking the fight to the enemy, and in Scandinavia, some of the burnt mounds may have doubled-up as cremation pyres.[11] One mound, located on the island used by the inhabitants of Pryssgården to bury their dead, had a spiral design of stones fashioned at its base, mirroring the tunnel that gave access to the otherworld.[12]

If people were journeying to negotiate with the dead, it is likely that they did so armed with gifts and offerings. As we have already seen, this was a time when many metal items were consigned to rivers and wet places, but there were also others that were buried in the ground. A detailed study of Sussex in southern England shows that these metal hoards were usually placed between the settlement and the burnt mounds, as if people wanted to pass by and reaffirm their offering every time they visited the burnt mound.[13] Since many of these items would have previously been placed in graves, it seems that people had taken what was once given to the newly dead and were now offering it instead to the ancestral dead. At Bargeroosterveld in the Netherlands, for example, a small open building was constructed within a raised bog.[14] Since it was surrounded by a ring of stones, had horned ends to its roof beams, and was made using a distinctive broad-bladed ritual axe, it seems likely that it was the focus for ceremonies, perhaps even for approaching the dead. It is not surprising, therefore, that there were three bronze hoards around it, offerings, maybe, to appease their spirits.[15] Similarly, at Tauberbischofsheim-Hochhausen in Germany, a wooden post served as a focus for more metal deposits, concentrating, most appropriately, on spiral-decorated ornaments.[16]

At Bargeroosterveld, the wet location of the site probably served as a suitable portal to the otherworld, whereas at Tauberbischofsheim-Hochhausen, it may have been the post itself that allowed access to this realm. We have seen similar beliefs at Durrington Walls in chapter 23, where a post at the centre of a maze may have also marked the route to the otherworld. In Wales, many burnt mounds were situated next to standing stones, and it is possible that these pillars served a similar purpose.[17] In the south-west of England, distinctive natural outcrops sometimes replaced artificially positioned stones. At Kynance Gate, for example, an outcrop that had formed the focus for offerings in the Neolithic and early Bronze Age became the central axis of a later village. It was as if people wanted their entire existence to revolve around this outcrop; a portal, perhaps, to the otherworld. However, unlike the outcrop at Kynance Gate, most burnt mounds were situated away from settlements in the sort of liminal locations we have come to associate with otherworldly portals.

Some burnt mounds in Cambridgeshire in eastern England formed part of larger ceremonial complexes and these could sometimes include upside-down trees.[18] This is very similar to another nearby site, named with no more accuracy than its famous namesake: Seahenge.[19] I did not get to see this enigmatic monument as it was excavated from the Norfolk sands, but I visited it later in its holding tanks at Flag Fen. It looked a very sorry sight and had lost much of what had once made it so special. Fifty-five split oak posts formed a circle, bark-side outwards, with a huge upside-down oak tree at its centre. The roots reached at least a metre into the air. Although it was made in the early Bronze Age (it can be dated exactly by its timbers to 2049 BC), there are signs that it was still in use in later periods. A trackway dating to the middle Bronze Age crossed a creek nearby and, with an absence of houses in the vicinity, it is likely that people were coming here to visit the monument. The immediate area, now almost inundated by the sea, would have been wet, marshy ground, exactly the sort of liminal location we might expect to find a site such as this. Moreover, in Ireland, similar structures were also constructed and these date to the middle Bronze Age.[20]

The upside-down tree, which formed the main focus of Seahenge, has parallels in other Eurasian traditions. The Sámi, for example, placed upside-down trees into the earth either to mark the position of offerings to the spirits or as offerings themselves.[21] The tree, mirroring the upside-down boats we explored in chapter 29, provided a portal to the otherworld and, presumably, allowed safe passage for the offerings that were left around it. For the Evenks of Siberia, it was not offerings but the shaman who passed through the portal, and upside-down trees were arranged to form a 'river' along which the shaman journeyed to the otherworld.[22] It was likely that Seahenge was used in the same way, perhaps with people lying upon the inverted bole of the tree as they let their spirit be pulled to the otherworlds. Intriguingly, near to Seahenge is a similar circle of posts with two large timbers at the centre.[23] Hollows on the upper sides of both timbers may have been designed to hold a coffin or other platform and perhaps this was where the dead were once laid out, allowing their souls an easy path to the afterlife.[24]

At the burnt mounds people used steam to induce trance, but at places such as Seahenge, they likely used other means. From the middle Bronze Age onwards, rye cultivation expanded significantly, ostensibly because of the more demanding soil conditions combined with an increasingly cool and wet climate.[25] However, with rye comes a parasite fungus called ergot, which is powerfully hallucinogenic.[26] Perhaps this gave people an added incentive to adopt the new crop?

Throughout our exploration of the portals to the otherworld, those individuals that would have made the actual journeys, the shamans of the time, have remained elusive. However, damp conditions in two graves in Denmark, at Maglehøj and Hvidegård, have preserved the belongings of two individuals who may have been shamans themselves. Both were buried with bags attached to their belts containing a collection of small amulets and animal parts – seemingly a collection of magical objects.[27] Many relate to the three worlds a shaman journeys through or to those creatures that appear to follow the shaman's cycle of death and rebirth. Snake remains, for example, were carried by both individuals. These were also people of status: the woman had bronze items left with her cremated remains and the man had a sword. Moreover, the clothing in the man's grave has parallels with the outfit worn by two bronze figurines from Grevensvænge, thought to form part of a set showing a ritual on board a boat. The figurines have a distinct flap to their shirts, which mirrors that worn by the Hvidegård man.[28] In addition, each figure wears a horned helmet, identical to the full-sized examples from Viksø that we considered in chapter 30. Each also carries a broad-bladed ritual axe, the same type of tool that probably fashioned the sanctuary at Bargeroosterveld. As the ritual they were engaged in took place on a boat, perhaps it portrayed a journey to the otherworld; maybe it was even something the Hvidegård shaman enacted himself.

From the middle of the Bronze Age, it seems that journeys to the otherworld took place with increasing frequency; the conflict between the living and the dead was clearly not going to be settled quickly. It required a radical shift in the way people thought about the world and their place within it. We shall return to see its resolution, but this will not be until near the end of the next great age, that of Iron. For now, the scene needs to be set for the dawn of a new people in central Europe: the Celts. How and why they arose is a tale as titanic in scale as it was in effect. For us, perhaps events are best viewed as the gods might have seen them: from a vantage high in the sky.

PART FIVE

DIVIDING THE LAND:
THE IRON AGE

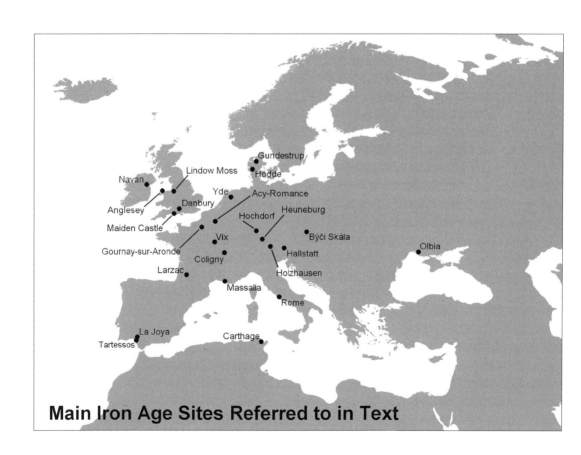

Main Iron Age Sites Referred to in Text

Chapter 36

SEEING WITH THE EYES OF THE GODS

With the eyes of the gods, the changes we see as we look down from our heavenly realms do not concern individuals or even groups of people, but entire nations and whole populations. Through the Bronze Age, we see the rise of the Minoans on their island home of Crete and, after their collapse around 1400 BC, the rise of Mycenaean royalty and their palaces on the mainland to the north.[1] There are routes of trade that fan out from these palaces but they quickly grow faint and indistinct as they head inland. Some seem to cross the entire continent to reach Britain but it is hard to see clearly from this distance. Sometime around 1200 BC we see long ships set sail from the Levant, scything across the waves and attacking all who cross their path. These are the Sea Peoples, and among them are the Philistines, the ancient origin of our modern word.[2] The Egyptians will erect a carving at Thebes showing Ramesses III smiting at those pirates he had captured, but in truth, the devastation they bring will be too much for these early civilisations.[3] We watch as the Sea Peoples lay waste to the region.[4]

The collapse of Mycenae was the end of an era and, as we have already seen, led to a diaspora of techniques and ideas that infiltrated far from their Aegean home. It is possible that the system was so dependent on commerce and the provision of sumptuous items to sustain the image of its rulers, that once the Sea Peoples had disrupted the trade, it had little else to fall back upon. The Mediterranean grows quiet beneath us and passes into what is called the Greek Dark Age. Looking closely, however, there seems little that is dark about it, as people are flourishing, increasing their numbers, and extending their farming to cover the land with a patchwork of worked fields.[5] After 1100 BC, there are more ships leaving the Levant and we fear at first that it is the Sea Peoples returning, but these ships are different. Some, that seem to hug the shore, have horse-head prows, while the hulls of others are so deep that they look like bathtubs floating on the ocean. The largest ships have battering rams at their prows and, with a galley full of oars, it is clear that they could inflict serious damage on any that got in their way.[6] However, these are not pirates but traders: the Phoenicians of the Levantine coast.

Looking hard at their homeland, we can only see a thin strip occupied by the Phoenicians, and most of this seems to revolve around a few major cities.[7] To the east, and bearing irrepressibly down upon them, is the vast territory of the Assyrians. No wonder the people looked to the sea for their fortune; the famed cedars of Lebanon gave them ample wood for their ships. We watch as Phoenician crafts dock at the cities and unload their cargoes. Most comprise raw materials and silver is particularly abundant. Ferried to the craftworkers who throng the city streets, we watch as they fashion a dazzling array of cups, bowls, jewellery, and ivory plaques, most destined to be given to the Assyrians in tribute. Now we know why the Phoenician ships ply the waves in such numbers: they have a hungry neighbour to feed.

Following one ship as it departs Sidon, the largest of the cities, it sails first to Cyprus, then to Crete, then past Sicily to Sardinia and, finally, on to southern Spain.[8] So this is where all that silver comes from: parts of the Iberian Peninsula, as we know, are seamed with it. We watch as the ship arrives at Gades, now called Cádiz, and the crew melt into the places that sailors always congregate. However, the captain has other plans and is royally entertained by the local leaders. These are the Tartessos people. Like the Phoenicians, they are a trading community, although it is sometimes hard to tell the two groups apart since the local leaders seem determined to imitate their exotic partners in every way.[9] It is likely that the visiting sea captain will be told of the grave at La Joya, where a particularly renowned leader was buried with a cart made from walnut with gold hubcaps and a silver-encased draught pole. Ivory carvings and copious drinking vessels also accompanied the man.[10] It is likely to be a story the captain has heard before but he will accommodate his hosts; after all, he will have a hold full of silver and ivory come the morning tide. In addition, he has a daughter with him; it would not be the first marriage between these groups and the girl will probably have far better prospects in Spain than she would at home.[11]

Increasing activity in the Aegean catches our eyes and we wrench our gaze away from Spain. It is the Greeks, emerging from their Dark Age with a flourish. Burgeoning populations require more land and colonisers sail to settle the Turkish coast. Back in Greece, cities arise, the fabled 'polis', where state and citizens combine to create a formidable unit.[12] Armies emerge and we can see the dust the hoplite soldiers make as they perform their manoeuvres. It will not be long before they have a real enemy to fight.[13]

The Greeks form colonies around the Black Sea and along the north Mediterranean coast, whereas the Phoenicians claim the southern coast as their own, founding new cities such as Carthage in Tunisia.[14] Founded in 814 BC, it was to receive an influx of immigrants after 574 BC when the Phoenician homeland fell to another Near Eastern power: the Babylonians. From this point on, the Phoenicians will abandon the eastern Mediterranean and Carthage will become the base for their new Punic empire. It is from here that Hannibal will later emerge to defeat the nascent Romans at Canae. For now, the Phoenician search for trade takes them into the Atlantic, although the old routes have vanished and Britain now looks across the Channel for commerce, whereas Ireland sits in forlorn isolation.[15]

The Greeks are on the move again, this time into southern Italy, where they form an uneasy existence with the Etruscans to the north. These are another trading peoples who, like the Tartessos from Iberia, rely upon the abundance of metal ores within their lands to trade for luxury items from overseas. Despite their unease within the Italian peninsula, the extensive cemeteries where the Etruscans bury their dead are full of pottery from Athens.[16] The trading reach of the Etruscans stretches along the northern shores of the Mediterranean (west of Italy), and it must come as something of a shock, therefore, when the Greeks found Massalia (modern Marseille) in 540 BC.[17] It will come to dominate trade in the western Mediterranean and, with boats forging up the Rhone, will also open the massive trading potential of central Europe. No wonder the Etruscans are infuriated, and we watch as they vent their anger on the Greek settlements in southern Italy. The cacophony of ship against ship and the screams of those sailors meeting their ends make us shiver, but when the tempest subsides, it is the Greeks who emerge triumphant. The destruction of their fleet at Cumae in 474 BC effectively ends the Etruscan role as a Mediterranean power. We will leave them to lick their wounds, but they will be back using a very different strategy of attack.

The Greeks then suffer the same fate as the earlier Phoenicians, with an aggressive neighbour, in their case Persia, hammering at the door to their homeland. The Persians will be repulsed in time but Greek refugees flood into Massalia and the city thrives. Since the Persians block routes to the east and the Phoenicians still control the west, the new inhabitants of Massalia look north for their trading partners: to the Urnfield people with whom we are familiar. We know that these people are always looking for new ways to flaunt their status and the Greeks quickly assess what will be in greatest demand – drinking sets and a new beverage for them to hold: wine. Gallons and gallons move north to fuel an ever more inebriated population. What comes back in return puzzles us for a while until you realise the pale blocks are not marble but salt, a valuable commodity for storing food in the cities of the Mediterranean. However, with no sea, just where did the Urnfield people get it?

We search hard until we spot a place in the Austrian Alps that provides an answer: mines. Hallstatt, both the location of the mines and the name given to all central European peoples at this time, provided over 2 million cubic metres of salt. The cemetery next to the mine saw 2000 people laid in the earth, testament to the physical demands of the mine. However, while some of these people were clearly wealthy, the majority, perhaps the miners themselves, were poor, and it speaks of the close solidarity of the workforce that they were even buried at all.[18] Or perhaps there was another reason that these people were buried: they worked all their life in the otherworld of the mines; maybe something of the sacred adhered to them and they were honoured for it? In addition to salt, the miners may have also turned their attention to iron ore. In the beginning, this new metal remained the preserve of the wealthy, with the ingots found only in royal centres.[19] Over time, people found that iron ore cropped up almost everywhere and it lost some of its former cachet. For now, however, it remains a metal of distinction.

The people we see hoarding the objects from Massalia make little attempt to understand or even appreciate what they receive. For them, it seems that more is better, just like nouveau riche anywhere. They ape those they see as superior and disregard the consequences. We watch as one of the old Urnfield villages, the Heuneburg in Germany, is surrounded by walls.[20] Unfortunately, the initial attempt is deemed insufficient and they are rebuilt using Mediterranean designers and techniques. We find it hard to stifle our mirth as the first mud bricks are laid, and, when the walls are complete, what bakes hard in the Greek sun now slowly washes away under the rains of winter. Somewhat chastened, the leader orders them to be rebuilt once more, this time using old methods. The fort is well situated to take control of the trade routes from east to west and also from south to north across the Alpine passes. There are craftspeople within the fort, mainly metalworkers, and it is striking that they congregate around the south-eastern entrance. Clearly, despite their haste for what the Mediterranean can offer, people have not forgotten the old beliefs. The graves surrounding the Heuneburg will be looted of their treasures in time but it is not gold or silver that catches our eyes but silk: its first ever appearance in central Europe.[21]

Another grave beckons for our attention, at Hochdorf, in Germany.[22] We watch as items are carried into the tomb, a wooden chamber excavated over 2m into the ground. There is a bronze couch upon which the chieftain will be laid to rest, a four-wheeled cart and trapping for its horses, although thankfully not the horses themselves. There is also tableware and gold-encased drinking horns for nine (the ideal number for a Greek symposium) and a huge cauldron. However, despite all the Greek trappings, the cauldron holds mead; it seems that this chieftain wants to appear a sophisticated Mediterranean without giving up his favourite tipple. The mead itself has not yet fermented and requires another year to finish. Clearly, this was a drink exclusively for the afterlife.[23] There are few armaments in the grave, only hunting weapons. The Greek princes did not need arms since they had an army to fight for them; their pleasures were hunting and feasting. The Hochdorf chieftain was unlikely to have had the same lifestyle and yet this is how he wanted to be preserved for posterity. It was an image rather than reality.

Women were also honoured at this time. Looking further west to Vix in France, a woman is set out in her tomb around 500 BC. She has all the usual trappings: a four-wheeled cart, sumptuous jewellery, and an enormous wine mixer, or 'krater', clearly obtained from the Greeks.[24] It could hold the equivalent of 1,500 modern bottles of wine; clearly, she expected to entertain lavishly in the afterlife, although in this world, the bronze walls of the krater might have collapsed if it was filled to capacity.[25] As with the Hochdorf mead, its use was reserved for the afterlife.

Like the Mycenaeans before them, the Hallstatt economy was fragile. All the items obtained from the Greeks were concentrated in the hands of a few chiefs, women as well as men. While they we able to obtain these items, they could use them to buy the support of their retinue and so maintain their positions.[26] It was a precarious existence and perhaps this was why it reacted so badly to the changes that were afoot further south.

Looking down on the seas of the Mediterranean, we see a massive fleet sail towards Greece; these are the Persians, intent to follow up their victories at Thermopylae and Artemisium.[27] The united Greek cities are heavily outnumbered and yet they still face the invaders, trapping them in the straits at Salamis in 480 BC, where the vast number of Persian ships causes confusion and panic. The Greeks emerge as victors and the Persians withdraw, leaving only a small army that is picked off the next year. It is a staggering victory and we watch as the Greeks celebrate madly: the world is now at their feet. Except that, to our astonishment, their unity is quickly forgotten and the region is plunged into yet more conflict with Athens and Sparta as the main protagonists in the Peloponnesian War, lasting from 431 until 404 BC.[28] At its end, both sides are finished and Greek pride now rests with Macedonia to the north, where the king we spy annexing more conquests to his kingdom will soon have a son born for greatness: Alexander.

That is all in the future, for while the Greeks have been busy killing each other, the wily Etruscans, who first lost their trade to Massalia and were then slammed out of the Mediterranean by the Greek fleet, have not been idle. Forging trade routes north of their territory, across the Alpine passes and into the heart of Europe, they bypass the Hallstatt nobles, who are wedded to trade with the Greeks, and befriend those on the northern periphery. These people, living in a sweeping arc from western France through to the Czech Republic, are well positioned to intercept those items that flow from the northern lands: gold, tin, amber, furs, and, to our horror, even slaves.[29] No longer able to maintain their status as intermediaries, and thereby having nothing to trade, the Hallstatt elite crash, pulling the fortunes of Massalia down with them. Those central Europeans now controlling the trade start to build their own fortunes, first by obtaining bronze vessels from the Etruscans (and also by copying their love of the two-wheeled chariot), but then, very quickly, by finding their own style. Called La Tène for the site in Switzerland where their distinctive art was first discovered, these were the Celts, the masters of Iron Age Europe. Theirs was a return to the old warrior ethic: fighting, feasting, and, if the Roman historians are to be believed, lots of fornicating. Our heads are spinning with so much activity over such a short period of time and we step down from the heavens to assume our mortal forms. However, our adventures are far from over. A feast has been called and a new champion will be proclaimed. We must hurry if we are to take our seats in time.

Chapter 37

AN INVITATION
TO THE FEAST

We sit, or rather recline, upon thick pelts of bear, wolf, and deer. Two jugs of strong wine lie before us on a low table. The hall is filling with powerful men wearing heavy tunics of plaid wool. Their moustaches hang low over sneering mouths and swords drape menacingly at their waists. Nobody disarms to enter. The women accompanying them are tall and look just as powerful, bedecked with an array of dazzling jewellery. Their manner is haughty and they observe any lesser companion with contempt. Once all have settled before the fire-pit, some jostling for positions that they deem slightly better than those left vacant, two slave boys bring in the main dish. It is a boar, cooked whole with its tusks still glinting in the firelight. There is much raucous appreciation shown at its entrance and jugs of wine are thumped onto tables, some overturning their contents, which soak into the floor. An older man stands, his simple garb suggestive of priesthood, and, raising his dagger, he slices a hunk of flesh from the boar's rump. He holds it aloft and speaks powerfully to the room. His tale seems to be one of valour as there is much cheering and envious looks towards a tall, powerful young man waiting for the priest's call. The hero, for this is what the young man appears to be, moves forward to claim his meat. But just then there is a shout behind us and another springs forward to challenge this young upstart, his sword held aloft. It is an older man, his scarred arms telling of many past glories. The young hero immediately pulls his sword and the two champions, the current and the deposed, leap to each other with a clash of iron on iron. The diners scatter as the two men slash at each other, each trying to land the killer blow. At last, the young man opens a wound across the chest of the older, who falls, blood bubbling from his mouth. Other men rush forward, pulling him away before he hits the ground. It is not only his reign as champion that has been taken by the young man tonight, but also his life. The diners return to their positions with broad grins and the feast continues. The young hero eats his meat with the arrogant pride of youth, the juices staining his tunic a deep red.

During the Bronze Age, we have seen how aggression, feasting, and alcohol became the touchstones for society. After an interlude of Hallstatt chieftains who tried their best to emulate the civilisations of the south, we now return to these enduring themes. For the Celts of the Iron Age, the warrior ethic was paramount and to be declared champion, and receive the hero's portion of meat, was something to fight and even die for.[1] Yet there was also a transparency and honesty about such brutality. Disputes flared but were resolved quickly, the result witnessed by the entire community.

Despite their swaggering arrogance and fiery temperament, sharing lay at the heart of a Celtic feast. The entire population was invited to attend and even strangers were offered food and drink before anyone asked their business.[2] In addition to the hero's portion, which exposed a single individual for particular acclaim, there were many other ways that the Celts flaunted their status. Moustaches were only worn by the nobles, probably those of the chieftain's warband, while common men shaved or allowed only a light beard to grow.[3] Perhaps the hair drew attention to the mouth and gave emphasis to their utterings. Both men and women dripped in gold, including neck-rings, called 'torcs', wrist and arm rings, and even gold sewn into their tunics.[4] While common people drank beer, the nobles quaffed wine, an import from the Etruscan traders further south.[5] Like the Hallstatt chiefs before them, it is likely that the Celts thought wine superior because of its exotic origins and drank it to show off their position and connections.[6]

For the host of the feast, presumably the leader of those attending, distributing wealth and largesse on such a lavish scale was essential to retain status. Some of those attending even bargained their own lives for items they would hurriedly distribute before having their throats slit.[7] For most, affluence was measured in cattle and gold, whereas the chiefs also needed an entourage, a warband around them, and loyalty was only assured through offering generous hospitality and making copious gifts.[8] Lest anyone should forget past acts of munificence, Bards, the Celtic historians and storytellers, were on hand to recite past deeds and to lavish praise on any of standing.[9] They could be richly rewarded, even having bags of gold thrown at their feet, and this was incentive for the tales to grow ever longer, allowing the warriors to bask in their own inflated glory.[10]

From an analysis of Celtic graves in the Czech Republic, it appears that men were either buried as warriors, with their weapons beside them, or with nothing at all.[11] Status, it seems, could only be accrued from battle. Women were buried wearing lavish jewellery, with rings and bands encircling necks, arms, wrists, fingers, waists, and even ankles.[12] However, these women were no wilting wallflowers and were equal to men in most matters, including leadership. Onomāris, for example, took leadership of her people when the men were too timid to do so.[13] Perhaps the status of women rose as the men were often away seeking glory in battle, leaving the administration of the community in their hands.[14]

Raiding was probably endemic in the Celtic world and the demand for slaves from their Greek and Etruscan trading partners gave sufficient incentive to venture into hostile territory. However, changes in the years leading to 400 BC meant that trade reduced, particularly as the Etruscans became occupied with the growing power of their Roman neighbour, and the Greeks were off with Alexander conquering the world. Trade was essential to maintain the existence of the leaders and their retinue. After all, wealth was readily distributed among the population and then consigned to the ground upon their deaths.[15] Without new items, the system would collapse, which was the fate that befell the Hallstatt chiefs. Fortunately, the Celts had a solution: what they could not obtain through trade, they took through raiding. The Etruscans were about to get a nasty shock.

To the Iron Age Celt, battle was everything. Prowess was proven, booty was collected, and stories ensured that it was all remembered. The main weapons were a sword and spear, with defence provided by a helmet, a large shield, and, in later periods, a mail shirt. Apart from this, and a torc around their necks, many warriors entered battle completely naked.[16] This was likely to have been deeply symbolic, perhaps as a stripping of individual identity to become a single body of war. However, nakedness is often a means utilised by shamans when seeking contact with the otherworld.[17] Possibly the warriors were invoking the gods of war to come to their aid or preparing to enter the otherworld of death themselves. Since they drank large quantities of alcohol before battle, and worked themselves into a frenzy with dances and the blaring of trumpets,[18] perhaps the ecstatic state they reached was comparable to trance and they prepared for both in similar ways. Certainly, alcohol was said to turn warriors into maniacs and strike fear into the hearts of those who faced them.[19] Perhaps this transformation was even thought to mirror that of the alcohol itself, as fruit and water slowly turned into an intoxicating mix? Since it is likely that women controlled the production of alcohol, maybe this also enhanced their status within the group.

Before the battle frenzy found its outlet, the champions of the Celts, those warriors who had been honoured with the hero's portion at the feasts, would emerge from the ranks, probably borne by chariot, and call for a worthy opponent to fight in single combat.[20] All the while, these champions would parade before the company and cry out tales of their prowess in battle. They might also tell of the feats of their ancestors, perhaps even calling down spirits to guide their sword hands in combat. Once the formalities were over, the Celtic hoard would descend on the enemy in a cacophonic surging mass of bodies, running and screaming with no fear of death and with the lust for glory propelling them onwards. It was a tactic that caused many to turn and run.[21]

Even if naked, the Celts retained the torcs around their necks. This may have been an arrogant display to the enemy, flaunting their heads as prizes if their opponents had the courage to take them. Stiffening their hair with lime may have served a similar purpose.[22] However, heads may also have taken on a spiritual significance, perhaps because they were believed to be the seat of the soul; the heads of defeated enemies were often collected in battle and preserved.[23] In one instance, the head of a defeated Roman consul-designate was so prized that it was made into a cup to give libations at a temple.[24] At Entremont in France, people decorated a shrine with carved heads, some set around a seated figure, perhaps a god, while they nailed real severed heads into niches designed for the purpose.[25]

Some helmets had animals attached to their crests, particularly birds and boars.[26] Symbols of boars, and especially their tusks, were a common amulet, especially at the time of upheavals when the Celts began to expand their range.[27] The boar was a ferocious advocacy in the hunt and perhaps people were calling on these powers when carrying the amulet. Birds may have been seen as comrades in arms, not only since the scavenging crows took the remains of the dead from the battlefield, but also because of a more direct involvement. According to contemporary historians, a crow that was perched on an opponent's helmet flew and attacked a Celtic warrior, disgorging his eyes and causing his death.[28] A helmet from Ciumeşti in Romania, which holds an enormous bird with wings that would flap as the wearer ran, may directly allude to such a tale.[29]

Birds also augured the future and there are other records showing that whole populations would follow the flight of birds when seeking new lands to settle.[30] The reasons for these migrations were varied. Escalating populations and dissent created by too many warriors with too little to do may have caused the initial unrest, but the love of battle and desire for booty (especially following the reduction in trade) provided ample incentive to move.[31] Visitors to the lands of the Etruscans spoke of the riches to be found in the south,[32] and so the first incursions were into their territory. The town of Mediolanum was founded by these raiders and is still thriving today as Milan.

From these newly conquered lands, the Celts sallied forth on raids deep into Italy, even, in 390 BC, sacking Rome itself.[33] The city was ransomed for 1000lb of gold. When the Romans objected to the weights of the Celts being heavier than those of the Romans, Brennus, the leader of the invaders, flung his sword onto the scales with a cry: woe to the vanquished.[34] Forging into the Balkans, Celtic emissaries were brought before Alexander himself, and when asked what they most feared, they replied that they only feared the sky falling upon them.[35] Nevertheless, an equal fear of Alexander kept the Celtic raids in check, but after his death they sought to sack the wealth of the Oracle at Delphi. The wily Greeks left the surrounding villages well provisioned and, drinking their spoils long into the night, the fearsome warriors were too hung over to martial an effective fight. Even without the fabled intervention of Apollo, the swords of the Greeks were too much for the weary Celts and they fled, a fortuitous hailstorm finishing what the Greeks had started.[36] Following their defeat, the Celts scattered, some even reaching Turkey and founding the province of Galatia. Brennus did what any defeated Celtic leader would have done in similar circumstances: he took his own life. Battle may have been where status and renown was achieved but it was also where reputations were crushed, and with the imagined satires of Bards ringing in the ears, many chose an immediate end.[37]

Catuvolcus, an ageing chief of the Eburones people, facing attack by Caesar during the subjugation of his lands at the end of the Iron Age, could not face another battle and so killed himself by eating yew, a deadly poison.[38] Since this event was recorded by the Roman victors, rather than the indigenous Celts, it is likely that it hides deeper meanings. Eburone, the name of the group, is taken from the Celtic word for the yew, and the tree may have had a mystical significance to the people even before Catuvolcus met his end. For the Celts, spiritual beliefs saturated every aspect of their lives and, like the birds that were said to augur the route of the migrations, it was impossible to conceive of anything without taking the supernatural into account. For the Celts, the otherworld of the spirits existed all around them.

Chapter 38

IMAGES OF THE SACRED

During the late Iron Age at Larzac in France, Severa, daughter of Tertiu, took a lead sheet and scratched onto its surface a most extraordinary tale.[1] A coven of witches had been cursed by another and sought the help of a wise woman to negate the spell and diffuse the tension. The lead was then moulded around the top of a burial urn containing a woman. Could the burnt remains have been the person who had made the curse, her death being the price for peace? It is a rare glimpse of the shadowy world of Celtic sorcery and magic and the role that women played within it.

Although Severa did not record it upon the lead sheet, the women of the coven might have sought their power from a more elevated female group. Many representations of goddesses, for example, show them grouped into three and this might have mirrored the arrangement of women in the covens.[2] The Larzac tablet mentions eight, possibly nine names, which would give three groups of three, a particularly significant number throughout the Celtic world.[3] Although we do not know the names of the individual triple goddesses, they were probably Mother or Earth deities ('Matronae' in Celtic), although some may have related to springs and wet places ('Saluviae' in Celtic). One of the most sacred springs was the source of the Seine, in France, where people left modelled body parts, perhaps as part of a healing ceremony.[4] It is striking that in many shamanic communities, healing is achieved through removing an intrusive spirit, thought to enter the body unbidden, which is drawn out and negated by being thrown into water (as we know, water is often seen as a portal to the otherworld).[5] The carved body parts in the Seine spring may have accumulated as people tried to cast off invading spirits, using a model as a surrogate for their own afflicted body.

As Caesar was conquering the Celts of Gaul (modern-day France), he recorded the names of many Celtic gods but, unfortunately, used only their equivalent Roman names to describe them.[6] More helpfully, he also noted that the Celts consider that they are all descended from a single ancestor god, whom Caesar called 'Dis'.[7] It may be that all ancestors were considered divine and we have already seen in the previous chapter that they could be invoked before battle, their deeds remembered and honoured by their descendents. Other Roman commentators were a little more forthcoming about the Celtic pantheon and Lucan records the names of three: Teutates, the god of the tribe, Taranis, the god of thunder and the sky, and Esus, the good or sun god.[8] A later commentator on Lucan's work adds a little more detail by revealing that each required sacrifices to be offered in different ways: Teutates by drowning, Taranis by burning, and Esus by hanging.[9] Each seems to equate with one of the traditional elements – water, fire, and air – with the Mother goddesses providing the fourth: earth (and possibly their own form of sacrifice, as many bodies were placed into disused storage pits).[10]

In charge of the sacrifices were the Druids, who, with the diviners or 'Vates', and the Bards we met in the previous chapter, formed the priesthood of the Celtic world.[11] It is likely that they formalised the roles that had previously fallen to the community shamans, although, as the witch covens demonstrate, it is likely that other people held roles that also required regular interaction with the supernatural.

According to Caesar, the centre for Druid learning was Britain, perhaps focused on Anglesey in Wales.[12] During the Roman subjugation of the Welsh tribes around AD 59, Anglesey was singled out for particularly savage treatment since it was reputed to be the last refuge of the Druids.[13] From Britain, the Druids spread into Gaul where they met once a year at Carutes, near Chartres, to elect their leader.[14] The discussions sometimes became heated and brawls could ensue; this was clearly a fighting priesthood. In fact, the Druids were at the forefront of resistance to Rome and it is probably no coincidence that the rebellion of the Gauls in 53 BC started at Carutes, the meeting place of the Druids. No wonder the Romans were so keen to wipe them out at Anglesey.

Training to become a Druid was arduous and could last several decades.[15] Emphasis was placed on memory rather than writing since this was considered the best way to develop the brain; entire tracts of history and lore had to be learnt by rote. Work was undertaken in groves, woodland clearings, and the association between Druids and trees may reflect the origin of their name, thought to mean 'knowledge of the oak'.[16] Within these groves, Druids also learnt about the celestial bodies and their movement across the sky.[17] During the Bronze Age, we saw how people thought that the sun travelled across the heavens in a boat pulled by a horse or water birds and it is likely that the Druids built their own knowledge around this ancient foundation. For the Celts, the sun was often represented as a spoked wheel and it is striking that on many coins, horses were associated with spoked wheels, and at Pogny and Catulauni, both in France, torcs had engraved images of spoked wheels with water birds gathered around them.[18] Clearly, the old traditions still carried considerable weight. However, the Druids also claimed to know the will of the gods and perhaps this allowed them a more personal involvement in the order of the world. A sword scabbard found at Hallstatt in Austria (but dating to the La Tène period at around 500 BC), was beautifully engraved with a parade of cavalry, but on either side were two figures holding a spoked wheel.[19] Circles above and below the wheel may represent the passage of the sun across the sky and through the underworld of night, and it is clear that the figures, confidently holding the wheel in both hands, were now intimately involved in that journey. This may have been why many people carried small amulets of spoked wheels: it allowed them to feel a personal involvement in a timeless event.[20] This provided certainty among the vagaries of life and, by taking the amulet with them to their graves, perhaps people also hoped that the sun might lead them swiftly to the afterlife, a belief that originated in the Neolithic.

The vagaries of life could also be reduced by obtaining knowledge of the future and this task appears to have fallen to Celtic women. While there are references to female Druids, most sources tell of women's role in divination.[21] Perhaps the most renowned was Veledā, the seer with so much power that she concluded a treaty with the Romans on behalf of her people, and in time became akin to a goddess.[22] Earlier, she had foretold the defeat of the Roman legion (that led to the need for a peace treaty), which is why she was fêted with such renown. To divine the future, Veledā may have watched the flow of water across the surface of specially made 'spoons'. These have been discovered across the Celtic world and comprise a flat surface, often etched into four quarters, with a hole for the water to drain.[23] It is likely that the flow of water across the quarters would have meant something to the observer, just like the flow of water across the carved rocks or the jumping rings across the Sámi drum we explored in chapter 29.

The division of the surface of the spoon into four may mirror the division of the world according to the cardinal points. It may also unlock the meaning of a stone carving from Kermaria-en-Pont-l'Abbé in France, which was divided vertically into three, the lower section seemingly marked by waves, with the flat top of the stone separated into four quarters by a cross.[24] It is likely that this represented the cosmos as the Celts believed it to be, with three vertical plains representing the lowerworld, middleworld and upperworld, and all further divided according to the cardinal points. If the Druids did know the mysteries of the universe, then that knowledge was recorded on stones such as this.

Many Celtic women were buried with mirrors in their graves and while this might seem a suitable accoutrement for the fairer sex (one Roman historian records how he had to berate his mistress for painting herself like a Celtic hussy), it is likely that they had a deeper meaning.[25] Mirrors are used in shamanic practice to induce trance, and, rather like the modern crystal balls, if they are used to focus concentration, shapes begin to appear on their surface.[26] This may be why many mirrors had phosphenes engraved on their surface, emphasising their role in accessing the wisdom of the otherworld.[27]

Other methods of divination were not so benign and there are records of women cutting open the body of a sacrificial victim and discerning the future within the entrails.[28] Siculus, another Roman historian, records only that the seers performed the sacrifice (without stating whether they were women) but helpfully notes that the convulsions of the limbs and spurting of blood were also considered significant.[29] At other times, women merely slit the throats of captives and drained the blood into cauldrons.[30] It is revealing that cauldrons were often deposited into lakes and bogs

and perhaps there was a circularity about draining the liquid of a person before placing the entire assemblage into water.

It is likely that the cauldrons were offerings to the gods, but they were not the only
items thrown into lakes. At Llyn-Cerrig-Bach, on the Druid stronghold of Anglesey,
weapons, chariot parts, horse harnesses, tools, and trumpets were all left in the water,
along with parts from two cauldrons.[31] These may have been offered as part of the
Druid ceremonies that took place on the island but, in other instances, war booty was
also given to the gods. In exchange for victory, the spoils of war were promised and
then either left in water or more formally placed in the newly emerging temples.[32]
An incredible find at Hjortspring in Denmark, where a boat was filled with weapons
and left in a bog, probably represents a prize of battle.[33] Even the treasure looted from
Delphi was brought to Toulouse and left piled in the precinct of the temple. There
were clear strictures against touching it, however, with infringements punishable by
torture and death.[34]

Despite this, death was not the worst punishment that could be inflicted. According
to Caesar, the very worst was to be excluded from sacrifice and, presumably, from the
favour of the gods.[35] Death itself held no fear as the belief in the afterlife (and potential future reincarnation) was so strong.[36] Indeed, gambling debts could be set off for
repayment in the next world, and people threw letters onto funeral pyres in the belief
that they could reach the afterlife and be read by deceased relatives.[37]

People may have used other methods to reach the otherworld while alive and
several hallucinogenic drugs have been found at Iron Age sites, including henbane,
opium, and ergot.[38] The fluid, otherworldly nature of Celtic art may have been
inspired by trance journeys where tendrils of plants wrap around items and occasionally reveal an animal outline or a human face, as if caught in transition from one form
to another.[39] The dragons that were engraved on sword scabbards were clearly creatures from the otherworld (and it is telling that they are often placed on either side of
a tree symbol).[40] Others, such as vultures, which were given the remains of the dead
to carry away in Spain, or bears, whose claws were buried with women and children
in the early Iron Age, were probably thought to be spirit helpers.[41] Some images
may even depict shapeshifting, such as the bronze statue of a man from Bouray-sur-
Juine in France that has cloven feet, or the figure on the Gundestrup cauldron from
Denmark, which has antlers.[42]

The Gundestrup figure also holds a torc in his hand and wears another around
his neck; clearly this was an important individual. He is also surrounded by animals
and appears to sit at the base of a tree. This is a similar tableau to that engraved
on the Trialeti goblet we explored in chapter 24. Like the Georgian example, the
Gundestrup cauldron may also show a shaman shapeshifting into animal form before
ascending the world-tree and journeying to the otherworld. It is intriguing that the
cauldron, despite being found in a bog in Denmark (the land of the Germanic tribes),
had its origins far to the south in Thrace, the area around modern-day Bulgaria. This
explains why some of the imagery, such as elephants and gryphons, seem out of place
in Iron Age Denmark, whereas others appear to portray recognisable Celtic scenes.

One in particular shows a line of warriors beneath a horizontal tree, waiting to be thrust head-first into a cauldron, before riding away above the tree. A dog guards the access to the cauldron. The warriors are similar to those depicted on the Hallstatt scabbard and appear to be a Celtic war hoard. Perhaps those beneath the tree are dead and await revival by a god through emersion in the cauldron, with the tree and dog marking the portal between this world and the other. It is also curious that a medieval Welsh story uses the same theme of a cauldron bringing dead warriors back to life after their emersion within it.[43] The depictions on the outside of the cauldron are all faces with small scenes interspersed between them. Perhaps these were likenesses of the gods and the scenes served to identify them to a non-literate people? Inside the cauldron are other images but these are more involved, including the two scenes described above. It is almost as if the vessel was designed so that the teachings of the gods could only be sought once their images had been passed. Perhaps the deepest mystery of all was only revealed at the base of the cauldron where a bull was shown in the act of sacrifice. Was this the price of the knowledge contained within the vessel or was it prescient of the eventual fate of the cauldron, itself to be sacrificed and left, deliberately dismantled, in a bog in Denmark?

We shall probably never know how the cauldron managed to travel almost the entire length of Europe. It may have been war booty, but the specific form of the images makes it more likely to have been a stupendous diplomatic gift. Its mix, however, of both western and eastern influences provides an appropriate curtain raiser for our next foray into the steppe lands of the Far East of Europe. A new people have arisen and they are every bit as flamboyant and as bellicose as the Celts. A king has died and we are mourning his passing when a strange transgendered figure joins us.

Chapter 39

MOUNTED WARRIORS AND TRANSVESTITE PRIESTS

We sit in a small tent in the middle of grassland so expansive that it only stops when it finally reaches the horizon. There are several other people with us: fierce warriors weighed down with weapons, and several women, striking in their finery. A metal plate is set over the fire and all eyes watch as a small, bent man enters. His face betrays his sex, although the clothes he wears are those of a woman. I turn to you with surprise, although everyone else seems oblivious. The small man takes a handful of seeds from a small pouch by his waist and throws them onto the plate. They immediately start to smoke, and the soft, sweet smell of cannabis assails us. It is not long before our heads start to swim and our thoughts turn to the burial mound a short way from the tent, except that this time it is not the dead king that lies at the centre of the burial chamber, but his spirit. Around the mound are the spirits of 50 horses and riders, each strangled, preserved, and stuffed before being mounted on stakes. The horses have their legs hanging in the air and the riders are perched upright on their backs. They are the honour guard for the departed king. Their eyes seem to bore into ours as the cannabis forces us deeper into their realm; it is an uncomfortable and unnerving experience.

Herodotus, a Greek historian who travelled widely throughout the Mediterranean region, wrote profusely about the people he observed. At around 550 BC, during a visit to the Black Sea trading outpost of Olbia at the mouth of the River Bug in the Ukraine, he heard stories about, and probably met, some of the nomadic peoples of the Eurasian steppes: the Scythians. From his account comes the description of the funeral and burial of the king whose tomb we have just visited.[1] What we did not see, but Herodotus records, were the other retainers and attendants that were slaughtered to accompany the king to the afterlife, including a concubine, a cupbearer, a cook, a groom, a messenger, and other assorted flunkies. Wherever the king was headed, it seems clear that he was not going alone.

The Scythians moved into the Black Sea region around 600 BC from lands further east. They were truly nomadic, following their herds on horseback while searching for the best grazing sites. When we left the steppes at the end of chapter 24, people had only just domesticated the horse and it seemed unlikely that they had realised its potential for riding. Much has changed in the intervening years.

Horses were probably used to pull wagons long before they were ridden; they were easier to lead than draught cattle and could go longer distances. It was likely an easy step to substitute one species for the other.[2] Utilising the power of the horse allowed people to move locations and seek out the best grazing for their animals. The steppes provided a fickle environment and hard winters and summer droughts could cause catastrophic losses to those who could not move somewhere better. Mobility allowed people to flourish.[3] Wagons became a sign of status, with many following their owners to the grave. Huge barrows, or 'kurgans', were needed to contain the vehicles; even dismantled, they were large. The drama of this new lifestyle filtered west and entranced the people of central Europe. We have already seen in chapter 27, for example, how the tumulus tradition took its cue from the wagons and kurgans of the east. Even the first Beaker communities in eastern Europe adopted the battleaxe as a sign of status, another trait copied from the people of the steppes.[4] However, despite increased mobility, it is likely that for much of the Bronze Age, the people of the steppes were not completely nomadic, and varied their livelihoods between keeping cattle and growing crops.[5] It was a cautious but successful strategy.

By the start of the late Bronze Age, around 1500 BC, large kurgans, and the wagons inside them, disappeared, and for a short time there was more equality in the way people were buried.[6] This may have been because of the development of new ways to flaunt status: instead of using horses to pull their wagons, people had learnt to ride them instead. No wonder wagons were now dismissed as passé. Horse riding certainly began in the steppes, probably around the rivers Don and Volga in southern Russia.[7] However, the craze spread like fury and bridles and cheek-pieces (used to control the horse when riding but not when harnessed) rapidly appeared across the region. A new age, far more significant to these people than either the coming of bronze or iron, had begun.

Increased mobility through riding horses allowed people to range further and faster, seeking out new sites while the convoy of wagons trundled behind. In the main, people pushed south and west towards the rich grasslands of the Black Sea coast. Herodotus provides a name for the people who settled the area: the Cimmerians.[8] Even having found a place to call home, however, the Cimmerians did not stop their wandering and they pushed further west into Hungary, where lively trading probably preceded a more permanent presence.[9] It is possible that the chiefs of the Hallstatt people obtained horses from these Cimmerian traders. As we have seen, the horse was considered a prestigious animal even by the earlier Urnfield people, although most were likely limited to traction. The versatile two-piece bits that allowed for control when riding only emerged with the rise of the Hallstatt chiefs; being mounted must have added to their image considerably.[10] They may have even started wearing specialist riding attire: trousers.

The Cimmerians did not lack battle experience. Indeed, they served as mercenaries for the Assyrian empire that so plagued the Phoenicians in chapter 36, and yet, by around 800 BC, their borders were under threat from a new people to emerge from the east. These were the Scythians we met at the start of this chapter, and, for them, sharing the land was not an option. In the space of 200 years, the Cimmerians were all but driven into the sea.[11]

The Scythians probably originated deep in the Siberian steppes.[12] Like the Cimmerians, they were a nomadic people who likely came west because of drought in their homeland and its attendant disruption to communities reliant on access to good grazing land.[13] Spreading through southern Russia and the Ukraine, some reached the Black Sea coastal region, where the favourable conditions allowed them to thrive. Those of highest standing built immensely rich tombs, like the one we visited at the beginning of this chapter. Herodotus called these people the Royal Scythians on account of their great wealth.[14]

The decline of the Assyrian empire removed competition to Scythian supremacy in the region. In fact, the Scythian king, Partatua, even asked the Assyrian king, Asarhaddon, for his daughter's hand in marriage.[15] After searching through sheep's entrails for a divinely inspired response, Asarhaddon agreed. In reality, he had little choice. It is not recorded how his daughter felt about moving from the refined comforts of her youth to living on horseback with a barbarian king as her husband, but Herodotus records that her son, King Madyas, later returned to help the Assyrians fight the Medians, so perhaps her new life was not too unbearable.[16]

The decline of the Assyrians, and their eventual fall in 614 BC, undoubtedly helped secure Scythian supremacy in the region but it was perhaps the Greek trading port at Olbia (the city visited by Herodotus) that enabled them to build their fortune. The Greeks wanted grain and fish, both of which were abundant in the region, as well as cattle, slaves, iron, and, of course, horses. The Scythians were expert breeders and their animals were justifiably renowned. What the Greeks offered in return became evident when a shipwreck was found in a tributary of the River Dnieper in Ukraine. The young boat-hand went down with his cargo, which was mostly wine and valuable vessels to drink it from. Like the Celts of central Europe, the Scythians were heavy drinkers and their wild parties were the talk of the Mediterranean world.[17] Over time, the Greek craftworkers began to fathom the Scythian taste for decorative artwork and produced some of the finest treasures known from this period. Some were fashioned from the metal the Scythian kings loved above all others: gold.[18]

Many of the rich burials contained copious quantities of gold, as well as every other luxury that the deceased may have required. Some kurgans seemed to cover great warehouses stuffed with every conceivable comfort, including weapons, wagons, and, perhaps most treasured of all, wine stores.[19] Attendants were sacrificed to join their master or mistress in death, including the mummified honour guard we saw at the start of the chapter. The kurgan was a surrogate dwelling for its occupant, possibly the only permanent residence he or she had ever known.[20] The covering mound, sometimes 100m wide and 20m high, comprised turfs taken from the best pastures in the region, sometimes being brought several kilometres to the burial site. This was grazing for the afterlife.[21] Stelae were often placed on top of the mounds, perhaps representing the spirit of the deceased. Certainly, at sanctuaries in the Ustyurt region of Kazakhstan, several stelae were erected inside circles, with tables for offerings laid before them.[22] However, like the warrior images we have seen before, the stelae on the graves emphasise weaponry and sexual prowess before individual identity; faces were rarely depicted in detail.[23]

In addition to the stone stelae, there was another way that people may have approached the dead: by taking what Herodotus describes as a 'vapour bath'.[24] These are similar to the burnt mound sites we explored in chapter 35, except that the Scythians did not rely on steam alone to transport them to the otherworld, they also burnt cannabis seeds.[25] No wonder Herodotus records those experiencing the vapour as howling with delight. When we experienced the vapour bath at the beginning of the chapter, it was a transvestite figure, which Herodotus calls an 'enaree', who brought the seed.[26] Hippocrates fleshes out the details of these androgynous figures, suggesting that they received serious damage to their manhood through riding and therefore lived the rest of their lives as women.[27] This seems to equate to the initiatory sickness experienced by many shamans when they are first called to their vocation.[28] Moreover, many who are called to be shamans often lived their lives in the guise of the opposite gender, just like the Scythian enarees.[29] One of their roles appears to have been prophecy, with thrown rods or the twists of lime bark telling of future events.[30] They may have also escorted the dead to the afterlife and even been possessed by disembodied spirits, roles recorded for the shamans of their descendents, the Ossetians, in historical times.[31] Certainly, some Scythian art shows female figures, possibly the enarees, dancing in frenzied rituals while clutching the heads of animals or weapons, possibly under the influence of cannabis, and journeying to the otherworld of death.[32]

A drug-induced frenzy may have also been the prelude for Scythian warriors before riding to battle.[33] The mounted warriors would have certainly been a terrifying sight as they thundered across the plains, heavily armoured in iron-scaled suits and armed to the teeth with weapons. First, they would draw their bows and shoot arrows, bringing what Ovid, the Greek poet, called 'double-death'.[34] He was probably referring to the Scythian habit of dipping their arrows into poison formed from decomposed snake, excrement, and putrefied blood; it must have been an agonising way to die.[35] Next, they would throw spears, or use lances to pinion their foes. If that failed, there was a long sword, a short sword, an axe, a chain flail, and, last, but just as deadly in their hands, a whip.[36] If they were out to get you, they got you. The warriors would collect the heads of the slain, both to prove the kill and thereby collect a fair share of the booty when it was divided at the end of the battle, and also to preserve them as drinking cups.[37] The very finest were even gilded in silver. The skin was often peeled away from the head, and once preserved, formed trophies that the Scythians tied to the bridles of their horses. Occasionally, these were sewn together to form an elaborate cloak or, presumably to save time on the needlework, the whole body could be flayed and worn instead.[38] It must have paralysed their enemies with fear.

Some bodies may have been preserved because of the designs tattooed into the flesh. Mummified bodies from Pazyryk in Tuva, at the far east of the Scythian range, show an array of animals gliding sinuously across the skin, the flexing of muscles doubtless enhancing the visual effect.[39] However, it is likely that the designs had a deeper purpose than mere decoration.[40] We saw in chapter 28 how the Ob-Ugrians tattooed bird images to serve as spiritual guides to the bearer. The Scythian motifs were likely to have been considered in a similar way. Indeed, much of the animal art decorating golden implements seems to have an otherworldly quality, often appearing to be flying rather than running, or shifting from one state to another in lithe and effortless movements. While some animals, such as the gryphon, are clearly mythical, the majority of the species depicted originated from the forest hinterlands rather than the steppes themselves.[41] Perhaps this physical remove enhanced their liminal, otherworldly nature?

Some animals were sacrificed as offerings to the gods, generally meeting their end through strangulation before being boiled in cauldrons (or, if none were available, in their own gut lining).[42] The cauldron seems to have been an important item for the Scythians, and Herodotus tells of the war leaders mixing bowls of wine of which only those who had killed in battle were allowed to partake; those excluded sat apart in disgrace.[43] When on the battlefield, a victorious warrior was supposed to drink the blood of the first enemy he killed, although how easy this was in the heat of conflict is not recorded.[44] Bonds between allies were sealed through a ritual drink of wine mixed with the blood of both parties and there are touching scenes of two burly warriors pressed close and simultaneously drinking from the same cup to seal their troth.[45] Blood and wine was also a suitable offering to the god of war, symbolised by an upraised iron sword set within a shrine of stacked brushwood. Libations were poured over the metal and, to add more colour to festivities, the severed hands of slaughtered prisoners were tossed into the air.[46]

If men could live their lives as women, then certain women were also able to take on the traditional roles of men. These were the fabled Amazon warriors, man killers, who, despite their near-mythical status, appear to have been a regular part of Scythian life.[47] Many women were buried with weapons, most often the bow, which would have been easier for them to use than the heavier items. Moreover, they clearly still valued their femininity as they also took cosmetics and perfume with them to the afterlife. Even spindles appear in some graves, perhaps demonstrating that, for all their masculine traits, they could still perform work that would more usually fall to a woman.[48]

The Sarmatian people, who were the next group to emerge from the Siberian steppes, also had female warriors and had a trick that perhaps even the formidable Scythians had not considered. During infancy, the right breast was seared off with a red-hot blade in order that their bow arm might grow stronger.[49] These Sarmatians were clearly made of stern stuff and they swept aside the Scythians from their Black Sea territories at around 400 BC. The king and his nobles were deposed, settlements were flattened, and the Greek trading port of Olbia suffered a slow but ultimately terminal decline.[50]

The Sarmatian hoards spread east into China and west into Europe and this is where we must also go. At the end of the Bronze Age, there was unfinished business in the north of the continent, where we left the living and the dead at loggerheads over the ownership of the land. That conflict has not abated and its effects still hang like a pall over the land.

Chapter 40

LIFE IN THE NORTH

A little before 300 BC, a boat slipped out of Massilia harbour and onto the Mediterranean Sea. Whether its departure attracted much attention is hard to say, but perhaps there were wives and girlfriends of the crew watching it go and offering prayers to Poseidon to look after their sweethearts. For this ship was undertaking a journey to the very ends of the world, and without divine intervention, its sailors must surely perish. Passing through the straits of Gibraltar, the small craft would make its way up the Atlantic coast before circumnavigating Britain and visiting the legendary Thule, somewhere north of the Arctic Circle. Among those undertaking the voyage was a Greek geographer named Pytheas. It is his record of the voyage, now only surviving in parts copied by other writers, that reveals the audacity of the undertaking.[1]

Setting out a little after Pytheas, we shall undertake a similar journey, making our way up the Atlantic façade and observing the people in the north of the continent. Taking a last look at the city of Massilia as our ship catches the evening wind, we head west, hugging the coast as Gaul gives way to Spain.

At first, the towns we pass along the eastern Spanish coast look very similar to Massilia; walls enclose urban houses, some ostentatiously large, and people seem occupied with trade and specialist crafts.[2] Pytheas would have felt very at home had he landed at one of these towns. If he had stayed for dinner, he may have found himself eating off Greek plates, such was the volume of trade with the Greek world.[3] Further west, Greek influence wanes as we pass towns that owe their origins to the Phoenicians, now based in their new Tunisian home of Carthage. The most accessible silver mines (that we saw give their wealth to the Tartassos people in chapter 36), are now exhausted and some of the past splendour has gone from the towns. Mass-produced Greek pottery floods the region and provides a semblance of prosperity but it will not be until 237 BC, when the Carthaginians invade and take over administration of southern Iberia, that fortunes will change. For now, however, trade is opportunistic and fortune fickle. A shipwreck off the harbour of Palma de Mallorca, dating to around 350 BC, revealed a variety of trade items ranging from millstones to bronze wine-drinking vessels. Scratched inventories in Greek and Punic (Carthaginian) show that trade was exploited wherever and whenever it could be found.[4]

Passing through the straits of Gibraltar, we enter the vast ocean of the Atlantic. From here, we will hug the coast of Portugal and avoid the worst of the surging waves. This was an important trade route in former times, with copper and tin pouring into the markets of the Mediterranean. Now it is quiet but for the odd Carthaginian ship picking up business where it can. The local people got used to a steady supply of luxury items when they traded with the Tartessos people further south. With the decline of the mines, this trade also declined and communities turned to another form of wealth: land. Settlements proliferated and marked out their domains into ordered fields.[5] Crops were cultivated and the harvest stored in enormous quantities. Perhaps this was a means of showing off: the modern equivalent of an extravagant sword? Stone effigies of bulls and pigs were erected throughout the land, the engraved inscriptions seeking divine protection for the animals grazed in the vicinity, but they may have also carried another message: this land is taken, it belongs to us. No longer represented by weapons and fancy armour, people now took their identity from the land that they worked.

Further north, where the Atlantic cuts back into the continent to form a massive shelf, other people are also concentrating upon the land. We spent last night at one of their hilltop towns; its location meant that we could see the walls long before we reached its entrance. Inside lived the Castro peoples, named after the Latin word for castle, aptly describing their fortified homes.[6] Numerous houses bunched together behind the sturdy walls, with none seemingly any different from the other. Nevertheless, from the gold we saw a few people wearing as we ate our supper, some clearly had more wealth than others.[7] People seemed to grow crops and keep livestock; evidently this was what occupied the lives of most. A few small workshops echoed to the sound of metalworking; their inhabitants seemingly specialising in their craft. As we left the town, you noticed rows of upright stones set before the walls. This was a 'chevaux-de-frise', so-called since it is thought to be designed to stop a cavalry charge. They are a feature of the entire Atlantic façade and demonstrate once again that across the millennia, people who lived near the sea shared ideas as well as trade.[8]

Sailing up the French coast, we come to a wide estuary where the River Garonne meets the sea. There are plenty of boats plying its waters and, from the shouts we hear echoing across its surface, most seem to be Greek traders. Until the time of the Celtic migrations (which we explored in chapter 36), Massilia obtained metals from the west via the trade routes of the River Rhone. Wishing to avoid the rampaging Celts, the Greeks, quite sensibly, abandoned trade up the Rhone and sought new avenues to replace it. To access the metal ores of the Atlantic west, they likely sailed along the River Aube, with an overland portage to reach the Garonne, and from there to the Atlantic sea.[9] The vessels we spy are likely filled with bronze and tin from the lands to the north.

It takes an uncomfortable night, followed by an even worse day, until we reach the shores of Armorica, modern-day Brittany. Fortunately, the storm we have sailed through has now dissipated and we get a clear view of the numerous fortifications that seal off short lengths of the cliff-top peninsula. When we stop to spend the night at one of the small villages that dot the landscape, our meal is served from crockery that seems too fine for the standard of house we sit in. Sadly, this is all that remains from the once lucrative trade with the Celtic people of the Marne valley to the east.[10] Fine pottery and metal vessels were imported in return for the mineral wealth of the earth. Like the Greek trade along the River Rhone, however, it was the Celtic migrations that put paid to Armorican dreams of riches. They must have been mightily relieved when Pytheas passed this way and grateful for the Greek traders that followed in his wake.

Sailing the short stretch of channel that separates Britain from its smaller namesake, there seems little change, either to the shape of the rugged coastline or the fortified peninsulas that erupt from it. There is a chill in the air, and this is part of a long-term trend that will drive farming communities from the upland regions and cause them to move closer to the coast. We can just see some of these new settlements, still only comprising a few houses nestling together, but their enclosing boundaries seem unnecessarily elaborate.[11] Perhaps these small settlements with multiple rings of banks and ditches are the way people define themselves within the land? Elsewhere, huts are scattered among fields and we can see people tending to their livestock. Fortunately, the wetter climate will improve the grazing for these beasts, but only at the loss of crop cultivation. It is in balancing the two that fortunes will be made, and occasionally lost. Stopping off at one of these settlements, we are startled to see met-alworking occurring within one of the huts.[12] In the Bronze Age, such activity took place at the edge of the settlement, or in liminal, boundary locations. The change of metal has ruptured these traditions and ironworking now seems suitable to be under-taken within the home.

As we leave the south-western peninsula and head along the south coast of Britain, making the occasional foray inland to the chalk hills beyond the coast, most of the land seems to be worked by the scattered farms that crowd the landscape.[13] Many of these are substantial holdings and it is evident that the houses have probably occupied the same site for many generations. When we last visited this region, at the end of the Bronze Age, the pervading power of the dead, coupled with the belief that they owned the land, forced people to abandon their farms and move on. Clearly, the living have made inroads in their struggle for the land. Indeed, cemeteries appear absent and, but for a few bones (especially skulls) kept within the houses, the dead seem to have vanished altogether. However, the change to iron may have even helped people in their struggle with the dead; the new metal better reflecting the message that people wanted to portray about themselves.

Iron was probably never seen as a replacement for bronze; the umbrella term 'metal' is a modern construct and, for people of the past, iron may have been in the same category as wood, bone, or antler.[14] Bronze, or rather the copper from which it arose, was an exotic metal, telling of far-off places and beliefs. We saw in chapter 30 how owning a bronze sword was a mark of sophistication and an acknowledgement of contacts with people far away. Iron was different. Rather than being exotic, iron was local, sometimes even gathered straight from the fields in which people planted their crops.[15] In farming communities, where status arose from owning the land, iron better reflected the obsessions of the time; wearing an iron sword may have been akin to 'wearing' your field. It is also telling that during the last stages of the Bronze Age, there was more and more recycling of metal.[16] Perhaps this was a desperate effort to make the old metal reflect the local nature of the new? Moreover, given the increasingly agrarian outlook, the buried hoards of bronze metalwork seemed to focus on axes in the north and sickles further south, both tools of the agricultural trade.[17] Ironworking was probably still considered to be a special process, however, and the piles of slag heaped at the edge of the bog at Welham Bridge may have been an attempt to return the residue of the process back to the location from which the ore was originally collected.[18] The fact that the heap resembled an earlier burial cairn may not have been coincidental. At the Titelberg hillfort, far to the south of Luxembourg, a baby was placed into the smelter pit at a metal foundry, perhaps demonstrating that the entire process of metal production was still linked with the imagery of birth and death.[19]

Among the scattered farms we visit are altogether more massive settlements, the so-called hillforts, often perched atop a rise and surrounded by several circuits of banks and ditches. Our journey does not allow us the time to explore these places in any detail and so we make a note to return later, when we might pass through some of the massive gates and explore the interior. For now, our travels take us further along the channel and then left, into the North Sea.

The first thing we notice is that the enclosure ditches and large houses that we explored in chapter 31 appear to have disappeared from the east of England. All that remain are small farms set within large expanses of cultivated land. There are no enclosure ditches, and from what we can tell, the farms shift their location every so often.[20] This seems very similar to the wandering farmsteads that we observed in chapter 33, where the house was abandoned after the death of the household head and the land returned to the dead.

Across the sea, in a broad arc from Scandinavia to the Low Countries, houses also continued to be abandoned and replaced elsewhere every generation or so.[21] It all seems rather pointless to our eyes and, in some regions, it will not be until the late Iron Age that permanent settlements will be built and the living will finally claim ownership of the land.[22] When houses were eventually rebuilt in the same location, the structure was often burnt before being cleared, and perhaps this was a means of disrupting the usual sequence of events and easing the tension of what the survivors were about to do.[23] It may even have mirrored the cremation rite afforded to people when they died. It is telling that all this happened at a time when communal cemeteries had disappeared and the dead were buried within the settlement.[24] Bringing the dead into the settlement allowed them to be contained and controlled. It may be for similar reasons that ironworking was also brought within the confines of the settlement boundaries.

Within Denmark, the collapse of the bronze trade meant that the old chiefs lost the means of maintaining their power.[25] Items were left in wet places or buried in the ground but they were now fewer and of poorer quality. Wealth was concentrated with the Celts in the south and it is only in those regions with something to trade that fortunes could be amassed. In the Netherlands, for example, some people were able to obtain fancy horse trappings by trading the salt that they collected from the sea.[26] Elsewhere, wherever there was trade, rich burials sporadically emerged, often with items obtained from the Celts.

There is one region, however, where there was a concentration of wealthy burials: Yorkshire. We soon pass by on our journey north and marvel at the large square barrows that dot the landscape. One of our travelling companions tells us that the people bury their leaders with weapons and a cart, just like the Celts to the south.[27] We wonder if this could be an offshoot of the La Tène people, but there are differences that make this unlikely: we are told that the burial cart is dismantled here, whereas the Celts leave it whole; the barrows are square and not round; and the houses are undifferentiated and quite ordinary. These people are not Celts, although perhaps they have heard stories of these far-off people and wished that they were. As we might expect, many of the barrows were located near rivers (the better for the soul to reach the afterlife), but many of the watercourses only run in winter and are dry during the summer.[28] Perhaps this seasonality reminded people of the agricultural cycle and the image of death and rebirth it represented. However, it is unlikely that people wanted the dead to be reborn literally; in some instances, they even speared the corpse to make sure.[29]

As we sail further north, we briefly pass another band of hillforts in southern Scotland. These match those we have seen in the south and, curiously, we are told that many are deliberately burnt upon abandonment.[30] This seems to mirror the houses on the continent and we wonder whether the reasons for it are the same.

Sailing around the tip of Scotland is another storm-tossed voyage and we are glad to reach the isles off the western coast. As we approach land, we are struck by a substantial stone-built house that looms over the shore. Over time, houses such as this will develop into 'brochs', tall towers, several storeys high.[31] Although they looked formidable, they were unlikely to have withstood a direct attack. All a besieger needed to do was set a fire at the door. However, their location, set in a liminal zone between land and sea, hints that perhaps they had a different role, and represented more than mere houses. Once our voyage is over, we will return to this place, and explore these towers further.

Chapter 41

AROUND THE HOUSES

The broch is just close enough to the sea that the sound of the waves provides an almost mesmerising backdrop to the early spring morning. As we approach the door to the tower, we are overwhelmed by its sheer size; in this flat landscape it seems almost to skim the passing clouds. The sun has now risen and we can feel the warmth on our backs. You point out that the doorway must face east, a direction that we know is significant. Stooping to enter, we have to pass through a narrow passageway that extends through the thick outer wall. The interior is dark, the circular space broken up by partitions and cupboards built from the same stone as the walls. We are forced to turn left by a large stone partition and you point out that we now walk in the same direction that the sun will shortly take through the sky. We wonder if there might be a connection. Avoiding a low trough filled with grain, and another filled with water, we circle round the interior of the broch, passing doors set into the wall and stairs leading up to higher floors. Eventually, we come to a small hole in the floor and a flight of rough steps heading down. You nudge me to go first and I descend slowly, allowing my eyes to get used to the darkness. Almost at once, I feel earth beneath my feet, and crouching to fit inside the cramped space, touch something with my foot. Looking down, it is a bone. I point it out to you and you nod in confirmation: we can both recognise human remains by now. However, the space under the broch looks strangely familiar. We have seen its like before: one night when we sat outside a Neolithic tomb and witnessed the burial of a woman. This tomb is the same. But why would people build their broch over an old tomb and even provide stairs down into it? Even more macabre, why would they leave the bones in place? We climb the stairs back into the broch with many questions unanswered.

The sunwise direction in which people were forced to move around the broch seems to be deliberate as it was a commonly repeated design throughout the Scottish isles.[1] In fact, there is even a Gaelic word for it: 'deosil' (pronounced 'djee-zhul' and meaning sunwise or clockwise). Anyone entering the accommodation at Bu, for example (a broch that may have had its origins in the early Iron Age), would have been faced with a small entrance hall with several doors leading from it. By taking the door on the left, thereby moving deosil around the interior, a visitor would reach the main living area, with a central hearth, cooking trough, and stone cupboards. Moving further around the broch (and also accessed via the entrance hall by turning right) was a long, curved room, which was paved. This may have been where people slept, as the clear floors would allow several individuals to stretch out in comfort.[2] Intriguingly, the stones forming the walls at Dun Vulan, and, in common with many other brochs, the stairs giving access to the upper floors, spiralled in a deosil direction.[3] Whatever someone did within the broch, it seems that they were constantly orientated according to the path of the sun. Perhaps this was believed to be the correct and natural order of the world, as opposed to its opposite, known as 'widdershins' (a Saxon word adopted into Gaelic, meaning anticlockwise), which often carries negative connotations.

The sun may have emphasised the life contained within the broch in opposition to the realm of death, which people may have believed lay beneath their feet. As we have seen ourselves, sometimes this was literally true, and at Howe, the broch was positioned directly over a Neolithic chambered tomb.[4] This was no accident since the entrance to the broch aligned exactly with the entrance to the tomb, and people even dug an access to the burial chamber and cleared out its contents. As if to acknowledge that this was a place of death, however, the Iron Age occupants left a cup-marked stone in the passage that they dug and may have even buried their own dead there.[5] At Quanterness, another broch built over a chambered tomb, the original entrance passage into the chamber was retained and even the contents were left in place.[6]

We have seen already that from the late Bronze Age people brought selected human bones into their houses, perhaps as a way of bringing the dead closer and thereby seeking to control their influence. This was also true of the Scottish brochs and roundhouses, where bones are concentrated around the entrance passageways.[7] It is probable that these bones belonged to identifiable people (or, at least, people may have believed them to be). The remains in the Neolithic tombs, by contrast, would have been from distant strangers and would have formed only an amorphous ancestral presence. By placing their dwellings over the tombs, perhaps people were extending their control over the dead to include all deceased, ancient as well as recent.[8]

Some tombs that were not covered by later houses, such as the Calf of Eday, were the focus for feasting during the Iron Age, as copious pottery and animal bones were discarded around them.[9] Moreover, at Unival the chamber of a tomb was incorporated into an Iron Age roundhouse and used as a cooking pit.[10] We have seen in chapter 33 how there may have been a conceptual link between cooking food and 'cooking' the dead, and this may have been another way that Iron Age people sought to assert their authority and control over the deceased. However, there may have been even more at stake. Receiving food that had been cooked in a place associated with the dead may have been equated with creating life out of death, (a theme that also harks back to the Bronze Age). It may even relate to the brochs themselves, which, as we have seen, were located in an unproductive, almost dead zone between the cultivated land and the sea.[11] Anyone approaching the broch passed through this dead zone before being faced with the soaring intensity of life represented by the broch (the walls were even tapered near the top to emphasise the height). The fact that people knew that under the broch may have been a tomb of ancestral dead could only have heightened the drama.

The broch may have formed an 'axis mundi': an interface where the lowerworld, middleworld, and upperworld came together. The lowerworld was beneath the broch, and where there was no tomb that the occupants could enter, steps were sometimes dug to small cisterns, which often filled naturally with water.[12] While these may have been wells, it would surely have been far more convenient to dig a conventional shaft and use a bucket rather than risk descending dark, slippery steps. Moreover, a similar structure was dug into an actual burial mound at Mine Howe; the small cistern at its base again filling with water.[13] Perhaps the water represented the final portal to the otherworld, a place where people could go to access this alternative realm? In other chambers under settlements (known by the French word 'souterrain' since they are found all along the Atlantic coast to France), the presence of cup-marked stones may have served a similar purpose.[14]

In addition to the lowerworld under the broch, the structure also allowed people to go up by climbing the stairs to the upper floors. At Gurness, Dun Vulan and Dun Mor Vaul, such steps survive, and are placed opposite the main entrance, in the west of the broch.[15] This was a clear reversal of the main entrance, and if ascending the stairs was believed to be akin to entering the realm of the upperworld, such opposition would have been highly significant. As we have already seen, the otherworld is often believed to take the opposite form to this world.

Brochs were highly symbolic structures, and anyone entering their confines was immediately assailed with images of life, death, and the mediating influence of the otherworld. In fact, people may not have lived in the brochs at all, but reserved their use for ritual gatherings, perhaps to mark significant times of the year. It is curious that in the late Iron Age small villages emerge around the walls of some brochs.[16] While these may have been built by people wanting to be close to the possible occupants of the broch, the houses appear entirely self-contained and there seems little need for them to have been built there. Unless, however, the broch did not house a single family, but was a communal space used by the entire group for their gatherings and rituals. Certainly, the effort expended to build them (estimated at 100 people working for three months) suggests that they were community affairs.[17]

When we entered the broch, we noticed that the doorway faced east; this characteristic was repeated for the vast majority of Iron Age houses and, indeed, for many other structures.[18] It was even reflected in the continental long-houses, where the majority were aligned to the east during the Iron Age.[19] This was a subtle but definite change from the south-eastern orientation that prevailed during the Bronze Age. Moreover, it was clearly a deliberate decision, as the village at Hijken in the Netherlands demonstrates.[20] During the Bronze Age, all the houses were orientated towards the south-east, but when the village was rebuilt during the Iron Age, every house was constructed to align to the east. However, while there was a definite change in the direction of alignment from the Bronze Age, the reasons behind it may not have altered. In chapter 32, we saw how houses were aligned to the south-east so that the rising sun at the midwinter solstice could enter the interior and thereby introduce themes of regeneration and rebirth into the domestic sphere. This was also probably true in the Iron Age, except that, with an eastern alignment, this now happened twice a year, at the spring and autumn equinoxes, rather than just once a year as before. Rather than abandoning the Bronze Age traditions, people were actually emphasising their effect.

By aligning their houses with the rising sun, people were allowing its influence to enter their realm. Moreover, as the sun made its daily journey through the southern sky, people occupied the southern part of their homes. In many roundhouses, the majority of everyday items have been found in the south of the dwelling, suggesting that this is where people spent their days.[21] Like the brochs we explored at the start of the chapter, people entering the roundhouse would have turned left to enter the living quarters. Since the continental long-houses (that were split between a living area and a byre, the latter usually positioned at the eastern end) usually had two entrances, centrally placed along the long sides, it is more difficult to discern a pattern, especially since many lack preserved floors. However, at Heltborg, in Denmark, the long-house was arranged so that the earth floor of the byre led to the north entrance and the clay floor of the living area led to the south entrance.[22] People would have therefore entered the house from the south, with their stock entering from the north. This meant that to reach the living quarters, a visitor would turn left, just like the occupants of the roundhouses.

As we have seen in chapter 27, when the sun set in the west, people probably believed that it continued its journey into the otherworld, passing out of sight in the north, before rising once again in the east. Owing to the paucity of items found in the north of the houses, people likely had their beds in this area. Again, their daily use of the house mirrored the journey of the sun, and, when it was in the north, people occupied the northern part of their houses. They may have even extended the metaphor: since life was situated in the south, death may have been seen to occupy the north. There is certainly an immediate similarity between the repose of sleep and that of death, but it is also revealing that when the people of Cladh Hallan buried the mummies we met in chapter 34, the majority were placed in the north of the houses.[23]

People in the Iron Age were ordering their lives through the arrangement of their houses. There were places occupied by the living and, perhaps more importantly, there were places reserved for the dead. This ordering principle may have been set by the sun, but it was maintained by the people. It was the living who were now at the centre of the world and the dead, with their claims over the land, were increasingly pushed to its margins.

We leave the broch and stand on the shoreline, watching the sun as it climbs high in the sky. Having no other means of judging time, we have begun to plan our own lives around its movements and hail its presence each morning like an old friend. We are even beginning to believe that it really does journey to the otherworld at night. However, our travels are not yet complete and, now, we need to move south. In our earlier forays from the ship that brought us to these shores, we decided that we would take a closer look at the hillforts. As we begin our long trudge to reach them, we wonder if they will prove as strange as the brochs.

Chapter 42

WALKING THE LABYRINTH

Whereas the height of the broch made it impressive to behold, the hillfort is on another scale altogether. We spend an age panting up the hill just to reach the entrance, and then marvel at the rings of banks and ditches that seem to spread out on every side. You point to the entrance and, sure enough, it is aligned to the east; we smile at the predictable familiarity. Stepping inside the hillfort, there are a few houses crammed around its edge, but these look flimsy and nothing like the roundhouses we have seen elsewhere. It is not even clear if any are lived in; they look so bedraggled. Instead, the bulk of the interior is divided between small thatched granaries to our left, and what appear to be covered pits to our right. Just then, a cart rumbles by and we move to the side of the track to let it pass. It stops by one of the granaries and two women start to gather some of the grain and load it onto the back of the cart. They do not take long and leave before we manage to reach them. However, we notice more carts entering and more granaries are opened to dispense their grain. There is an almost constant bustle of activity, although nobody ventures over to the huge pits in the north. It is as if these are out of bounds for the visitors.

Although hillforts probably originated in the late Bronze Age, they primarily date to the Iron Age, around 600 to 400 BC.[1] After that, many were abandoned, although those that remained were refashioned and in many cases made larger.[2] While it is tempting to see them as the residences of chiefs, rather like the Heuneburg we explored in chapter 36, there is very little evidence to support this. Although some of the earliest hillforts may have contained large houses, these disappear in later forms, and dwellings became flimsy and insubstantial.[3] Moreover, unlike the Heuneburg, there were no rich graves near hillforts, or, indeed, any other sign of elite occupation, such as craft workshops or significant weaponry. Even the massive banks and ditches that encircle the hillforts may have been more for display than for actual use. Not all hillforts, for example, were in the best defensive positions and some were even over-looked by adjacent high ground.[4] At Maiden Castle, a hillfort in southern England with massive earthworks around it, the amount of dead ground created by the banks and ditches could never have been successfully defended.[5] A sling may have powered a stone across the distance, and there are certainly caches of suitable stones within the interior, but these do not occur when the earthworks were at their greatest extent.[6] Similarly, at Danebury, also in southern England (the hillfort we visited at the start of the chapter), at the time when the main gate was burnt, ostensibly as part of an attack, the slingstones were all lying somewhere else.[7] Either people were very forgetful about where they had stashed their ammunition, or the hillforts were not actually attacked at all and the burning has to be interpreted in other ways.

When we looked at the hillforts in Scotland in chapter 40, we noticed that many had been burnt. This occurred at such high temperatures that the rock vitrified. This requires such skill and effort that it could never have happened in battle.[8] It was more likely part of an abandonment ritual and the same was probably true at Danebury, with the gate burnt to mark the remodelling of the hillfort around 400 BC.[9]

The Scottish hillforts also reveal another trait that is not easy to explain in conventional terms. Many of the enclosures pass through several stages of development, from wooden fences to earthen banks.[10] There is no particular reason for this (people had been building banks for millennia, so they knew how to do it). Moreover, some wooden fences were so makeshift they would have decayed very rapidly, providing no protection whatsoever.[11] Rather than developing defensive capabilities, perhaps the boundary was designed to reflect the increasing permanence and durability of the hillfort and also of the people themselves as they sought to retain their land through more than one generation? The hillfort became a visual metaphor reflecting the needs of the people.

If hillforts were not the fortified castles of the elite, it does not appear that they housed many ordinary people either. While some hillforts such as Hod Hill in southern England and Moel y Gaer in Wales, contained houses across the whole of the interior,[12] at Danebury, as we saw ourselves, the houses were restricted to the edge and many of these were flimsy structures.[13] With some hillforts, there may have even been more houses gathered around the outside than in the interior, perhaps mirroring the arrangement at the brochs we explored in the previous chapter.[14] Moreover, like the brochs, the hillforts may have been reserved for communal gatherings, their interiors left clear for very specific activities.

In contrast to the houses, the facilities for grain storage on the hillforts were impressive. Granaries (identified from their distinctive four-post design and the remains of grain left around them)[15] were massive and grew more enormous over time.[16] The relative frequency of granaries in hillforts far outweighs that on other sites, suggesting that perhaps these were communal supplies. However, many of the farmsteads around the hillforts were entirely independent and had a mixed farming strategy that could cope with losses and shortages. There would have been little incentive, therefore, for communities to join such a redistributive network and, yet, people definitely brought their grain to hillforts. At Danebury, for example, where detailed analysis is available, the grain was gathered from a variety of locations and was probably processed elsewhere before being brought to the hillfort.[17] Just why were people doing this?

When we walked around Danebury at the start of the chapter, we noticed that the granaries were located in the south of the hillfort and the storage pits in the north. Two other excavated hillforts in southern England, at Winklebury and Maiden Castle, also follow this arrangement.[18] If people had come to collect and deposit grain in the granaries (it would probably not have kept past a single season), the south of the hillfort would have been a hive of activity, with people regularly coming and going. This matches the arrangement of the roundhouses that we examined in the previous chapter, where the area associated with everyday activities was to the south. It seems that at both houses and hillforts, life was represented in the south. Conversely, in the hillforts, the northern part was reserved for underground grain storage. Since this was likely long-term storage (the grain was only preserved if a considerable quantity was packed into the pit and sealed; the outer grain would rot but the majority would survive), it is likely that this was the seed crop for sowing the following season.[19] By placing the grain underground, out of sight, and leaving it through the winter months, the grain may have been considered to reside in the otherworld, perhaps, even be dead. In the roundhouses, the north of the house was associated with the realm of death and it seems that the same was true for the hillforts. As if to emphasise this, after the storage pits were emptied in the spring, their contents were sometimes replaced with human remains.[20] Perhaps the life of a human was given in return for the life of the grain. We have come across similar beliefs before, in chapter 33, where life was considered a finite resource that must be kept in balance. Moreover, the remains were placed rather than thrown into the pits, and where the body was entire, their heads were mostly aligned to the north: the direction of death.[21] We will explore more about the people that were placed in the pits in the next chapter but, for now, it is enough to note their involvement in emphasising the arrangement of the hillfort: life in the south and death in the north.

Anyone entering a hillfort through its eastern entrance would have been faced with images of life on their left and images of death on their right; the same arrangement as in the roundhouses. The Celts were said to turn to the right when they honoured their gods, and since we have already seen that deceased ancestors may have assumed a mantle of divinity, this would also have been an appropriate description for how someone should behave in the hillforts.[22] It may also be why most of the human remains in the pits (when not entire) were from the right side of the body: the side associated with death.[23] Even before entering the hillfort, its underlying arrangement would have been clear; the southern earthworks at Danebury, for example, were faced in chalk, providing a startling contrast to the sombre earth tones of the north.[24]

By visiting the hillfort to deposit and collect grain, people would have become personally involved within its symbolism. Their very presence would have brought the place to life, rather like actors on a stage, and the eastern entrance would have ensured that a visitor was properly orientated for the imagery of the hillfort to make sense. Moreover, at dawn, it would also have allowed them to turn around and note the position of the sunrise as it changed through the year.

At the spring equinox, for instance, the sun would have risen directly through the entrance. In the days thereafter, it would rise in the north of the hillfort, the half associated with death, until, at the midsummer solstice, having reached its maximum trajectory, the sun would 'die' and begin its slow descent south. Crossing the entrance at the autumn equinox, it would sink further and further south, until, at the midwinter solstice, it would reach its lowest ebb before being 'reborn' once more and beginning its slow climb back to the north. Perhaps these times were marked and celebrated and this was when the houses within the hillfort were occupied (an Iron Age equivalent of Durrington Walls)?[25] The sun would have brought together all the oppositions evident in the hillfort – south and north, left and right, life and death – and joined them in an eternal, unbroken whole. Life would emerge from death just as surely as death would emerge from life. These were common themes in the Iron Age but they had never been played out on such a massive scale before. The hillforts were theatres with a single programme: emphasising permanence with an unbroken cycle of death and renewal. This was where people came to shout out their claims to the land and demonstrate that they too were a permanent fixture within it.

At the centre of many hillforts were small shrines and this may have been where people approached the otherworld themselves, perhaps leaving offerings to the denizens that resided there.[26] In Ireland, however, it seems that some hillforts may have been designed solely for this purpose, such as Navan in Ulster.

An external bank and inner ditch was the first sign a visitor would have that this was not a usual place.[27] As we saw in chapter 23, Neolithic people constructed similar forms in which to contain their rituals and it is likely that the Iron Age people were doing the same.[28] It also reversed the standard arrangement around settlements, hinting that, perhaps, the interior was not entirely of this world. At the heart of Navan was a huge structure of 269 posts in four concentric rings. The arrangement was walled but probably not roofed and the floor was left rough and unfinished.[29] We have come across a similar structure before, at Durrington Walls during the Neolithic, and, once again, we steel ourselves to enter a labyrinth.[30]

It is so dark that it is difficult to see the entrance to the ring of posts. They rise like some primeval forest barring our way. Once inside, the route is obvious and we stumble forward over the rough earth floor. A few flashes of firelight outside the ring show where people rest after walking the route themselves. Walking slowly, concentrating on each step, our minds still. The air around us feels close and heavy. I try to count how many circuits we have walked, but it is impossible to get any bearings in the maze of posts. Our thoughts stray and we feel light-headed and dizzy. I want to lie down but can feel your presence behind me and I struggle to keep moving. My mind seems to be floating above my body, as if it is undertaking a journey of its own. I struggle to retain my consciousness and I wonder if you feel the same. At last, we reach the centre: a massive post that seems to disappear into the sky. This is the portal between the worlds and we know that, with little effort, we could let go of our floating spirits and they would climb the post and depart for the otherworld. We struggle to restrain them and it is a relief that the way out of the labyrinth is a straight path ahead of us, cutting across the rings of posts and returning us to our own world.

Shortly after the labyrinth at Navan was completed, its interior was filled with limestone blocks, themselves perhaps reused from a burial cairn.[31] This would explain the odd addition of human bone.[32] The walls were then burnt, the white of the stone emerging from the flames just like the bones of people during cremation. Finally, the cairn was covered with earth, some of it gathered from some distance. The structure had now become a burial mound, the portal to the otherworld sealed beneath its surface.

In an effort to further their claims to the land, people seemed to be far more eager to confront the otherworld and the dead spirits that resided there. The hillforts became places where the entire cosmos was laid bare in a production that was both orchestrated and played out by its occupants. However, the increasing confidence of the living can perhaps best be judged in their treatment of the dead, and, in places, this treatment became quite staggeringly gruesome. Be prepared to enter the gates of Iron Age hell.

Chapter 43

THE GATES
TO IRON AGE HELL

We stand before a square fenced-compound, its entrance, once again, facing east. A man passes us leading an elderly cow, its body so emaciated that it is a wonder it managed to walk here at all. Following him through the large, heavy gates, we notice a ditch running round the inside of the fence. But then it is not so much the ditch that holds our attention than what lies within it. Bones of every description cover its base, some still red with rotting gore. The flies lift over the freshest pieces as we pass and the foulest smell assails us. I hear you gag in disgust. An almost complete horse skeleton lies near the entrance, together with several cattle skulls. However, you point to something more ominous near the corner of the ditch and I wince as I see it. Several human arm and leg bones lie either side of a skull. Swallowing hard, we move on. At the centre of the compound is a small shelter with an arc of pits beneath it. The central pit is the largest and the man with the heifer is lifting its cover. Flies swarm out and, peeking in, all we can see is a pile of bones and putrid flesh. The smell is revolting. The man strokes his cow and speaks to it softly. Its eyes roll back in panic and the man fights to control it as he draws the knife that will end its life. We know that, once dead, the beast will be butchered and thrown into the pit. We do not stay to watch.

Our brief visit was to the so-called sanctuary site at Gournay-sur-Aronde, one of several in northern France.[1] Although, as we noticed, the ditched and fenced enclosure was orientated to the east, this was only an approximation and was noticeably askew. By contrast, the internal arrangement of pits ignored the orientation of the entrance and, instead, faced exactly east. This would have meant that people entering the enclosure would have had to reposition themselves before approaching the central arc of pits. This was likely a very deliberate ploy and, perhaps, represented a perfect inner world within the sanctuary, contrasted with its imperfect surroundings. Like the hillforts, the architecture determined that people became actors in their own performance; every move choreographed to be meaningful.

The perfection of the inner realm of the sanctuary was also reflected in the arrangement of body parts in the surrounding ditch. Initially, remains were placed in the central pit where they rotted until the bones could be pulled apart. The dismembered remains were then thrown into the appropriate section of the surrounding ditch. Cattle skulls were left around the entrance, sheep parts were placed in the middle of the sides, and human remains were put at the corners. There also appear to have been other rules: sheep remains were always accompanied by pig bones, horses tended to be entire, and cattle either comprised solely the skull and spine or were elderly beasts that had little meat left on them.[2] Dogs were placed in the ditch as it was filled with earth, just before the site was abandoned. The treatment of cattle is especially revealing as skulls and spines are not found on contemporary settlement sites and, presumably, they were brought to the sanctuary already butchered. The pigs and sheep may have also been processed apart from the sanctuary, the meat, presumably, being eaten. However, elderly animals were brought whole and probably slaughtered on site. If these were offerings to the gods, then perhaps their divine sensibilities might have felt slightly cheated.

When the meat from the younger animals, whose remains were destined for the sanctuary, was eaten by the community, it may have been as part of a formal ceremony. Although the bones at most sanctuaries were raw, at Mirebeau the bones had been cooked, perhaps as part of such a feast.[3] It is also revealing that almost all of the animals within the sanctuaries were domestic, with virtually no wild animals appearing at all.[4] Only at Digeon were wild animals significantly represented and, even then, the majority were deer, a beast whose status may have been ambiguous if the herds were managed and controlled by people.[5] It seems that people were only bringing to the sanctuaries what was theirs to give. We have seen similar beliefs before, in chapter 11, where Mesolithic hunters believed that the Master of the Animals was in charge of all wild creatures and controlled their numbers accordingly. By the Iron Age, certain animals were domesticated, of course, and it was now humans that assumed the role of master over them. Clearly, if the remains left at the sanctuary were offerings, people could only give what they controlled: domestic stock. Wild animals were the preserve of the Master of the Animals, and therefore could not be given.[6]

In additional to animal remains, weapons were also left at the sanctuaries, perhaps as sacrificial offerings. Certainly, the same items appear in many high-status graves of the corresponding period, showing that these were clearly considered to be prestigious objects.[7] Curiously, the treatment of the weapons at the sanctuaries seems to mirror that afforded to the animal remains. Initially, they were thrown into pits or were hung on the eastern wall until they had decayed sufficiently to be broken or bent and placed in the boundary ditch.[8] It seems that this was the standard pattern for sacrifices and, as we know, the ritualised dismemberment of both animals and weapons may have ensured that they became whole again in the otherworlds. If they were indeed offerings to gods, then this would have been essential. Intriguingly, weapons placed in graves were unbroken until the sanctuaries were established, when more items reveal deliberate damage.[9] Perhaps people were trying to make their own individual offerings, thus seeking to bypass communal rituals?

While the sanctuaries may have contained sacrificed offerings, it is the strict ordering of the remains that is most striking. As in the hillforts, people seem to be attempting to order and arrange the world according to their own needs and beliefs and were, quite literally, putting the dead in their place. This is particularly clear at Ribemont, where a small structure inside the sanctuary enclosure was constructed from over 2000 human arm and leg bones, with the token addition of 12 horse bones.[10] It is likely that broken weapons were hung on its outside walls and, at the very centre of the structure, there was a pit filled with human ashes. This gruesome building ordered the remains of the dead in a manner that had never been attempted before. During the Bronze Age, the house was intimately linked with certain individuals, so that when they died, their dwelling had to die with them and become a house for the dead. At Ribemont, this imagery took another step, and, instead of being a house *for* the dead, the house was now *of* the dead, constructed from their remains. The message from those who built it was clear: here is the domain of the dead – all else is ours.

It is significant that many sanctuary sites seemed to focus around a pit. At Gournay-sur-Aronde the offerings were first placed in pits, and at Ribemont the bone house was centred on a pit containing human ashes. It may have been that the pit, rather than the surrounding structure, was the most important aspect of the sanctuaries and this was why, at Gournay-sur-Aronde, the pits, and not the entrance to the enclosure, were aligned exactly east.[11] Pits were also important on a similar type of site known as 'Viereckschanzen', a singularly unhelpful name since it merely means a four-sided enclosure.[12] Like the hillforts, they seem to straddle the boundary between ritual and domestic use, highlighting again the paucity of such a division when it is applied to the past.[13] Many Viereckschanzen contain shafts within their confines, some extremely deep. At Holzhausen in Germany, for example – the first Viereckschanze to be formally excavated – three shafts were discovered at 8, 19, and 40m deep.[14] At the base of the smallest was an upright post, with traces of blood and gore still clinging to its surface. Before being thrown into the pit, the post may have marked a place where animals were sacrificed, forming a familiar portal to the otherworld so that the offerings would rapidly pass from this realm to the other. The pit may have formed another portal and this was why they formed the focus of both sanctuaries and Viereckschanzen. By placing the post within the pit at Holzhausen, people were bringing together two portals, perhaps strengthening the significance of the site. Incredibly, at Stanwick in southern Britain, a similar 8m shaft dating to the late Bronze Age also had a post placed within it, and, as at Holzhausen, the post was smeared with blood.[15] While the time and geographical distance between the two sites rules out a direct connection, if the beliefs behind them stemmed from a similar understanding of the world (resulting, in part, from trance journeys) then such coincidences become easier to explain.

At Fellbach-Schmiden, also in Germany, a shaft had animal carvings at its base, which had perhaps fallen in from once decorating its exterior.[16] It is also possible, however, that these were surrogate sacrifices and stood for the animals they represented.

At Acy-Romance in France, all the themes of these ritual places seem to converge.[17] The site comprised a settlement with associated cemetery, and in this regard was quite unremarkable. However, within the settlement was a D-shaped sanctuary. The arrangement of animal remains around it was very similar to other sites, with cattle skulls and attached spines inside the enclosure and sheep remains (excluding skulls and spines) outside it. Alongside was a row of buildings, possibly shrines, one of which had a shaft at its heart, although most of the items recovered there were also found around the houses. If these were shrines, then they formed an extension to everyday activities rather than falling outside them. To the north of the enclosure, the direction associated with death in the hillforts, was a group of 19 bodies, all men and all probably sacrificed. The bodies were aligned on the enclosure ditch, indicating that even after the grisly act of sacrifice, people still wanted to order the dead.

In the previous chapter we came across other human remains, which were placed in grain storage pits. Although they are known from France,[18] the most detailed analysis has occurred in southern England.[19] As we have seen, the bodies were often hacked to pieces after death, although some might have also had a violent end beforehand. A number were bound, or had their hands tied, while others were covered with large blocks of stone, holding their remains firmly in place. Although clothing would not have survived in the pits, the lack of any fastenings suggests that the people were left naked. Like the bodies at Acy-Romance, most were adults, with children only found in shallow scoops at the top of the pits after they had been filled, as if parents wanted their offspring to be close to the people at their base. Some pits contained the remains of birds, such as ravens, perhaps placed there as guides to the afterlife.[20] In chapter 38 we saw how the dead in Spain were given to vultures for a similar purpose. Some of the bodies at Danebury had been branded with a red-hot sword on their face, most often on the left side.[21]

It seems clear that these were special people and that they were marked (sometimes quite literally with branding on their faces) for special treatment. If they were sacrifices, and some had definitely been decapitated at the point of death, their location within the storage pits suggests that they had a special role to fulfil. This was where the dead grain of winter transformed into the living seed of spring, its death leading to eventual rebirth. The specialists in these matters were the shamans, and if that is what the people in the pits were, then perhaps they met their deaths willingly, knowing that they had tasks to fulfil which went beyond their mortal confines. More will become clear in chapter 45, when we consider another group of sacrificed individuals and place each aspect surrounding the death of the pit bodies into a wider context.

Towards the end of the Iron Age, sanctuaries and Viereckschanzen were increasingly associated either with major towns or chiefly settlements.[22] At Montmartin in France, for example, a high-status settlement had its own sanctuary sealed within it, and at Bopfingen in Germany, a Viereckschanze was located inside a major town.[23] Even at Gournay-sur-Aronde, an oppida (Caesar's term for a fortified town in the Classical style) developed next to the sanctuary, as if certain people were trying to control and appropriate its role. In southern England, although shrines were still constructed at hillforts (the largest shrine at Danebury, for example, and those at South Cadbury, were probably constructed after the hillforts were abandoned),[24] others moved to large and, in particular, 'royal' towns where the emerging aristocracy lived. Hayling Island, for example, was such a place and had its own shrine with associated offerings of weapons and animal remains.[25] It seems that the attempt by the elite to appropriate the role of the sanctuaries by taking broken weapons to the grave, had now accelerated and ritual was now contained within the chief settlements, and presumably also controlled by those that lived there: the aristocracy.

It seems that as soon as the living had felt secure in their claims to the land, the thoughts of the elite had turned to their own advancement. Their motivation for such social climbing lay far to the south, where a new people offered the delights of civilisation to those who would ape their ways. However, these people were not like the Mediterranean powers of the past; they were not happy simply to trade with the north, they wanted to own and control it. The living may have subjugated the dead and made their remains into macabre bone houses, but their victory was soon to ring hollow. A force was emerging that would rip apart the traditions of the Iron Age, and eventually subjugate both the living and the dead in equal measure. The emerging aristocracy were about to see their new world fall apart.

Chapter 44

STORM IN THE SOUTH

Julius Caesar was 42 years old when he began his conquest of Gaul. He was 51 by the time it was over and he could declare that peace prevailed. Along the way, out of 3 million fighting Gauls, he had killed a million, taken another million as slaves, and left an untold number maimed and injured. As Caesar discovered: when there is nobody left to fight, you have peace.[1]

Caesar led the army of Rome, or at least the part that was allotted to him. At the time, it was the most powerful force in the world, but this had not always been so. When we left the Mediterranean in chapter 40, the Greeks and the Carthaginians were the forces to be reckoned with; Rome was just another Italian city with a dream of grandeur. That changed with Hannibal, the Spanish Carthaginian who came within a sword's width of defeating the nascent power of Rome and altering the course of European history. That he failed was to prove disastrous for Carthage when Rome took revenge in the Third Punic War. Hannibal's home city of Carthage was not just conquered, it was wiped off the map. The Greeks, meanwhile, rapidly gave way to their more powerful neighbour and fell under Roman sway. Rome now controlled the region and, with good reason, rechristened the Mediterranean as *Mare Nostrum*: Our Sea.[2]

The ruthlessness shown at Carthage set the tone for Roman military might and, yet, it also pulled Rome into a spiral of war and conquest that was to last another 300 years before Hadrian called a halt to expansion and built the wall through England that still bears his name.[3] Barry Cunliffe, an expert on this period, sees the spiral originating with the need for men to join the army and fight the wars.[4] This inevitably led to depopulation of rural areas and, as a consequence, families that could no longer manage to farm without their men, migrated to the cities. Rome, for example, had a population of 1 million by the turn of the millennium. These people needed to be fed and, after an edict in 58 BC, wheat was freely provided to all. This welfare state needed to be paid for, of course, which it was through taxes collected from conquered lands.[5] Meanwhile, the wealthy families (their affluence being sizably supplemented through war loot) snapped up the now empty countryside and created vast estates.[6] They needed people to farm them, and if these people also came free it would allow for greater profits. The demand for slaves rocketed: over a million worked in Italy by 50 BC, most originating from the conquered territories.[7] The threat of insurrection was an ever-present fear but after 6000 slaves had been crucified following the revolt led by Spartacus in 73 BC, it would have taken a brave soul to try it. Besides, their owners found that a well-kept slave would breed more readily, thus adding to the workforce with little additional outlay. These estates also needed an outlet for their produce, and where better than a pacified land where people craved the trappings of civilisation?[8] Populations could also be supplemented by resettling retired soldiers, keeping many grumpy and possibly disaffected old men out of harm's way.

It was not only slave revolts that gave Rome nightmares, but also the memories of the Celts and their sack of the city in 390 BC. The words of Brennus still rang loud in many ears. Therefore, when a complex sequence of events was initiated by tribes migrating from the north in 120 BC, the citizens of Rome had reason to catch their breath.[9] The Cimbri and Teutones, both Germanic tribes, moved south from Denmark and onto a collision course with Rome. In 113 BC, the wandering Cimbri attacked the Celtic kingdom of Noricum (now a part of Austria), a valuable trading partner for Rome.[10] The Roman army was sent out to crush the Celts and, somewhat unexpectedly, was roundly defeated. The Cimbri, instead of pillaging Rome as its population feared, then moved west into Gaul, making sure to sack the wealth of northern Iberia on the way. Rome attempted to put them down twice more, and twice more were defeated, until Gauis Marius took the army by the collective scruff of its neck, injected some much needed reform, and set it loose once more. This time, the Celts were obliterated and Rome exhaled as one. It was another shock that was to weigh heavily in the years to follow.

After 100 BC, much of central Europe remained quiet. Oppida, the large towns described by Caesar, emerged, and these seemed to combine civic organisation with manufacturing output.[11] After raiding, the Celts seem to have found another forte in craftwork. They still drank, however, and wine poured into Gaul at a rate of 10 million litres a year. From the remains of the storage vessels, or amphorae, around the metalworking sites, either the smiths were inebriated while they worked or there was a connection between wine and the transformation of metal. Perhaps the production of one was linked to the other, or maybe the magical nature of metalworking was heightened with alcohol?[12]

The recorded rate of one slave per amphora of wine was probably optimistic but the Romans certainly knew the importance of commerce.[13] On the slightest pretence, the army was mobilised to secure trade routes, first into northern Italy and then into southern Gaul. The route to Britain, via the rivers Aube and Garonne, which we sailed in chapter 40, was still important and this too was brought under Roman control.[14] For a while, all was well.

It was the Germans again who started the trouble.[15] In a convoluted sequence of events, the Suebi, a German tribe led by Ariovistus, crossed the Rhine (to the

Romans, all Germans should remain on their side of the Rhine) to help the Sequani, a Celtic tribe, with their grievances with the Aedui. Meanwhile, the Helvetii, another Celtic tribe from Switzerland, wanted to move west to enjoy some sea air. It all coincided with a triumvirate being formed in Rome, where three of the wisest heads were brought together in the hope that they would lay their personal differences aside and put Rome first. One member was Julius Caesar, who, upon being elected Governor of Gaul (or, at least, the parts Rome legitimately controlled), lost no time in spinning wild tales about the whole country being lost to the German menace if Ariovistus and his kin were not driven back to the far side of the Rhine. In truth, he desperately needed a military campaign to distinguish himself from the other triumvirate members and this was his chance. The shock of previous incursions from barbarian hoards weighed heavily and Caesar was empowered to take necessary steps to resolve the issue. He set out in 58 BC. Nine years later, and having conquered Gaul as far as the English Channel, he considered the job done.[16]

Pushing back the Suebi, persuading the Helvetii to go home, and knocking collective heads together to quieten the Sequani and Aedui, was quickly accomplished and Caesar immediately headed north to invade Britain – a plan that, had it worked, would have secured him legendary status ahead of his time. Initially, he struck out from Belgium, where people friendly to Rome provided him with a stable platform. Caesar was canny, and rather than just lay the country to waste, he planned his campaigns carefully so that resistance was defeated without upsetting trade routes. These he maintained for later Roman exploitation. Those in the south spotted his ploy and immediately objected. Caesar had to abandon thoughts of Britain and head south to extinguish the insurrection. It was to be three more years of revolt and war before he managed to return.

One tactic that Caesar used to maintain the subjugation of tribes was to send the sons of prominent leaders to Rome for education. This was not a euphemism – Caesar meant what he promised. Of course, it probably helped to guarantee the good behaviour of the parents but it also indoctrinated a group of influential youngsters to the ways of Rome. Allies were made this way and it was a far-reaching policy that, chillingly, showed that Roman presence was no short-term arrangement. The advantages of a classical education meant that some leaders even willingly sent their offspring to Rome. While Caesar was doing his best to destroy the old way of life, it seems that some among the Celtic elite were also hastening its downfall.[17]

The elite may have thought that their position was inviolate. After all, the most serious impediment to building their fortunes had now been removed: the living had wrested ownership of the land away from the dead. Across northern Europe, houses were now rebuilt in the same place, even in those regions along the North Sea, which only two centuries ago were abandoned and rebuilt every generation or so.[18] In some places, such as Thy in Denmark, the rebuilt houses formed mounds, with the new house positioned on top of the debris of the old, as if people wanted to emphasise their newly won freedoms.[19] However, for some, the emphasis on permanence and inheritance did not just apply to the land that they farmed but also to the power that they wielded. Not only was land passed down through families but so too was position and influence and, consequently, family dynasties began to emerge.

We saw in the previous chapter how rich burials appeared at this time, just as broken weapons were given to the gods in ritual settings, some were now taking them to the grave, assuming a role that had previously been the preserve of ritual specialists, presumably the Vates and Druids. The preponderance of grooming items within the same graves, the like of which we have not seen since the beautiful warriors of the Bronze Age, suggests that these people wanted to be admired when laid out in the grave and presumably remembered for the broken weapons that they held.[20]

Within certain settlements, houses appear that were set apart from others by fences or ditches.[21] Knowing what we do about the importance of enclosure, it was a powerful message of individuality and permanence. Within southern England, a new type of house emerged, and unlike the majority, these were rectangular. Anyone living in one would have stood out, which is presumably what they wanted, and John Creighton, a specialist on this period, knows why. The youngsters that had been sent to Rome for their upbringing had begun to return and they brought new ideas and customs with them. Decades before the Claudian invasion of AD 43, Rome had arrived in Britain.[22] Graves now betrayed their Roman influence, and in a manner similar to the broken weapons, Creighton interprets the numerous vessels that often accompany the dead as tools with which to perform Roman sacrifices.[23] Again, the elite were challenging the hegemony of the Druids and may even have turned their backs on the Celtic gods, preferring instead the Roman deities. Certainly, in Denmark, items appear in graves that were previously placed in rivers or bogs, presumably as offerings to the gods. Perhaps the people doing this even believed that they were divine themselves?[24]

The elite may still have dispensed bounty to the people, even tossing gold at their feet as we saw in chapter 37, but there was now a subtle difference to their largesse. Their gifts were now coinage, and stamped upon every one was the face and name of the chief, or as the paramount leaders increasingly liked to style themselves, *Rex* – king.[25] There was never any doubt about where the riches originated, even if they were reused. Again, there were attempts to usurp the role of the Druids and many of the coins had phosphenes incorporated into their designs, often alongside images showing shapeshifting beasts, or images of the sun.[26] Even the food the elite consumed aped the traditions of Rome, with pig becoming the choice delicacy.[27] Pigs also had the added attribute of having no other use besides eating; they were another means of displaying decadence.

There were even changes in those parts that Caesar avoided: the lands of the so-called Germans, north of the Rhine. Finding them mad for war, he later concluded that their temperament made them ungovernable.[28] Perhaps it was a compliment? Fences appeared around some settlements in Denmark around 200 BC, although the locations of these early villages still seemed to shift over time.[29] It was not until a little later that single large houses appeared and formed the focus of new permanent settlements, such as Hodde, also in Denmark.[30] Here, the large house was set within its own enclosure and, from the remains of fine pottery found around it, its owners clearly hosted lavish entertainment.[31] Perhaps this was another way of distributing largesse, with those that received it beholden to the occupiers of the large house? Caesar, for example, writes of clientage in his memoires, a system whereby people worked the land for a leader, who would house and feed them in return and also ensure their safety in times of strife.[32]

Clientage may have been the manner in which much of the countryside was organised, in places giving the rising elite their first taste of political power. In urban and more densely populated areas, it seems that a tribal council of elders made decisions, with strict rules limiting the power of any single family.[33] Clearly, the threat of dynasties forming was taken seriously, and since some of these elders were likely to have been Druids (the training was so lengthy that almost by definition, practising Druids would have been old), the threats to the religious hierarchy would not have gone unnoticed. Indeed, Caesar records two occasions when a wannabe king was executed for his impudence.[34] Perhaps this was why many of the rich graves arose outside the oppida: the emerging aristocracy were putting distance between themselves and the traditions that they were challenging.[35]

However, there was one occasion when a leader could emerge to take individual and far-reaching control over the tribes: war. The Roman offensive had given the burgeoning elite exactly what they needed to seize power. It is perhaps revealing that many of the rich graves of the time contain cavalry equipment, and horses seem to have taken on the symbolism of leadership, often appearing on coins.[36] Caesar even comments that there were just two classes of people at the time: Druids and Knights.[37] It seems that in times of war, the former handed power to the latter. This certainly happened in Gaul, when Vercingetorix, whose own father had been one of those put to death for designs of kingship, was hailed as leader of all the tribes.[38] Like Hannibal before him, Vercingetorix came within a whisper of success before his last, desperate stand at Alesia ended with him prostrate before the all-powerful Caesar. The defeated Celt was shipped back to Rome in chains and had to wait five long years in prison before being present at Caesar's homecoming triumph. His starring role was to be strangled to death.

In southern England, Caesar's conquest of Gaul led to increased trade, and people used this time of bounty to make themselves rich. However, time was not on their side, and it is likely that they knew it. Richard Bradley suggests that people can either submit to the passing of time or seek to control it.[39] In the past, time was measured by the sun, its movement across the sky determining the arrangement of the Iron Age world. People would have observed the same movement, year upon year, until they found themselves in a timeless present, where everything seemed held in an eternal cycle. In the decades before the turn of the millennium, people started to order time differently and a calendar appeared at Coligny in southern France.[40] Divided into months and days, it also showed agricultural festivals, determined by date and not by the celestial seasons. Revealingly, swords started to have images of the sun and moon engraved upon them, as if the elite wanted to demonstrate their control over these heavenly bodies.[41] It is almost as if they were attempting to steal time itself. Moreover, the language of the calendar was Latin, not Celtic; it was another spear in the side of tradition.

The Druid elders were the last line of defence against the onslaught of Rome; their destruction would come later. Meanwhile, the elite had been proved wrong: Rome was no friend. What the Romans brought was not civilisation but enslavement.[42] By the turn of the millennium, Rome had over 2 million slaves and needed more every year. What were the people to do? The solution was as dramatic as it was shocking. Blood would have to flow like never before.

Chapter 45

THE STAIN OF BLOOD

It is dusk and the mist rolls off the moor to cocoon the village where we have spent the day. We now wait with the rest of the community for the woman to appear. When she finally steps out of her house into the chill of the evening, her body is covered only by a thin woollen cloak; beneath it she is quite naked. As she briefly turns, we notice that her hair has been roughly cut from the right side of her head; on the left side it still falls to her shoulders. Her gait is unsteady and it is clear that her spine twists as if the bones have grown crooked. As she passes close to where we stand, we notice that she is young; we are later told that she has seen only 16 summers. She does not look at the community as she heads purposefully towards the moor. We follow her route, keeping a respectful distance behind her. Once the woman arrives at the edge of the peat, she is joined by two others, a woman and a man. She shrugs off her cloak, and, her body looking pale in the fading light, leans forwards so that her head draws close to the man. He slips a thin band around her neck and, wrapping it three times about her, pulls it taught: a slipknot betraying its deadly intent. The woman immediately stiffens, her muscles contorting against the pressure to her throat. Phlegm forms on her lips and her eyes grow wide in alarm, and yet she makes no attempt to resist what is happening. The man pulls the band still tighter and the woman spasms; her back twists painfully and it is clear that she is losing her grip on this world. Suddenly she falls, and the man catches her limp form almost tenderly. His accomplice, who has stood unmoved all this time, immediately draws a knife and plunges it into the still form of the dying woman. The blade finds an artery and blood begins to pour from the wound, its colour a dull black in the crepuscular light. All around us, people are silent; our own thudding heartbeats are the only sounds we hear.

Peat cutting not only provides material for burning, it also occasionally reveals a perfectly preserved body. These bodies date to all periods of the past but there seems to have been a concentration of them during the transition from the late Iron Age to the period of Roman domination.[1] Although there was considerable variety among the events leading to death, there are several characteristics which suggest that there was a definite pattern to the executions. Strangest of all of these were the victims' apparent willingness to die. There were very few signs of struggle or resistance, as if people accepted or even acquiesced to their fate.[2] Perhaps the respect with which their remains were treated after death, often being laid in the bog with care, sometimes even on a prepared bed of cotton grass, offered a sense of comfort and reassurance?[3] However, it is also possible that in the mind of the victim, they did not expect to die at all, regardless of the horrendous treatment that was meted out to them. Despite giving up their lives, these people may have expected to transcend death, their souls surviving their corporeal form to journey permanently to the otherworlds. The fact that they were killed, and their mortal remains placed within the watery confines of a bog, possibly assisted the transition from one world to the other. These were the shamans of the community, maybe even members of the Druid priesthood, and they had work to attend to on behalf of those they had left behind.

There are many characteristics of the bog bodies that match what we know of historical shamans. The woman who we saw killed, known as Yde Girl because of her young age and from the region of the Netherlands in which she was found, displays several of these idiosyncrasies. We noticed that she walked with a pronounced gait, and this was because she suffered from idiopathic scoliosis, a condition that would have emerged and steadily worsened during adolescence.[4] Zweeloo Woman, also from the Netherlands, walked with a similar gait on account of having shortened limbs, a condition called dyschondrosteosis, that would have also emerged during adolescence.[5] Kayhausen Boy, from Germany, was another adolescent who could not walk properly.[6] In shamanic communities, such afflictions are often believed to be a sign of having been touched by the spirits, similar to the initiatory sickness we explored in chapter 39.[7] Such people lived on the margins of their communities and these liminal locations are immediately associated with the boundaries that the shamans cross from one world to the other. Perhaps the afflictions in the bog bodies were especially significant because they emerged at adolescence, when a child crosses another boundary to adulthood? Other odd physical characteristics were also celebrated by shamanic communities, such as having an extra finger or thumb.[8] This may be why Lindow Man, from England, who we met in the introduction to this book, was chosen to die: he had a second thumb.[9] Lindow Man had also let his fingernails grow, and these were well manicured, suggesting that he did little manual work.[10] To the Nenets of Siberia, long fingernails were a sign of a person's calling to shamanism. They were a visual reminder of the status of the shaman as well as removing their owners from heavy physical work.[11] Even among the bog bodies, several show signs of having had a comfortable existence. Some bodies, such as Borremose Woman II and Haraldskjær Woman, both from Denmark, were well nourished and even plump.[12] Others, such as Grauballe Man and Borremose Man, both also from Denmark, had notably unblemished hands.[13] These people would have served their communities all their lives and so perhaps it was to be expected that they would have been looked after (although Windeby Girl, from Germany, had marks on her bones revealing times when food was short, so existence was not always easy).[14] However, the last journey that the bog bodies undertook for their communities was particularly special and it ended their lives. What was so terrible that it would have driven them to such extreme lengths?

In the previous chapter, we saw how the irrepressible power of Rome was marching north to conquer and subjugate more and more of free Europe. Even in those places that Rome did not reach, such as the lands of the Germans north of the Rhine, Roman influence was still apparent and the elites of the tribes had turned their backs on the spirits and were even seeking to usurp their position. Something had to be done and it was the people whose remains lie in the bogs that were prepared to give the ultimate sacrifice. They entered permanently into the otherworlds in order to beg the spirits for their aid. With their shamans gone, however, it was vital that the communities they left behind remember their sacrifice and keep alive the memory of the old ways. This was probably why the bog bodies died in such horrific ways: so that the people would remember what they had witnessed forever.

As we have seen ourselves, the death of the bog bodies was dramatic. Yde Girl was strangled and stabbed, while Lindow Man was garrotted and clubbed and still had his throat slashed, unleashing a torrent of blood. Others were strangled, hanged, or simply decapitated.[15] It is curious that most of the treatment centred on the head, as if this made the violence more prominent and visible for those watching the unfolding drama. What people witnessed was designed to be shocking and psychologists have long recognised the ability of the mind to remember such events with startling accuracy.[16] Furthermore, traumatic events are more likely to retain their vividness, becoming sharper with time and this is especially true of extreme violence.[17] A striking backdrop, such as at the edge of a bog, only adds to later recall.[18] Moreover, even after death, the violence to the bog bodies did not stop, and many were stabbed or hacked even as they lay inert on the ground. Huldremose Woman, from Denmark, had her limbs hacked off after death, and Borremose Woman II had her skull smashed.[19] This violence seems particularly gratuitous, unless it also fits the pattern of a shaman's journey to the otherworld.

In many shamanic communities, when first meeting his or her helping spirits, the shaman is ritually 'killed' and dismembered.[20] This is a common experience of trance and is probably caused by the disintegration of the self and the fear impulse of the amygdala that we explored in chapter 5. During dismemberment, the initiate may be defleshed, hacked into pieces, and even boiled in a cauldron.[21] Interestingly, at Býči Skála, in the Czech Republic, 40 Iron Age individuals, mostly women, had been dismembered in a cavern. At the centre of the remains was a cauldron. The similarity to shamanic initiation is further enhanced by pieces of dismembered horse which were found among the human remains – an animal which was, as we have already seen, readily associated with crossing between the worlds.[22] It is likely that the brutal slaying and dismemberment of the bog bodies was part of their journey to the otherworlds: what was happening to their souls was enacted physically on their bodies. The slaying of these individuals became an appalling performance.

In order to set the scene for their killing, the bog bodies may have prepared as they would have done for any other shamanic journey. While each individual would have had different habits, leading to significant variety in detail, there are certain themes that are still evident. Many individuals met their deaths naked, or with just a token item of clothing, some worn inside out.[23] Tolland Man, for example, wore only a cap, and Lindow Man had an armband of fox fur, itself perhaps relating to an animal totem. Elling Woman, from Denmark, had a cape, worn inside out.[24] Many historical shamans also undressed before journeying to the spirits, or wore token items of clothing, such as a hat, or put their clothes on back-to-front.[25] Some bog bodies were bound before death, such as Kayhausen Boy, who was bound with his own clothing, or Elling Woman, who had her feet tied.[26] Windeby Girl, from Germany, by contrast, was blindfolded.[27] Again, this reflects historical shamanic practice, with binding or blindfolding often part of the journey to the otherworld.[28] In many cases, the shamans were expected to free themselves of their bonds with the aid of the spirits.[29] With the bog bodies, binding could also occur after death and some bodies were fixed into the bog with hurdles. Others were covered with branches or stones.[30] Perhaps this was to emphasise that while the body was immovable, the soul of the individual was flying free?

When we witnessed the death of Yde Girl, we noticed that half of her head had been shaved; the same happened to Windeby Girl. Huldremose Woman and Borremose Woman II were completely scalped before death but their severed locks were then left with the body.[31] In other cases, the hair was not cut and Elling Woman, for example, had a very elaborate coiffure.[32] The emphasis given to hair matches the violence inflicted on the skull and seems to echo the Celtic preoccupation with the head that we explored in chapter 37. Certainly, in shamanic communities, the head and, by extension, the hair, is often seen as containing the soul of an individual.[33] Cutting the hair is, therefore, akin to freeing the soul.

Some bog bodies may have even heightened their experiences through ingesting hallucinogenic drugs. Grauballe Man, for example, had eaten ergot before his death, a powerful hallucinogen that we explored in chapters 35 and 38. However, more recent research has questioned whether the amount ingested was sufficient to induce trance by itself.[34]

Most bog bodies were buried alone in the bog but at Weerdinge, in the Netherlands, two men were found arm-in-arm.[35] For some, this immediately brought to mind the account of the Roman historian Tacitus, who commented that the punishment for homosexuality was drowning in a bog.[36] While Tacitus may have had his facts correct, in that some of the bog bodies were homosexual, his comment that they were being punished for it was, perhaps, an assumption too far. We have seen in chapter 39 how those who crossed gender and sexual boundaries were often believed to have the same ability to cross the boundary between the worlds and become a shaman. Whether the same was true of the bog bodies becomes more apparent when we consider other figures found in the bogs.

Wooden figurines were left in the bogs during the period just prior to that of the bog bodies, perhaps revealing the increasing tempo of a tradition that eventually led to the real bodies we have been looking at.[37] Certainly, the treatment of the figurines seems to match that of the bog bodies. The Ballachulish figurine from Scotland, for example, was covered with wickerwork and poles, the Bad Doberan figurine from Germany was covered with branches, and the Foerlev Nymølle and Broddenbjerg figurines, both from Denmark, were covered with stones.[38] The Rebild Skovmose figurine, from Denmark, was found with a large piece of woven material, possibly imitating the capes found with some of the bog bodies.[39] The Corlea figurine from Ireland, and also one of the Wittemoor figurines from Germany, had less weathering on the neck than on the rest of the body, suggesting that something had been tied around it, possibly in imitation of strangling that was later meted out to the bog bodies.[40] It seems that, before the concentration of actual bodies left in the bogs, the wooden figurines provided surrogates.

Most figurines were roughly carved, only broadly approximating a human shape, and this may have served to emphasise those features that were represented, such as the sexual organs. Moreover, in many cases, all that remains is a pubic hole, which may have been designed to hold a phallus, thereby signifying a male, or may have simply been a vulva, thereby signifying a female.[41] However, it is possible that the figurine could have been different sexes at different times, or even neither. We have already seen how crossing such boundaries is an attribute particularly associated with shamanism. One of the earliest historically recorded gods to have emerged from the lands of the bog bodies was Odin, and it is curious that he also straddled gender roles in his quest for shamanic knowledge.[42] This knowledge only came when Odin gave up an eye and it is striking that the Ballachulish figurine, the Ralaghan figurine from Ireland, and one of the Roos Carr figurines from England, were all damaged in this way.[43] Furthermore, while the Broddenbjerg figurine from Denmark was not damaged, its left eye was almost blank, possibly indicating blindness.[44]

All of these figurines were damaged in the left eye and this brings to mind the bodies buried in the disused grain storage pits that we met in chapter 43, which were branded, often above the left eye. Indeed, some of the figurines, such as the Ussen figurine from the Netherlands and the Bad Doberan figurine from Germany, were even found in pits.[45] This seems to draw the traditions of the bog bodies and the pit bodies together and it is striking that many of the features of the pit bodies we explored in chapter 43, such as the violence of their deaths, their dismemberment, their binding, their nakedness, and the fact that many were weighed down with stones, mirrors the characteristics of the bog bodies. There is even the likelihood that some of the individuals were disabled and had difficulty walking, again mirroring characteristics of the bog bodies.[46] However, if the bogs held particular resonance as places where the veil to the otherworld was thin, the storage pits were also resplendent with images of death and rebirth; heady locations indeed for those who expected to live on in the otherworlds.

The individuals killed and then placed into storage pits or abandoned to the bog were the shamans of the communities, perhaps representing or even being overseen by the Druidic priesthood. The drama of their last moments and the savagery of their deaths meant that they would be remembered. Through them, the spirits would remain central to people's lives. It was a last, desperate gamble to stop the advance of Rome but, ultimately, it was doomed to fail. The sacrifice of these people was for nothing.

As the life of the woman gives way, the man lowers her limp form to the ground. He lays her in the marsh almost with tenderness, his kindness in stark contrast to his murderous act. There is still no sound from those about us: no cries, no keening, no exclamation. People only bow their heads in honour of what the woman has done for them. But how do we make sense of what we have witnessed this night? I turn to you. We do not belong in this world. It is time to return home.

Coda

IN THE GRIP OF
THE EAGLE

The Druid stands high above the shore as the might of Rome assembles on the far bank. She knows that they have come for her and all those of her kind. The massed ranks of her warband crowd before her, shrieking their curses to the winds and clamouring to be the first at the foe, should he finally dare cross to their island home. Carynxes boom and a thunderous beat is played out through the clash of sword on shield. In that moment, the Romans are fearful; she can feel it. Suddenly, the Roman commander, the one they call Paulinus, unleashes his ballistae and vats of burning oil crash among the warriors. Iron bolts follow, pinioning flesh to shield as more brave warriors fall. Panic rises like bile through the ranks. Then, and only then, does the army of Rome come forward. Flat-bottomed boats ferry the troops, while the cavalry wade or even swim to the battle. The warriors unleash spears with their curses but they have little impact against a Roman shield. Too soon, the army reaches the shore and forms a cruel line of spike and shield. The warriors of the tribes surge to meet them and the battle boils. Too many brave warriors throw themselves upon the line, wasting their life's blood to the slash of a Roman sword. The Druid lifts her hands to the heavens and, invoking all the spirits of old, hurls her own curses into the maelstrom. Around her, others scream invective and the women tear at their clothes in fury. Some fly towards the battle carrying brands of fire, as if their heat might drive the hated soldiers back into the sea. But the Roman line is like iron and, inexorably, it moves up the shore as the warriors are forced to retreat. The Druid shrieks her entreaties to the spirits: crush this foe, let him not defile our groves. But, in her heart, she knows that nothing will stop the grip of the eagle. Many will die, in battle and in the violent aftermath; the sacred groves will burn. Will everything of the Druid's world end this day?

Tacitus writes of the attack on Anglesey, the home of the Druids, and the terrible repercussions that followed.[1] He describes the fear of the Romans, the dreadful curses of the watching Druids, the frenzied women with their flaming brands, the crossing of the army and, finally, the destruction of the groves. One might think he was even there. Tacitus excuses the massacre on Anglesey because of the Druids'

236

penchant for human sacrifice, but the Romans gave far more to the gods in their arenas, so he is probably being economical with the truth. More likely was that the Druids had become too powerful and were inciting revolt. We saw in chapter 38 how they had provided a rallying point for resistance to occupation in Gaul and it is likely that they were now doing the same in Britain.[2] Their adherence to the spirits also conflicted with Rome, where noble families traced their bloodlines back to the gods themselves. We have seen in chapter 44 how the elite of the unconquered lands had started to take for themselves what had once been offered to the gods and perhaps these people considered themselves equally divine. If so, then it was a Roman belief. Some may have even adopted Roman gods; the cults of Mars and Hercules, for example, had no Celtic equivalent and yet became popular in Gaul with the advance of Rome.[3]

Prasutagus may have also worshipped Roman gods; he certainly seemed to assist the Romans in quashing a revolt among his tribe, the Iceni, in 48 AD.[4] That may have been why he was made king shortly thereafter: the Romans rewarding a dependable ally. When he died in 60 AD, his wife expected to inherit his lands for herself and for her daughters, but the rules of Rome did not work like that. The lands were forfeit, the protesting wife flogged, and her daughters raped for their impertinence. With the army otherwise occupied crushing the Druids in Anglesey, it was a grave mistake. The scorned wife rose up to foment a revolt that came within a spear's length of crushing the Romans in Britain. Her name was Boudica.[5]

Before battle, Cassius Dio tells us that Boudica sought the help of the goddess of war, Andraste, as well as releasing a hare from the folds of her cloak to divine the outcome of the conflict.[6] It seems clear that, for her, the spirits of old were still alive to the fortunes of their followers. Moving to sack the Roman settlements of Colchester, London, and possibly also St Albans, Boudica's cruel and bloody advance was only halted when Suetonius Paulinus, the conqueror of Anglesey, was recalled with his troops and met the revolt somewhere in the English Midlands.[7] Boudica's warriors were so sure of victory that they encircled the battlefield with carts in order that those watching could get a better view.[8] These were the same carts that later prevented their escape as their force was crushed by the might of Rome. If anything, the aftermath was more brutal than it had been on Anglesey and even the spectators and baggage animals were slain, perhaps in revenge for Boudica's earlier atrocities.[9] The suppression of the tribes of Britain continued until Paulinus was recalled and replaced with a man of gentler temperament.[10] The veteran general was not a man for whom forgiveness came easily.

With the Druids gone, and seemingly the last flame of rebellion extinguished, was this to be the end of the spirits and the beliefs we have traced since the Ice Age? New research in the lands of the Dobunni, the Iron Age tribe of the Cotswolds, suggests otherwise.

From studying the carvings left by the Iron Age Dobunni, and the rich graves dating to the Roman occupation, Stephen Yeates from the University of Oxford has noticed that the people seemed to venerate a goddess holding a vessel.[11] As we have seen in chapter 38, cauldrons and other vessels were often left in bogs or lakes, probably as prestigious gifts to the spirits. Moving forward into the early medieval period, the people occupying the Dobunni lands became known as 'Hwicce', a name Stephen Yeates has broken down to mean 'witches of the sacred vessel'.[12] Witches were those who interacted with the supernatural and it may be that the vessel they venerated was the same as that held sacred by the Dobunni many hundreds of years previously. It may even have been that the goddess herself remained unchanged; it seems that in other regions where the Celtic gods were superseded by Roman equivalents, goddesses retained their unique identity.[13] While much changed for the people of the Cotswolds from the pre-Roman Iron Age to the early medieval period, it seems that their spiritual beliefs retained a degree of continuity. Even the church minsters followed the same divisions of the land laid out by the Dobunni, and the Christian crosses that eventually became the focus of religious veneration may have been no more than transcribed tree-posts, the gateways to another world for count-less generations.[14]

In those lands not occupied by the Romans, such as Ireland, the Druids may have remained unmolested, eventually becoming part of the Celtic church itself.[15] Certainly, Druids were featured in the Irish Law tracts until at least the sixth century AD.[16] Even some of the old beliefs may have survived, such as shapeshifting and rein-carnation. The fact that an ecclesiastic, Augustinus Hibernicus, recalls these practices with such polemic, suggests that they were still widespread beliefs at the time of his writing in the seventh century AD.[17]

In Gaul, Pliny records that the Druids were put down during the reign of Tiberius, in the early years of the first century AD.[18] Nevertheless, in the imperial biographies, the existence of female Druids was recorded from the third century AD, showing that there may have been pockets where the old beliefs survived.[19] However, both of these references are to seership and it may be that only this least offensive aspect of Druidry (at least to Roman eyes) was allowed to continue. The apparently odious practice of human sacrifice disappeared, except for a curious tale told by an eighth-century historian of early Britain, Nennius. He records that, in the fifth century AD, when King Vortigern could not build a tower without it collapsing, his wise men, perhaps his Druids, recommended that no building could stand until a child was sacrificed and its blood covered the ground.[20] As in Gaul, perhaps these wise men also included wise women and, if so, then it may explain why King Alfred passed laws in the ninth century AD that banned women from contact with magic.[21] The seeds of the later witch trials had been sown.

From the Scandinavian lands of the far north, we have already met Odin, one of the gods of the native religion, and seen his connection with earlier shamanic practice. Indeed, the Viking tradition seems to be replete with shamanism and it is curious that the last surviving shamanic peoples in Europe, the Sámi, also come from these lands.[22] However, whether shamanism was ever practised by the Anglo-Saxons to the south, is a moot point.[23] The Norse sagas suggest that it could have been, with Thorbjorg, the female seer, carrying a bag of magical amulets[24] that seem to mirror objects found in many graves of the Anglo-Saxons.[25] Over time, however, paganism gave way to a new religion.

The widespread adoption of Christianity into Europe changed the experience of spirituality, with the Church and priesthood now providing the medium for approaching the divine. However, for ordinary people, such change may not have been as marked as first appears. The Druids had established the role of a priesthood during the Iron Age and many churches were built in places that had been sacred for centuries. The greater change was the attitude that the otherworlds were locations people only visited on death and, even then, the route that they took depended on their deeds throughout life and their acceptance of the Christian doctrine. Similarly, spirits became either entities of extreme good – the angels and the saints – or else extreme evil – the devils and the demons. Again, however, this would not have been difficult for people to understand (the spirits always were capricious), but accusations of consorting with such evil was a new development, leading to the persecution and execution of scores of innocents during the early modern period.[26] The sixteenth and seventeenth centuries saw a confused attitude towards spirituality, with witchcraft and anything associated with it condemned, at the same time that popular magic flourished.[27] The protestant reformation sought to remove this ambiguity and introduce a more rational way of looking at the world. Science was in the ascendancy and the subsequent era of enlightenment did much to banish superstition.[28]

Such banishment extended into those parts where shamanic beliefs still held sway, such as the Sámi lands in the far north of Scandinavia. Following traditions that may have survived for millennia, the conversion of the Sámi was as sudden as it was brutal.[29] It is ironic, therefore, that while much of the ethnographic past of Europe was being destroyed, the same zeal led to the discovery and celebration of a far older material past. In time, the practice of archaeology, or at least of antiquarianism, was born. Bizarrely, the newfound interest in the past did not stop solely at uncovering ancient remains but also led to attempts to reconstruct how those remains might once have been used. Early antiquarians were not only pioneering excavators, some were also revivalist Druids.[30]

Today, there are revivals of a myriad of traditions, most claiming a degree of association, if not authenticity, with the past. Among them is shamanism. While its re-emergence in Siberia, and, to a far lesser extent, in the lands of the Sámi, is often accepted as legitimate,[31] its introduction into Western society receives a far more ambiguous response.[32] Anthropologist Merete Jakobsen, for example, compares Western shamanism with historical Inuit traditions and concludes that it is doubtful that what is offered today is really shamanism at all.[33] This is a curious reaction, since, as this book has shown, shamanism emerges from the neurophysiology of every modern human, whether he or she lived in the Palaeolithic, a historical Inuit community, or even in the heart of a modern metropolis. What differs is how these experiences are interpreted, used, and reflected in the ideas and lifestyles of those adopting them and not whether it is even possible to have the experiences in the first place. To conclude that shamanism is only real if it was practised in the past (historically or archaically) or is practised only in certain parts of the world is to set parameters that bear no relation to the authenticity of the experience or the efficacy of its results.

The experience of trance is a natural, useful, and convenient resource that lies within the capabilities of virtually everyone living today. The otherworlds are domains that can be accessed by all. Throughout the preceding pages, we have seen myriad examples of how the ancient people of Europe identified and represented their experiences of trance and the enlarged view of reality that this gave them. Although these representations changed over time, even today their underlying tenets cannot easily be dismissed. Our minds, after all, are identical to theirs. However, whether we call the denizens of the otherworlds hallucinations or spirits depends to a large extent on our personal inclinations – shared neurophysiology can only take us so far. No amount of evidence will ever disprove the existence of the spirits across thousands of years of prehistory, just as no amount of evidence can ever disprove their existence today. What determines our own stance depends upon what we *believe*, and that is as true today as it has been throughout all human history. Did those that inhabited the Palaeolithic caves really see spirits, or did the painted walls merely reflect their own projections back at them? Their attitude seems clear; ours may be more variable. But then, people have always made the world by how they believe it to be; make believe makes belief, makes belief.

NOTES

Chapter 1

1. Arsuaga, Bermúdez de Castro, and Carbonell (1997) and discussion in Stringer and Andrews (2005) pp.152–3.
2. Stringer and Gamble (1993) chapter 3.
3. Gamble (1999) pp.175–94 examines the climate at the time of the Neanderthals.
4. Johanson and Edgar (1996) pp. 211–33 contains details of the best-preserved bodies.
5. Heim (1976).
6. Trinkus (1983) pp.401–13.
7. Solecki (1975).
8. Solecki (1972) p.178.
9. Movius (1953) pp.25–8.
10. Boule (1911–13).
11. Rak, Kimbel and Hovers (1994) pp.314–5.
12. Confusingly called the Berekhat Ram figurine, it is only 3cm tall. Marshak (1997); d'Errico and Nowell (2000).
13. For additional examples from Italy see Marquet and Lorblanchet (2003) and Milliken (2007) p.341.
14. Stringer and Gamble (1993) pp.158–9 for red ochre and Mithen (2005) pp.229–30 for manganese dioxide.
15. Turk, Dirjec and Kavur (1997) for the finding of the flute, and Kunej and Turk (2000) pp.249–64 for an analysis of the sounds it made.
16. J. Renfrew (2009) pp.54–6.

Chapter 2

1. Sommer (1999).
2. Movius (1953) pp.48–9.
3. Chase and Dibble (1987) pp.277–9.
4. The flint tools of the Neanderthals, called Mousterian, are easily differentiated from those of modern humans, called Aurignacian. However, in a handful of sites in France and Spain, a hybrid type of flint tool has been discovered, called Châtelperronian, that although rooted in the Mousterian tradition had clear modifications copied from the more advanced Aurignacian tradition. This is clearly the work of Neanderthals since

examples of these tools have been found with a Neanderthal burial. The Châtelperronian Neanderthals were the very last of their kind and are known to have copied other aspects of modern human behaviour, such as ornamentation. Chase (2007) provides an overview of the Châtelperronian.

5. This is called the 'Independent Invention Hypothesis', d'Errico (2003) pp.194–201; Langley, Clarkson and Ulm (2008).
6. This is called the 'Acculturation Hypothesis', Mellars (2005) pp.20–3; Hublin (2007); Tostevin (2007).
7. Stringer and Gamble (1993) pp.74–94 provides a physical description of Neanderthals.
8. Mithen (1998) chapter 8.
9. Wynn and Coolidge (2004).
10. Morley (2006).
11. Mithen (2005) chapter 15.
12. Lewis-Williams (2009) pp.136–8 comments on the morality of such criticism and the objections it can generate.
13. Zubrow (1989).
14. Richards and Schmitz (2008).
15. Marean (2007).
16. There is evidence that the very last Neanderthals were pushed to the southern reaches of Spain, where they hung on for a last few thousand years. Papers in Stringer, Barton and Finlayson (2000).
17. Klein (2009) pp.571–3.
18. Stringer and Gamble (1993) pp.161–8 think it unlikely that Neanderthals would have stored food for later consumption but there are some caves with unexplained pits that could have served this purpose, particularly at Combe Grenal, le Moustier and la Quina. Whether Neanderthals would have had the mental capacity to think through the implications of storage is another matter.
19. J. Renfrew (2009) pp.53–4 suggests that such cannibalism may even indicate ritual behaviour.
20. Only at Saint Césaire is there evidence of a Neanderthal having been brought to a cave to be buried. Bar-Yosef (2007) pp.210–11.
21. Stringer and Gamble (1993) p.160, comment that no Neanderthal burials have ever been found from open sites (where it would have been easier to dispose of the body in other ways), unlike modern human burials, where a number are known.
22. Duarte et al. (1999).
23. Genetic analysis indicates that there is negligible Neanderthal DNA in modern human populations, or even those who lived at the same time as the last Neanderthals: Caramelli et al. (2003), Lalueza-Fox et al. (2005). However, others claim that this is as a result of vanishingly small samples and such inter-breeding was probably commonplace; Neanderthals did not die out, therefore, but became a small part of us. Zilhão (2006).

Chapter 3

1. Bader (1978).
2. White (1993) pp.289–94.
3. *Ibid.* p.294.
4. Jacobi and Higham (2008). Most of the early modern burials of the Upper (later) Palaeolithic date to the Gravettian period, between 27,000 and 23,000 years ago, but the Red Lady may now belong to the earlier Aurignacian period, between 35,000 and 27,000 years ago.

5. Although the burial is referred to as the Red Lady, it is, in fact, a man. When the body was first discovered by William Buckland in 1823, he identified it as a customs officer, murdered by smugglers. By the time of his publication, this had changed to the far racier story that *she* was a prostitute servicing the Roman encampment on the bluff above the cave. In the event, neither story was correct, but the name Red Lady prevailed. Sommer (2007) provides a history of the find and its aftermath.
6. Aldhouse-Green (2000) provides a 'definitive' report.
7. Jenílek, Pelísek and Valoch (1959).
8. Bancroft Hunt (2003) chapter 1.
9. Oliva (1996).
10. The term 'shaman' has been used throughout the book to indicate a spiritual practitioner, notwithstanding the debate regarding the suitability of the term outside a historical Siberian context. Kehoe (2000).
11. Binant (1991) pp.127–31.
12. Svoboda (2006).
13. She had scoliosis of the spine, a deformed right leg, osteoarthritis to her arms and scaly red skin.
14. Commenting on this phenomenon, Taylor (2002) notes that three individuals at Barma Grande in Italy had osteophytosis, a body at Cro Magnon in France had the cancer-like condition histiocytosis X, and a skeleton from Ohalo 2 in Israel had chronic degenerative disease.
15. Lewis (1989) chapter 3.
16. Mussi (2001) p.256.
17. Mussi (1986) pp.548–9.
18. Svoboda et al. (1994) pp.459.
19. Emmerling, Geer and Klíma (1993).
20. Aldhouse-Green and Aldhouse-Green (2005) p.42; Klein (2009) p.694.
21. Aldhouse-Green and Aldhouse-Green (2005) p.40; Gamble (1999) p.409.
22. Aldhouse-Green and Aldhouse-Green (2005) pp.41–2 relates the covering of burials at this time to the later tradition of Sámi bear burials when the animal was covered to stop it rising again. However, Hoffecker (2002) pp.215–7 points out that in areas of tundra, where the ground is frozen below a metre or so, shallow burials are likely to have survived only if they had been covered in this way, with any others becoming easy prey for carnivores or being destroyed by frost heave. The sample may, therefore, be unrepresentative.

Chapter 4

1. Hominin is a term including human and *Australopithecine* species. Johanson and Maitland (1981) for the excavation of Lucy.
2. There are many books about human evolution but a good introduction is Stringer and Andrews (2005).
3. Leakey et al. (1995).
4. Dart (1967).
5. Grine (1988).
6. Leakey, Tobias and Napier (1964).
7. Dubois (1924); Rukang and Shenlong (1983). *H. erectus* may have given rise to the remarkable, diminutive species *H. floresiensis* (nicknamed 'the hobbit'), that lived until 12,000 years ago on the island of Flores in Indonesia. Brown et al. (2004).
8. Tools, but no human remains, have now been found in Pakefield and Happisburgh in

eastern England, dating to about 700,000 years ago (and possibly providing indirect evidence for a new variant of human, *H. antecessor*). Parfitt et al. (2005). Džaparidze et al. (1989) for the Dmanisi remains of *H. erectus*.

9. Gamble (1999) pp.123–4.

10. *H. heidelbergensis* may have evolved from *H. erectus* or, possibly, from yet another variant of human that spread out of Africa at approximately the same time, *H. ergaster*. A comprehensive study of *H. heidelbergensis* was undertaken at Boxgrove in southern England. Pitts and Roberts (1997).

11. Thorne and Wolpoff (1992).

12. Stringer and McKie (1996) pp.112–69.

13. For example, Oppenheimer (2003) pp.346–8.

14. The discussion of the brain comes from Mithen (1996), particularly chapter 4.

15. The gene associated with speech and language is FOXP2. Enard et al. (2002).

16. Mithen (2005) chapter 16.

17. Edelman (1994) pp.117–23.

18. *Ibid.* pp.131–6.

19. Wynn and Coolidge (2007).

20. Bourguignon (1973) p.11.

21. D'Aquili and Newberg (1999) pp.161–2.

22. Rossano (2007) p.51.

23. McClenon (2002) p.31.

24. Jablonka and Lamb (1995) pp.191–228 for the role of epigenetic inheritance systems in adaptive evolution.

25. Ludwig (1969) pp.18–20.

26. Such a positive trait (the ability to enter trance) would have given certain individuals better chances of survival and reproduction. Therefore, under the theory of natural selection, it would have been replicated and refined over time.

Chapter 5

1. It is the neurophysiology of the brain that is universal to all humans, meaning that the sensation of trance will be identical to all those who experience it. However, these sensations will be interpreted according to the cultural expectations and norms of those experiencing it. Accordingly, the universality of shamanism is neurological only. Culturally, it can be very different. Winkelman (1986).

2. Nunez and Srinivasan (2006) pp.215–43 on brain rhythms and Kasamatsu and Hirai (1966) for a case study of brain rhythm changes in deep meditative states.

3. The following is taken from D'Aquili and Newberg (1999) pp.23–7.

4. Heinze (1993).

5. I am following the stages of trance outlined by Siegel and Jarvik (1975).

6. Knoll et al. (1963); Oster (1970); Tyler (1978); Walker (1981).

7. Kellog, Knoll and Kugler (1965).

8. Graziand, Andersen and Snowden (1994).

9. Horowitz (1975) pp.183–6.

10. For example, Dobkin de Rios (1996) pp.131–2.

11. Halifax (1982) pp.23–4 and pp.86–7.

12. Lewis-Williams and Dowson (1990) p.10; Harner (1968) p.28.

13. Hoppál (1992); Basilov (1984) pp.48–9; Diószegi (1960) p.62.

14. D'Aquili and Newberg (1999) pp.100–1.

15. Slade and Bentall (1988) pp.69–70.

16. *Ibid.* p.114.
17. Siegel (1978) p.311.
18. Tooby and Cosmides (1992) pp.94–108 and Boyer (2000) for the theory, and Bourdieu (1990) and Bloch (1998) for worked examples.
19. Jung (1959).
20. Laughlin, McManus and d'Aquili (1992) for the theory and Swanson (1973) for an ethnographic example.
21. The distinction between the otherworld and the afterlife is too fine for it to be recognised in prehistory. People may have believed them to be the same place or viewed the afterlife as a separate realm contained within the otherworld. Different modern shamanic societies conceive of both possibilities although it is usually accepted that, when journeying to the otherworld, the shaman can interact with the dead. To make things easier, throughout the book, the otherworld will define the realm that is accessible by the shaman (which may also include interaction with the dead) whereas the afterlife will define the particular place where the dead reside.
22. Vitebsky (1995) pp.68–9.
23. Pearson (2002) p.97.
24. Harner and Tryon (1992).
25. McClenon (2002) pp.47–52.
26. In a study of people who had experienced spontaneous out-of-body experiences (i.e. those who were not predisposed to look for it), 88 per cent reported beneficial changes, including a heightened sense of spirituality. Mitchell (1985) p.68.

Chapter 6

1. Much of the information for this chapter comes from the comprehensive survey of cave art by Jean Clottes (2008).
2. Upon seeing the Hall of the Bulls at Lascaux, Pablo Picasso is reputed to have said, 'We have invented nothing'.
3. Henshilwood et al. (2002).
4. Donald (1991).
5. C. Renfrew (2009), although Henshilwood (2009) pp.41–5 thinks that the key changes occurred in Africa despite there being no evidence of a comparable 'symbolic explosion'.
6. Lewis-Williams and Dowson (1989).
7. Lewis-Williams and Dowson (1988); Clottes and Lewis-Williams (1996); Lewis-Williams (2002).
8. Bahn is perhaps the most vociferous opponent (2001) and Helvenston and Bahn (2002), although he is joined by Hodgson (2008).
9. Lewis-Williams and Dowson (1994) p.214.
10. Clottes (2008) pp.46–9.
11. *Ibid.* pp.106–7.
12. *Ibid.* pp.196–9.
13. Lewis-Williams (2002) p.37.
14. Clottes (2008) pp.124–5.
15. *Ibid.* pp.278–9 & pp.72–3.
16. Clottes (2009) pp.202–9.
17. Lewis-Williams (2002) p.216.
18. Sharpe and Van Gelder (2006).
19. Snow (2006).
20. Dowson (1998) p.73.

21. Mithen (2009) p.31 sees the images and the mind as developing in tandem, each inform-
    ing and being reflected in the other.
22. Lewis-Williams (2002) p.224.
23. Clottes (2008) pp.40–3.
24. *Ibid.* pp.120–1.
25. Lewis-Williams (1997).

Chapter 7
1. All quotes given to *National Geographic* News, 17 December 2003.
2. Conard (2003).
3. Clottes (2008) pp.54–5.
4. Zvelebil (1997) p.37; Zvelebil and Jordan (1999) p.109 & p.118.
5. Hahn (1993).
6. Dowson and Porr (2001).
7. Hamilton Cushing (1999).
8. Hahn (1986) pp.234–5.
9. Dowson and Porr (2001) p.169.
10. *Ibid.*
11. Hahn (1993) p.232.
12. Soffer and Vandiver (1997).
13. Soffer, Vandiver, Klíma and Svoboda (1993) pp.268–9.
14. Vandiver, Soffer, Klíma and Svoboda (1989) p.1007.
15. Ovsyannikov and Terebikhin (1994) p.54.
16. Clottes (2008) pp.66–7 and White (2003) for an assessment of prehistoric art.
17. All Palaeolithic female figurines are given the unfortunate moniker 'Venus', White (2003)
    pp.54–5.
18. Clottes (2008) pp.74–5.
19. *Ibid* p.74.
20. Tarassov (1995).
21. Praslov (1993).
22. Gvozdover (1995) pp.24–5. The pit also contained other items, including a 'wand' and the
    foot bone of a wolf fashioned from ivory, leading the excavator to believe that the entire
    assemblage had a ritual or magical use.
23. Mussi, Cinq-Mars and Bolduc (2000) pp.110–2.

Chapter 8
1. White (1989a) p.218.
2. Gamble (1999) p.329.
3. Henry-Gambier and White (2006).
4. Gamble (1999) pp.329–30; Morphy (1989).
5. White (1997) pp.96–7.
6. White (1989b) p.377.
7. Henshilwood et al. (2004).
8. Vanhaeren et al. (2006). The beads were found in graves from Skhul and Qafzeh in Israel,
   dating to between 120,000 and 80,000 years ago, suggesting the existence of modern (or,
   as they are sometimes called, transitional) humans long before Cro-Magnons moved into
   Europe at least 40,000 years later. It seems that modern humans might have migrated out
   of Africa during a warm period between glaciations around 125,000 years ago. When the

next (and last) Ice Age began, these people either died out or moved south again, leaving the region free to be colonised by the Neanderthals.

9. Stiner (1999).
10. *Ibid.* p.735.
11. Gamble (1999) p.319.
12. Stiner (1999) p.750.
13. Gamble (1999) p.319.
14. Kopytoff (1986).
15. Warnier (2001) pp.7–10, and for examples see Gosden and Marshall (1999).
16. Hoffecker (2002) p.175.
17. White (2003) pp.122–3 & pp.146–7; Hoffecker (2002) p.235. Although no research has been undertaken comparing these geometric designs directly to phosphenes, the similarity is persuasive. Moreover, the explosion of this style as opposed to naturalistic representation may be a continuation of the tradition begun with cave art.
18. This analysis of beads comes from Kuhn and Stiner (2007).
19. Kuhn et al. (2001) p.7645.
20. d'Errico and Vanhaeren (2007) p.280, for the argument, and in the next paper in the same edited volume, White (2007) p.293, against the argument.

Chapter 9
1. Boserup (1965).
2. Davies (2001, 2007).
3. *Ibid.*
4. The early settlements of northern Iberia are a little harder to account for but the Rhone and Garonne rivers are potential conduits, with coastal hops where necessary.
5. Davies (2001) p.212.
6. Although Descartes is often given an almost personal responsibility for such divisions – stemming from his famous separation of body and mind – in reality, the main thrust of the entire Enlightenment was to classify, understand, and, hence, divide. Heidegger has done much to restore this imbalance in the European philosophical tradition, particularly in relation to landscape formation (1962) pp.78–90.
7. Casey (1996).
8. Ingold (1993).
9. The following discussion is taken from Gamble (1999) chapter 3.
10. The Inuit are known for naming locations after single noteworthy events. My favourite is in Baffin Island: *The Place Where Two Men Kissed and the Caribou Got Away*.
11. David (2002) pp.13–28.
12. Mauss (1988).
13. Mithen (1996) p.198.
14. Farbstein and Svoboda 2007 for a recent review of this imagery in Eastern Europe.
15. White (2003) pp.146–7; Hoffecker (2002) p.235.

Chapter 10
1. Mithen (2003) p.120.
2. Currant, Jacobi and Stringer (1989).
3. Cook (1991).
4. Charles and Jacobi (1994) pp.13–14.
5. Ripoll and Muñoz (2007).

6. There are around 90 figures within Church Hole at Creswell Crags. There are bird forms (or extremely stylised women, according to one of the discoverers), a bison head, possible bears, a headless horse, a possible ibis, but the finest image is of a complete stag with head and antlers clearly engraved but like so much Palaeolithic art, truncated lower legs and no hooves.
7. After the discoveries at Creswell, more images have been found at Gough's Cave and at nearby Aveline's Hole. However, these engravings comprise scratched geometric shapes rather than animals and may date to a later period; the research is ongoing, Mullen and Wilson (2005a and b).
8. It used to be thought that the reindeer calved in northern Germany before moving to southern Sweden for winter grazing, but new research has questioned this assumption, Aaris-Sørensen, Mühldorff and Brinch Petersen (2007).
9. Bokelmann (1991) pp.77–8.
10. *Ibid.* The spear-thrower almost acts as an extension to the arm as the spear is hooked into its end and then spear and spear-thrower are thrust forward.
11. Terberger (2006) p.31.
12. Pigeot (1987).
13. Pigeot (1990).
14. White (2003) p.107.
15. Mithen (2003) p.130–1 provides a different reconstruction for the use of the panels, although retaining the ceremonial setting and shamanic overtones.
16. Bosinski and Fischer (1980).
17. Bosinski (1984).
18. Bosinski, d'Errico and Schiller (2001).
19. Clottes (2008) pp.214–5.
20. Fiedorczuk et al. (2007).
21. Bokelmann (1991) pp.78–9.

Chapter 11
1. Huntley and Webb (1988) pp.352–60.
2. Clarke (1954).
3. Petersson (1951).
4. Malmer (1966–8).
5. Mithen (2003) pp.139–40.
6. Mellars and Dark (1998) pp.211–2.
7. Conneller (2004).
8. *Ibid.* There are also Mesolithic stone engravings from the Netherlands, which show people dancing. Although the figures depicted are not wearing antler headdresses, similar masks to those at Star Carr have been found in the wetlands of northern Germany: Verhart (2008) pp.166–7. Baldick (2000) p.32 provides an example of historical shamans using the pelt and heads of deer for both hunting disguises and to shapeshift into the minds of their prey.
9. Mithen (2003) p.529. Note 11 comments that the site maintains an 'unhealthy obsession' among Mesolithic specialists.
10. Jordan (2003) p.101 & p.119.
11. *Ibid.* p.118.
12. Conneller and Schadla-Hall (2003) pp.101–2.
13. Karsten and Nilsson (2006) pp.117–20.
14. Warren (2005) p.109.

15. Karsten and Nilsson (2006) pp.161–7. Artificial structures dating to the Mesolithic are rare, but if they were of wood then perhaps it is just that the remains are now lost. Intriguingly, Stonehenge is thought to have originated with three massive posts (totem poles?) on the site of the modern car park, which also date to the Mesolithic. Allen (1995).
16. Jordan (2003) p.136, also Zvelebil (2008) p.43.
17. Warren (2003).
18. Jordan (2003) pp.118–9; Rival (1998).
19. Warren (2005) p.89.
20. *Ibid.* p.69.
21. Conneller and Schadla-Hall (2003) p.102.
22. Barton et al. (1995).

Chapter 12
1. Since the division of Yugoslavia, Lepenski Vir now lies in Serbia.
2. Bonsall (2008) pp.230–40.
3. *Ibid.* p.252.
4. Radovanović (1996) p.119.
5. Borić (2005) p.58.
6. Radovanović (1996) p.55.
7. *Ibid.* p.314. There is also the suggestion that people bred dogs as a food source. Bonsall (2008) p.261.
8. Meiklejohn and Zvelebil (1991) pp.132–3.
9. Radovanović (2000).
10. Borić and Stefanović (2004).
11. *Ibid.* p.529.
12. Radovanović (2000) p.334 & p.341.
13. *Ibid.* pp.334–5.
14. Radovanović (1996) pp.138–59.
15. Radovanović (1997). Although there is absolutely no evidence that the people of Lepenski Vir took hallucinogenic drugs, henbane, a common weed that turns up in later archaeological deposits, apparently gives the imbiber the sensation and appearance of turning into a fish (information from Giovanni Della Porta, *Natural Magic*, VIII, 2). Could the people of Lepenski Vir have known about this? If so, what did it bring to their shapeshifting experiences?
16. Borić (2005) p.58.
17. Radovanović (2000) p.336.
18. Radovanović (2000).
19. Borić and Stefanović (2004) p.539.
20. Whittle (1996) pp.24–9.

Chapter 13
1. Brown (1993) pp.14–6. Evans, of course, went on to find lasting fame by excavating Knossos on Crete.
2. Bradley (2000) pp.3–5.
3. Jordan (2003) p.146.
4. Gurina (1956).
5. Norlander-Unsgaard (1985).
6. Malmer (1960) pp.128–332.
7. Jordan (2003) p.227.

8. Zvelebil and Jordan (1999) p.114.
9. *Ibid.*
10. Zvelebil (2003) p.13.
11. Aldhouse-Green and Aldhouse-Green (2005) pp.72–3.
12. Zvelebil (1997) pp.44–5.
13. Eliade (1954).
14. Eidlitz (1969).
15. Bradley (1998a) p.25 also draws on the symbolism of antlers.
16. *Ibid.* p.25 & fig. 8.
17. Larsson (1983) pp.78–81.
18. Zvelebil (1997) p.45.
19. Maula (1990).
20. Albrethsen and Brinch Petersen (1976) pp.8–9.
21. Jacobs (1995) pp.392–3.
22. Mithen (1994) pp.120–1. Mithen also comments that areas next to water may have been favoured habitation sites (and, by extension, burial sites) because of their access to numerous food resources.

Chapter 14
1. Larsson (1988).
2. Rowley-Conwy (1998).
3. *Ibid.* p.200; Whittle (1996) p.154.
4. Mithen (2003) p.175.
5. Schleidt and Shalter (2003).
6. Nobis (1979).
7. Davis and Valla (1978).
8. Miklosi (2007) pp.97–101.
9. Price (2003) pp.25–6.
10. Mithen (1994) pp.106–7.
11. Clutton-Brock and Noe-Nygaard (1995) analyse the evidence for the use of dogs at one of the very earliest Mesolithic sites at Star Carr.
12. Larsson (1990).
13. Verhart (2008) p.175.
14. Radovanović (1999).
15. Dolukhanov (2008) p.295.
16. There is even the likelihood that the minds of dogs altered to better suit their new environment. Some of the behavioural cues that they understand, such as the attentional state of their owners, were once thought to be exclusively the preserve of humans and it is likely that dogs learnt these habits from us. Udell and Wynne (2008) examine this and other examples.
17. Whittle (1996) p.197.

Chapter 15
1. Gkiasta et al. (2003).
2. Childe (1925) p.15.
3. Gronenborn (2007).
4. Perlès (2001) pp.38–63.
5. For example, Cole (1965).
6. Thomas (2003).

7. Barnard (2007).
8. There is other evidence for incipient domestication during the Mesolithic. For example, Zvelebil (1998) p.15 suggests that Mesolithic hunter-gatherers had tamed (but not domesticated) pigs in the Baltic region. Furthermore, there is evidence that a bear was tamed and kept tethered at Grande Rivoire in France, presumably in connection with the widespread veneration of bears at this time. Chaix, Bridault and Picavet (1997).
9. Tresset and Vigne (2007) p.202. Pots were also ritually deposited as special items within the houses at Lepenski Vir. Garašanin and Radovanović (2001).
10. Scarre (2007) pp.256–7.
11. In addition to totem poles and standing stones, shell middens (huge piles of empty shells) are also thought to have been monumental in purpose, Warren (2007) pp.312–6, and in Portugal they continued from the Mesolithic into the Neolithic, Stiner et al. (2003).
12. Tilley (2007).
13. It is also likely that Mesolithic hunter-gatherers already managed natural plants to maximise returns, even if they did not domesticate them. Zvelebil (1994).

Chapter 16

1. Zvelebil (2004a) p.45.
2. Boguki (2000) p.212.
3. Price (2000) p.290.
4. Zvelebil (1998) pp.16–21.
5. *Ibid.*
6. Whittle (1996) pp.174–6.
7. Mithen (2003) p. 175.
8. Frayer (1997).
9. Jennbert (1998) p.34.
10. Bonsall (2008) p.274. The marriage alliances imply a peaceful co-existence between hunter-gatherers and farmers and there is certainly no evidence of increased injuries in the burial remains that might be expected if there was violent opposition, *Ibid.* p.276. However, Mithen (2003) p.166 notes that the elaboration of the half-human half-fish carvings at the time of transition and the fact that they were now placed near the entrance to the dwellings rather than hidden away in the interior, suggests some degree of resistance towards the farmers.
11. Bentley, Chikhi and Price (2003) p.64; Bentley (2007) pp.129–32.
12. Seielstad et al. (1998).
13. Zvelebil and Lillie (2000) pp.66–7.
14. *Ibid.*
15. Zvelebil (2008) p.54.
16. Bonsall et al. (2002).
17. Larsson (2007) pp.604–7; Jochim (2000) pp.195–6 notes similar environmental pressures and their effects on the Mesolithic communities in central Europe during the time of transition.
18. Price (2000) p.271.
19. Thomas (2007).

Chapter 17

1. Moore, Hillman and Legge (2001).
2. *Ibid.* pp.461–71 & pp.519–20. There is evidence that people were already managing wild sheep populations through careful selection of those they killed: the old, the weak, and those with unfavourable traits being taken first.

3. Whittle (1996) p.40. Gkiasta et al. (2003) for dates.
4. Erdoğu (2003).
5. The classic work in this regard is Ammerman and Cavalli-Sforza (1971).
6. For example, Borić (2005) pp.19–21; Budja (2004).
7. Tringham (2000).
8. Gimbutus, Winn and Shimabuku (1989).
9. The degree of sedentism during the early Neolithic in Greece is still debated. Halstead (2005).
10. Bailey (2000) pp.44–6.
11. *Ibid.* pp.53–5.
12. At Polyanitsa in Bulgaria, for example, access to the inner rooms of some houses was through six or seven outer rooms (*Ibid.* pp.157–9). The so-called shrine at Nea Nikomedeia (Rodden and Wardle (1996)), which contained hoards of tools and materials, may have been a means through which the new focus on activities within the house was marked and celebrated. They may have even been offerings to a household spirit. Whittle (1996) p.59.
13. Tringham (2005).
14. *Ibid.* p.105.
15. Bailey (2000) p.157.
16. *Ibid.* p.81.
17. This is suggested by Bailey (2000) p.80, but see also Sherratt (1991) for similar ideas.
18. Nanoglou (2008).
19. People also made model houses, furniture, and tools, which may have been used in such performances, again emphasising identity through actions. Bailey (2000) p.95.
20. Bailey (2000) pp.116–24.
21. Papers in Fol and Lichardus (1988) (and especially Grave 36).
22. Bailey (2000) p.230. Stahl (1989) relates these designs to the phosphenes seen in trance

Chapter 18

1. Zvelebil (2004b) and the papers in part 2 of the same volume for a good summary of the opposing views.
2. Beneš (2004) pp.147–9.
3. *Ibid.* p.146.
4. Kind (1989) p.460.
5. Whittle (1996) pp.162–7; Lenneis (2004).
6. Modderman (1988) pp.94–7.
7. These ideas are from Bradley (2002) pp.21–3.
8. Whittle (1996) p.162.
9. *Ibid.* p.167.
10. Bradley (2007) p.348.
11. For the excavation of the burials, Coblenz (1956).
12. Whittle (1996) p.167.
13. Marciniak (2004) pp.137–8.
14. Bradley (2002) pp.26–8.
15. *Ibid.*
16. Bentley (2007) pp.124–9.
17. Wahl and König (1987) for the excavation report; Bentley et al. (2008) for the analysis. The separate groups have been identified through individuals bearing associated isotopic signatures.

18. Bentley (2007) p.129.
19. Golitko and Keeley (2007).
20. Whittle (1996) p.173.
21. Bogucki (2000) p.202.
22. Marciniak (2004) p.133–7.

Chapter 19
1. Korek (1951).
2. van Vuure (2005). Aurochs survived in Europe until 1627, when the last cow died in Poland.
3. Bollongino and Burger (2007).
4. Lewis-Williams and Pearce (2005) p.145.
5. Hodder (1990) p.35.
6. Mellaart (1967) pp.77–130 refers to these ornamented rooms as shrines but Lewis-Williams and Pearce (2005) p.105 think that such a distinction between ritual and profane would have been meaningless to the inhabitants and that ritual would have imbued every aspect of people's existence.
7. Cauvin (2007) pp.25–33, pp.67–72, & pp.126–7 expands on similar ideas.
8. Lazarovici et al. (1985) pp.34–42.
9. Vlassa (1963) pp.490–4.
10. Marciniak (2004) p.135.
11. *Ibid.* pp.132–3.
12. Pollex (1999).
13. Thomas (1999a) pp.26–9.
14. Hodder (1990) p.250.
15. Ashbee, Smith and Evans (1979) pp.245–9.
16. From the *Secret Life of Genghis Khan*, cited in Baldick (2000) p.98.

Chapter 20
1. Whittle (1996) p.176.
2. Boelicke et al. (1988) pp.891–931; Kuper et al. (1977) pp.81–106.
3. Hodder (1990) p.111.
4. Svodín and Bučany properly belong to the Lengyel culture, the equivalent of the SBK in Slovakia, Pavúk (1991) pp.348–50.
5. Whittle (1996) pp.266–70.
6. Bradley (1998a) p.71.
7. *Ibid.* p.80; Hodder (1990) p.224.
8. Bradley (1998a) p.80.
9. Andersen (2002) p.8. There are also signs that in Britain and Ireland pottery took on a more individualised character at this time. Bradley (2007) p.74.
10. Whittle, Pollard and Grigson (1999). The subsequent analysis of the site is taken from their interpretations in chapters 17 and 18.
11. The occurrence of cattle in the inner ditches and pigs in the outer seems to mirror their respective positions in tombs where cattle bones could be placed inside the tomb but pig bones remained outside.
12. Pryor (1988) p.295.
13. At Maiden Castle causewayed enclosure in southern England, flint axes were finished and transformed into completed items. Edmonds (1993) pp.119–21.

Chapter 21

1. Podborský (2002).
2. Quoted from Pettitt and Zvelebil (2009).
3. Bradley (1998a) pp.44–5.
4. Hodder (1990) pp.150–3, provides eight points of comparison between long-houses and long mounds.
5. Midgley (1992) chapter 5.
6. Also Modderman (1988) p.118.
7. Midgley (2005) pp.84–8.
8. *Ibid.* pp.82–4; Field (2006) pp.102–6.
9. Midgley (2005) p.95.
10. *Ibid.* pp.95–8.
11. Metcalf and Huntington (1991) part II.
12. Field (2006) p.140; Thomas (1999a) p.137.
13. Thomas (1999a) pp.146–9; Reilly (2003).
14. Bradley (1998a) chapter 4.
15. Watson and Keating (1999); Watson (2001). The drumming may also have affected those observing events, causing sensations of trance which, owing to the surroundings, would have probably led to experiences that matched those of the shamans. This would have engendered closer understanding of the role of the shamans and have given credibility to what they did.
16. Dronfield (1995).
17. Lewis-Williams and Pearce (2005) p.219.
18. Bradley (2009) pp.67–71.
19. Bradley et al. (2001). Some of the later chambered tombs in Orkney even take their distinctive ground plan from houses, Bradley (2007) pp.108–9.
20. Bradley and Philips (2008).
21. Patton (1990).
22. Powell and Daniel (1956) pp.16–8.
23. Also Lewis-Williams and Pearce (2005) pp.189–91.
24. Thomas (1999a) p.148.
25. O'Kelly (1992) for the tomb (pp.123–6 for the slot above the entrance); Lewis-Williams and Pearce (2005) pp.229–31 for the analysis.

Chapter 22

1. This chapter follows the idea of Johnston (1999), that the cursus and associated monuments sealed an existing route through the land and prevented further use.
2. For example, Barclay, Brophy and MacGregor (2002); Brophy and Barclay (2004).
3. Brophy (2006). Cross (2003) pp.198–200 suggests that similar structures in Ireland were feasting halls.
4. Brophy (2006) pp.85–8.
5. Thomas (2006) p.230.
6. This sequence is apparent at Holywood North. Thomas (1999b), with interpretation in Thomas (2006).
7. In shamanic societies, everything has a spirit: people, objects, and even abstract entities, such as a community. Vitebsky (1995) pp.12–4.
8. Thomas (1999a) p.52.
9. Barclay and Maxwell (1998) (pp.20–1 for the long mound).
10. *Ibid.* pp.50–2.
11. Stukeley (1740) p.41.

12. Barclay and Bayliss (1999) p.20.
13. Tilley (1994) pp.172–96.
14. Barret, Bradley and Green (1991) p.50.
15. Gibson (1999) p.132; Brophy (1999) p.128, (2000) pp.64–6; Barclay and Hey (1999) p.73.
16. Chapman (2005).
17. Bailloud et al. (1995) pp.48–68.
18. This is according to Roughley (2004) p.165 who has reconstructed the now much-disturbed landscape through digital means.
19. Mens (2008) pp.29–32.
20. Giot et al. (1979) pp.415–25.
21 The analysis is taken from Bradley (2002) pp.106–7.
22. Bradley (1997) chapter 3.

Chapter 23

1. This may have been to hold power in rather than to keep intruders out, Hodder (1990) p.264.
2. Parker Pearson (2007) p.133.
3. Bradley (2007) p.106.
4. Bradley (1998a) p.102.
5. *Ibid.* p.110.
6. *Ibid.* p.111–3.
7. Barclay and Russell-White (1993) pp.76–88.
8. Harding (2003) pp.31–2.
9. Thomas (1999a) pp.113–20.
10. Wainwright and Longworth (1971) provides the excavation report for both Durrington Walls and Woodhenge.
11. Richards (2004) pp.242–3.
12. These themes are explored in Parker Pearson and Ramilisonina (1998).
13. Pollard (1995).
14. Thomas (1996) p.203.
15. Gibson (2005) pp.107–16.
16. Odner (1992) p.63.
17. Parker Pearson et al. (2007).
18. Parker Pearson et al. (2009).
19. In contrast, the southern timber circle within Durrington Walls was aligned to the winter solstice sunrise. Woodhenge, however, spoils this neat dichotomy and matches Stonehenge; perhaps this is why it was included within the walls of the henge?
20. Harding (2003) pp.63–8 has other examples.
21. *Ibid.* p.76.
22. Whittle (1997) pp.53–138.
23. Pitts (2001).
24. Darvill (2007).

Chapter 24

1. Dolukhanov (2002) pp.15–7.
2. Much of the information for this chapter comes from Kohl (2007), which provides a comprehensive overview of the region in English.
3. *Ibid.* pp.42–4.

4. Dolukhanov (2002) p.17.
5. Kohl (2007) pp.40–3.
6. Dolukhanov (2002) p.17.
7. Todorova (1995) pp.89–91.
8. Kohl (2007) p.84.
9. *Ibid.* p.53.
10. *Ibid.* p.67–72.
11. Bailey (2000) pp.214–7.
12. The description of the Maikop burial is taken from Phillips (1965) pp.30–4.
13. Kohl (2007) p.75.
14. *Ibid.* p.75.
15. Dolukhanov (2002) pp.20–1.
16. Kohl (2007) pp.114–5.
17. Tiratsian (1992) p.39.
18. Phillips (1965) pp.37–8.
19. Halifax (1982) pp.84–5.
20. Kohl (2007) p.75.
21. Govedarica and Kaiser (1996) review these and other designs.
22. Olsen (2000) p.201.
23. *Ibid.* pp.191–2.
24. Anthony and Brown (2000) pp.80–1.
25. Levine (1999); Kuzmina (2000); and papers in part 2 of Levine, Renfrew and Boyle (2003).

Chapter 25
1. Conrad Spindler was in charge of Ötzi following the discovery and his book (1994, for the English translation) provides details of the discovery, analysis, and background to the find, although recent research has now superseded some of his conclusions.
2. Müller et al. (2003).
3. Peintner, Poder and Pümpel (1998) p.1846.
4. Dickson et al. (2000). It would have also staunched wounds, such as the cut to Ötzi's hand.
5. Spindler (1994) part IV chapter 7.
6. Barfield (1995) pp.157–9.
7. Nerlich et al. (2003).
8. Oeggl et al. (2007).
9. Egarter Vigl and Gostner (2002); Pernter et al. (2007).
10. Lippert et al. (2007).
11. Spindler (1994) pp.206–13.
12. Whittle (1996) pp.117–8.
13. *Ibid.* pp.352–3.
14. Sherratt (1994) p.174.
15. De Grooth (1997).
16. Edmonds (1995) pp.63–5; Topping (2005).
17. *Ibid.* pp.66–8.
18. *Ibid.* p.81.
19. Bradley (2000) p.80.
20. Pétrequin et al. (2006).
21. Bradley et al. (1992).
22. Spindler (1994) p.209.

Chapter 26

1. Price et al. (2004). The analysis shows that men, women, and children were all mobile, presumably moving as part of family groups. However, appreciably more women than men moved away from the area in which they were raised, suggesting that they may have relocated on marriage.
2. Fitzpatrick (2003). It is possible that the man's son lay in another grave close by.
3. Whittle (1996) pp.284–6.
4. Davis and Payne (1993).
5. Turek (2006) pp.175–6.
6. Case (2004).
7. Nocete (2006).
8. Guerra-Doce (2006) p.252 gives examples of beakers being used in the smelting process. Chapman (1990) pp.159–67 reviews the development of the industry in Iberia.
9. Cardoso, Querré and Salanova (2005).
10. O'Brien (2004).
11. Taylor (1970).
12. Heyd (2007) p.332.
13. *Ibid.* pp.341–51.
14. Fokkens, Achterkamp and Kuijpers (2008).
15. Turek (2004).
16. For example, Rojo-Guerra et al. (2006) p.262.
17. J. Thomas (2005) p.174 & p.183.
18. Guerra-Doce (2006) p.249.
19. Vander Linden (2006) p.325–6.
20. For example, Shepherd (1986) p.15.
21. Brück (2004) sees people defined by their interpersonal connections rather than as individuals.
22. Similar ideas are explored in van der Beek (2004) pp.187–8.
23. Mizoguchi (1993).
24. Grave 1 at Landau-Südost, in Germany, for example, was for a small boy but had a range of adult items possibly including a full-size bow, which would also account for the size of the grave. Husty (2004).
25. Bradley (2007) p.150.
26. Fitzpatrick (2004).
27. Evans, Chenery and Fitzpatrick (2006).
28. The Amesbury Archer also had a withered left leg owing to an old wound to his knee. If the bluestones of Stonehenge were reputed to have healing properties, as explored in chapter 23, this may provide another reason for why the archer was drawn there.

Chapter 27

1. Sopp (1999) p.238.
2. Harding (2000) p.220.
3. For example, Shennan (1995).
4. Harding (2000) pp.76–84.
5. Bradley (1998b) pp.88–9.
6. Cunliffe (2008) pp.185–203 provides a good analysis of the trade at the time.
7. With little excavation of comparable burials without a covering mound, however, it is difficult to say if such burial was uniformly afforded to those of high status. In some areas,

for example, there were no barrows and yet it hardly seems likely that they would have been without leaders, Harding (2000) pp.98–9.
8. *Ibid.* p.220.
9. Wels-Weyrauch (1989).
10. Kristiansen (1998) pp.370–84 provides an overview of the societies of the Carpathians including the settlement of Spissky Sturtok.
11. Kuznetsov (2006).
12. Kristiansen (1998) pp.371–4.
13. Lull (2000) p.589.
14. Chapman (1990) p.84–5 examines El Argar, the archetypal Bronze Age site in the region.
15. *Ibid.* p.195.
16. Chapman (1984), Montero (1993).
17. Mathers (1994) pp.44–5.
18. O'Sullivan (2005) pp.169–218.
19. Eogan (1994) pp.28–39.
20. Briard (1984) pp.131–41.
21. Woodward (2002) p.1043.
22. Although rich graves existed elsewhere in Britain from about 2000 BC, there is a striking density within the Wessex region and particularly around Stonehenge.
23. Needham (2000) p.170 analyses the graves from Brittany and N. Thomas (2005) p.287 & p.299 provides a good example from the Wessex tradition.
24. Needham (2000) pp.176–81.
25. Helms (1998) pp.66–171.
26. van de Noort (2006).
27. Meller (2002 and subsequent papers in the same volume). Pásztor and Roslund (2007) also consider the disc a symbolic rather than a realistic interpretation of the heavens.
28. Coles (1993) outlines the images and Kristiansen (2004) considers their role in actual voyages.
29. Randsborg (1993). The idea that the slabs could depict a journey comes from Cunliffe (2008) p.221.

Chapter 28
1. Harding (2000) p.112 for discussion.
2. *Ibid.* pp.400–1.
3. Kristiansen (1998) pp.113–4.
4. *Ibid.*
5. *Ibid.* p.93.
6. Cunliffe (2008) p.267 imagines the scene.
7. Brown and Kulik (1977).
8. Wright and Gaskell (1992) p.276.
9. Wilhelm, Gerlach and Simon (1990).
10. Broholm (1944) for analysis.
11. Needham and Woodward (2008) p.6.
12. Bergmann (1982) pp.96–110.
13. Neugebauer (1991) p.131.
14. Kubach-Richter (1978–79).
15. Baldick (2000) p.154.
16. Napolskikh (1992); Linkola and Linkola (2000) p.24.
17. Piggott (1983) pp.109–16; Pare (1992) pp.28–30.
18. Eluére (1998) p.134.

Chapter 29

1. From the remains of tools left at the site, the images at Alta appear to have been chipped into the rock using a chisel or quartz point. At other locations, a faint trace of pigment suggests that some carvings were painted, and today, most are enhanced in this manner to aid viewing. Sveen (1996).
2. Eliade (1964) chapter 8.
3. We have already seen many manifestations of this cosmology, such as crossing water or entering a cave to reach the lowerworld, ascending to the sky (through birds or cremation) to reach the upperworld, and the existence of an *axis-mundi*, such as a tree, to link them.
4. Helskog (1999).
5. Coles (2005) pp.100–19; Coles (2006) provides two case studies from Sweden of sea level change and its effect on the rock carvings on the shoreline. Also Bradley (2009) pp.177–9.
6. Terebikhin (1993).
7. Bradley et al. (2002); Bradley (2006) p.378.
8. Bolin (2000) pp.161–2.
9. Bradley et al. (2002); Hauptman Wahlgren (1998).
10. Coles (2002) p.244; Coles (2004) p.191; Bradley (2009) pp.197–8 suggests that images would have also been animated by snow, sea spray, and fire.
11. Kaul (1998) pp.188–95.
12. Kaplan (1975).
13. Dunn (1973); Czigány (1980).
14. Kähler Holst, Breuning-Madsen and Rasmussen (2001).
15. Capelle (1986).
16. Widholm (1998) p.76; Bradley et al. (2002) p.117.
17. Bradley (1997; 1999).
18. Waddington (1998).
19. Hedengran (1990).
20. Coles (2004) p.191.
21. Kaul (1998) pp.263–5.
22. Müller (1903).
23. Kaul (1998) pp.242–4.
24. Bradley (2009) p.129.
25. Bradley (2006) p.375.
26. Wihlborg (1977–78).
27. Goldhahn (1999) p.95.
28. Bäckman and Hultkranz (1978) p.16.
29. Helskog (1987).
30. Bäckman and Hultkranz (1978) pp.67–8.
31. Pentikäinen (1987).
32. Sommarström (1989) pp.126–7.
33. Johansen (1979).
34. Lahelma (2008) pp.37–40.
35. Lahelma (2007).

Chapter 30

1. This custom was recorded by Rasmussen (1908) pp.111–2.
2. Atran (1990) p.59.
3. Harvey (2005).
4. Barber (2003) pp.101–7.

5. Childs (1991); Collett (1993); Reid and MacLean (1995); Bekaert (1998).
6. Budd and Taylor (1995).
7. Bradley (1998b) p.xix.
8. For example, O'Sullivan (1997) pp.119–20.
9. Gingell (1992) pp.109–11; Needham (1980).
10. Kaul (1985).
11. Siikala (1978) p.241 & p.316; also Czaplicka (1914) p.199.
12. Khushi (2000).
13. Williams (2001) pp.184–6.
14. Lynn (1977).
15. Hansen (1991) pp.87–99.
16. Needham (1981) pp.37–40.
17. Gosden and Marshall (1999) p.174; also Kopytoff (1986) for similar ideas.
18. Rohl and Needham (1998) use lead-isotope analysis to show the origin of the metal used in southern Britain.
19. Bradley (1998b) pp.132–5 discusses this difference.
20. Butler and Sarfatij (1970–71); Needham (1990) for examples.
21. Kristiansen (2002) pp.329–30 makes similar comments.
22. See Ehrenberg (1980); Hansen (1991) pp.27–54; Jensen (1993); Scurfield (1997); Davis (1999); Bourke (2001).
23. For example, Bradley (2007) pp.185–6.
24. Torbrügge (1970–1) pp.41–7.
25. Pryor (2001) pp.421–9; Bradley (2007) pp.203–4 for a review of other examples.
26. Pryor (2001) pp.423–6.
27. York (2002) shows that 68 per cent of swords placed in the Thames in the late Bronze Age were broken beforehand.
28. Nebelsick (2000).
29. Bradley and Gordon (1988); ter Schegget (1999).

Chapter 31
1. Harding (2000) pp.275–8.
2. Harding (1999) p.162.
3. Jensen (1998) p.94–7.
4. Harding (2000) p.285–7.
5. Kristiansen and Larsson (2005) pp.288–91. Giles (2008) p.66 suggests that spiral and maze-like designs on weapons may have been a means to trap an enemy and render them unable to resist.
6. Kristiansen (2002) p.323.
7. Norling-Christensen (1946).
8. Coles (1962) pp.181–5.
9. Kristiansen (1984; 2002); Bridgeford (1997); York (2002).
10. Osgood, Monks and Toms (2000) p.30.
11. Müller-Karpe (1956) has details of a burial where the deceased was laid out and then burnt on a wheeled cart (predictably, the cart also carried images of water birds). Coles (2002) examines similar vehicles in Scandinavian rock art.
12. Crouwel (1981).
13. Burström (1999).
14. Jorge and Almeida (1980).
15. Bradley (1998c) pp.243–58.

16. Galan Domingo (1993).
17. González García (2009) p.63.
18. Gomez De Soto (1993).
19. These ideas come from Treherne (1995). The subsequent cremation may also have added to the drama of the occasion, as we saw in chapter 28.
20. Sørensen (1997).
21. Jockenhövel (1999).
22. Hrala, Sedláek and Vávra (1992).
23. Reinerth (1928) pp.31–9.
24. Osgood Monks and Toms (2000) pp.65–6.
25. Vladár (1973) pp.277–93.
26. Mathers (1994) pp.42–3.
27. Bradley (2007) pp.206–10.
28. Buckley and Hedges (1987).
29. Bond (1988).
30. Yates (2001).

Chapter 32

1. Brück (1999a) p.155.
2. Bradley (2002) p.76.
3. Oswald (1997) makes similar comments for doorway alignments in the Iron Age.
4. Lindström (1997) p.116; Williams (2001) pp.105–6.
5. Audouze and Büchsenschütz (1991) p.132.
6. Zimmermann (1999).
7. Barker (1999) p.279.
8. Williams (2001) pp.107–8.
9. Audouze and Büchsenschütz (1991) p.160.
10. Brongers (1976) provides plans for 115 fields in the Netherlands. The majority, where orientation can be ascertained, were aligned to the south-east.
11. Bradley (2002) p.77.
12. Yates (2007) p.136.
13. Nielsen (1984) provides plans for 55 fields in Denmark. The majority were aligned to the south-west with a smaller percentage to the south-east.
14. Fleming (1987) pp.190–1; Bradley (2007) p.188.
15. Bradley (2007) pp.188–9.
16. Field (2001) p.59.
17. Lohof (1994) pp.104–6.
18. Roymans and Kortlang (1999) pp.44–9 who also liken the mounds to the long-houses, mirroring the symbolism we explored during the Neolithic.
19. Some bodies were cremated and some long-mounds contained several bodies, although often only one primary interment.
20. Verlinde (1985) pp.284–5.
21. *Ibid.* pp.246–61; with analysis of additional long-mounds in Williams (2001) pp.111–2.
22. For examples see Simon's Ground (White, 1982), Itford Hill (Holden, 1972), and South Lodge (Barrett, Bradley and Green (1991) pp.168–81).
23. Bradley (1998a) pp.155–7.
24. For examples see Down Farm ring ditch (Barrett, Bradley and Green (1991) pp.211–4), Itford Hill (Holden, 1972), Kinson Barrow 3 (Knocker, 1958), Latch Farm (Piggott, 1938) and the Landford Barrow (Preston and Hawkes, 1933).

25. Predictably, these are known as linear boundaries because they are straight and form boundaries. Field (2001) pp.60–1.
26. *Ibid.*; Bradley, Entwistle and Raymond (1994) p.141.

Chapter 33
1. Audouze and Büchsenschütz (1991); Brück (1999b).
2. Brück (1999a) p.146.
3. Gerritsen (1999).
4. *Ibid.* p.84.
5. Nowakowski (1991) for Penhale Moor; Brück (2006) for discussion.
6. Bradley (1981); Fokkens (1997).
7. Brück (2006) pp.303–5; Williams (2001) pp.134–5 for specific sites.
8. Brück (1999a) p.152; Williams (2001) pp.136–7.
9. Brück (1995).
10. Barrett, Bradley and Green (1991) p.157.
11. Jones (2008).
12. Jones (1998/9).
13. Svanberg (2005).
14. Boysen and Andersen (1983); Pedersen (1986).
15. Bokelmann (1977).
16. The analysis is from Bradley (2005) pp.53–5.
17. *Ibid.* p.53.
18. Williams (2003).
19. Drewett (1982) pp.382–90 for Black Patch, and Williams (2001) pp.139–40 for list of sites.
20. Brück (2006) p.304.
21. Ladle and Woodward (2003) p.275.
22. For the relevant excavation reports see Ratcliffe-Densham and Ratcliffe-Densham (1961); Green (1987); Papworth (1992); Gingell (1992); Barrett, Bradley and Green (1991).
23. Brück (2001) p.155.
24. *Ibid.*
25. Bradley (2005) pp.23–8 considers such ritual ploughing. Haggaerty (1991) p.67 for Machrie Moor.
26. Thrane (1984).
27. Johnston (2000); Jones (2008).
28. Brück (2001) p.154.
29. Cunliffe and Poole (2000a) pp.79–80.
30. This idea is taken from Bloch and Parry (1982).
31. Roymans (1995) p.34 makes a similar point.
32. Williams (2001) p.326 for examples from Britain, Denmark, and the Netherlands.
33. Russell (1996).

Chapter 34
1. Chamberlain and Parker Pearson (2001) chapter 1.
2. *Ibid.* chapter 3.
3. All information on Cladh Hallan is from Parker Pearson et al. (2005).
4. Painter (1995).
5. Bradley and Gordon (1988) p.504.
6. Cooney and Grogan (1994) p.147.

7. Needham (1992) p.61.
8. Peters (2000).
9. Jennbert (1991–92) p.92.
10. Kooi (1979) p.134.
11. McKinley (1997) p.137.
12. *Ibid*. p.142.
13. Kaliff (1998).
14. *Ibid*. pp.186–8; Sandagergård in Denmark, that we explored in chapter 30, may be another.
15. Benton (1931) pp.206–7; Brück (1995) p.260 suggests that the skulls were hung from the walls and ceiling.
16. *Ibid*.
17. Wells and Hodgkinson (2001).
18. Fokkens (1997) p.366.
19. Roymans (1995) p.6.
20. Holtorf (1998) p.30.
21. Clay (1927) p.468; Piggott (1938) p.181.
22. Brück (1995) p.249.
23. Brossler, Early and Allen (2004) pp.124–5; Cotton and Frere (1968) (Brück (1995) p.271 identifies one skull fragment as being worked into an amulet).
24. Brück (1995) pp.257–60.
25. Broholm (1953).
26. Bradley and Ellison (1975) p.34 for Rams Hill and re-dating by Needham and Ambers (1994), placing the ditch at the beginning of the later Bronze Age. Papworth (1992) p.54 for Crab Farm. Pitt Rivers (1898) p.240 for South Lodge where a large urn was preserved unbroken in the ditch due to the rapidly accumulating silt.
27. Thomas (1997).

Chapter 35

1. Bucko (1998).
2. Allen (1994).
3. Ó Drisceóil (1988).
4. Harding (2000) p.312.
5. For example, Gleirscher (1996).
6. Zachrisson and Iregren (1974) p.83.
7. This idea was first put forward by Barfield and Hodder (1987).
8. Winkelman (1986) p.186; Slade and Bentall (1988) pp.30–2.
9. Balázs (1996) for this and other examples.
10. Bradley (2008) p.216.
11. Kaliff (1998).
12. Runcis (1999).
13. Dunkin (2001).
14. Waterbolk and van Zeist (1961).
15. Butler (1960).
16. Wamser (1984).
17. Bradley (2008) p.216.
18. Mark Knight cited in Brennand and Taylor (2003) p.71.
19. Brennand and Taylor (2003).
20. O'Sullivan (1996) pp.64–5.

21. Fjellström (1985) p.47; Vorren (1985) pp.75–6.
22. Anisimov (1963) pp.87–9.
23. Brennand and Taylor (2003) pp.10–2.
24. A similar arrangement was found around a Beaker period grave at Dolní Věstonice, in the Czech republic, suggesting that Seahenge may have formed part of a far wider tradition. Dvořák et al. (1996) grave 44.
25. Chambers and Jones (1984).
26. Katzung (2007) p.274.
27. The woman's belt-purse held two horse's teeth, some marten bones, the claw-joint of a lynx, bones from a fawn or lamb, a piece of bird's windpipe, snake vertebrae, two burnt fragments of bone (possibly human), a twig of rowan, aspen charcoal, two quartz pebbles, a lump of clay, two pieces of pyrites, a piece of bronze foil, and a piece of bronze wire. The man's belt-purse held an amber bead, a red stone, a conch with suspension hole, a conifer die, a piece of flint, various dried roots and bark, the tail of a grass snake, the claw of a falcon, bronze tweezers, a bronze razor, a fire-lighting flint, and a second leather pouch with the jaw of a squirrel or weasel, and a gut wound round some stones (possibly from a bird's gizzard). Kaul (1998) pp.16–7.
28. *Ibid.* pp.18–20.

Chapter 36

1. Dickinson (1994) covers both civilisations.
2. Dothan and Dothan (1992).
3. Sandars (1978) pp.124–37.
4. Liverani (1987).
5. Snodgrass (1971).
6. Casson (1986) chapter 5.
7. Markoe (2000).
8. Aubet (1993) chapter 4.
9. For a comprehensive study of the region, Morgenroth (2004).
10. Garrido (1970 and 1978).
11. López Castro (2006).
12. Whitley (2001) chapter 8.
13. Papers in Hanson (1991).
14. Boardman (1980) chapters 5 and 6; Lancel (1995).
15. Cunliffe (2001) chapter 8.
16. Haynes (2005) pp.162–4.
17. Papers in Bats et al. (1992).
18. Kristiansen (1998) pp.228–30.
19. *Ibid.* pp.212–6.
20. Kimmig (1983).
21. Riek and Hundt (1962) pp.204–9.
22. Biel (1985).
23. Körber-Grohne (1985) pp.121–22.
24. Joffroy (1954).
25. Fischer (1982) pp.45–6.
26. Nash (1985) pp.46–9 for similar ideas.
27. Green (1996).
28. Bagnall (2004).
29. Nash Briggs (2003).

Chapter 37

1. The details of Celtic feasts were recorded by Posidonius, who wrote in the first century BC. His first-hand records have not survived but were used as source material by later historians, including Athenæus in *Deipnosophistae* 4.36 and 4.40. (see Koch (2005) for translations of most of the literary sources for this chapter).
2. Athenæus, *Deipnosophistae* 4.15 and 4.37; Siculus 5.28.
3. Siculus 5.28.
4. Siculus 5.27.
5. Athenæus, *Deipnosophistae* 4.36.
6. Arnold (1999).
7. Athenæus, *Deipnosophistae* 4.40.
8. Cunliffe (1997) pp.105–7.
9. Athenæus, *Deipnosophistae* 4.49.
10. Athenæus, *Deipnosophistae* 4.37 tells of a Bard who was late for his Lord's feast and yet, upon arriving, recited a brilliant poem admonishing his own tardiness. The Lord was so impressed, he tossed a bag of gold from his chariot as he left, leading the Bard to compose another verse lauding that even his Lord's chariot left behind tracks of gold.
11. Kristiansen (1998) pp.337–8.
12. Biel (1981); Lorentzen (1993).
13. *Tractatus De Mulieribus Claris in Bello* (translated by Koch (2005) p.42). Boudica and Cartimandua were later female leaders although both only assumed the role following the death or capture of their husbands. Ellis (1995).
14. Arnold (1995) pp.159–61.
15. Kristiansen (1998) pp.320–1.
16. Polybius, *History* 2.28.3–10.
17. For example Siikala (1978) p.134; Jacobsen (1999) p.73.
18. Polybius *History* 2.29.5–9.
19. Siculus 5.26.2–3.
20. Siculus 5.29.
21. Livy, *Ab Urbe Condita* 5.28–9 tells of the collapse of the Romans before the Celtic onslaught.
22. Siculus 5.28.
23. Siculus 5.29.
24. Livy, *Histories* 23.24.
25. Benoit (1981) pp.51–99.
26. Cunliffe (1997) p.98; and compare the images on the Gundestrup Cauldron in Kaul 1995.
27. Pauli (1975).
28. Recorded by Livy, *Histories* 7.26.
29. Cunliffe (1997) p.98.
30. Trogus, *Historiae Philippicae* 20.4.1–3; Livy *Histories* 5.34: 1–4.
31. Trogus, *Historiae Philippicae* 20.4.1–3 and 5.7–8; Livy *Histories* 5.33: 2–6 and 5.34: 1–4.
32. Trogus, *Historiae Philippicae* 22.2.5.
33. The raid on Rome is told by Livy *Ab Urbe Condita* 5.38–9 and 5.41.
34. *Ibid.* 5.48.
35. Strabo, *Geography* 7.3.8.
36. Trogus *Historiae Philippicae* 24.6–8.
37. Compare the self-inflicted fates of Florus and Sacrovir after defeat in Gaul and Boudica in Britain.
38. Caesar, *The Conquest of Gaul* 6.31.

Chapter 38

1. Lejeune (1984); Koch (2006) pp.1105–7 for a translation of the text.
2. Cunliffe (1997) p.187.
3. Arnold (1999) pp.76–8.
4. Martin (1965).
5. Vitebsky (1995) pp.98–103 for shamanic healing; Harner (1980) chapter 7 for spirit extractions.
6. Caesar, *The Conquest of Gaul* 6.17.
7. *Ibid.* 6.18.
8. Lucan, *Pharsalia* 1.422–65.
9. See Cunliffe (1997) p.185.
10. Cunliffe (1993).
11. Strabo, *Geography* 4.4.4; Caesar *The Conquest of Gaul* 6.13–14.
12. Caesar, *The Conquest of Gaul* 6.13.
13. Tacitus, *Annals* 14.29–30.
14. Caesar, *The Conquest of Gaul* 6.13.
15. *Ibid.* 6.14 for Druid training.
16. Lucan, *Pharsalia* 3.372–417; Cunliffe (1997) p.190.
17. Pomponious Mela, *De Situ Orbis* 3.2.18–19.
18. Green (1997a) pp.8–10; Green (1986) p.42.
19. Kruta (2004) pp.60–1.
20. Green (1986) p.41.
21. Vopiscus, *Numerianus* 14 and *Aurelianus* 63.4.5; Lampridius, *Alexander Severus* 59.5 both refer to female Druids although it is unclear whether they belonged to the pre-Roman Celtic tradition.
22. Tacitus, *Histories* 4.61 and 4.66. Veledā's people, the Bructeri, lived east of the Rhine, and were therefore regarded as Germans by Tacitus, but it is likely that they shared many traditions with the Celts.
23. Green and Green (2005) pp.140–1; Kruta (2004) p.150.
24. Kruta (2004) pp.148–9.
25. Arnold (1995) pp.154–5.
26. For examples, Shirokogoroff (1935) p.299; Eliade (1964) pp.153–4.
27. Creighton (2000) pp.49–50.
28. Strabo, *Geography* 7.2–3.
29. Siculus, *Histories* 5.31.
30. Strabo, *Geography* 7.2–3.
31. Fox (1946).
32. Tacitus, *Annals* 14.57.
33. Rosenberg (1937).
34. Strabo, *Geography* 4.1.13; Caesar, *The Conquest of Gaul* 6.17.
35. Caesar, *The Conquest of Gaul* 6.13.
36. Siculus, *Histories* 5.28.
37. *Ibid.* Pomponious Mela, *De Situ Orbis* 3.2.18–19.
38. Creighton (2000) p.52.
39. Green (2001).
40. Kruta (2004) pp.200–1.
41. Aelian, *De Ora Natura Animali* 10.22; Marco Simón (2008); Schönfelder (1994).
42. Cunliffe (1997) p.203; Kaul (1995).
43. Translation by Davies (2007) p.32.

Chapter 39

1. Herodotus, *Histories* 4.71–3.
2. Kohl (2007) p.142.
3. *Ibid.* chapter 4.
4. Kristiansen (1998) p.190.
5. Otchir-Goriaeva (2002).
6. Kohl (2007) pp.178–9.
7. Priakhin and Besedin (1999).
8. Herodotus, *Histories* 4.12; Bouzek (1983).
9. Metzner-Nebelsick (2000).
10. Kossack (1988).
11. Cunliffe (2008) pp.302–9 provides an overview of changes in the region.
12. See Legrand and Bokovenko (2006) for possible origins.
13. Kristiansen (1998) p.195.
14. Herodotus, *Histories* 4.20.
15. Taken from a cuneiform tablet recording the question put to the sun god and answered through the entrails of a sheep. Rolle (1989) p.71.
16. Herodotus, *Histories* 1.103: King Madyas, son of King Protothyes (identified as Partatua).
17. Rolle (1989) pp.92–3.
18. *From the Lands of the Scythians: Ancient Treasures from the Museums of the USSR 3000 BC– 100 BC* [Exhibition Catalogue]. New York, Metropolitan Museum of Art.
19. Kristiansen (1998) p.278.
20. Koryakova (2000) p.15.
21. Rolle (1989) pp.32–4.
22. Olkhovskiy (2000).
23. Rolle (1989) p.36.
24. Herodotus, *Histories* 4.73–4.
25. Equipment for cannabis inhalation has been found at the eastern end of the Scythian territory at Pazyryk, in Tuva, Rolle (1989) p.94.
26. Herodotus, *Histories* 1.105 and 4.67; Ustanova (1999) pp.76–80.
27. Hippocrates, *Airs, Waters, Places* section 22.
28. Lewis (1989) chapter 3.
29. Bleibtrau-Ehrenberg (1970).
30. Herodotus, *Histories* 4.67.
31. Eliade (1964) pp.394–6.
32. Davis-Kimball (2000) p.226.
33. Rolle (1989) p.94.
34. Ovid, *Tristia* 5.10.
35. Rolle (1989) p.65.
36. *Ibid.* pp.66–7.
37. Herodotus, *Histories* 4.64–5.
38. *Ibid.*
39. Rudenko (1970) pp.109–14.
40. Brentjes (2000).
41. Phillips (1965) pp.62–3.
42. Herodotus, *Histories* 4.60–1.
43. *Ibid.* p.66.
44. *Ibid.* p.64.
45. Rolle (1989) pp.61–2.

46. Herodotus, *Histories* 4.62.
47. *Ibid.* p.110.
48. Rolle (1989) pp.86–9.
49. If Hippocrates, *Airs, Waters, Places* section 17 is to be believed.
50. Sulimirski (1970) pp.100–1.

Chapter 40
1. Cunliffe (2002).
2. Grau Mira (2003); Belarte (2008).
3. Harrison (1988).
4. Arribas et al. (1987) pp.605–50.
5. Álvarez-Sanchís (2000).
6. Queiroga (2003).
7. The preponderance of these settlements may have been a means to reduce conflict over unequal wealth; isolationism being chosen instead of war and the division of communities rather than internal expansion. Sastre (2008).
8. Ralston (2006) pp.85–8.
9. Cunliffe (2008) p.347.
10. Cunliffe (2000).
11. Cunliffe (2005) chapter 13.
12. Kestor, on Dartmoor, is one of the first settlements of the south-west to reveal ironworking within one of the houses, Fox (1954).
13. Cunliffe (2005) chapter 12.
14. Sørensen (1989) p.195.
15. Hingley (1997) p.10.
16. Bradley (1998b) pp.147–54.
17. Briard (1976) pp.571–4; Sommerfeld (1994).
18. Halkon and Millet (1999) pp.75–95.
19. Rowlett et al. (1982).
20. Hill (1999).
21. Jensen (1982) p.204; Gerritsen (1999).
22. For example, Fokkens (1998) p.129; also comments in Roymans and Theuws (1999).
23. Williams (2003) pp.237–8.
24. Gerritsen (1999) p.92.
25. Jensen (1982) p.257.
26. Fokkens (1998) pp.122–3.
27. Stead (1991).
28. Bevan (1999) p.126.
29. Parker Pearson (1999) p.56.
30. Ralson (2006) chapter 7.
31. Armit (2003).

Chapter 41
1. Parker Pearson and Sharples (1999) pp.19–22; Armit (2003) pp.42–4.
2. Hedges (1987a); Armit (2003) p.43 thinks that the space may have been a byre.
3. Parker Pearson and Sharples (1999) p.352.
4. Ballin Smith (1994).
5. *Ibid.* p.33 & p.281.

6. Renfrew (1979) pp.181–95.
7. Hingley (1996) p.233 & p.241.
8. Also Hingley (1999) p.247.
9. Calder (1936–37); (1938–39).
10. Scott (1948).
11. Parker Pearson and Sharples (1999) pp.10–2.
12. Armit (2003) pp.108–9.
13. *Ibid.*
14. Hingley (1992) p.29.
15. Hedges (1987b) p.19; Parker Pearson and Sharples (1999) p.353; MacKie (1974) p.14.
16. Armit (2003) pp.95–100.
17. *Ibid.* p.76. The hillforts we explore in the next chapter may be comparable places for community gatherings.
18. Oswald (1997); Parker Pearson (1996) p.120.
19. Williams (2001) pp.105–6.
20. Harsema (1992).
21. *Ibid.* pp.119–21. Even if the items were left on abandonment rather than being dropped when the house was in use, they still reflect the way that people believed their houses should be, with the living area located in the south. Webley (2007).
22. Bech (1985) p.141.
23. Parker Pearson et al.(2005) p.533.

Chapter 42
1. Cunliffe (2005) pp.384–7.
2. *Ibid.* pp.388–96.
3. Bradley (2007) pp.247; Bambridge (1998).
4. Collis (1996) pp.88–9; Bowden and McOmish (1989) p.15 provides examples.
5. Bowden and McOmish (1987) pp.77–8.
6. Sharples (1991a) p.83.
7. Cunliffe (1995) p.94. Crickley Hill is one of the few hillforts where episodes of burning and slingstone use appear to match. Dixon (1994) p.105 & pp.115–6.
8. Ralson (2006) chapter 7.
9. Avery (1986) reviews the evidence but prefers to see the fires as part of attacks on the hillforts.
10. Rideout (1992) p.4.
11. Reynolds (1982) p.47.
12. Richmond (1968) pp.19–25; Guilbert (1976) pp.306–12.
13. Cunliffe (1984) pp.173–89.
14. Bradley (2007) p.251.
15. Gent (1983).
16. Cunliffe and Poole (1991a) pp.116–39.
17. Cunliffe (1995) p.90.
18. *Ibid.* pp.41–2; Smith (1977) p.40; Sharples (1991b) p.74.
19. Cunliffe (1995) pp.48–50.
20. Hill (1995).
21. Whimster (1981) p.14.
22. Athenæus, *Deipnosophistae* 4.36.
23. Hill (1995) p.106.
24. Fitzpatrick (1997) p.78.

25. Bradley (2007) p.251.
26. For example, Downes (1997).
27. Collis (1977).
28. Waterman (1997) p.1.
29. *Ibid.* pp.35–59.
30. Newman (1996).
31. The sequence is described by Waterman (1997) pp.49–59.
32. Lynn (1992) pp.37–9.

Chapter 43

1. Brunaux, Meniel and Poplin (1985).
2. Brunaux (1988) p.120.
3. Meniel (1987) p.129.
4. *Ibid.* p.121.
5. Green (1992) p.22.
6. Zvelebil and Jordan (1999) p.109.
7. Rapin (1993).
8. Rapin and Brunaux (1988) discusses the treatment of the weapons left at Gournay-sur-Aronde where this pattern was followed.
9. Rapin (1993) pp.295–7.
10. Cadoux (1984).
11. See similar comments in Roymans (1990) p.73.
12. Bittel, Schiek and Müller (1990); Wieland (1999).
13. Bradley (2005) pp.16–23 for discussion.
14. Schwartz (1962) pp.22–34.
15. Fox (1928; 1930).
16. Planck (1982) pp.138–47.
17. Lambot and Méniel (2000).
18. For example, Delattre (2000).
19. All examples are taken from Wilson (1981) and Whimster (1981), supplemented by the many Danebury examples in Cunliffe and Poole (1991b) and Cunliffe (1995).
20. For example, Richardson (1951) p.129; Smith (1977) p.59; Cunliffe and Poole (1991b) pp.479–82; Cunliffe and Poole (2000b) p.152.
21. Cunliffe and Poole (1991b) pp.429–31.
22. Kristiansen (1998) pp.350–6.
23. Brunaux and Méniel (1997) pp.108–94; Krause and Wielandt (1993).
24. Cunliffe and Poole (1991a) pp.238–9; Downes (1997) p.151.
25. King and Soffe (1998).

Chapter 44

1. Caesar, *The Conquest of Gaul.*
2. Cornell (1995); Lancel (1995) pp.361–427.
3. Opper (2008) chapter 2.
4. Cunliffe (2008) pp.366–9.
5. Hopkins (1980).
6. Hopkins (1978) pp.48–56.
7. Ibid. pp.99–106.
8. Brunt (1971) pp.20–41.

9. Described in Cunliffe (1997) pp.221–2.
10. Alfödy (1974) pp.35–8.
11. Collis (1984).
12. Loughton (2009) pp.91–2 and also p.93, linking the treatment of amphorae to the agricultural cycle.
13. Siculus, *Histories* 5.26.
14. Ebel (1976) pp.64–95.
15. Described in Cunliffe (1997) pp.238–9.
16. Caesar, *The Conquest of Gaul* tells the story in his own words and Goudineau (1990) provides a commentary.
17. Cunliffe (1997) p.108.
18. Jensen (1982) pp.204–14; Fokkens (1998) p.129; Gerritsen (1999) p.91.
19. Bech (1985).
20. Eckardt (2008) pp.114–8.
21. Creighton (2000) pp.16–7.
22. Creighton (2000).
23. *Ibid.* p.199.
24. Parker Pearson (1993) p.224.
25. Creighton (2000) pp.176–88.
26. *Ibid.* pp.35–54; Williams and Creighton (2006).
27. Meniel (1987) p.74 for cuisine and p.117 for inclusion in graves.
28. Tacitus, *Germania* 14; Todd (1992).
29. Grøntoft, in Denmark, was among the first fenced settlements. Becker (1965).
30. Hvass (1985).
31. *Ibid.* p.175.
32. Caesar, *The Conquest of Gaul* 6.11–12; discussed in Champion (1995) p.92.
33. Cunliffe (1997) pp.231–2.
34. Caesar, *The Conquest of Gaul* 1.2–4; 7.4.
35. Cunliffe (1997) p.232.
36. For example Creighton (2000) pp.15–17 and pp.101–5.
37. Caesar, *The Conquest of Gaul* 6.13–14.
38. *Ibid.* Book 7.
39. Bradley (1991) p. 209.
40. Le Contel and Verdier (1997).
41. Fitzpatrick (1996).
42. Comments attributed to the general Agricola in Tacitus, *Agricola* 21.

Chapter 45

1. van der Sanden (1996) provides the best introduction to bog bodies. Usually, the bodies are named after the place in which they were found.
2. Fischer (1979).
3. For example, Tollund Man was laid out as if he was merely sleeping, and Borremose Woman II (found 1948) and Søgårds Mose Man I (found 1942) were each laid on a bed of cotton grass. All these bodies were found in Denmark. Glob (1969) p.31 & p.96; Fischer (1979).
4. van der Sanden (1996) p.138.
5. *Ibid.* p.141.
6. *Ibid.*
7. Schmidt (1987) p.63.

8. For example, Basilov (1997) p.8; Diószegi (1998a) p.2.

9. Brothwell and Bourke (1986) p.56.

10. Bourke (1986) p.51.

11. Donner (1920) p.7.

12. Fischer (1980) p.181; Andersen and Geertinger (1984) p.111.

13. van der Sanden (1996) p.177; Fischer (1980) p.180.

14. Called Harris lines, these are discussed in van der Sanden (1996) p.112.

15. Williams (2002) p.94.

16. Brown and Kulik (1977) call this 'flashbulb memory' since the entire scene is remembered as if it had been captured on camera.

17. The condition is called 'hypermnesia', Scrivner and Safer (1988).

18. Geiselman et al. (1985).

19. van der Sanden (1996) pp.162–3.

20. Vitebsky (1995) pp.59–63.

21. For examples, Siikala (1978) p.22; Diószegi (1960) p.62; (1998b).

22. Poulik and Nekvasil (1969) pp.38–49.

23. Williams (2002) pp.96–7.

24. Fischer (1999) p.94; Budworth et al. (1986) p.40.

25. For example, Siikala (1978) p.134; Jakobsen (1999) p.73; Donner (1920), Bonser (1917) p.170.

26. van der Sanden (1996) p.93; Fischer (1979).

27. Glob (1969) p.114.

28. For example, Weyer (1932) pp.437–8; Jakobsen (1999) p.23 & p.64; Siikala (1978) p.190.

29. For example, Rasmussen (1998) pp.63–5.

30. Williams (2002) p.95.

31. Brothwell, Liversage and Gottlieb (1990) pp.175–7; Fischer (1980) p.181.

32. Fischer (1979).

33. For example, Humphrey and Onon (1996) pp.80–1 & p.214; Donner (1920) pp.2–6; Siikala and Hoppál (1992) p.3; Baldick (2000) p.154.

34. Helbaek (1958); Harild, Robinson and Hudlebusch (2007) pp.175–6 conclude that the sclerotia consumed were within current European Union limits for bread flour.

35. Uytterschaut (1990) p.187.

36. Tacitus, *Germania* 12.

37. Coles (1990); Capelle 1995.

38. Coles (1990) p.320; van der Sanden (1996) p.175; Glob (1969) pp.180–2.

39. Riismøller (1952).

40. Raftery (1996) pp.285–7; Capelle (1995) p.18.

41. Green (1997b) p.202.

42. Solli (1999).

43. Coles (1990).

44. Aldhouse-Green (2000) p.19.

45. van der Sanden (1988) p.107; (1996) p.175.

46. For example, Hooper in Cunliffe and Poole (1991b) pp.427–8.

Coda

1. Tacitus, *Annals* 14.29–30.

2. Discussed in chapter 38; Webster (1999).

3. Derks (1998) chapter 3.

4. Tacitus, *Annals* 12.31.

5. Hingley and Unwin (2005).
6. Dio, *Roman History* 63.6.1–4.
7. Tacitus, *Annals* 14.32–3; Hingley and Unwin (2005) chapter 3 finds evidence for burning at Colchester and London but is less conclusive for St Albans.
8. Tacitus, *Annals* 14.34.
9. *Ibid.* 14.36–7.
10. Tacitus, *Agricola* 16.
11. Yeates (2008) pp.137–43.
12. *Ibid.* pp.143–5.
13. Derks (1991) presents evidence from lower Germany.
14. Yeates (2008) pp.61–88 & pp.117–8.
15. Ryan (1992) pp.206–7, pp.376–7 & pp.408–9.
16. Patterson (1995) p.135 & note 5 on p.136.
17. Augustinus Hibernicus, *De Mirabilibus Sacrae Scripturae* 1.17. St Isidor of Seville in *De Ordine Creaturarum* 10.8–10 refers to similar beliefs.
18. Pliny, *Natural History* 30.4.
19. *Historia Augusta*, 'The Lives of Carsus, Carinus and Numerian' 14.3.f and 'The Life of Aurelian' 44.4.
20. Nennius *Historia Brittonum* pp.40–2.
21. Meaney (1989) p.20.
22. Price (2002).
23. Wilson (1992) and Hines (1997) provide a comprehensive account from both perspectives.
24. *Saga of Eirik the Red* 4.81–8.
25. Meaney (1981).
26. Levack (2006).
27. For example, Thomas (2003).
28. *Ibid.* chapter 22, although Parish and Naphy (2003) detect continuation of much of the superstition within the reformed Church.
29. Rydving (1995) pp.54–68.
30. Hutton (2009) chapter 12.
31. For example, Hutton (2001) chapter 12.
32. Wallis (2003).
33. Jakobsen (1999).

BIBLIOGRAPHY

Unless otherwise stated, all books are published in London.

Aaris-Sørensen, K., R. Mühldorff and E. Brinch Petersen, 2007, 'The Scandinavian Reindeer (*Rangifer tarandus* L.) After the Last Glacial Maximum: Time, Seasonality and Human Exploitation', *Journal of Archaeological Science* 34, 914–23.

Albrethsen, S. and E. Brinch Petersen, 1976. 'Excavation of a Mesolithic Cemetery at Vedbæk, Denmark', *Acta Archaeologica* 47, 1–28.

Aldhouse-Green, M. and S. Aldhouse-Green, 2005, *The Quest for the Shaman: Shape-Shifters, Sorcerers and Spirit-Healers of Ancient Europe*, Thames and Hudson.

Aldhouse-Green, M., 2000, *Seeing the Wood for the Trees: The Symbolism of Trees and Wood in Ancient Gaul and Britain*, Aberystwyth, University of Wales.

Aldhouse-Green, S. (ed.), 2000, *Paviland Cave and the 'Red Lady': A Definitive Report*, Bristol, Western Academic and Specialist Press.

Alföldy, G., 1974, *Noricum*, Routledge.

Allen, D., 1994, 'Hot Water and Plenty of It', *Archaeology Ireland* 8, 8–9

Allen, M., 1995, 'Before Stonehenge' in Cleal, R., K. Walker and R. Montague (eds) *Stonehenge in its Landscape. Twentieth-Century Excavations*, English Heritage, 41–62.

Álvarez-Sanchís, J., 2000, 'The Iron Age in Western Spain (800 BC–AD 50): An Overview', *Oxford Journal of Archaeology* 19, 65–89.

Ammerman, A. and L. Cavalli-Sforza, 1971, 'Measuring the Rate of Spread of Early Farming in Europe', *Man* 6, 674–88.

Andersen, N., 2002, 'Neolithic enclosures of Scandinavia' in Varndell, G. and P. Topping (eds) *Enclosures in Neolithic Europe: Essays on Causewayed and Non-Causewayed Sites*, Oxford, Oxbow, 1–10.

Anderson S. R. and P. Geertinger, 1984, 'Bog Bodies Investigated in the Light of Forensic Medicine', *Journal of Danish Archaeology* 3, 111–119.

Anisimov, A., 'The shaman's tent of the Evenks and the origin of the shamanistic rite' in Michael, H. (ed.), 1963, *Studies in Siberian Shamanism*, Toronto, Arctic Institute of North America, 84–123.

Anthony, D. and D. Brown, 2000, 'Eneolithic Horse Exploitation in the Eurasian Steppes: Diet, Ritual and Riding', *Antiquity* 74, 75–86.

Armit, I., 2003, *Towers in the North: The Brochs of Scotland*, Stroud, Tempus.

Arnold, B., 1995, '"Honorary Males" or Women of Substance? Gender, Status, and Power in Iron-Age Europe', *Journal of European Archaeology* 3, 153–68.

Arnold, B., 1999, '"Drinking the Feast": Alcohol and the Legitimisation of Power in Celtic Europe', *Cambridge Archaeological Journal* 9, 71–93.

Arribas, A., G. Trias, D. Cerdá and J. de la Hoz, 1987, *El Barco de el Sec (Calvià, Mallorca). Estudio de los Materiales*, Palma de Mallorca, Universitat de Les Balears.

Arsuaga, J., J. Bermúdez de Castro and E. Carbonell, 1997, 'The Sima de los Huesos Hominid Site', *Journal of Human Evolution* 33, 105–421.

Ashbee, P., I. Smith and J. Evans, 1979, 'Excavation of Three Long Barrows Near Avebury, Wiltshire', *Proceedings of the Prehistoric Society* 45, 207–300.

Atran, S., 1990, *Cognitive Foundations of Natural History: Towards an Anthropology of Science*, Cambridge, Cambridge University Press.

Aubet, M., 1983, *The Phoenicians and the West: Politics, Colonies and Trade*, Cambridge, Cambridge University Press.

Audouze, F. and O. Büchsenschütz, 1991, *Towns, Villages and Countryside of Celtic Europe: From the Beginning of the Second Millennium to the End of the First Century BC*, Batsford.

Avery, M., 1986, 'Stoning and Fire at Hillfort Entrances of Southern Britain', *World Archaeology* 18, 216–30.

Bäckman, L. and Å. Hultkrantz, 1978, *Studies in Lapp Shamanism*, Stockholm, Stockholm Studies in Comparative Religion.

Bader, O., 1978, *Sunghir*, Moscow, Nauka.

Bagnall, N., 2004, *The Peloponnesian War: Athens, Sparta, and the Struggle for Greece*, New York, St Martin's Press.

Bahn, P., 2001, 'Save the last trance for me: an assessment of the misuse of shamanism in rock art studies', in Francfort, H.-P. and R. Hamayon (eds), *The Concept of Shamanism: Uses and Abuses*, Budapest, Akadémiai Kiadó.

Bailey, D., 2000, *Balkan Prehistory: Exclusion, Incorporation and Identity*, Routledge.

Bailloud, G., C. Boujot, S. Cassen and C-T. Le Roux, 1995, *Carnac. Les Premières Architectures de Pierre (Patrimoine au Présent)*, Paris, Caisse Nationale des Monuments Historiques et des Sites.

Balázs, J., 1996, 'The Hungarian shaman's technique of trance induction', in Diószegi, V. and M. Hoppál (eds), *Folk Beliefs and Shamanic Traditions in Siberia*, Budapest, Akadémiai Kiadó, 26–48.

Baldick, J., 2000, *Animal and Shaman: Ancient Religions of Central Asia*, New York, New York University Press.

Ballin Smith, B., 1994, *Howe: Four Millennia of Orkney Prehistory. Excavations 1978–1982*, Edinburgh, Society of Antiquaries of Scotland Monograph 9.

Bambridge, K., 1998, *Going Round the Houses: A Closer Look at the Roundhouse Evidence of Iron Age Hillforts*, University of Reading, Unpublished MA Thesis.

Bancroft Hunt, N., 2003, *Shamanism in North America*, New York, Firefly Books.

Barber, M., 2003, *Bronze and the Bronze Age: Metalwork and Society in Britain c.2500–800 BC*, Stroud, Tempus.

Barclay, A. and A. Bayliss, 1999, 'Cursus monuments and the radiocarbon problem', in Barclay, A. and J. Harding (eds), *Pathways and Ceremonies: The Cursus Monuments of Britain and Ireland*, Oxford, Oxbow, 11–29.

Barclay, A. and G. Hey, 1999 'Cattle, cursus monuments and the river: the development of ritual and domestic landscapes in the Upper Thames Valley', in Barclay, A. and J. Harding (eds), *Pathways and Ceremonies: The Cursus Monuments of Britain and Ireland*, Oxford, Oxbow, 67–76.

Barclay, G. and C. Russell-White, 1993, 'Excavations in the Ceremonial Complex of the Fourth to Second Millennium BC at Balfarg/Balbirnie, Glenrothes, Fife', *Proceedings of the Antiquaries of Scotland* 123, 43–210.

Barclay, G. and G. Maxwell, 1998, *The Cleaven Dyke and Littleour: Monuments in the Neolithic of Tayside*, Edinburgh, Society of Antiquaries of Scotland.

Barclay, G., K. Brophy and G. MacGregor, 2002, 'Claish, Stirling: An Early Neolithic Structure in its Context', *Proceedings of the Society of Antiquaries of Scotland*, 132, 65–137.

Barfield, L., 1995, 'Burials and boundaries in Chalcolithic Italy', in Malone, C. and S. Stoddart (eds) *Papers in Italian Archaeology IV: Volume 2*, Oxford: British Archaeological Reports (International Series) 1452, 152–76.

Barfield, L. and M. Hodder., 1987, 'Burnt Mounds as Saunas, and the Prehistory of Bathing', *Antiquity* 61, 370–9.

Barker, G., 'Cattle-keeping in ancient Europe: to live together or apart?', in Fabech, C. and J. Ringtved (eds) 1999, *Settlement and Landscape*, Moesgård, Jutland Archaeological Society, 273–80.

Barnard, A., 2007 'From Mesolithic to Neolithic modes of thought', in Whittle, A. and V. Cummings (eds), *Going Over: The Mesolithic – Neolithic Transition in North-West Europe*, Oxford, Proceedings of the British Academy 144, 5–19.

Barrett, J., R. Bradley and M. Green, 1991, *Landscape, Monuments and Society: The Prehistory of Cranborne Chase*, Cambridge, Cambridge University Press.

Barton, N., P. Berridge, M. Walker and R. Bevins, 1995, 'Persistent Places in the Mesolithic Landscape: An Example from the Black Mountain Uplands of South Wales', *Proceedings of the Prehistoric Society* 61, 81–116.

Bar-Yosef, O., 2007, 'The dispersal of modern humans in Eurasia: a cultural interpretation', in Mellars, P., K. Boyle, O. Bar-Yosef and C. Stringer (eds), *Rethinking the Human Revolution*, Cambridge, McDonald Institute Monographs, 207–17.

Basilov, V., 1984 'The study of shamanism in Soviet ethnography', in Hoppál, M. (ed.) *Shamanism in Eurasia*, Göttingen, Edition Herodot, 46–63.

——, 1997, 'Chosen by the spirits', in Mandelstam Balzer, M. (ed.) *Shamanic Worlds: Rituals and Lore of Siberian and Central Asia*, North Castle Books, 3–48.

Bats, M., G. Bertucchi, G. Conges and H. Treziny, 1992, *Marseille Greque et la Gaule*, Aix-en-Provence, Études Massaliètes 3.

Bech, J.-H., 1985, 'The Iron Age Village Mound at Heltborg, Thy', *Journal of Danish Archaeology* 4, 129–46.

Becker, C., 1965, 'Ein Früheisenzeitliches Dorf bei Gröntoft, Westjütland: Vorbericht Über dei Ausgrabungen 1961–63', *Acta Archaeologica* 36, 209–22.

Bekaert, S., 1998, 'Multiple Levels of Meaning and the Tension of Consciousness: How to Interpret Iron Technology in Bantu Africa', *Archaeological Dialogues* 5, 6–29.

Belarte, M., 2008, 'Domestic Architecture and Social Differences in North-Eastern Iberia During the Iron Age (c.525–200 BC)', *Oxford Journal of Archaeology* 27, 175–99.

Beneš, J., 2004, 'Palaeoecology of the LBK: the earliest agriculturalists and the landscape of Bohemia', in Lukes, A. and M. Zvelebil (eds) *LBK Dialogues: Studies in the Formation of the Linear Pottery Culture*, Oxford, British Archaeological Reports (International Series) 1304, 143–9.

Benoit, F., 1981, *Entremont*, Paris, Ophrys.

Bentley, A., 2007, 'Mobility, specialisation and community diversity in the Linearbandkeramik: isotopic evidence from the skeletons', in Whittle, A. and V. Cummings (eds), *Going Over: The Mesolithic – Neolithic Transition in North-West Europe*, Oxford, Proceedings of the British Academy 144, 117–40.

Bentley, A., L. Chikhi and T. D. Price, 2003, 'The Neolithic Transition in Europe: Comparing Broad Scale Genetic and Local Scale Isotopic Evidence', *Antiquity*: 77, 63–6.

Bentley, A., J. Wahl, T. D. Price and T. Atkinson, 2008, 'Isotopic signatures and hereditary traits: snapshot of a Neolithic community in Germany', *Antiquity* 82, 290–304.

Benton, S., 1931, 'The Excavation of the Sculptor's Cave, Covesea, Morayshire', *Proceedings of the Society of Antiquaries of Scotland* 65, 177–216.

Bergmann, J., 1982, *Ein Gräberfeld der Jüngeren Bronze- und Älteren Eisenzeit bei Vollmarshausen, Kr. Kassel: Zur Struktur und Geschichte einer Vorgeschichtlichen Gemeinschaft im Spiegel ihres Gräberfeldes*, Marburg, N.G. Elwert Vorlag.

Bevan, B., 1999, 'Land – life – death – regeneration: interpreting a middle Iron Age landscape in eastern Yorkshire', in Bevan, B. (ed.), *Northern Exposure: The Iron Age in Northern Britain*, Leicester, Leicester Archaeology Monographs No. 4, 123–47.

Biel, J., 1981, 'Tracht und Bewaffnung', In Bittel, K., W. Kimmig and S. Schiek (eds), Die Kelten in Baden-Württemberg, Stuttgart, Konrad Theiss Verlag, 138–59.

Biel, J. (ed.), 1985, *Der Keltenfürst von Hochdorf*, Stuttgart, Konrad Theiss Verlag.

Binant, P., 1991, *Les Préhistoire de la Mort: les Premières Sépultures en Europe*, Paris, Editions Errance.

Bittel, K., S. Schiek and D. Müller, 1990, *Die Keltischen Viereckschanzen*, Stuttgart, Konrad Theiss Verlag.

Bleibtrau-Ehrenberg, G., 1970, 'Homosexualität und Transvestition im Schamanismus', *Anthropos* 65, 189–228.

Bloch, M., 1998, *How We Think They Think: Anthropological Approaches to Cognition, Memory and Literacy*, Oxford, Westview Press.

Bloch, M. and J. Parry, 1982, 'Death and the regeneration of life', in Bloch, M. and J. Parry (eds), *Death and the Regeneration of Life*, Cambridge, Cambridge University Press, 1–44.

Boardman, J., 1980, *The Greeks Overseas: Their Early Colonies and Trade*, Thames and Hudson.

Boelicke, U., D. von Brandt, J. Lüning et al., *Der bandkeramische Siedlungsplatz Langweiler 8, Gemeinde Alderhoven, Kreis Düren*, Köln, Rheinische Ausgrabungen 28 (1988).

Bogucki, P., 2000, 'How agriculture came to north-central Europe', in Price, T.D. (ed.), *Europe's First Farmers*, Cambridge, Cambridge University Press, 197–218.

Bokelmann, K., 1977, 'Ein Bronzezeitlicher Hausgrundriß bei Handewitt, Kreis Schleswig-Flensburg', *Offa* 34, 82–9.

Bokelmann, K., 1991, 'Some new thoughts on old data on humans and reindeer in the Arensburgian tunnel valley in Schleswig-Holstein, Germany', in Barton, N., A. Roberts and D. Roe (eds) *The Late Glacial in North-West Europe: Human Adaptation and Environmental Change at the End of the Pleistocene*, CBA Research Report 77, 72–81.

Bolin, H., 2000, 'Animal Magic: The Mythological Significance of Elks, Boats and Humans in North Swedish Rock Art', *Journal of Material Culture* 5, 153–76.

Bollongino, R. and J. Burger, 2007, 'Neolithic cattle domestication as seen from ancient DNA', in Whittle, A. and V. Cummings (eds), *Going Over: The Mesolithic – Neolithic Transition in North-West Europe*, Oxford, Proceedings of the British Academy 144, 165–87.

Bond, D., 1988, *Excavation at the North Ring, Mucking, Essex: A Late Bronze Age Enclosure*, Chelmsford, East Anglian Archaeology Report No. 43.

Bonsall, C., 2008, 'The Mesolithic of the Iron Gates', in Bailey, G. and P. Spikins (eds), *Mesolithic Europe*, Cambridge, Cambridge University Press, 238–79.

Bonsall, C., M. Macklin, D. Anderson and R. Payton, 2002, 'Climate Change and the Adoption of Agriculture in North-West Europe', *European Journal of Archaeology* 5, 9–23.

Bonser, W., 1917, 'Some Notes on the Magic of the Finns', *Man* 17, 169–72.

Borić, D., 2005, 'Deconstructing essentialisms: unsettling frontiers of the Mesolithic-Neolithic Balkans', in Bailey, D., A. Whittle and V. Cummings (eds), *(Un)settling the Neolithic*, Oxford, Oxbow, 16–31.

Borić, D. and S. Stefanović, 2004, 'Birth and Death: Infant Burials from Vlasac and Lepenski Vir', *Antiquity* 78, 526–46.

Borić, I., 2005, 'Body Metamorphosis and Animality: Volatile Bodies and Boulder Artworks from Lepenski Vir', *Cambridge Archaeological Journal* 15, 35–69.

Boserup, E., 1965, *The Conditions of Agricultural Growth: The Economics of Agrarian Change under Population Pressure*, George Allen and Unwin.

Bosinski, G., 1984, 'The mammoth engravings of the Magdalenian site of Gönnersdorf (Rhineland, Germany)', in Bandi, H.-G., W. Huber, M.-R. Sauter and B. Sitter (eds), *La Contribution de la Zoologie et de l'Ethologie a l'Interprétacion de l'Art des Peuples Chasseurs Préhistorique*, Fribourg, Editions Universitaires, 295–322.

Bosinski, G. and G. Fischer, 1980, *Mammut und Pferdedarstellungen von Gönnersdorf*, Weisbaden, Franz Steiner.

Bosinski, G., F. d'Errico and P. Schiller, 2001, *Die Gravierten Frauendarstellungen von Gönnersdorf*, Stuttgart, Franz Steiner.

Boule, M., 1911–13, 'L'Homme Fossile de La Chapelle-aux-Saints', *Annales de Paléontologie* 6 (1911), 109–72; 7 (1912), 105–92; 8 (1913), 1–72.

Bourdieu, P., 1990, *The Logic of Practice*, Cambridge, Cambridge University Press.

Bourguignon, E., 1973, 'Introduction: a framework for the comparative study of altered states of consciousness', in Bourguignon, E. (ed.) *Religion, Altered States of Consciousness and Social Change*, Columbus, Ohio University Press, 3–25.

Bourke, J., 1986, 'The medical investigation of Lindow Man', in Stead, I., J. Bourke and D. Brothwell (eds), *Lindow Man – The Body in the Bog*, British Museum Publications, 46–51.

Bourke, L., 2001, *Crossing the Rubicon: Bronze Age Metalwork from Irish Rivers*, Galway, National University of Ireland.

Bouzek, J., 1983, 'Caucasus and Europe and the Cimmerian Problem', *Sbornik Národniho Muzea v Praze* (Series A) 37, Part 4.

Bowden, M. and D. McOmish, 1987, 'The Required Barrier', *Scottish Archaeological Review* 4, 76–84.

Bowden, M. and D. McOmish, 1989, 'Little Boxes: More About Hillforts' *Scottish Archaeological Review* 6, 12–16.

Boyer, P., 2000, Functional Origins of Religious Concepts: Ontological and Strategic Selection in Evolved Minds, *Journal of the Royal Anthropological Institute* 6, 195–214.

Boysen, A. and S. Andersen, 1983, 'Trappendal: Barrow and House from the Early Bronze Age', *Journal of Danish Archaeology* 2, 118–26.

Bradley, R., 1981, '"Various styles of urn" – cemeteries and settlement in southern England *c.*1400–1000 BC', in Chapman, R., I. Kinnes and K. Randsborg (eds), *The Archaeology of Death*, Cambridge, Cambridge University Press, 93–104.

Bradley, R. 1997, 'Death by Water: Boats and Footprints in the Rock Art of Western Sweden', *Oxford Journal of Archaeology* 16, 315–24.

Bradley, R., 1991, 'Ritual, Time and History', *World Archaeology* 23, 209–19.

Bradley, R., 1998a, *The Significance of Monuments: On the Shaping of Human Experience in Neolithic and Bronze Age Europe*, Routledge.

Bradley, R., 1998b, *The Passage of Arms: An Archaeological Analysis of Prehistoric Hoards and Votive Deposits*, Oxford, Oxbow.

Bradley, R., 1998c, 'Invisible Warriors – Galician Weapon Carvings in their Iberian Context', in Fábregas Valcarce, R. (ed.), *A Idade do Bronce en Galicia: Novas Perspectivas*, Sada, Edicións do Castro.

Bradley, R., 1999, 'Dead soles', in Gustafsson, A. and H. Karlsson (eds), *Glyfer och Arkeologiska Rum – en Vänbok till Jarl Nordbladh*, Göteborg, Gotarc, 661–6.

Bradley, R., 2000, *An Archaeology of Natural Places*, Routledge.

Bradley, R., 2002, *The Past in Prehistoric Societies*, Routledge.

Bradley, R., 2005, *Ritual and Domestic Life in Prehistoric Europe*, Routledge.

Bradley, R., 2006, 'Danish Razors and Swedish Rocks: Cosmology and the Bronze Age Landscape', *Antiquity* 372–389.

Bradley, R., 2007, 'Houses, bodies and tombs', in Whittle, A. and V. Cummings (eds), *Going Over: The Mesolithic – Neolithic Transition in North-West Europe*, Oxford, Proceedings of the British Academy 144, 347–55.

Bradley, R., 2007, *The Prehistory of Britain and Ireland*, Cambridge, Cambridge University Press.

Bradley, R., 2009, *Image and Audience: Rethinking Prehistoric Art*, Oxford, Oxford University Press.

Bradley, R. and A. Ellison, 1975, *Rams Hill: A Bronze Age Defended Enclosure and its Landscape*, Oxford, British Archaeological Reports (British Series) 19.

Bradley, R. and K. Gordon, 1988, 'Human Skulls from the River Thames: Their Dating and Significance', *Antiquity* 62, 503–9.

Bradley, R. and T. Philips, 2008, 'Display, disclosure and concealment: The Organisation of Raw Materials in the Chambered Tombs of Bohuslän', *Oxford Journal of Archaeology* 27, 1–14.

Bradley, R., A. Jones, L. Nordenborg Myhre and H. Sackett, 2002, 'Sailing Through Stone: Carved Ships and the Rock Face at Revheim, Southwest Norway', *Norwegian Archaeological Review* 35, 109–18.

Bradley, R., P. Meredith, J. Smith and M. Edmonds, 1992, 'Rock Physics and the Stone Axe Trade in Neolithic Britain', *Archaeometry* 34, 323–33.

Bradley, R., R. Entwistle and F. Raymond, 1994, *Prehistoric Land Divisions on Salisbury Plain: The Work of the Wessex Linear Ditches Project*, English Heritage.

Bradley, R., T. Philips, C. Richards and M. Webb, 2001, 'Decorating the Houses of the Dead: Incised and Pecked Motifs in Orkney Chambered Tombs', *Cambridge Archaeological Journal*, 45–67.

Brennand, M. and M. Taylor, 2003, 'The Survey and Excavation of a Bronze Age Timber Circle at Holme-next-the-Sea, Norfolk, 1998–9', *Proceedings of the Prehistoric Society* 69, 1–84.

Brentjes, B., 2000, '"Animal style" and shamanism: problems of pictorial tradition in northern in central Asia', in Davis-Kimball, J., E. Murphy, L. Koryakova and L. Yablonsky (eds), *Kurgans, Ritual Sites, and Settlements: Eurasian Bronze and Iron Age*, Oxford, British Archaeological Reports (International Series) 890, 259–68.

Briard, J., 1976, 'Les civilisations de l'Age du Bronze en Armorique', in Guilaine, J. (ed.), *La Préhistoire Française II: Les Civilisations Néolithiques et Protohistoriques de la France*, Paris, Éditions du Centre National de la Recherche Scientifique, 561–74.

Briard, J., 1984, *Les Tumulus d'Armorique*, Paris, L'Âge du Bronze en France 3.

Bridgeford, S., 1997, 'Mightier than the pen? (An edgewise look at Irish Bronze Age swords)', in Carman, J. (ed.), *Material Harm: Archaeological Studies of War and Violence*, Glasgow, Cruithne Press, 95–115.

Broholm, H., 1944, *Danmarks Bronzealder 1. Kultur og Folk i den Ældre Bronzealder*, Copenhagen, Nordisk Forlag.

Broholm, H., 1953, *Danske Oldsager IV: Yngre Bronzealder*, Copenhagen, Gyldendalske Boghandel.

Brophy, K., 1999, 'The Cursus monuments of Scotland', in Barclay, A. and J. Harding (eds), *Pathways and Ceremonies: The Cursus Monuments of Britain and Ireland*, Oxford, Oxbow, 119–29.

Brophy, K., 2000, 'Water coincidence? Cursus monuments and rivers', in Ritchie, A. (ed.), *Neolithic Orkney in its European Context*, Cambridge, McDonald Institute, 59–70.

Brophy, K., 2006, 'From Big Houses to Cult Houses: Early Neolithic Timber Halls in Scotland', *Proceedings of the Prehistoric Society* 73, 75–96.

Brophy, K. and G. Barclay, 2004, 'A Rectilinear Timber Structure and Post-Ring at Carsie Mains, Meikleour, Perthshire', *Tayside and Fife Archaeological Journal* 10, 1–22.

Brossler, A., R. Early and C. Allen, 2004, *Green Park (Reading Business Park): Phase 2 Excavations 1995 – Neolithic and Bronze Age Sites*, Oxford, Oxford Archaeology.

Brothwell, D. and J. Bourke, 1986, 'The human remains from Lindow Moss 1987–8', in Turner, R. and R. Scaife (eds), *Bog Bodies: New Discoveries and New Perspectives*, Trustees of British Museum Press, 52–61.

Brothwell, D., D. Liversage and B. Gottlieb, 1990, 'Radiographic and Forensic Aspects of the female Huldremose Body', *Journal of Danish Archaeology* 9, 157–78.

Brown, A., 1993, *Before Knossos … Arthur Evans's Travels in the Balkans and Crete*, Oxford, Ashmolean Museum.

Brown, P., T. Sutikna, M. Morwood et al., 2004, 'A New Small-Bodied Hominin from the Late Pleistocene of Flores, Indonesia', *Nature* 431, 1055–61.

Brown, R. and J. Kulik., 1977, 'Flashbulb Memories', *Cognition* 5, 73–99.

Brück, J., 1995, 'A Place for the Dead: The Role of Human Remains in Late Bronze Age Britain', *Proceedings of the Prehistoric Society* 61, 245–77.

Brück, J., 1999a, 'Houses, Lifecycles and Deposits on Middle Bronze Age Settlements in Southern England', *Proceedings of the Prehistoric Society* 65, 145–66.

Brück, J., 1999b, 'What's in a settlement? Domestic practice and residential mobility in Early Bronze Age southern England', in Brück, J. and M. Goodman (eds), *Making Places in the Prehistoric World: Themes in Settlement Archaeology*, UCL Press, 52–75.

Brück, J., 2001, 'Body metaphors and technologies of transformation in the English middle and late Bronze Age', in Brück, J. (ed.), *Bronze Age Landscapes: Tradition and Transformation*, Oxford, Oxbow, 149–60.

Brück, J., 2004, 'Material Metaphors: The Relational Construction of Identity in Early Bronze Age Burials in Ireland and Britain', *Journal of Social Archaeology* 4, 307–33.

Brück, J., 2006, 'Fragmentation, Personhood and the Social Construction of Technology in Middle and Late Bronze Age Britain', *Cambridge Archaeological Journal* 16, 297–315.

Brunaux, J.-L., 1988, *The Celtic Gauls: Gods, Rites and Sanctuaries*, Seaby.

Brunaux, J.-L., and P. Méniel, 1997, *Le Résidence Aristocratique de Montmartin (Oise) du IIIᵉ au IIᵉ s. av. J.-C.*, Paris, Éditions de la Maison des Sciences de l'Homme.

Brunaux, J.-L., P. Meniel and F. Poplin, 1985, *Gournay I. Les Fouilles sur le Sanctuaire et L'Oppidum (1975–1984)*, Amiens Revue Archéologique de Picardie Numéro Spécial 180F.

Brunt, P., 1971, *Social Conflicts in the Roman Republic*, W.W. Norton.

Buckley, D. and J. Hedges, 1987, *The Bronze Age and Saxon Settlements at Springfield Lyons, Essex: An Interim Report*, Essex, Essex County Council.

Bucko, R., 1998, *The Lakota Ritual of the Sweat Lodge: History and Contemporary Practice*, Lincoln, University of Nebraska Press.

Budd, P. and T. Taylor, 1995, 'The Faerie Smith Meets the Bronze Industry: Magic Versus Science in the Interpretation of Prehistoric Metalworking', *World Archaeology* 27, 133–143.

Budja, M., 2004, 'The Neolithicisation of the Balkans: where in the puzzle?', in Lukes, A. and M. Zvelebil (eds), *LBK Dialogues: Studies in the Formation of the Linear Pottery Culture*, Oxford, British Archaeological Reports (International Series) 1304, 37–48.

Budworth, G., M. McCord, A. Priston and I. Stead, 1986, 'The artefacts', in Stead, I., J. Bourke and D. Brothwell (eds), *Lindow Man – The Body in the Bog*, British Museum Publications, 38–40.

Burström, M., 1999, 'On earth as in heaven. Images of the divine as ideological messages in Bronze Age society', in Gustafsson, A. and H. Karlsson (eds), *Glyfer och Arkeologiska Rum – en Vänbok till Jarl Nordbladh*, Göteborg, Gotarc Series A, 625–31.

Butler, J., 1960, 'A Bronze Age Concentration at Bargeroosterveld', *Palaeohistoria* 8, 103–26.

Butler, J. and H. Sarfatij, 1970–1, 'Another Bronze Ceremonial Sword by the Plougrescant-Ommerschans Smith', *Berichten van de Rijksdienst voor het Oudheidkundig Bodemonderzoek* 20–21, 301–10.

Cadoux, J.-L., 1984, 'L'Ossuaire Gaulois de Ribemont-sur-Ancre (Somme): Premières Observations, Premières Questions', *Gallia* 42, 53–78.

Calder, C., 1936–7, 'A Neolithic Double-Chambered Cairn of the Stalled Type and Later Structures on the Calf of Eday, Orkney', *Proceedings of the Society of Antiquaries of Scotland* 71, 115–56.

Calder, C., 1938–9, 'Excavations of Iron Age Dwellings on the Calf of Eday, Orkney', *Proceedings of the Society of Antiquaries of Scotland* 73, 167–85.

Capelle, T., 1986, 'Schiffsetzungen', *Prähistorische Zeitschrift* 61, 1–63.

Capelle, T., 1995, *Anthropomorphe Holzidole in Mittel- und Nordeuropa*, Lund: Scripta Minora, Regiae Societatis Humanorum Litterarum Lundensis 1.

Caramelli, D., C. Lalueza-Fox, C. Vernesi et al., 2003, 'Evidence for a Genetic Discontinuity Between Neanderthals and 24,000-year-old Anatomically Modern Europeans', *Proceedings of the National Academy of Sciences of the USA* 100, 6593–7.

Cardoso, J., G. Querré and L. Salanova, 2005, 'Bell beaker relationships along the Atlantic coast', in Prudêncio, I., I. Dias and J. Waerenborgh (eds), *Understanding People Through Their Pottery*, Lisbon, Instituto Português de Arqueologia, 27–31.

Case, H., 2004, 'Beakers and the Beaker culture', in Czebreszuk, J. (ed.), *Similar but Different: Bell Beakers in Europe*, Poznań, Adam Mickiewicz University, 11–34.

Casey, E., 1996, 'How to get from space to place in a fairly short stretch of time: phenomenological prolegomena', in Feld, S. and K. Basso (eds), *Senses of Place*, Santa Fe, School of American Research Press, 13–52.

Casson, L., 1995, *Ships and Seamanship in the Ancient World* [New Edition], Baltimore, The Johns Hopkins University Press.

Cauvin, J., 2007, *The Birth of the Gods and the Origins of Agriculture*, Cambridge, Cambridge University Press.

Chaix, L., A. Bidault and R. Picavet, 1997, 'A Tamed Brown Bear (*Ursus actos* L.) of the Late Mesolithic from la Grande Rivoire (Isère, France)?', *Journal of Archaeological Science* 24, 1067–74.

Chamberlain, A. and M. Parker Pearson, 2001, *Earthly Remains: The History and Science of Preserved Human Bodies*, British Museum Press.

Chambers, F. and M. Jones, 1984, 'Antiquity of Rye in Britain', *Antiquity* 58, 219–24.

Champion, T., 1995, 'Power, politics and status', in Green, M. (ed.), *The Celtic World*, Routledge, 85–94.

Chapman, H., 2005, 'Rethinking the "Cursus Problem" – Investigating the Neolithic Landscape Archaeology of Rudston, East Yorkshire, UK, Using GIS', *Proceedings of the Prehistoric Society* 71, 159–70.

Chapman, R., 1984, 'Early metallurgy in Iberia and the Western Mediterranean: Innovation, Adoption and Production', in Waldren, W., R. Chapman, J. Lewthwaite and R. Kennard (eds), *The Deya Conference of Prehistory: Early Settlement in the Western Mediterranean Islands and their Peripheral Areas*, Oxford, British Archaeological Reports (International Series) 229, 1139–61.

Chapman, R., 1990, *Emerging Complexity: The Later Prehistory of South-East Spain, Iberia and the West Mediterranean*, Cambridge, Cambridge University Press.

Charles, R and R. Jacobi, 1994, 'The Late Glacial Fauna from the Robin Hood Cave, Creswell Crags: A Re-assessment', *Oxford Journal of Archaeology* 13, 1–32.

Chase P. and H. Dibble, 1987, 'Middle Palaeolithic Symbolism: A Review of Current Evidence and Interpretations', *Journal of Anthropological Archaeology* 6, 263–96.

Chase, P., 2007, '"The significance of 'acculturation' depends on the meaning of "culture"', in Mellars, P., K. Boyle, O. Bar-Yosef and C. Stringer (eds), *Rethinking the Human Revolution*, Cambridge, McDonald Institute Monographs, 55–65.

Childe, V. G., 1925, *The Dawn of European Civilisation*, Routledge & Kegan Paul.

Childs, T., 1991, 'Style, Technology and Iron Smelting Furnaces in Bantu-Speaking Africa', *Journal of Anthropological Archaeology* 10, 332–59.

Clarke, J., 1954, *Excavations at Star Carr: An Early Mesolithic Site at Seamer, Near Scarborough, Yorkshire*, Cambridge, Cambridge University Press.

Clay, R., 1927, 'A Late Bronze Age Urn-Field at Pokesdown, Hants', *The Antiquaries Journal* 7, 465–84.

Clottes, J., 2008, *Cave Art*, Phaidon.

Clottes, J., 2009, 'Sticking bones into cracks in the Upper Palaeolithic', in Renfrew, C. and I. Morley (eds), *Becoming Human: Innovation in Prehistoric Material and Spiritual Culture*, Cambridge, Cambridge University Press, 195–211.

Clottes, J. and D. Lewis-Williams, 1996, *The Shamans of Prehistory: Trance and Magic in the Painted Caves*, Paris, Le Seuil.

Clutton-Brock, J. and N. Noe-Nygaard, 1990, 'New Osteological and C-Isotope Evidence on Mesolithic Dogs: Companions to Hunters and Fishers at Star Carr, Seamer Carr and Kongemose', *Journal of Archaeological Science* 17, 643–53.

Coblenz, W., 1956, 'Skelettgräber von Zauschwitz, Kreis Borna', *Arbeits- und Forschungsberichte der Sächsischen Bodendenkmalpflege* 5, 57–119.

Cole, S., 1965, *The Neolithic Revolution*, British Museum.

Coles, B., 1990, 'Anthropomorphic Wooden Figures from Britain and Ireland', *Proceedings of the Prehistoric Society* 56, 315–33.

Coles, J., 1962, 'European Bronze Age Shields', *Proceedings of the Prehistoric Society* 28, 156–90.

Coles, J., 1993, 'Boats on the Rocks', in Coles, J., V. Fenwick and G. Hutchinson (eds), *A Spirit of Enquiry: Essays for Ted Wright*, Essex, Wetland Archaeology Research Project, 23–31.

Coles, J., 2002, 'Chariots of the Gods? Landscape and Imagery at Frännarp, Sweden', *Proceedings of the Prehistoric Society* 68, 215–246.

Coles, J., 2004, 'Bridge to the Outer World: Rock Carvings at Bro Utmark, Bohuslän, Sweden', *Proceedings of the Prehistoric Society* 70, 173–206.

Coles, J., 2005, *Shadows of a Northern Past: Rock Carvings of Bohuslän and Østfold*, Oxford, Oxbow.

Coles, J., 2006, 'Beacon on the Ridge. Rock Carvings at Kasen Lövåsen, Bohuslän, Sweden', *Proceedings of the Prehistoric Society* 72, 319–39.

Collett, D., 1993, 'Metaphors and representations associated with pre-colonial iron-smelting in Eastern and Southern Africa', in Shaw, T., P. Sinclair, B. Andah and A. Okpoko (eds), *The Archaeology of Africa: Food, Metals and Towns*, Routledge, 499–511.

Collis, J., 1977, 'Iron Age Henges?', *Archaeologia Atlantica* 2, 55–63.

Collis, J., 1984, *Oppida: Earliest Towns North of the Alps*, Sheffield, J.R. Collis Publications.

Collis, J., 1996, 'Hill-forts, Enclosures and Boundaries', in Champion, T. and J. Collis (eds), *The Iron Age in Britain and Ireland: Recent Trends*, Sheffield, J.R. Collis Publications, 87–94.

Conard, N., 2003, 'Palaeolithic Ivory Sculptures from Southwestern Germany and the Origins of Figurative Art', *Nature* 426, 830–2.

Conneller, C., 2004, 'Becoming Deer. Corporeal Transformations at Star Carr', *Archaeological Dialogues* 11, 37–56.

Conneller, C. and T. Schadla-Hall, 2003, 'Beyond Star Carr: The Vale of Pickering in the 10th Millennium BP', *Proceedings of the Prehistoric Society* 69, 85–106.

Cook, J., 1991, 'Preliminary report on marked human bones from the 1986–1987 excavations at Gough's Cave, Somerset, England', in Barton, N., A. Roberts and D. Roe (eds), *The Late Glacial in North-West Europe: Human Adaptation and Environmental Change at the End of the Pleistocene*, CBA Research Report 77, 160–8.

Cooney, G. and E. Grogan, 1994, *Irish Prehistory: A Social Perspective*, Dublin, Wordwell.

Cornell, T., 1995, *The Beginnings of Rome: Italy and Rome from the Bronze Age to the Punic Wars (c. 1000–264 BC)*, Routledge.

Cotton, M. and S. Frere., 1968. Ivinghoe Beacon Excavations, 1963–65, *Records of Buckinghamshire* 18, 187–260.

Creighton, J., 2000, *Coins and Power in Late Iron Age Britain*, Cambridge, Cambridge University Press.

Cross, S., 2003, 'Irish Neolithic settlement architecture – a reappraisal', in Armit, I., E. Murphy, E. Nelis and D. Simpson (eds) *Neolithic Settlement in Ireland and Western Britain*, Oxford, Oxbow, 195–202.

Crouwel, J., 1981, *Chariots and Other Means of Land Transport in Bronze Age Greece*, Amsterdam, Allard Pierson Series, Volume 3.

Cunliffe, B., 1984, *Danebury: An Iron Age Hillfort in Hampshire. Volume 1 – The Excavations 1969–1978: The Site*, Council for British Archaeology Research Report No. 52.

Cunliffe, B., 1993, *Fertility, Propitiation and the Gods in the British Iron Age*, Amsterdam, Universiteit van Amsterdam.

Cunliffe, B., 1995, *Danebury: An Iron Age Hillfort in Hampshire. Volume 6: A Hillfort Community in Perspective*, York, Council for British Archaeology Research Report No. 102.

Cunliffe, B., 1997, *The Ancient Celts*, Oxford, Oxford University Press.

Cunliffe, B., 2000, 'Brittany and the Atlantic Rim in the Later First Millennium BC', *Oxford Journal of Archaeology* 19, 367–86.

Cunliffe, B., 2001, *Facing the Ocean: The Atlantic and its Peoples*, Oxford, Oxford University Press.

Cunliffe, B., 2002, *The Extraordinary Voyage of Pytheas the Greek: The Man Who Discovered Britain*, Walker & Co.

Cunliffe, B., 2005, *Iron Age Communities in Britain*, [Fourth Edition], Routledge.

Cunliffe, B., 2008, *Europe Between the Oceans. Themes and Variations 9000 BC–AD 1000*, New Haven, Yale University Press.

Cunliffe, B. and C. Poole, 1991a, *Danebury: An Iron Age Hillfort in Hampshire. Volume 4 – The Excavations 1979–1988: The Site*, Council for British Archaeology Research Report No. 73.

Cunliffe, B. and C. Poole, 1991b, *Danebury: An Iron Age Hillfort in Hampshire. Volume 5 – The Excavations 1979–1988: The Finds*, Council for British Archaeology Research Report No. 73.

Cunliffe, B. and C. Poole, 2000a, *The Danebury Environs Programme: Volume 2 – Part 4: New Buildings, Longstock, Hants, 1992 and Fiveways, Longstock, Hants, 1996*, Oxford, Oxford Committee for Archaeology Monograph No. 49.

Cunliffe, B. and C. Poole, 2000b, *The Danebury Environs Programme: Volume 2 – Part 3: Suddern Farm, Middle Wallop, Hants, 1991 and 1996*, Oxford, Oxford Committee for Archaeology Monograph No. 49.

Currant, A., R. Jacobi and C. Stringer, 1989, 'Excavations of Gough's Cave, Somerset, 1986–7', *Antiquity* 63, 131–6.

Czaplicka, M., 1914, *Aboriginal Siberia: A Study in Social Anthropology*, Oxford, Clarendon Press.

Czigány, L., 1980, 'The Use of Hallucinogens and the Shamanistic Tradition of the Finno-Ugrian People', *The Slavonic and East European Review* 58, 212–17.

d'Aquili, E. and A. Newberg, 1999, *The Mystical Mind: Probing the Biology of Religious Experience*, Minneapolis, Fortress Press.

d'Errico, F., 2003, 'The Invisible Frontier: A Multiple Species Model for the Origin of Behavioural Modernity', *Evolutionary Anthropology* 12, 188–202.

d'Errico, F. and A. Nowell, 2000, 'A New Look at the Berekhat Ram Figurine: Implications for the Origin of Symbolism', *Cambridge Archaeological Journal* 10, 123–67.

d'Errico, F. and M. Vanhaeren, 2007, 'Evolution or revolution? New evidence for the origin of symbolic behaviour in and out of Africa', in Mellars, P., K. Boyle, O. Bar-Yosef and C. Stringer (eds), *Rethinking the Human Revolution*, Cambridge, McDonald Institute Monographs, 275–86.

Dart, R., 1967, *Adventures with the Missing Link*, Philadelphia, The Institutes Press.

Darvill, T., 2007, Message in the Stones, *Current Archaeology* 212, 12–19.

David, B., 2002, *Landscapes, Rock-Art and the Dreaming*, Leicester, Leicester University Press.

Davies, S., 2007, *The Mabinogion*, Oxford, Oxford University Press.

Davies, W., 2001, 'A Very Model of a Human Industry: New Perspectives on the Origins and Spread of the Aurignacian in Europe', *Proceedings of the Prehistoric Society* 67, 195–217.

Davies, W., 2007, 'Re-evaluating the Aurignacian as an expression of modern human mobility and dispersal' in Mellars, P., K. Boyle, O. Bar-Yosef and C. Stringer (eds), *Rethinking the Human Revolution*, Cambridge, McDonald Institute Monographs, 263–74.

Davis, R., 1999, 'Bronze Age Metalwork from the Trent Valley: Newark, Notts. to Gainsborough, Lincs', *Transactions of the Thoroton Society of Nottinghamshire* 103, 25–48.

Davis, S. and F. Valla., 1978, 'Evidence for Domestication of the Dog 12,000 Years Ago in the Natufian of Israel', *Nature* 276, 608–10.

Davis, S. and S. Payne, 1993, 'A Barrow Full of Cattle Skulls', *Antiquity* 67, 12–22.

Davis-Kimball, J., 2000, 'Enarees and women of high status: evidence of ritual at Tillya Tepe (northern Afghanistan)', in Davis-Kimball, J., E. Murphy, L. Koryakova and L. Yablonsky (eds), *Kurgans, Ritual Sites, and Settlements: Eurasian Bronze and Iron Age*, Oxford, British Archaeological Reports (International Series) 890, 223–39.

de Grooth, M., 1997, 'Social and Economic Interpretations of the Chert Procurement Strategies of the Bandkeramik settlement at Heinheim, Bavaria', *Analecta Praehistorica Leidensia* 29, 91–8.

Delattre, V., 2000, 'De la Relégation Sociale à l'Hypothèse des Offrandes: l'Exemple des Dépôts en Silos Protohistoriques au confluent Seine-Yonne (Seine-et-Marne)', *Révue Archéologique du Centre de la France* 39, 5–30.

Derks, T., 1991, 'The perception of the Roman pantheon by a native elite: the example of votive inscriptions from lower Germany', in Roymans, Nico and Frans Theuws (eds), *Images of the Past: Studies on Ancient Societies in Northwestern Europe*, Amsterdam, Amsterdam University Press, 235–65.

Derks, T., 1998, *Gods, Temples and Religious Practices: The Transformation of Religious Ideas and Values in Roman Gaul*, Amsterdam, Amsterdam University Press.

Dickinson, O., 1994, *The Aegean Bronze Age*, Cambridge, Cambridge University Press.

Dickson, J., K. Oeggl, T. Holden et al., 2000, 'The Omnivorous Tyrolean Iceman: Colon Contents (Meat, Cereals, Pollen, Moss and Whipworm) and Stable Isotope Analyses', *Philosophical Transactions: Biological Sciences* 355, 1843–49.

Diószegi, V., 1960, *Tracing Shamans in Siberia: The Story of an Ethnographical Research Expedition*, Oosterhout, Anthropological Publications.

Diószegi, V., 1998a, 'Shamanism', in Hoppál, M. (ed.), *Shamanism: Selected Writings of Vilmos Diószegi*, Budapest, Akadémiai Kiadó, 1–9.

Diószegi, Vilmos, 1998b, 'How to become a shaman among the Sagais', in Hoppál, Mihály (ed.), *Shamanism: Selected Writings of Vilmos Diószegi*, Budapest, Akadémiai Kiadó, 27–35.

Dixon, P., 1994, *Crickley Hill. The Hillfort Defences*, Nottingham, University of Nottingham.

Dobkin de Rios, M., 1996, *Hallucinogens: Cross-Cultural Perspectives*, Prospect Heights, Waveland Press.

Dolukhanov, P., 2002, 'Alternative revolutions: hunter–gatherers, farmers and stock-breeders in the northwestern Pontic area', in Boyle, K., C. Renfrew and M. Levine (eds), *Ancient Interactions: East and West in Eurasia*, Cambridge, McDonald Institute for Archaeological Research, 13–24.

Dolukhanov, P., 2008, 'The Mesolithic of European Russia, Belarus, and the Ukraine', in Bailey, G. and P. Spikins (eds), *Mesolithic Europe*, Cambridge, Cambridge University Press, 280–301.

Donald, M., 1991, *Origins of the Modern Mind: Three Stages in the Evolution of Culture and Cognition,* Cambridge, MA., Harvard University Press.

Donner, K., 1920, 'Ornements de la Tête et de la Chevelure. Quelques mots sur leur Signification', *Journal de la Société Finno-Ougrienne* 37, 1–23.

Dothan, T. and M. Dothan, 1992, *People of the Sea: The Search for the Philistines*, New York, Macmillan.

Downes, J., 1997, 'The shrine at South Cadbury Castle: belief enshrined?', in Gwilt, A. and C. Haselgrove (eds), *Reconstructing Iron Age Societies: New Approaches to the British Iron Age*, Oxford, Oxbow Monograph 71, 145–52.

Dowson, T., 1998, 'Rock art: handmaiden to studies of cognitive evolution', in Renfrew, C. and C. Scarre (eds), *Cognition and Material Culture: The Archaeology of Symbolic Storage*, Cambridge, McDonald Institute for Archaeological Research, 67–76.

Dowson, T. and M. Porr, 2001, 'Special objects – special creatures: shamanistic imagery and the Aurignacian art of south-west Germany', in Price, N. (ed.) *The Archaeology of Shamanism*, Routledge, 165–77.

Drewett, P., 1982, 'Later Bronze Age Downland Economy and Excavations at Black Patch, East Sussex', *Proceedings of the Prehistoric Society* 48, 321–400.

Dronfield, J., 1995, 'Migraine, Light and Hallucinogens: the Neurocognitive Basis of Irish Megalithic Art', *Oxford Journal of Archaeology* 14, 261–75.

Duarte, C., J. Maurício, P. Pettitt et al., 1999, 'The Early Upper Palaeolithic Human Skeleton from the Abrigo do Lagar Velho (Portugal) and Modern Human Emergence in Iberia', *Proceedings of the National Academy of Sciences of the USA* 96, 7604–9.

Dubois, E., 1924, 'On the Principal Characters of the Cranium and the Brain, the Mandible and the Teeth of *Pithecanthropus erectus*', *Koninklijke Nederlandsche Akademie van Wetenschappen te Amsterdam* 27, 265–78.

Dunkin, D., 2001, 'Metalwork, Burnt Mounds and Settlement on the West Sussex Coastal Plain: A Contextual Study', *Antiquity* 75, 261–2.

Dunn, E., 1973, 'Russian Use of *Amanita muscaria*: A Footnote to Wasson's *Soma*', *Current Anthropology* 14, 488–92.

Dvořák, P., A. Matějíčková, J. Peška, and I. Rakovský, 1996, *Gräberfelder der Glockenbecherkultur in Mähren II (Bezirk Břeclav): Katalog der Funde*, Brno, Olomouc.

Džaparidze, V., G. Bosinski, T. Bugianišvili et al., 1989, 'Der altpaläolithische Fundplatz Dmanisi in Georgien (Kaukasus)', *Jahrbuch des Römisch-Germanischen Zentralmuseums Mainz* 36, 67–116.

Ebel, C., 1976, *Transalpine Gaul: The Emergence of a Roman Province*, Leiden, E.J. Brill.

Eckardt, H., 2008, 'Technologies of the body: Iron Age and Roman grooming and display', in Garrow, D., C. Gosden and J.D. Hill (eds), *Rethinking Celtic Art*, Oxford, Oxbow, 113–28.

Edelman, G., 1994, *Bright Air, Brilliant Fire: On the Matter of the Mind*, Harmondsworth, Penguin.

Edmonds, M., 1993, 'Interpreting causewayed enclosures in the past and the present', in Tilley, C. (ed.), *Interpretative Archaeology*, Berg, 99–142.

Edmonds, M., 1995, *Stone Tools and Society: Working Stone in Neolithic and Bronze Age Britain*, Batsford.

Egarter Vigl, E. and P. Gostner, 2002, 'Report of Radiological-Forensic Findings on the Iceman', *Journal of Archaeological Science* 29, 323–6.

Ehrenberg, M., 1980, 'The Occurrence of Bronze Age Metalwork in the Thames: An Investigation', *Transactions of the London and Middlesex Archaeological Society* 31: 1–15.

Eidlitz, K., 1969, 'Food and Emergency Food in the Circumpolar Area', *Studia Ethnographica Uppsaliensia* 32.

Eliade, M., 1954, *The Myth of Eternal Return*, Princeton, Princeton University Press.

Eliade, M., 1964, *Shamanism: Archaic Techniques of Ecstasy*, Arkana.

Ellis, P., 1995, *Celtic Women: Women in Celtic Society and Literature*, Constable.

Eluére, C., 1998, 'The world of the gods in the Bronze Age', in Demakopoulou, K., C. Eluére, J. Jensen et al. (eds), *Gods and Heroes of the European Bronze Age*, Thames and Hudson, 132–6.

Emmerling, E., H. Geer and B. Klíma, 1993, 'Eine Mondkalenderstab aus Dolní Věstonice', *Quartär* 43/44, 151–62.

Enard, W., M. Przeworski, S. Fisher et al., 2002, 'Molecular Evolution of *FOXP2*, A Gene Involved in Speech and Language', *Nature* 418, 869–72.

Eogan, G., 1994, *The Accomplished Art: Gold and Gold-Working in Britain and Ireland During the Bronze Age*, Oxford, Oxbow.

Erdoğu, B., 2003, 'Visualising Neolithic Landscape: The Early Settled Communities in Western Anatolia and Eastern Aegean Islands', *European Journal of Prehistory* 6, 7–23.

Evans, J., A Chenery and A. Fitzpatrick, 2006, 'Bronze Age Childhood Migration of Individuals Near Stonehenge, Revealed by Strontium and Oxygen Isotope Tooth Enamel Analysis', *Archaeometry* 48, 309–21.

Farbstein, R. and J. Svoboda, 2007, 'New Finds of Upper Palaeolithic Decorative Objects from Předmostí, Czech Republic', *Antiquity* 81, 856–64.

Fiedorczuk, J., B. Bratlund, E. Kolstrup and R. Schild, 2007, 'Late Magdalenian Feminine Flint Plaquettes from Poland', *Antiquity* 311, 97–105.

Field, D., 2001, 'Place and memory in Bronze Age Wessex', in Brück, J. (ed.), *Bronze Age Landscapes: Tradition and Transformation*, Oxford, Oxbow, 57–64.

Field, D., 2006, 'Earthen Long Barrows: The Earliest Monuments in the British Isles', Stroud, Tempus.

Fischer, C., 1979, 'Moseligene fra Bjældskovdal', *Kuml* 1979: 7–44.

Fischer, C., 1980, 'Bog bodies of Denmark', in Cockburn, A. and E. Cockburn (eds), *Mummies, Diseases and Ancient Cultures*, Cambridge, Cambridge University Press, 177–93.

Fischer, C., 1999, 'The Tollund Man and the Elling Woman and other bog bodies from central Jutland', in Coles, B., J. Coles and M. Schou Jørgensen (eds), *Bog Bodies, Sacred Sites and Wetland Archaeology*, Exeter, Wetland Archaeology Research Project, 93–7.

Fischer, F., 1982, 'Frühkeltische Fürstengräber in Mitteleuropa' *Antike Welt: Zeitschrift für Archäologie und Kulturgeschichte* 13 (Sondernummer), 2–72.

Fitzpatrick, A., 1996, 'Night and Day: The Symbolism of Astral Signs on Later Iron Age Anthropomorphic Short Swords', *Proceedings of the Prehistoric Society* 62, 373–98.

Fitzpatrick, A., 1997, 'Everyday life in Iron Age Wessex', in Gwilt, A. and C. Haselgrove (eds), *Reconstructing Iron Age Societies: New Approaches to the British Iron Age*, Oxford, Oxbow Monograph 71, 73–86.

Fitzpatrick, A., 2003, 'The Amesbury Archer', *Current Archaeology* 184, 146–52.

Fitzpatrick, A., 2004, 'The Boscombe Bowmen: Builders of Stonehenge', *Current Archaeology* 193, 10–6.

Fjellström, P., 1985, 'Sacrifices, burial gifts and buried treasures: function and material', in Bäckman, L. and Å. Hultkrantz (eds), *Saami Pre-Christian Religion: Studies on the Oldest Traces of Religion Among the Saamis*, Stockholm, Almqvist and Wiksell, 43–60.

Fleming, A., 1987, 'Coaxial Field Systems: Some Questions of Time and Space', *Antiquity* 61, 188–202.

Fokkens, H., 1997, 'The Genesis of Urnfields: Economic Crisis or Ideological Change?', *Antiquity* 71, 360–73.

Fokkens, H., 1998, *Drowned landscape: The Occupation of the Western Part of the Frisian-Drentian Plateau, 4400BC–AD500*, Amersfoort, Rijksdienst voor het Oudheidkundig Bodemonderzoek.

Fokkens, H., Y. Achterkamp and M. Kuijpers, 2008, 'Bracers or Bracelets? About the Functionality and Meaning of Bell Beaker Wrist-guards', *Proceedings of the Prehistoric Society* 74, 109–140.

Fol, A. and J. Lichardus (eds), 1988, *Macht, Herrschaft und Gold: Das Gräberfeld von Varna (Bulgarien) und die Anfänge einer Neuen Europäischen Zivilisation*, Saarbrücken, Moderne Galerie des Saarland-Museums.

Fox, A., 1954, 'Celtic Fields and Farms on Dartmoor, in the Light of Recent Excavations at Kestor', *Proceedings of the Prehistoric Society* 20, 87–102.

Fox, C., 1928, 'A Bronze Age Refuse Pit at Swanwick, Hants', *Antiquaries Journal* 8, 331–6.

Fox, C., 1930, 'The Bronze Age Refuse Pit at Swanwick: Further Finds', *Antiquaries Journal* 10, 30–3.

Fox, C., 1946, *A Find of the Early Iron Age from Llyn Cerrig Bach, Anglesey*, Cardiff, National Museum of Wales.

Frayer, D., 1997, 'Ofnet: evidence for a Mesolithic massacre', in Martin, D. and D. Frayer (eds), *Troubled Times: Violence and Warfare in the Past*, Amsterdam, Gordon & Breach, 181–216.

Galan Domingo, E., 1993, *Estelas, Paisaje y Territorio en el Bronce Final del Suroeste de la Península Ibérica*, Madrid, Editorial Complutense.

Gamble, C., 1999, *The Palaeolithic Societies of Europe*, Cambridge, Cambridge University Press.

Garašanin, M. and I. Radovanović, 2001, 'A Pot in House 54 at Lepenski Vir I', *Antiquity* 75, 118–25.

Garrido, J., 1970 and 1978, *Excavaciones en la Necrópolis de La Joya, Huelva*, Excavaciones Arqueológicas en España, Volumes 71 and 96.

Geiselman, E., R. Fisher, D. MacKinnon and H. Holland, 1985, 'Eyewitness Memory Enhancement in the Police Interview: Cognitive Retrieval Mnemonics Versus Hypnosis', *Journal of Applied Psychology* 70, 401–12.

Gent, H., 1983, 'Centralised Storage in Later Prehistoric Britain', *Proceedings of the Prehistoric Society* 49, 243–67.

Gerritsen, F., 1999, 'To Build and Abandon: The Cultural Biography of Late Prehistoric Houses and Farmsteads in the Southern Netherlands', *Archaeological Dialogues* 6, 78–114.

Gibson, A., 1999, 'Cursus monuments and possible cursus monuments in Wales: avenues for research (or roads to nowhere?)', in Barclay, A. and J. Harding (eds), *Pathways and Ceremonies: The Cursus Monuments of Britain and Ireland*, Oxford, Oxbow, 130–40.

Gibson, A., 2005, *Stonehenge and Timber Circles*, Stroud, Tempus.

Giles, M., 2008, 'Seeing red: the aesthetics of martial objects in the British and Irish Iron Age', in Garrow, D., C. Gosden and J.D. Hill (eds), *Rethinking Celtic Art*, Oxford, Oxbow, 59–77.

Gimbutus, M., S. Winn and D. Shimabuku, 1989, *Achilleion: A Neolithic Settlement in Thessaly, Greece*, Los Angeles, UCLA.

Gingell, C., 1992, *The Marlborough Downs: A Later Bronze Age Landscape and its Origins*, Devizes, Wiltshire Archaeological and Natural History Society Monograph 1.

Giot, P.-R., J. L'Helgouac'h and J.-L. Monnier, 1979, *Préhistoire de la Bretagne*, Rennes, Ouest France.

Gkiasta, M., T. Russell, S. Shennan and J. Steele, 2003, 'Neolithic Transition in Europe: The Radiocarbon Record Revisited', *Antiquity* 77 45–62.

Gleirscher, P., 1996, 'Brandopferplätze, depotfunde und symbolgut im Ostalpenraum während der Spätbronze- und Früheisenzeit', in Huth, V. (ed.), *Archäologische Forschungen zum Kultgeschehen in der Jüngeren Bronzezeit und Frühen Eisenzeit Alteuropas*, Bonn, Habelt.

Glob, P., 1969, *The Bog People: Iron Age Man Preserved*, Faber and Faber.

Goldhahn, J., 1999, 'Rock art and the materialisation of a cosmology – the case of the Sagaholm barrow', in Goldhahn, J. (ed.) *Rock Art as Social Representation*, Oxford, British Archaeological Reports (International Series) 794, 77–100.

Golitko, M. and L. Keeley, 2007, 'Beating Ploughshares Back Into Swords: Warfare in the *Linearbandkeramik*', *Antiquity* 81, 332–42.

Gomez De Soto, J., 1993, 'Cooking for the elite: feasting equipment in the Late Bronze Age', in Scarre, C. and F. Healy (eds), *Trade and Exchange in Prehistoric Europe*, Oxford, Oxbow, 191–7.

González García, F., 2009, 'Between Warriors and Champions: Warfare and Social Change in the Later Prehistory of the North-Western Iberian Peninsula', *Oxford Journal of Archaeology* 28, 59–76.

Gosden, C. and Y. Marshall, 1999, 'The Cultural Biography of Objects', *World Archaeology* 31, 169–78.

Goudineau, C., 1990, *César et la Gaule*, Paris, Errance.

Govedarica, B and E. Kaiser, 1996, 'Die Äneolithischen Abstrakten und Zoomorphen Steinzepter Südost- und Osteuropas', *Eurasia Antiqua* 2, 59–103.

Grau Mira, I., 2003, 'Settlement Dynamics and Social Organisation in Eastern Iberia During the Iron Age (Eighth–Second Centuries BC)', *Oxford Journal of Archaeology* 22, 261–79.

Graziand, M., R. Andersen and R. Snowden, 1994, 'Tuning of MST Neurons to Spiral Motions', *The Journal of Neuroscience* 14, 54–67.

Green, C., 1987, *Excavations at Poundbury, Dorchester, Dorset 1966–1982. Volume 1: The Settlements*, Dorset Natural History and Archaeological Society Monograph Series, Number 7.

Green, M., 1986, *The Gods of the Celts*, Stroud, Sutton.

Green, M., 1991, 'Cosmovision and Metaphor: Monsters and Shamans in Gallo-British Cult-Expression', *European Journal of Archaeology* 4, 203–32.

Green, M., 1992, *Animals in Celtic Life and Myth*, Routledge.

Green, M., 1997a, 'The symbolic horse in pagan Celtic Europe: an archaeological perspective', in Davies, S. and N. Jones (eds), *The Horse in Celtic Culture: Medieval Welsh Perspectives*, Cardiff, University of Wales Press, 1–22.

Green, M., 1997b, 'Images in Opposition: Polarity, Ambivalence and Liminality in Cult Representation', *Antiquity* 71, 898–911.

Green, P. 1996, *The Greco-Persian Wars*, Berkley, University of California Press.

Grine, F (ed.), 1988, *Evolutionary History of the 'Robust' Australopithecine*, New York, Aldine de Gruyter.

Gronenborn, D., 2007, 'Beyond the models: 'Neolithisation' in central Europe', in Whittle, A. and V. Cummings (eds), *Going Over: The Mesolithic – Neolithic Transition in North-West Europe*, Oxford, Proceedings of the British Academy 144, 73–98.

Guerra-Doce, E., 2006, 'Exploring the Significance of Beaker Pottery Through Residual Analysis', *Oxford Journal of Archaeology* 25, 247–59.

Guilbert, G., 1976, 'Moel y Gaer (Rhosesmor) 1972–1973: an area excavation of the interior', in Harding, Derek (ed.), *Hillforts. Later Prehistoric Earthworks in Britain and Ireland*, Academic Press, 303–17.

Gurina, N., 1956, *Oleneostrovskii Mogil'nik*, Moscow, Akademiya Nauk.

Gvozdover, M., 1995, *Art of the Mammoth Hunters: The Finds from Avdeevo*, Oxford, Oxbow.

Haggarty, A., 1991, 'Machrie Moor, Arran: Recent Excavations at Two Stone Circles', *Proceedings of the Society of Antiquaries of Scotland* 121, 51–94.

Hahn, J., 1986, *Kraft und Aggression. Die Botschaft der Eiszeitkunst im Aurignacien?* Tübingen, Archaeologica Venatoria.

Hahn, J., 1993, 'Aurignacian and Gravettian art in central Europe', in Knecht, H., A. Pike-Tay and R. White (eds), *Before Lascaux: The Complete Record of the Early Upper Palaeolithic*, Boca-Raton, CRC Press, 229–57.

Halifax, J., 1982, *Shaman: The Wounded Healer*, Thames and Hudson.

Halkon, P. and M. Millet, 1999, *Rural Settlement and Industry: Studies in the Iron Age and Roman Archaeology of Lowland East Yorkshire*, Leeds, Yorkshire Archaeological Society.

Halstead, P., 2005, 'Resettling the Neolithic: faunal evidence for seasons of consumption and residence at Neolithic sites in Greece', in Bailey, D., A. Whittle and V. Cummings (eds), *(Un)settling the Neolithic*, Oxford, Oxbow, 38–50.

Hamilton Cushing, F., 1999, *Zuni Fetishes* [New Edition], Las Vegas, K.C. Publications.

Hansen, S., 1991, *Studien zu den Metalldeponierungen während der Urnenfelderzeit im Rhein-Main-Gebiet*, Bonn, Habelt.

Hanson, V. (ed.), 1991, *Hoplites: The Classical Greek Battle Experience*, Routledge.

Harding, A., 1999, 'Warfare: a defining characteristic of the Bronze Age?', in Carman, J. and A. Harding (eds), *Ancient Warfare: Archaeological Perspectives*, Stroud, Sutton, 157–73.

Harding, A., 2000, *European Societies in the Bronze Age*, Cambridge, Cambridge University Press.

Harding, J., 2003, *Henge Monuments of the British Isles*, Stroud, Tempus.

Harild, J., D. Robinson and J. Hudlebusch, 2007, 'New Analysis of Grauballe Man's Gut Contents', in Asingh, P., *The Grauballe Man: An Iron Age Bog Body Revisited*, Aarhus, Aarhus University Press, 155–87.

Harner, M., 1968, 'The Sound of Rushing Water', *Natural History* 77, 28–33 and 60–1.

Harner, M., 1990, *The Way of the Shaman*, New York, Harper and Row.

Harner, S. and W. Tryon, 1992, 'Psychoimmunological effects of shamanic drumming', in Hoppál, M. and J. Pentikainen (eds), *Northern Religions and Shamanism: The Regional Conference of the International Association of the History of Religions: Selected Papers*, Budapest, Akadémiai Kiadó, 196–204.

Harrison, R., 1988, *Spain at the Dawn of History: Iberians, Phoenicians and Greeks*, Thames and Hudson.

Harsema, O.H., 1992, 'Bronze Age habitation and other archaeological remains near Hijken, Province of Drenthe, Netherlands', in Mordant, C. and A. Richard (eds), *L'Habitat et L'Occupation du Sol a L'Age du Bronze en Europe*, Paris, Editions du Comité des Travaux Historiques et Scientifiques, 71–87.

Harvey, G., 2005, *Animism: Respecting the Living World*, Hurst.

Hauptman Wahlgren, K., 1998, 'Encultured Rocks: Encounter with a Ritual World of the Bronze Age', *Current Swedish Archaeology* 6, 85–97.

Haynes, S., 2005, *Etruscan Civilisation: A Cultural History*, British Museum Press.

Hedengran, I., 1990, 'Skeppet i Kretsen: Kring en Symbolstruktur i Mälardalens Förhistoria', *Fornvännen* 85, 229–38.

Hedges, J., 1987a, *Bu, Gurness and the Brochs of Orkney. Part I: Bu*, Oxford, British Archaeological Reports (British Series) 163.

Hedges, J., 1987b, *Bu, Gurness and the Brochs of Orkney. Part II: Gurness*, Oxford, British Archaeological Reports (British Series) 163.

Heidegger, M., 1962, *Being and Time*, Oxford, Blackwell.

Heim, J-L., 1976, 'Les Hommes Fossiles de la Ferrassie I', *Archives de l'Institut de Paléontologie Humaine* 35, 1–331.

Heinze, R.-I., 1993, 'Shamanic states of consciousness: access to different realities', in Hoppál, M. and K. Howard (eds), *Shamans and Cultures*, Budapest, Akadémiai Kiadó, 169–78.

Helbaek, H., 1958, 'Grauballemandens Sidste Måltid', *Kuml*, 83–116.

Helms, M., 1998, *Ulysses' Sail: An Ethnographic Odyssey of Power, Knowledge and Geographical Distance*, Princeton, Princeton University Press.

Helskog, K., 1987, 'Selective depictions. A study of 3,500 years of rock carvings from Arctic Norway and their relationship to the Sami drums', in Hodder, I. (ed.), *Archaeology as Long Term History*, Cambridge, Cambridge University Press, 17–30.

Helskog, K., 1999, 'The Shore Connection. Cognitive Landscape and Communication with Rock Carvings in Northernmost Europe', *Norwegian Archaeological Review* 32, 73–94.

Helvenston, P. and P. Bahn, 2002, 'Desperately Seeking Trance Plants: Testing the "Three Stages of the Trance" Model', New York, RJ Communications.

Henry-Gambier, D. and R. White, 2006, 'Modifications artificielles des vestiges humains Aurignaciens de la Grotte des Hyenes et la Galerie Dubalen', in Cabrera, V. and F. Bernaldo de Quiros (eds), *El Centenario de la Cueva de El Castillo: El Ocaso de los Neandertales*, Madrid, Ministerio de Educacion y Ciencia, 71–88.

Henshilwood, C., 2009, 'The origins of symbolism, spirituality, and shamans: exploring Middle Stone Age material culture in South Africa', in Renfrew, C. and I. Morley (eds), *Becoming Human: Innovation in Prehistoric Material and Spiritual Culture*, Cambridge, Cambridge University Press, 29–49.

Henshilwood, C., F. d'Errico, R. Yates et al., 2002, 'Emergence of Modern Human Behavior: Middle Stone Age Engravings from South Africa', *Science*: 295, 1278–80.

Henshilwood, C., F. d'Errico, M. Vanhaeren et al., 2004, 'Middle Stone Age Shell Beads from South Africa', *Science* 304, 404.

Heyd, V., 2007, 'Families, Prestige Goods, Warriors & Complex Societies: Beaker Groups of the 3rd Millennium cal BC Along the Upper and Middle Danube', *Proceedings of the Prehistoric Society* 73, 327–79.

Hill, J.D., 1995, *Ritual and Rubbish in the Iron Age of Wessex: A Study on the Formation of a Specific Archaeological Record*, Oxford, British Archaeological Reports (British Series), 242.

Hill, J.D., 1999, 'Settlement, landscape and regionality: Norfolk and Suffolk in the pre-Roman Iron Age of Britain and beyond', in Davies, J. and T. Williamson (eds), *Land of the Iceni: The Iron Age in East Anglia*, Norwich, University of East Anglia, 185–207.

Hines, J., 1997, 'Religion: the limits of knowledge', in Hines, J. (ed.), *The Anglo-Saxons from the Migration Period to the Eighth Century: An Ethnographic Perspective*, Woodbridge, Boydell, 375–410.

Hingley, R., 1992, 'Society in Scotland from 700 BC to AD 200', *Proceedings of the Society of Antiquaries of Scotland* 122, 7–53.

Hingley, R., 1996, 'Ancestors and Identity in the Later Prehistory of Atlantic Scotland: The Reuse and Reinvention of Neolithic Monuments and Material Culture', *World Archaeology* 28, 231–43.

Hingley, R., 1997, 'Iron working and regeneration: a study of the symbolic meaning of metalworking in Iron Age Britain', in Gwilt, A. and C. Haselgrove (eds), *Reconstructing Iron Age Societies: New Approaches to the British Iron Age*, Oxford, Oxbow Monograph 71, 9–18.

Hingley, R., 1999, 'The creation of later prehistoric landscapes and the context of the reuse of Neolithic and earlier Bronze Age monuments in Britain and Ireland', in Bevan, B. (ed.), *Northern Exposure: The Iron Age in Northern Britain*, Leicester, Leicester Archaeology Monographs No. 4, 233–51.

Hingley, R. and C. Unwin, 2005, *Boudica: Iron Age Warrior Queen*, Hambledon Continuum.

Hodder, I., 1990, *The Domestication of Europe: Structure and Contingency in Neolithic Societies*, Oxford, Blackwell.

Hodgson, D., 2008, 'The Visual Dynamics of Upper Palaeolithic Cave Art', *Cambridge Archaeological Journal* 18, 341–53.

Hoffecker, J., 2002, *Desolate Landscapes: Ice-Age Settlement in Eastern Europe*, New Jersey, Rutgers University Press.

Holden, E., 1972, 'A Bronze Age Cemetery-Barrow on Itford Hill, Beddingham', *Sussex Archaeological Collection* 110, 70–117.

Holtorf, C., 1999, 'The Life-Histories of Megaliths in Mecklenburg-Vorpommern (Germany)', *World Archaeology* 30, 23–38.

Hopkins, K., 1978, *Conquerors and Slaves*, Cambridge, Cambridge University Press.

Hopkins, K., 1980, 'Taxes and Trade in the Roman Empire (200 BC–AD 400)', *Journal of Roman Studies* 70, 101–25.

Hoppál, M., 1992, 'Pain in shamanic initiation', in Hoppál, M. and J. Pentikainen (eds), *Northern Religions and Shamanism*, Budapest, Akadémiai Kiadó, 151–7.

Horowitz, M., 1975, 'Hallucinations: an information-processing approach', in Siegel, R. and L. West (eds), *Hallucinations: Behaviour, Experience, and Theory*, New York, Wiley, 163–95.

Hrala, J., Z. Sedláek and M. Vávra, 1992, 'Velim: A Hilltop Site of the Middle Bronze Age in Bohemia: Report on the Excavation 1984–90', *Památky Archeologické* 83, 288–308.

Hublin, J.-J., 2007, 'What can Neanderthals tell us about modern human origins?', in Mellars, P. K. Boyle, O. Bar-Yosef and C. Stringer (eds), *Rethinking the Human Revolution*, Cambridge, McDonald Institute Monographs, 235–48.

Humphrey, C. with U. Onon, 1996, *Shamans and Elders: Experience, Knowledge, and Power among the Daur Mongols*, Oxford, Oxford University Press.

Huntley, B. and T. Webb, 1988, *Vegetation History*, Dordrecht, Kluwer.

Husty, L., 2004, 'Glockenbecherzeitliche funde aus Landau a.d. Isar', in Heyd, V., L. Husty and L. Kreiner (eds), *Siedlungen der Glockenbecherkultur in Süddeutschland und Mitteleuropa*, Büchenbach, Dr Faustus, 15–102.

Hutton, R., 2001, *Shamans: Siberian Spirituality and the Western Imagination*, Hambledon and London.

Hutton, R., 2009, *Blood and Mistletoe: The History of Druids in Britain*, New Haven, Yale University Press.

Hvass, S., 1985, 'Hodde. Et Vestjysk Landsbysamfund fra Ældre Jernalder', Copenhagen, Universitetsforlaget i København Arkæologiske Studier Volume VII.

Ingold, T., 1993, 'The Temporality of the Landscape', *World Archaeology* 25, 152–74.

Jablonka, E. and M. Lamb, 1995, *Epigenetic Inheritance and Evolution: The Lamarckian Dimension*, Oxford, Oxford University Press.

Jacobi, R. and T. Higham, 2008, 'The "Red Lady" Ages Gracefully: New Ultrafiltration AMS Determinations from Paviland', *Journal of Human Evolution* 55, 898–907.

Jacobs, K., 1995, 'Return to Oleni'ostrov: Social, Economic and Skeletal Dimensions of a Boreal Forest Mesolithic Cemetery', *Journal of Anthropological Archaeology* 14, 359–403.

Jakobsen, M.D., 1999, *Shamanism: Traditional and Contemporary Approaches to the Mastery of Spirits and Healing*, New York, Berghahn Books.

Jenílek, J., J. Pelísek and K. Valoch, 1959, 'Der fossile Mensch Brno II', *Anthropos* 9, 5–30.

Jennbert, K., 1991–2, 'Changing Customs: Reflections on Grave Gifts, Burial Practices and Burial Rites During Period III of the Bronze Age in Southeast Scania', *Meddelanden från Lunds Universitets Historiska Museum*, 91–103.

Jennbert, K., 1998, '"From the inside": a contribution to the debate about the introduction of agriculture in southern Scandinavia', in Zvelebil, M., R. Dennell and L. Domanska (eds), *Harvesting the Sea, Farming the Forest: The Emergence of Neolithic Societies in the Baltic Region*, Sheffield, Sheffield Academic Press, 31–5.

Jensen, J., 1993, 'Metal deposits', in Hvass, Steen and Birger Storgaard (eds), *Digging the Past – 25 Years of Danish Archaeology*, Aarhus, Jutland Archaeological Society, 152–8.

Jensen, J., 1998, The heroes: life and death. In Demakopoulou, K., C. Eluére, J. Jensen et al. (eds), *Gods and Heroes of the European Bronze Age*, Thames and Hudson, 88–97.

Jochim, M., 2000, 'The origins of agriculture in south-central Europe', in Price, T.D. (ed.) *Europe's First Farmers*, Cambridge, Cambridge University Press, 183–218.

Jockenhövel, A., 1999, 'Bronzezeitlicher Burgenbau in Mitteleuropa. Untersuchungen zur Struktur Frümetallzeitlicher Gesellschaften', in *Orientalisch-Ägäische Einflüsse in der Europäischen Bronzezeit*, Mainz, Monographien des Römisch-Germanisches Zentralmuseums 15, 209–28.

Joffroy, R., 1954, *La Trésor de Vix*, Paris, Presses Universitaires de France.

Johansen, Ø., 1979, 'New Results in the Investigation of the Bronze Age Rock Carvings', *Norwegian Archaeological Review* 12, 108–14.

Johanson, D and B. Edgar, 1996, *From Lucy to Language*, Weidenfeld & Nicholson.

Johanson, D. and A. Maitland, 1981, *Lucy: The Beginnings of Humankind*, Harmondsworth, Penguin.

Johnston, R., 1999, 'An empty path? Processions, memories and the Dorset Cursus', in Barclay, A. and J. Harding (eds), *Pathways and Ceremonies: The Cursus Monuments of Britain and Ireland*, Oxford, Oxbow, 39–48.

Johnston, R., 2000, 'Dying, becoming, and being the field: prehistoric cairnfields in Northumberland', in Harding, J. and R. Johnston (eds), *Northern Pasts: Interpretations of the Later Prehistory of Northern England and Southern Scotland*, Oxford, British Archaeological Reports (British Series) 302, 57–70.

Jones, A., 1998/9, 'The Excavation of a Later Bronze Age Structure at Callestick', *Cornish Archaeology* 37–8, 5–55.

Jones, A., 2008, 'House for the Dead and Cairns for the Living; A Reconsideration of the Early to Middle Bronze Age Transition in South-West England', *Oxford Journal of Archaeology* 27, 153–74.

Jordan, P., 2003, *Material Culture and Sacred Landscape: The Anthropology of the Siberian Khanty*, Walnut Creek, Altamira Press.

Jorge, S. and C. Almeida, 1980, *A Estátua-Menhir Fálica de Chaves*, Porto, GEAP.

Jung, C., 1959, *The Collected Works. Volume 9, Part I: The Archetypes and the Collective Unconsciousness*, Routledge and Kegan Paul.

Kähler Holst, M., H. Breuning-Madsen and M. Rasmussen, 2001, 'The South Scandinavian Barrows with Well-Preserved Oak-Log Coffins', *Antiquity* 75, 126–36.

Kaliff, A., 1998, 'Grave Structures and Alters: Archaeological Traces of Bronze Age Eschatological Conceptions', *European Journal of Archaeology* 1, 177–98.

Kaplan, R., 1975, 'The Sacred Mushroom in Scandinavia', *Man* 10, 72–9.

Karsten, P. and B. Nilsson (eds), 2006, *In the Wake of a Woman: Stone Age Pioneering of North-eastern Scania, Sweden, 10,000–5000 BC, the Årup Settlements*, Stockholm, Riksantikvarieämbetet.

Kasamatsu, A. and T. Hirai, 1966, 'An electroencephalographic study on the Zen meditation (Zazen)', *Folia Psychiatrica et Neurologica Japonica* 20, 315–36.

Katzung, B., 2007, 'Histamine, serotonin and the ergot alkaloids', in Katzung, B. (ed), *Basic and Clinical Pharmacology* [Tenth Edition], New York, Lange Medical Books, 255–76.

Kaul, F., 1985, 'Sandagergård. A Late Bronze Age Cultic Building with Rock Engravings and Menhirs from Northern Zealand, Denmark', *Acta Archaeologica* 56, 31–54.

Kaul, F., 1995, 'The Gundestrup Cauldron Reconsidered', *Acta Archaeologica* 66, 1–38.

Kaul, F., 1998, *Ships on Bronzes: A Study in Bronze Age Religion and Iconography*, Copenhagen, National Museum Studies in Archaeology and History.

Kehoe, A., 2000, *Shamans and Religion: An Anthropological Exploration in Critical Thinking*, Prospect Heights, Waveland Press.

Kellog, R., M. Knoll and J. Kugler, 1965, 'Form-Similarity between Phosphenes and Preschool Children's Scribblings', *Nature* 208, 1129–30.

Khushi, A., 2000, 'The placenta and cord in other cultures', in Rachana, S. (ed.), *Lotus Birth*, Yarra Glen, Greenwood Press, 53–60.

Kimmig, W., 1983, *Die Heuneburg an der Oberen Donau*, Stuttgart, Konrad Theiss Verlag.

Kind, C.-J., 1989, *Ulm-Eggingen: Die Ausgrabungen 1982 bis 1985 in der Bandkeramischen Siedlung und der Mittelalterlichen Wüstung*, Stuttgart, Konrad Theiss Verlag.

King, A. and G. Soffe, 1998, 'Internal Organisation and Deposition at the Iron Age Temple on Hayling Island', *Proceedings of the Hampshire Field Club and Archaeological Society* 53, 35–47.

Klein, R., 2009, *The Human Career* [Third Edition], Chicago, Chicago University Press.

Knocker, G., 1958, 'Excavation of Three Round Barrows at Kinson, Near Bournemouth', *Proceedings of the Dorset Natural History and Archaeological Society* 80, 133–45.

Knoll, M., J. Kugler, O. Höfer and S. Lawder, 1963, 'Effects of Chemical Stimulation of Electrically-Induced Phosphenes on their Bandwidth, Shape, Number and Intensity', *Confinia Neurologica* 23, 201–26.

Koch, J., 2005, *The Celtic Heroic Age: Literary Sources for Ancient Celtic Europe and Early Ireland and Wales* [Fourth Edition], Aberystwyth, Celtic Studies Publications.

Koch, J., 2006, *Celtic Culture: A Historical Encyclopaedia*, Oxford, ABC-CLIO.

Kohl, P., 2007, *The Making of Bronze Age Eurasia*, Cambridge, Cambridge University Press.

Kooi, P., 1979, *Pre-Roman Urnfields in the North of the Netherlands*, Groningen, Wolters-Noordhoff.

Kopytoff, I., 1986, 'The cultural biography of things: commoditization as a process', in Appadurai, A. (ed.), *The Social Life of Things*, Cambridge, Cambridge University Press, 64–91.

Körber-Grohne, U., 1985, 'Pflanzliche und tierische Reste aus dem Fürstengrab von Hochdorf. Die Biologie als Hilfswissenschaft der Archäologie', in Biel, J. (ed.), *Der Keltenfürst von Hochdorf: Methoden und Ergebnisse der Landesarchäologie*, Stuttgart, Landesdenkmalmt Baden-Württemberg, 116–23.

Korek, J., 1951, 'Ein Gräberfeld der Badener Kultur bei Alsónmédi', *Acta Archaeologica Academiae Scientiarum Hungaricae* 1, 35–80.

Koryakova, L., 2000, 'Some notes about the material culture of Eurasian nomads', in Davis-Kimball, J., E. Murphy, L. Koryakova and L. Yablonsky (eds), *Kurgans, Ritual Sites, and Settlements: Eurasian Bronze and Iron Age*, Oxford, British Archaeological Reports (International Series) 890, 13–18.

Kossack, G., 1988, 'Pferd und Wagen in der Frühen Eisenzeit Mitteleuropas – Technik, Überlieferungsart und Ideeller Gehalt', *Münchener Beitrage zur Völkerkunde, Band 1* (Festschrift Laszlo Vajda.), München, Hirmer Verlag.

Krause, R. and G. Wielandt, 1993, 'Eine Keltische Viereckschanze bei Bopfingen am Westrand des Reises', *Germania* 71, 59–112.

Kristiansen, K., 1984, 'Krieger und Häuptlinge in der Bronzezeit Dänemarks. Ein Beitrag zur Geschichte des Bronzezeitlichen Schwertes', *Jarhbuch des Römisch-Germanischen Zentralmuseums Mainz* 31, 187–208.

Kristiansen, K., 1998, *Europe Before History*, Cambridge, Cambridge University Press.

Kristiansen, K., 2002, 'The Tale of the Sword – Swords and Swordfighters in Bronze Age Europe', *Oxford Journal of Archaeology* 21, 319–32.

Kristiansen, K., 2004, 'Sea faring voyages and rock art ships', in Clark, P. (ed.), *The Bronze Age Dover Boat in Context*, Oxford, Oxbow, 111–21.

Kristiansen, K. and T. Larsson, 2005, *The Rise of Bronze Age Society: Travels, Transmissions and Transformations*, Cambridge, Cambridge University Press.

Kruta, V., 2004, *Celts: History and Civilisation*, Éditions du Chêne-Hachette Livre.

Kubach-Richter, I., 1978–9, 'Amulettbeigaben in Bronzezeitlichen Kindergräbern', *Jahresbericht des Instituts für Vorgeschichte der Universität Frankfurt A.M.* 1978–9, 127–78.

Kuhn, S. and M. Stiner, 2007, 'Body ornamentation as information technology: towards an understanding of the significance of early beads', in Mellars, P., K. Boyle, O. Bar-Yosef and C. Stringer (eds), *Rethinking the Human Revolution*, Cambridge: McDonald Institute Monographs, 45–54.

Kuhn, S., M. Stiner, D. Reece and E. Güleç, 2001, 'Ornaments in the Earliest Upper Palaeolithic: New Perspectives from the Levant', *Proceedings of the National Academy of Sciences of the USA* 98, 7641–6.

Kunej, D. and I. Turk, 2000, 'New perspectives on the beginnings of music: archaeological and musicological analysis of a Middle Palaeolithic bone "flute"', in Wallin, N., B. Merker and S. Brown (eds), *The Origins of Music*, Cambridge, M.A., MIT Press, 235–68.

Kuper, R., H. Löhr, J. Lüning et al., 1977, *Der bandkeramische Siedlungsplatz Langweiler 9, Gemeinde Alderhoven, Kreis Düren*, Rheinische Ausgrabungen 18.

Kuzmina, E., 2000, 'The Eurasian steppes: the transition from early urbanism to nomadism', in Davis-Kimball, J., E. Murphy, L. Koryakova and L. Yablonsky (eds), *Kurgans, Ritual Sites, and Settlements: Eurasian Bronze and Iron Age*, Oxford, British Archaeological Reports (International Series) 890, 118–125.

Kuznetsov, P., 2006, 'The Emergence of Bronze Age Chariots in Eastern Europe', *Antiquity* 80, 638–45.

Ladle, L. and A. Woodward, 2003, 'A Middle Bronze Age House and Burnt Mound at Bestwall, Wareham, Dorset: An Interim Report', *Proceedings of the Prehistoric Society* 69, 265–77.

Lahelma, A., 2007, ' "On the Back of a Blue Elk": Recent Ethnohistorical Sources and "Ambiguous" Stone Age Rock Art at Pyhänpää, Central Finland', *Norwegian Archaeological Review* 38, 29–47.

Lahelma, A., 2008, *A Touch of Red: Archaeological and Ethnographic Approaches to Interpreting Finnish Rock Paintings*, Helsinki, Iskos 15.

Lalueza-Fox, C., M. Sampietro, D. Caramelli et al., 2005, 'Neanderthal Evolutionary Genetics: Mitochondrial DNA Data from the Iberian Peninsula', *Molecular Biology and Evolution* 22, 1077–81.

Lambot, B. and P. Méniel, 2000, 'Le centre communautaire et Cultuel du village Gaulois d'Acy-Romance dans son contexte regional', in Verger, S. (ed.), *Rites et Espaces en Pays Celte et Méditerranéen*, Rome, École Française de Rome, 7–139.

Lancel, S., 1995, *Carthage: A History*, Oxford, Blackwell.

Langley, M., C. Clarkson and S. Ulm, 2008, 'Behavioural Complexity in Eurasian Neanderthal Populations: A Chronological Examination of the Archaeological Evidence', *Cambridge Archaeological Journal* 18, 289–307.

Larsson, L., 1983, *Ageröd V. An Atlantic Site Bog in Central Scania*, Lund, Acta Archaeologica Lundensia.

Larsson, L., 1988, *The Skateholm Project I: Man and the Environment*, Stockholm, Acta Regiae Societatis Humaniorum Litterum Lundensis.

Larsson, L., 1990, 'Dogs in fraction – symbols in action', in Vermeersch, P. and P. Van Peer (eds), *Contributions to the Mesolithic in Europe*, Leuven, Leuven University Press, 153–60.

Larsson, L., 2007, 'The Mesolithic-Neolithic transition in Scandinavia', in Whittle, A. and V. Cummings (eds), *Going Over: The Mesolithic – Neolithic Transition in North-West Europe*, Oxford, Proceedings of the British Academy 144, 595–616.

Laughlin, C., J. McManus and E. d'Aquili, 1992, *Brain, Symbol and Experience: Toward a Neurophenomenology of Consciousness*, New York, Columbia University Press.

Lazarovici, G., Z. Kalmar, F. Draşoveanu and A. Luca, 1985, 'Complexul Neolitic de la Parţa', *Banatica* 1985, 7–71.

Le Contel, J. and P. Verdier, 1997, *Un Calendrier Celtique: Le Calendrier Gaulois de Coligny*, Paris, Éditions Errance.

Leakey, L., P. Tobias and J. Napier, 1964, 'A New Species of Genus *Homo* from Oldavai Gorge', *Nature* 202, 7–9.

Leakey, M., C. Feibel, I. McDougall and A. Walker, 1995, 'New Four-Million-Year-Old Hominid Species from Kanapoi and Allia Bay, Kenya', *Nature* 376, 565–71.

Legrand, S. and N. Bokovenko, 2006, 'The Emergence of the Scythians: Bronze Age to Iron Age in South Siberia', *Antiquity* 80, 843–79.

Lejeune, M., 1984, 'Deux Inscriptions Magiques Gauloises: Plomb de Chamalières; Plomb du Larzac', *Académie des Inscriptions et Belles-Lettres* 128, 703–713.

Lenneis, E., 2004, 'Architecture and settlement structure of the early Linear Pottery Culture in east central Europe', in Lukes, A. and M. Zvelebil (eds), *LBK Dialogues: Studies in the Formation of the Linear Pottery Culture*, British Archaeological Reports (International Series) 1304, 151–7.

Levack, B., 2006, *The Witch Hunt in Early Modern Europe* [Third Edition], Longman.

Levine, M., 1999, 'The origins of horse husbandry on the Eurasian steppe', in Levine, M., Y. Rassamakin, A. Kislenko and N. Tatarintseva (eds), *Late Prehistoric Exploitation of the Eurasian Steppe*, Cambridge, McDonald Institute for Archaeological Research, 5–58.

Levine, M., C. Renfrew and K. Boyle (eds), 2003, *Prehistoric Steppe Adaptation and the Horse*, Cambridge, McDonald Institute for Archaeological Research.

Lewis, I., 1989, *Ecstatic Religion: A Study of Shamanism and Spirit Possession* [Second Edition], Routledge.

Lewis-Williams, D., 1997, 'Agency, Art and Altered Consciousness: A Motif in French (Quercy) Upper Palaeolithic Parietal Art', *Antiquity* 71, 810–30.

Lewis-Williams, D., 2002, *The Mind in the Cave: Consciousness and the Origins of Art*, Thames and Hudson.

Lewis-Williams, D., 2009, 'Of people and pictures: the nexus of Upper Palaeolithic religion, social discrimination, and art', in Renfrew, C. and I. Morley (eds), *Becoming Human: Innovation in Prehistoric Material and Spiritual Culture*, Cambridge, Cambridge University Press, 135–58.

Lewis-Williams, D. and T. Dowson, 1988, 'The Signs of All Times: Entoptic Phenomena in Upper Palaeolithic Art', *Current Anthropology* 29, 201–45.

Lewis-Williams, D. and T. Dowson, 1989, *Images of Power: Understanding Bushman Rock Art*, Johannesburg, Southern Book Publishers.

Lewis-Williams, D. and T. Dowson, 1990, 'Through the Veil: San Rock Paintings and the Rock Face', *South African Archaeological Bulletin* 45, 5–16.

Lewis-Williams, D. and T. Dowson, 1994, 'Aspects of rock art research: a critical retrospective', in Dowson, T. and D. Lewis-Williams (eds), *Contested Images: Diversity in Southern African Rock Art Research*, Johannesburg, Witwatersrand University Press, 201–21.

Lewis-Williams, D. and D. Pearce, 2005, *Inside the Neolithic Mind: Consciousness, Cosmos and the Realm of the Gods*, Thames and Hudson.

Lindström, J., 1997, 'The Orientation of Ancient Monuments in Sweden: A Critique of Archaeoastronomy and an Alternative Explanation', *Current Swedish Archaeology* 5, 111–25.

Linkola, A. and M. Linkola, 2000, *Kolttasaamelaiset*, Inari, Inari Sámi Museum Publication No. 2.

Lippert, A., P. Gostner, E. Egarter Vigl and P. Pernter, 2007, 'Vom Lebun und Sterben des Ötztaler Gletschermannes, Neue Medizinische und Archäologische Erkenntnisse', *Germania* 85, 1–21.

Liverani, M., 1987, 'The collapse of the Near eastern regional system at the end of the Bronze Age: The case of Syria', in Rowlands, M., M. Larsen and K. Kristiansen (eds), *Centre and Periphery in the Ancient World*, Cambridge, Cambridge University Press, 66–73.

Lohof, E., 1994, 'Tradition and Change: Burial Practices in the Late Neolithic and Bronze Age in the North-Eastern Netherlands', *Archaeological Dialogues* 1, 98–132.

López Castro, J., 2006, 'Colonials, Merchants and Alabaster Vases: The Western Phoenician Aristocracy', *Antiquity* 80, 74–88.

Lorentzen, A., 1993, 'Frauen in keltischer Zeit', in Dannheimer, H. and R. Gebhard (eds), *Das Keltische Jahrtausend*, Mainz, Philipp von Zabern, 47–53.

Loughton, M., 2009, 'Getting Smashed: The Deposition of Amphorae and the Drinking of Wine in Gaul During the Late Iron Age', *Oxford Journal of Archaeology* 28, 77–110.

Ludwig, A., 1969, 'Altered states of consciousness', in Tart, C. (ed.), *Altered States of Consciousness: Book of Readings*, New York, Wiley, 9–22.

Lull, V., 2000, 'Argaric Society: Death at Home', *Antiquity* 74, 581–90.

Lynn, C. 1977, 'Trial Excavations at the King's Stables, Tray Townland, Co. Armagh', *Ulster Journal of Archaeology* 40, 42–62.

Lynn, C., 1992, 'The Iron Age Mound in Navan Fort: A Physical Realisation of Celtic Religious Beliefs?', *Emania* 10, 33–57.

MacKie, E., 1974, *Dun Mor Vaul: An Iron Age Broch on Tiree*, Glasgow, University of Glasgow Press.

Malmer, M., 1960, 'Monumental Art of Northern Sweden from the Stone Age: Nämforsen and Other Localities', Stockholm, Almqvist & Wiksell.

Malmer, M., 1966–1968, 'Die Mikrolithen in dem Pfeil-Fund von Loshult', *Meddelanden från Lunds Universitets Historika Museum*, 1966–1968, 249–55.

Marciniak, A., 2004, 'Everyday life at the LBK settlement: a zooarchaeological perspective', in Lukes, A. and M. Zvelebil (eds), *LBK Dialogues: Studies in the Formation of the Linear Pottery Culture*, Oxford, British Archaeological Reports (International Series) 1304, 129–41.

Marco Simón, F., 2008, 'Images of Transition: The Ways of Death in Celtic Hispania', *Proceedings of the Prehistoric Society* 74, 53–68.

Marean, C., 2007, 'Heading North: an Africanist perspective on the replacement of Neanderthals by modern humans', in Mellars, P., K. Boyle, O. Bar-Yosef and C. Stringer (eds), *Rethinking the Human Revolution*, Cambridge, McDonald Institute Monographs, 367–79.

Markoe, G., 2000, *Phoenicians*, British Museum Press.

Marquet, J-C. and M. Lorblanchet, 2003, 'A Neanderthal Face? The Proto-Figurine from La Roche-Cotard, Langeais', *Antiquity* 77, 661–70.

Marshak, A., 1997, 'The Berekhat Ram Figurine: A Late Acheulian Carving from the Middle East' *Antiquity* 71, 327–37.

Martin, R., 1965, 'Wooden Figures from the Source of the Seine', *Antiquity* 34, 247–52.

Mathers, C., 1994, 'Goodbye to all that? Contrasting patterns of change in the south-east Iberian Bronze Age *c*. 24/2200–600 BC', in Mathers, C. and S. Stoddart (eds), *Development and Decline in the Mediterranean Bronze Age*, Sheffield, J.R. Collis Publications, 21–71.

Maula, E. (ed.), 1990, *Swansongs, Rock Art from Lake Onega 4000–2000 BC*, Tartu, The Society of Prehistoric Art.

Mauss, M., 1969, *The Gift: Forms and Functions of Exchange in Archaic Societies* [Third Edition], Cohen and West.

McClenon, J., 2002, *Wondrous Healing: Shamanism, Human Evolution, and the Origin of Religion*, Dekalb, Northern Illinois University Press.

McKinley, J., 1997, 'Bronze Age 'Barrows' and Funerary Rites and Rituals of Cremation', *Proceedings of the Prehistoric Society* 63, 129–45.

Meaney, A.-L., 1981, *Anglo-Saxon Amulets and Curing Stones*, Oxford, British Archaeological Reports (British Series) 96.

Meaney, A.-L., 1989, 'Women, witchcraft and magic in Anglo-Saxon England', in Scragg, D. (ed.), *Superstition and Popular medicine in Anglo-Saxon England*, Manchester, Manchester Centre for Anglo-Saxon Studies, 9–40.

Meiklejohn, C. and M. Zvelebil, 1991, 'Health status of European populations at the agricultural transition and the implications for the adoption of farming', in Bush, H. and M. Zvelebil (eds), *Health in Past Societies: Biocultural Interpretations of Human Skeletal Remains in Archaeological Contexts*, Oxford, British Archaeological Reports (International Series) 567, 129–43.

Mellaart, J., 1967, *Çatal Hüyük: A Neolithic Town in Anatolia*, Thames and Hudson.

Mellars, P., 2005, 'The Impossible Coincidence: A Single-Species Model for the Origins of Modern Human Behaviour in Europe', *Evolutionary Anthropology* 14, 12–27.

Mellars, P. and P. Dark, 1998, *Star Carr in Context: New Archaeological and Palaeoecological Investigations at the Early Mesolithic Site of Star Carr, North Yorkshire*, Cambridge, MacDonald Institute of Archaeological Research.

Meller, H., 2002, Die Himmelsscheibe von Nebra – Ein Frühbronzezeitlicher Fund von Außergewöhnlicher Bedeutung, *Archäologie in Sachsen-Anhault* 1: 7–20.

Meniel, P., 1987, *Chasse et Elèvage chez les Gaulois (450–52, Av J. C.*, Paris, Editions Errance.

Mens, E., 2008, 'Refitting Megaliths in Western France', *Antiquity* 82, 25–36.

Metcalf, P. and R. Huntington, 1991, *Celebrations of Death: The Anthropology of Mortuary Ritual* [Second Edition], Cambridge, Cambridge University Press.

Metzner-Nebelsick, C., 2000, 'Early Iron Age pastoral nomadism in the Great Hungarian Plains: migration or assimilation? The Thraco-Cimmerian problem revisited', in Davis-Kimball, J., E. Murphy, L. Koryakova and L. Yablonsky (eds), *Kurgans, Ritual Sites, and Settlements: Eurasian Bronze and Iron Age*, Oxford, British Archaeological Reports (International Series) 890, 160–84.

Midgley, M., 1992, *TRB Culture*, Edinburgh, Edinburgh University Press.

Midgley, M., 2005, *The Monumental Cemeteries of Prehistoric Europe*, Stroud, Tempus.

Miklosi, A., 2007, *Dog Behaviour, Evolution, and Cognition*, Oxford, Oxford University Press.

Milliken, S., 2007, 'Neanderthals, Anatomically Modern Humans, and "Modern Human Behaviour" in Italy', *Oxford Journal of Archaeology* 26, 331–58.

Mitchell, J., 1985, *Out-of-Body Experiences: How Science is Helping us to Understand the Experience of Living Beyond the Body*, Wellingborough, Turnstone Press.

Mithen, S., 1994, 'The Mesolithic age', in Cunliffe, B. (ed.), *The Oxford Illustrated History of Prehistoric Europe*, Oxford, Oxford University Press, 79–135.

Mithen, S., 1996, *The Prehistory of the Mind: A Search for the Origins of Art, Religion and Science*, Thames and Hudson.

Mithen, S., 2003, *After the Ice: A Global Human History 20,000–5000 BC*, Weidenfeld and Nicolson.

Mithen, S., 2005, *The Singing Neanderthals: The Origins of Music, Language, Mind and Body*, Weidenfeld & Nicholson.

Mithen, S., 2009, 'Out of the mind: material culture and the supernatural', in Renfrew, C. and I. Morley (eds), *Becoming Human: Innovation in Prehistoric Material and Spiritual Culture*, Cambridge, Cambridge University Press, 123–34.

Mizoguchi, K., 1993, 'Time in the Reproduction of Mortuary Practices', *World Archaeology* 25, 223–35.

Modderman, P., 1988, 'The Linear Pottery Culture: Diversity in Uniformity', *Berichten van de Rijksdienst voor het Oudheidkundig Bodemonderzoek* 38, 63–139.

Montero, I., 1993, 'Bronze Age Metallurgy in Southeast Spain', *Antiquity* 67, 46–57.

Moore, A. G. Hillman and A. Legge, 2001, *Village on the Euphrates: From Foraging to Farming at Abu Hureyra*, Oxford, Oxford University Press.

Morgenroth, U., 2004, *Southern Iberia in the Early Iron Age*, Oxford, British Archaeological Reports (International Series) 1330.

Morley, I., 2006, 'Mousterian Musicianship? The Case of the Divje Babe I Bone', *Oxford Journal of Archaeology* 25, 317–34.

Morphy, H., 1989, 'From Dull to Brilliant: The Aesthetics of Spiritual Power Among the Yolngu', *Man* 24, 21–40.

Movius, H., 1953, 'The Mousterian Cave of Teshik-Tash, Southeastern Uzbekistan, Central Asia', *American School of Prehistoric Research Bulletin* 17, 11–71.

Mullen, G. and L. Wilson, 2005a, 'Cave Art in Somerset', *Current Archaeology* 197, 227.

Mullen, G. and L. Wilson, 2005b, 'Mesolithic Engravings at Cheddar Gorge', *Current Archaeology* 199, 360–1.

Müller, S., 1903, *Solbilledet fra Trundholm*, Copenhagen, Nordiske Fortidsminder.

Müller, W., H. Fricke, A. Halliday et al., 2003, 'Origin and Migration of the Alpine Iceman', *Science* 302, 862–66.

Müller-Karpe, H., 1956, 'Das Urnenfelderzeitliche Wagengrab von Hart a.d. Alz', *Bayerische Vorgeschichtsblätter* 21, 46–75.

Mussi, M., 1986, 'Italian Palaeolithic and Mesolithic Burials', *Human Evolution* 1, 545–56.

Mussi, M., 2001, *Earliest Italy: An Overview of the Italian Palaeolithic and Mesolithic*, New York, Kluwer.

Mussi, M., J. Cinq-Mars and P. Bolduc, 2000, 'Echoes from the mammoth steppe: the case of the Balzi Rossi', in Roebroeks, W., M. Mussi, J. Svoboda and K. Fennema (eds), *Hunters of the Golden Age: the Mid Upper Palaeolithic of Eurasia 30,000–20,000 BP*, University of Leiden, 105–24.

Nanoglou, S., 2008, 'Representation of Humans and Animals in Greece and the Balkans During the Earlier Neolithic', *Cambridge Archaeological Journal* 18, 1–13.

Napolskikh, V., 1992, 'Proto-Uralic world picture: a reconstruction', in Hoppál, M. and J. Pentikäinen (eds), *Northern Religions and Shamanism*, Budapest, Akadémiai Kiadó, 3–20.

Nash Briggs, D., 2003, 'Metals, Salt, and Slaves: Economic Links Between Gaul and Italy from the Eighth to the Late Sixth Centuries', *Oxford Journal of Archaeology* 22, 243–59.

Nash, D., 1985, 'Celtic territorial expansion and the Mediterranean world', in Champion, T. and J.V. Megaw (eds), *Settlement and Society: Aspects of West European Prehistory in the First Millennium BC*, Leicester, Leicester University Press, 45–67.

Nebelsick, L., 2000, 'Rent asunder: ritual violence in late Bronze Age hoards', in Pare, C. (ed.), *Metals Make the World Go Round: The Supply and Circulation of Metals in Bronze Age Europe*, Oxford, Oxbow, 160–75.

Needham, S., 1980, 'An Assemblage of Late Bronze Age Metalworking Debris from Dainton, Devon', *Proceedings of the Prehistoric Society* 46, 177–215.

Needham, S., 1981, *The Bulford-Helsbury Manufacturing Tradition. The Production of Stogursey Socketed Axes During the Later Bronze Age in Southern Britain*, British Museum Occasional Paper 13.

Needham, S., 1990, 'Middle Bronze Age Ceremonial Weapons: New Finds from Oxborough, Norfolk and Essex/Kent', *Antiquaries Journal* 70, 239–52.

Needham, S., 1992, 'The structure of settlement and ritual in the late Bronze Age of South-East Britain', in Mordant, C. and A. Richard (eds), *L'Habitat et L'Occupation du Sol a L'Age du Bronze en Europe*, Paris, Editions du Comité des Travaux Historiques et Scientifiques, 49–69.

Needham, S., 2000, 'Power Pulses Across a Cultural Divide: Cosmologically Driven Aquistion Between Armorica and Wessex', *Proceedings of the Prehistoric Society* 66, 151–207.

Needham, S. and A. Woodward, 2008, 'The Clandon Barrow Finery: A Synopsis of Success in an Early Bronze Age World', *Proceedings of the Prehistoric Society* 74, 1–52.

Needham, S. and J. Ambers, 1994, 'Redating Rams Hill', *Proceedings of the Prehistoric Society* 60, 225–44.

Nerlich, A., B. Bachmeier, A. Zink et al., 2003, 'Ötzi had a Wound on his Right Hand', *The Lancet* 362, 334.

Neugebauer, J.-W., 1991, *Die Nekropole F. von Gemeinlebarn, Niederösterreich. Untersuchungen zu den Bestattungssitten und zum Grabraub in der Ausgehenden Frühbronzezeit in Niederösterreich Südlich der Donau Zwischen Enns und Wienerwald*, Mainz, Zabern.

Newman, C., 1996, 'Woods, Metamorphosis and Mazes: The Otherness of Timber Circles', *Archaeology Ireland* 10, 34–7.

Nielsen, V., 1984, 'Prehistoric Field Boundaries in Eastern Denmark', *Journal of Danish Archaeology* 3, 135–63.

Nobis, G., 1979, 'Der älteste Haushunde lebte vor 14000 Jahren', *Umschau* 79: 610.

Nocete, F., 2006, 'The First Specialised Copper Industry in the Iberian Peninsula: Cabezo Juré (2900–2200 BC)', *Antiquity* 80, 646–57.

Norlander-Unsgaard, S., 1985, 'On gesture and posture, movements and motion in the Saami bear ceremonialism', in Bäckman, L. and Å. Hultkrantz (eds), *Saami Pre-Christian Religion: Studies on the Oldest Traces of Religion Among the Saamis*, Stockholm, Almqvist and Wiksell, 157–68.

Norling-Christensen, H., 1946, 'The Viksø Helmets. A Bronze Age Votive Find from Zealand', *Acta Archaeologica* 17, 99–115.

Nowakowski, J., 1991, 'Trethellan Farm, Newquay: The Excavation of a Lowland Bronze Age Settlement and Iron Age Cemetery', *Cornish Archaeology* 30, 5–242.

Nunez, P. and R. Srinivasan, 2006, *Electric Fields of the Brain: The Neurophysics of EEG* [Second Edition], Oxford, Oxford University Press.

Ó Drisceóil, D., 1988, 'Burnt Mounds: Cooking or Bathing?', *Antiquity* 62, 671–80.

O'Brien, W., 2004, *Ross Island. Mining, Metal and Society in Early Ireland*, Galway, National University of Ireland.

O'Kelly, C., 1992, *Newgrange: Archaeology, Art and Legend*, Thames and Hudson.

O'Sullivan, A., 1996, 'Later Bronze Age Intertidal Discoveries on North Munster Estuaries', *Discovery Programme Reports* 4, 63–72.

O'Sullivan, A., 1997, 'Interpreting the Archaeology of Late Bronze Age Lake Settlements', *The Journal of Irish Archaeology* 8, 115–21.

O'Sullivan, M., 2005, *Duma na nGiall: The Mound of the Hostages, Tara*, Bray, Wordwell.

Odner, K., 1993, *The Varanger Saami: Habitation and Economy AD 1200–1900*, Oslo, Scandinavian University Press.

Oeggl, K., W. Kofler, A. Schmidl et al., 2007, 'The Reconstruction of the Last Itinerary of "Ötzi", the Neolithic Iceman, by Pollen Analyses from Sequentially Sampled Gut Extracts', *Quaternary Science Reviews* 26, 853–61.

Oliva, M., 1996, 'Mladopalaeolitický hrob Brno II Jako Příspěvek k Počátkům Šamanismu' *Archeologické Rozhledy* 48, 353–84.

Olkhovskiy, V., 2000, 'Ancient sanctuaries of the Aral and Caspian regions: a reconstruction of their history', in Davis-Kimball, J., E. Murphy, L. Koryakova and L. Yablonsky (eds), *Kurgans, Ritual Sites, and Settlements: Eurasian Bronze and Iron Age*, Oxford, British Archaeological Reports (International Series) 890, 33–42.

Olsen, S., 2000, 'Reflections of ritual behaviour at Botai, Kazakhstan', in Jones-Bley, K., M. Huld and A. Della Volpe (eds), *Proceedings of the Eleventh Annual UCLA Indo-European Conference*, Washington, Institute for the Study of Man, 183–207.

Oppenheimer, S., 2003, *Out of Eden: The Peopling of the World*, Constable & Robinson.

Opper, T., 2008, *Hadrian: Empire and Conflict*, British Museum Press.

Osgood, R., S. Monks and J. Toms., 2000, *Bronze Age Warfare*, Stroud, Sutton.

Oster, G., 1970, 'Phosphenes', *Scientific American* 222, 83–7.

Oswald, A., 1997, 'A doorway on the past: practical and mystic concerns in the orientation of roundhouse doorways', in Gwilt, A. and C. Haselgrove (eds), *Reconstructing Iron Age Societies: New Approaches to the British Iron Age*, Oxford, Oxbow, 87–95.

Otchir-Goriaeva, M., 2002, 'Welchen Kultur und Wirtschaftstyp Repräsentieren die Bronzezeitlichen Funde in den Wolga-Manyč-Steppen?', *Eurasia Antiqua* 8, 103–33.

Ovsyannikov, O. and N. Terebikhin, 1994, 'Sacred space in the culture of the Arctic regions', in Carmichael, D., J. Hubert, B. Reeves and A. Schanche (eds), *Sacred Sites, Sacred Places*, Routledge, 44–81.

Painter, T., 1995, 'Chemical and microbiological aspects of the preservation process in *Sphagnum* peat', in Turner, R. and R. Scaife (eds), *Bog Bodies: New Discoveries and New Perspectives*, Trustees of British Museum Press, 88–99.

Papworth, M., 1992, 'Excavation and Survey of Bronze Age Sites in the Badbury Area, Kingston Lacy Estate', *Proceedings of the Dorset Natural History and Archaeological Society* 114, 47–76.

Pare, C., 1992, *Wagons and Wagon Graves from the Early Iron Age in Central Europe*, Oxford, Oxford University Committee for Archaeology.

Parfitt, S., R. Barendregt, M. Breda et al., 2005, 'The Earliest Record of Human Activity in Northern Europe', *Nature* 438, 1008–12.

Parish, H. and W. Naphy, 2003, *Religion and Superstition on Reformation Europe*, Manchester, Manchester University Press.

Parker Pearson, M., 1993, 'The Powerful Dead: Archaeological Relationships Between the Living and the Dead', *Cambridge Archaeological Journal* 3, 203–29.

Parker Pearson, M., 1996, 'Food, fertility and front doors in the First Millennium BC', in Champion, T. and J. Collis (eds), *The Iron Age in Britain and Ireland: Recent Trends*, Sheffield, J.R. Collis Publications, 117–32.

Parker Pearson, M., 1999, 'Food, Sex and Death: Cosmologies in the British Iron Age with Particular Reference to East Yorkshire', *Cambridge Archaeological Journal* 9, 43–69.

Parker Pearson, M., 2007, 'The Stonehenge Riverside Project: excavations at the east entrance of Durrington Walls', in Larsson, M. and M. Parker Pearson (eds), *From Stonehenge to the Baltic: Living with Cultural Diversity in the Third Millennium BC*, Oxford, British Archaeological Reports (International Series) 1692, 125–44.

Parker Pearson, M. and N. Sharples, 1999, *Between Land and Sea: Excavations at Dun Vulan, South Uist*, Sheffield, Sheffield Academic Press.

Parker Pearson, M. and Ramilisonina, 1998, 'Stonehenge for the Ancestors: The Stones Pass on the Message', *Antiquity* 72, 308–26.

Parker Pearson, M., A. Chamberlain, M. Jay et al., 2009, 'Who was Buried at Stonehenge?' *Antiquity* 83, 23–39.

Parker Pearson, M., A. Chamberlain, O. Craig et al., 2005, 'Evidence for Mummification in Bronze Age Britain', *Antiquity* 79, 529–46.

Parker Pearson, M., R. Cleal, P. Marshall et al., 2007, 'The Age of Stonehenge', *Antiquity* 81, 617–39.

Pásztor, E. and C. Roslund, 2007, 'An Interpretation of the Nebra Disc', *Antiquity* 81, 267–78.

Patterson, N., 1995, 'Clans are not primordial: pre-Viking Irish society and the modelling of pre-Roman societies in northern Europe', in Arnold, Bettina and D. Gibson (eds), *Celtic Chiefdom, Celtic State: The Evolution of Complex Social Systems in Prehistoric Europe*, Cambridge, Cambridge University Press, 129–36.

Patton, M., 1990, 'On Entoptic Images in Context: Art, Monuments, and Society in Neolithic Brittany', *Current Anthropology* 31, 554–8.

Pauli, L., 1975, *Keltischer Volksglaube: Amulette und Sonderbestattungen am Dürrnberg bei Hallein und im Eisenzeitlichen Mitteleuropa*, Munich, C.H. Beck.

Pavúk, J., 1991, 'Lengyel-culture fortified settlements in Slovakia', *Antiquity* 65, 348–57.

Pearson, J., 2002, *Shamanism and the Ancient Mind: A Cognitive Approach to Archaeology*, Walnut Creek, AltaMira Press.

Pedersen, J.-A., 1986, 'A New Early Bronze Age House-Site Under a Barrow at Hyllerup, Western Zealand', *Journal of Danish Archaeology* 5, 168–76.

Peintner, U., R. Poder and T. Pümpel, 1998, 'The Iceman's Fungi', *Mycological Research* 102, 1153–62.

Pentikäinen, J., 1987, 'The Saami shamanic drum in Rome', in Ahlbäck, T. (ed.), *Saami Religion*, Åbo, The Donner Institute for Research in Religious and Cultural History, 124–57.

Perlès, K., 2001, *The Early Neolithic in Greece: The First Farming Communities in Europe*, Cambridge, Cambridge University Press.

Pernter, P., P. Gostner, E. Egarter Vigl, and F. Rühli, 2007, 'Radiologic Proof for the Iceman's Cause of Death (ca. 5300 BP)', *Journal of Archaeological Science* 34, 1784–6.

Peters, F., 2000, 'Two Traditions of Bronze Age Burial in the Stonehenge Landscape', *Oxford Journal of Archaeology* 19, 343–58.

Petersson, M., 1951, 'Mikrolithen als Pfeilspitzen. Ein Fund aus dem Lilla Loshult-Moor Ksp. Loshult, Skåne', *Meddelanden från Lunds Universitets Historiska Museum*, 123–37.

Pétrequin, P., M. Errera, A-M. Pétrequin and P. Allard, 2006, 'The Neolithic Quarries of Mont Viso, Piedmont, Italy: Initial Radiocarbon Dates', *European Journal of Archaeology* 9, 7–30.

Pettitt, P. and M. Zvelebil, 2009, 'Europe's First Farmers: The Neolithic Burials from Vedrovice', *Current World Archaeology* 32, 26–34.

Phillips, E., 1965, *The Royal Hordes: Nomad Peoples of the Steppes*, Thames and Hudson.

Pigeot, N., 1987, *Magdaléniens d'Etiolles. Économie de Débitage et Organisation Sociale*, Paris, CNRS.

Pigeot, N., 1990, 'Technical and Social Actors: Flint Knapping Specialists and Apprentices at Magdalenian Etiolles', *Archaeological Review from Cambridge* 9, 126–41.

Piggott, C., 1938, 'A Middle Bronze Age Barrow and Deverel-Rimbury Urnfield, at Latch Farm, Christchurch, Hampshire', *Proceedings of the Prehistoric Society* 4, 169–87.

Piggott, S., 1983, *The Earliest Wheeled Transport: From the Atlantic Coast to the Caspian Sea*, Thames and Hudson.

Pitt Rivers, A., 1898, *Excavations in Cranborne Chase, near Rushmore on the Borders of Dorset and Wiltshire 1893–1896, Vol. IV*, printed privately.

Pitts, M., 2001, 'Excavating the Sanctuary: New Investigations on Overton Hill, Avebury', *Wiltshire Archaeological and Natural History Magazine* 94, 1–23.

Pitts, M. and M. Roberts, 1997, *Fairweather Eden: Life in Britain Half a Million Years Ago as Revealed by Excavations at Boxgrove*, Century.

Planck, D., 1982, 'Ein Neuentdeckte Keltische Viereckschanze in Fellbach-Schmiden, Rems-Murr-Kreis', *Germania* 60, 105–172.

Podborský, V. (ed.), 2002, *Dvě pohřebiště Neolitického lidu s Lineárni Keramikou ve Vedrovicích na Moravě*, Brno, Masarykovy Univerzity.

Pollard, J., 1995, 'Inscribing Space: Formal Deposition at the Later Neolithic Monument of Woodhenge, Wiltshire', *Proceedings of the Prehistoric Society* 61, 137–56.

Pollex, A., 1999, 'Comments on the Interpretation of the So-Called Cattle Burials of Neolithic Central Europe', *Antiquity* 73, 542–50.

Poulik, J. and J. Nekvasil, 1969, *Hallstatt a Býči Skála*, Brno, Akadamie Věd Archeologický Ústav.

Powell, T. and G. Daniel, 1956, *Barclodiad y Gawres: The Excavation of a Megalithic Chamber Tomb in Anglesey*, Liverpool, Liverpool University Press.

Praslov, N., 1993, 'Eine Neue Frauenstatuette aus Kalkstein von Kostenki I (Don, Russland)', *Archäologisches Korrespondenzblatt* 23, 165–73.

Preston, J. and C. Hawkes, 1933, 'Three Late Bronze Age Barrows on the Cloven Way', *The Antiquaries Journal* 13, 414–54.

Priakhin, A. and V. Besedin, 1999, 'The Horse Bridle of the Middle Bronze Age in the East European Forest-Steppe and the Steppe', *Anthropology and Archaeology of Eurasia* 38, 39–59.

Price, E., 2003, *Animal Domestication and Behaviour*, Cambridge, MA, CABI Publishing.

Price, N., 2002, *The Viking Way: Religion and War in Late Iron Age Scandinavia*, Uppsala, Uppsala University.

Price, T. D., 2000, 'The introduction of farming in northern Europe', in Price, T.D. (ed.), *Europe's First Farmers*, Cambridge, Cambridge University Press, 260–300.

Price, T.D., C. Knipper, G. Grupe and V. Smrcka, 2004, 'Strontium Isotopes and Prehistoric Human Migration: The Bell Beaker Period in Central Europe', *European Journal of Archaeology* 7, 9–40.

Pryor, F., 1998, *Etton. Excavations at a Neolithic Causewayed Enclosure near Maxey, Cambridgeshire, 1982–7*, English Heritage.

Pryor, F., 2001, *The Flag Fen Basin: Archaeology and Environment of a Fenland Landscape*, English Heritage.

Queiroga, F., 2003, *War and Castros: New Approaches to the Northwestern Portuguese Iron Age*, Oxford, British Archaeological Reports (International Series) 1198.

Radovanović, I., 1996, *The Iron Gates Mesolithic*, Ann Arbor, International Monographs in Prehistory.

Radovanović, I., 1997, 'The Lepenski Vir culture: a contribution to its ideological aspects', in *Antidoron Dragoslavo Srejović: Completis LXV Annis ab Amicis Collegis Discipulis Oblatum*, Belgrade, University of Belgrade, 85–93.

Radovanović, I., 1999, '"Neither Person Nor Beast" – Dogs in the Burial Practice of the Iron Gates Mesolithic', *Documenta Praehistorica* 26, 71–87.

Radovanović, I., 2000, 'Houses and Burials at Lepenski Vir', *European Journal of Archaeology* 3, 330–49.

Raftery, B., 1996a, *Trackway Excavations in the Mountdillon Bogs, Co. Longford, 1985–1991*, Dublin, Crannog Publications.

Rak, Y., W. Kimbel and E. Hovers, 1994, 'A Neanderthal Infant from Amud Cave, Israel', *Journal of Human Evolution* 26, 313–24.

Ralston, I., 2006, *Celtic Fortifications*, Stroud, Tempus.

Randsborg, K., 1993, 'Kivik, Archaeology and Iconography', *Acta Archaeologica* 64, 1–147.

Rapin, A., 1993, 'Destruction et mutilations des armes dans les necropoles et les sanctuaires au second Age du Fer: réflexions sur les rituels et leur description', in Cliquet, D., M. Remy-Watte, V. Guichard and M. Vaginay (eds), *Les Celtes en Normandie: Les Rites Funéraires en Gaule (IIIème - Ier Siècle Avant J.-C.)*, Revue Archéologique de l'Ouest Supplément No. 6, 291–8.

Rapin, A. and J.-L. Brunaux, 1988, *Gournay II: Boucliers et Lances et Dépôts et Trophées*, Paris, Revue Archeologique de Picardie.

Rasmussen, K., 1908, *The People of the Polar North: A Record* (Compiled from the Danish Originals and edited by G. Herring), Kegan Paul, Trench, Trübner and Co.

Rasmussen, K., 1998, 'An Angmagssalik Shaman's Magic Drum Séance (Edited from notes left by Knud Rasmussen)', *Shaman's Drum* 49, 63–5.

Ratcliffe-Densham, H. and M. Ratcliffe-Densham, 1961, 'An Anomalous Earthwork of the Late Bronze Age, on Cock Hill, Sussex', *Sussex Archaeological Collection* 99, 78–101.

Reid, A. and R. MacLean, 1995, 'Symbolism and Social Contexts of Iron Production in Karagwe', *World Archaeology* 27, 144–61.

Reilly, S., 2003, 'Processing the Dead in Neolithic Orkney', *Oxford Journal of Archaeology* 22, 133–154.

Reinerth, H., 1928, *Die Wasserberg Buchau. Eine Befestigte Inselsiedlung aus der Zeit 1100–800 v. Chr.*, Führer zur Urgeschichte 6.

Renfrew, C., 1979, *Investigations in Orkney*, Society of Antiquaries Research Report 38.

Renfrew, C., 2009, 'Situating the creative explosion: universal or local', in Renfrew, C. and I. Morley (eds), *Becoming Human: Innovation in Prehistoric Material and Spiritual Culture*, Cambridge, Cambridge University Press, 74–92.

Renfrew, J., 2009, 'Neanderthal symbolic behaviour?', in Renfrew, C. and I. Morley (eds), *Becoming Human: Innovation in Prehistoric Material and Spiritual Culture*, Cambridge, Cambridge University Press, 50–60.

Reynolds, D., 1982, 'Aspects of later timber construction in south-east Scotland', in Harding, D. (ed.), *Later Prehistoric Settlement in South-East Scotland*, Edinburgh, Edinburgh University Occasional Paper 8, 44–56.

Richards, C., 2004, *Dwelling Among the Monuments: The Neolithic Village of Barnhouse, Maeshowe Passage Grave and Surrounding Monuments at Stenness, Orkney*, Cambridge, McDonald Institute for Archaeological Research.

Richards, M. and R. Schmitz, 2008, 'Isotope Evidence for the Diet of the Neanderthal Type Specimen', *Antiquity* 82, 553–9.

Richardson, K., 1951, 'The Excavation of Iron Age Villages on Boscombe Down West', *Wiltshire Archaeological Magazine* 54, 123–68.

Richmond, I., 1968, *Hod Hill. Volume Two: Excavations Carried out Between 1951 and 1958 for the Trustees of the British Museum*, Trustees of the British Museum.

Rideout, J., 1992, 'Archaeological background', in Rideout, J., O. Owen and E. Halpin (eds), *Hillforts of Southern Scotland*, Edinburgh, Historic Scotland Monograph 1, 3–5.

Riek, G. and H. Hundt, 1962, *Der Hohmichele: Ein Fürstengrabhügel der Späten Hallstattzeit bei der Heuneburg*, Römische-Germanische Forschungen Bd. 25.

Riismøller, P., 1952, 'Froya fra Rebild', *Kulm* 1952, 119–32.

Ripoll, S. and F. Muñoz, 2007, 'The Palaeolithic rock art of Creswell Crags: prelude to a systematic study', in Pettit, P., P. Bahn, S. Ripoll and F. Muñoz (eds), *Palaeolithic Cave Art at Creswell Crags in European Context*, Oxford, Oxford University Press, 14–33.

Rival, L. (ed.), 1998, *The Social Life of Trees: Anthropological Perspectives of Tree Symbolism*, Oxford, Berg.

Rodden, R. and K. Wardle, 1996, *Nea Nikomedeia I: The Excavation of an Early Neolithic Village in Northern Greece 1961–1964*, The British School at Athens.

Rohl, B. and S. Needham, 1998, *The Circulation of Metal in the British Bronze Age: The Application of Lead Isotope Analysis*, British Museum Occasional Paper Number 102.

Rojo-Guerra, M., R. Garrido-Pena, Í. García-Martínez-de-Lagrán et al., 2006, 'Beer and Bell Beakers: Drinking Rituals in Copper Age Inner Iberia', *Proceedings of the Prehistoric Society* 72, 243–65.

Rolle, R., 1989, *The World of the Scythians*, Batsford.

Rosenberg, G., 1937, *Hjortspringfundet*, Copenhagen, Nordiske Fortidsminder III.

Rossano, M., 2007, 'Did Meditating Make us Human?', *Cambridge Archaeological Journal* 17, 47–58.

Roughley, C., 2004, 'The Neolithic Landscape of the Carnac Region, Brittany: New Insights from Digital Approaches', *Proceedings of the Prehistoric Society* 70, 153–72.

Rowlett, R., H. Thomas, E. Rowlett and S. Stout, 1982, 'Stratified House Floors on the Titelberg, Luxembourg', *Journal of Field Archaeology* 9, 301–12.

Rowley-Conwy, P., 1998, 'Cemeteries, seasonality and complexity in the Ertebølle of southern Scandinavia', in Zvelebil, M., R. Dennell and L. Domanska (eds), *Harvesting the Sea, Farming the Forest: The Emergence of Neolithic Societies in the Baltic Region*, Sheffield, Sheffield Academic Press, 193–202.

Roymans, N., 1990, *Tribal Societies in Northern Gaul: An Anthropological Perspective*, Amsterdam, Amsterdam University Press.

Roymans, N., 1995, 'The Cultural Biography of Urnfields and the Long-Term History of a Mythical Landscape', *Archaeological Dialogues* 2, 2–35.

Roymans, N. and F. Kortlang, 1999, 'Urnfield symbolism, ancestors and the land in the Lower Rhine region', in Theuws, F. and N. Roymans (eds), *Land and Ancestors: Cultural Dynamics in the Urnfield Period and the Middle Ages in Southern Netherlands*, Amsterdam, Amsterdam University Press, 33–61.

Roymans, N. and F. Theuws, 1999, 'Long-term perspectives on land and people in the Meuse-Demer-Scheldt region (1100BC–1500AD). An introduction', in Theuws, F. and N. Roymans (eds), *Land and Ancestors: Cultural Dynamics in the Urnfield Period and the Middle Ages in Southern Netherlands*, Amsterdam, Amsterdam University Press, 1–32.

Rudenko, S., 1970, *Frozen Tombs of Siberia: The Pazyryk Burials of Iron Age Horsemen*, J.M. Dent and Sons.

Rukang, W. and L. Shenglong, 1983, 'Peking Man', *Scientific American* 248, 78–86.

Runcis, J., 1999, 'Den mytiska geografin. Reflektioner kring skävstenhögar, mytologi och lanskaprum I Södermanland under bromsålder', in Olausson, M. (ed.), *Spiralens Öga. Tjugo Artiklar Kring Aktuell Bronsåldersforskning*, Stockholm, Riksantikvarieämbetet, 127–55.

Russell, M., 1996, 'Problems of Phasing: A Reconsideration of the Black Patch Middle Bronze Age "Nucleated Village"', *Oxford Journal of Archaeology* 15, 33–8.

Ryan, J., 1992, *Irish Monasticism: Origins and Early Development*, Dublin, Four Courts Press.

Rydving, H., 1995, 'The End of Drum-Time: Religious Change Among the Lule Saami, 1670s-1740s' [Second Edition], Uppsala, Acta Universitatis Upsaliensis.

Sandars, N., 1987, *The Sea Peoples: Warriors of the Ancient Mediterranean*, Thames and Hudson.

Sastre, I., 2008, 'Community, Identity, and Conflict: Iron Age Warfare in the Iberian Northwest', *Current Anthropology* 49, 1021–51.

Scarre, C., 2007, 'Changing places: monuments and the Neolithic transition in western France', in Whittle, A. and V. Cummings (eds), *Going Over: The Mesolithic – Neolithic Transition in North-West Europe*, Oxford, Proceedings of the British Academy 144, 243–61.

Schleidt, W. and M. Shalter, 2003, 'Co-evolution of Humans and Canids. An Alternative View of Dog Domestication: Homo Homini Lupus?', *Evolution and Cognoition* 9, 57–72.

Schmidt, M., 1987, 'Crazy wisdom: the shaman as mediator of realities', in Nicholson, Shirley (ed.), *Shamanism: An Expanded View of Reality*, Wheaton, IL, Quest Books, 62–75.

Schoetensack, O., 1908, *Der Unterkiefer des* Homo heidelbergensis *aus den Sanden von Mauer bei Heidelberg*, Leipzig, Wilhelm Engelmann.

Schönfelder, M., 1994, 'Bear-Claws in Germanic Graves', *Oxford Journal of Archaeology* 13, 217–27.

Schwartz, K., 1962, 'Zum Stand der Ausgrabungen in der Spätkeltischen Viereckschanze von Holzhausen', *Jahresbericht der Bayerischen Bodendenkmalpflege* 1962, 22–77.

Scott, W., 1948, 'The Chamber Tomb of Unival, North Uist', *Proceedings of the Society of Antiquaries of Scotland* 82, 1–49.

Scrivner, E. and M. Safer, 1988, 'Eyewitnesses Show Hypermnesia for Details about a Violent Event', *Journal of Applied Psychology* 73, 371–7.

Scurfield, C., 1997, 'Bronze Age Metalwork from the River Trent in Nottinghamshire', *Transactions of the Thoroton Society of Nottinghamshire* 101, 29–57.

Seielstad, M., E. Minch, E. Cavalli-Sforza and L. Cavalli-Sforza, 1998, 'Genetic Evidence for a Higher Female Migration Rate in Humans', *Nature Genetics* 20, 278–80.

Sharpe, K. and L. Van Gelder, 2006, 'Evidence for Cave Marking by Palaeolithic Children', *Antiquity* 310, 937–47.

Sharples, N., 1991a, 'Warfare in the Iron Age of Wessex', *Scottish Archaeological Review* 8, 79–89.

Sharples, N., 1991b, *Maiden Castle: Excavations and Field Survey 1985–6*, Historic Buildings and Monuments Commission for England Archaeological Report No. 19.

Shennan, S., 1995, *Bronze Age Copper Production of the Eastern Alps: Excavations at St. Veit-Klinglberg*, Bonn, Habelt.

Shepherd, I., 1986, *Powerful Pots: Beakers in North-East Prehistory*, Aberdeen, Anthropological Museum.

Sherratt, A., 1991, 'Sacred and profane substances: the ritual use of narcotics in later Neolithic Europe', in Garwood, P., D. Jennings, R. Skeats and J. Toms (eds), *Sacred and Profane*, Oxford, Oxford University Committee for Archaeology Monograph No. 32, 50–64.

Sherratt, A., 1994, 'The transformation of early agrarian Europe: the later Neolithic and Copper Ages, 4500–2500 BC', in Cunliffe, B. (ed.), *The Oxford Illustrated History of Prehistoric Europe*, Oxford, Oxford University Press, 167–201.

Shirokogoroff, S., 1935, *The Psychomental Complex of the Tungus*, Kegan Paul, Trench, Trubner and Co.

Siegel, R., 1978, 'Cocaine Hallucinations', *American Journal of Psychiatry* 135, 309–14.

Siegel, R. and M. Jarvik, 1975, 'Drug-induced hallucinations in animals and man', in Siegel, R. and L. West (eds), *Hallucinations: Behaviour, Experience and Theory*, New York, John Wiley, 81–161.

Siikala, A.-L., 1978, *The Rite Technique of the Siberian Shaman*, Helsinki, Academia Scientiarum Fennica.

Siikala, A.-L. and M. Hoppál, 1992, *Studies on Shamanism*, Budapest, Akadémiai Kiadó.

Slade, P. and R. Bentall, 1988, *Sensory Deception: A Scientific Analysis of Hallucination*, Croom Helm.

Smith, K., 1977, 'The Excavation of Winklebury Camp, Basingstoke, Hampshire', *Proceedings of the Prehistoric Society* 43, 31–129.

Snodgrass, A., 1971, *The Dark Age of Greece: An Archaeological Survey of the Eleventh to the Eighth Centuries BC*, Edinburgh, Edinburgh University Press.

Snow, D., 2006, 'Sexual Dimorphism in Upper Palaeolithic Hand Stencils', *Antiquity* 308, 390–404.

Soffer, O. and P. Vandiver, 1997, 'The ceramics from Pavlov I: 1957 Excavation', in Svoboda, J. (ed.), *Pavlov I. Northwest: The Upper Palaeolithic Burial and its Settlement Context*, Brno, Academy of Sciences of the Czech Republic, 383–401.

Soffer, O., P. Vandiver, B. Klíma and J. Svoboda, 1993, 'The pyrotechnology of performance art: Moravian Venuses and wolverines', in Knecht, H., A. Pike-Tay and R. White (eds), *Before Lascaux: The Complete Record of the Early Upper Palaeolithic*, Boca-Raton, CRC Press, 259–75.

Solecki, R., 1972, *Shanidar: The Humanity of Neanderthal Man*, Allen Lane.

Solecki, R., 1975, 'Shanidar IV, A Neanderthal Flower Burial in Northern Iraq', *Science* 190, 880–1.

Solli, B., 1999, 'Odin the queer? On ergi and shamanism in Norse mythology', in Gustafsson, A. and H. Karlsson (eds), *Glyfer och Arkeologiska Rum – en Vänbok till Jarl Nordbladh*, Göteborg, Gotarc Series A, 341–9.

Sommarström, B., 1985, 'Pointers and clues to some Saami drum problems', in Bäckman, L. and Å. Hultkrantz (eds), *Saami Pre-Christian Religion: Studies on the Oldest Traces of Religion Among the Saamis*, Stockholm, Almqvist and Wiksell, 139–56.

Sommer, J., 1999, 'The Shanidar IV "Flower Burial": A Re-evaluation of Neanderthal Burial Ritual', *Cambridge Archaeological Journal* 9, 127–9.

Sommer, M., 2007, *Bones and Ochre: The Curious Afterlife of the Red Lady of Paviland*, Cambridge, MA, Harvard University Press.

Sommerfeld, C., 1994, *Gerätegeld Sichel: Studiem in Monetären Struktur Bronzelicher Horte in Nördlichen Mitteleuropa*, Berlin, Walter de Gruyter.

Sopp, M., 1999, *Die Wiederaufnahme älterer Bestattungsplätze in den nachfolgenden vor- und früge- schichtlichen Perioden in Norddeutschland*, Bonn, Habelt.

Sørensen, M., 1989, 'Ignoring innovation – denying change: the role of iron and the impact of external influences on the transformation of Scandinavian societies 800–500 BC', in van der Leeuw, S. and R. Torrence (eds), *What's New? A Closer Look at the Process of Innovation*, Unwin Hyman, 182–202.

Sørensen, M., 1997, 'Reading Dress: The Construction of Social Categories and Identities in Bronze Age Europe', *Journal of European Archaeology* 5, 93–114.

Spindler, C., 1994, *The Man in the Ice*, Weidenfeld & Nicholson.

Stahl, Pr., 1989, 'Identification of Hallucinatory Themes in the Late Neolithic Art of Hungary', *Journal of Psychoactive Drugs* 21, 101–12.

Stead, I., 1991, *Iron Age Cemeteries in East Yorkshire: Excavations at Burton Fleming, Rudston, Garton-on-the-Wolds, and Kirkurn*, English Heritage.

Stiner, M., 1999, 'Palaeolithic Mollusc Exploitation at Riparo Mochi (Balzi Rossi, Italy): Food and Ornaments from the Aurignacian Through Epigravettian', *Antiquity* 73, 735–54.

Stiner, M., N. Bicho, J. Lindly and R. Ferring, 2003, 'Mesolithic to Neolithic Transitions: New Results from Shell-Middens in the Western Algarve, Portugal', *Antiquity* 77, 75–86.

Stringer, C. and C. Gamble, 1993, *In Search of the Neanderthals: Solving the Puzzle of Human Origins*, Thames and Hudson.

Stringer, C. and P. Andrews, 2005, *The Complete World of Human Evolution*, Thames and Hudson.

Stringer, C. and R. McKie, 1996, *African Exodus*, Jonathan Cape.

Stringer, C., R. Barton and J. Finlayson (eds), 2000, *Neanderthals on the Edge*. Oxford, Oxbow.

Stukeley, W., 1740, *Stonehenge: A Temple Restor'd to the British Druids*, Innys and Manby.

Sulimirski, T., 1970, *The Sarmatians*, Thames and Hudson.

Svanberg, F., 2005, 'House symbolism in aristocratic death rituals of the Bronze Age', in Artelius, T. and F. Svanberg (eds), *Dealing with the Dead: Archaeological Perspectives on Prehistoric Scandinavian Burial Ritual*, Stockholm, National Heritage Board, 73–98.

Sveen, A., 1996, *Rock Carvings, Jieprialuokta Hjemmeluft, Alta*, Trykkforum Finnmark.

Svoboda, J., 2006, 'The burials: ritual and taphonomy', in Trinkaus, E. and J. Svoboda, *Early Modern Human Evolution in Central Europe: The People of Dolní Věstonice and Pavlov*, Oxford, Oxford University Press, 15–26.

Svoboda, J., J. Ložek, H. Svobodová and P. Škrdla, 1994, 'Předmostí After 110 Years', *Journal of Field Archaeology* 21, 457–72.

Swanson, G., 1973, 'The Search for a Guardian Spirit: A Process of Empowerment in Simpler Societies', *Ethnology* 12, 359–78.

Tarassov, L., 1995, 'Les statuettes féminines de Gagarino', in Delporte, H. (ed.) *La Dame de Brassempouy: Ses Ancêtres, ses Contemporaines, ses Héritieres*, Liege, ERAUL, 239–47.

Taylor, J., 1970, 'Lunulae Reconsidered', *Proceedings of the Prehistoric Society* 36, 38–81.

Taylor, T., 2002, *The Buried Soul: How Humans Invented Death*, Fourth Estate.

ter Schegget, M., 1999, 'Late Iron Age human skeletal remains from the River Meuse at Kessel: a river cult place?', in Theuws, F. and N. Roymans (eds), *Land and Ancestors: Cultural Dynamics in the Urnfield Period and the Middle Ages in Southern Netherlands*, Amsterdam, Amsterdam University Press, 199–240.

Terberger, T., 2006, 'From the first humans to the Mesolithic hunters in the northern German lowlands – current results and trends', in Møller Hansen, K. and K. Buck Pedersen (eds), *Across the Western Baltic*, Vordingborg, Sydjællands Museum, 23–56.

Terebikhin, N., 1993, 'Cultural Geography and the Cosmology of the Saami', *Acta Borealia* 10, 3–17.

Thomas, J., 1996, *Time, Culture and Identity: An Interpretative Archaeology*, Routledge.

Thomas, J., 1999a, *Understanding the Neolithic*, Routledge.

Thomas, J., 1999b, 'The Holywood cursus complex, Dumfries: an interim account 1997', in Barclay, A. and J. Harding (eds), *Pathways and Ceremonies: The Cursus Monuments of Britain and Ireland*, Oxford, Oxbow, 107–118.

Thomas, J., 2003, 'Thoughts on the 'Repacked' Neolithic Revolution', *Antiquity*: 77, 67–74.

Thomas, J., 2005, 'Transforming Beaker Culture in North-West Europe; Processes of Fusion and Fission', *Proceedings of the Prehistoric Society* 71, 171–217.

Thomas, J., 2006, 'On the Origins and Development of Cursus Monuments in Britain', *Proceedings of the Prehistoric Society* 72, 229–41.

Thomas, J., 2007, 'Mesolithic-Neolithic transitions in Britain', in Whittle, A. and V. Cummings (eds), *Going Over: The Mesolithic – Neolithic Transition in North-West Europe*, Oxford, Proceedings of the British Academy 144, 423–39.

Thomas, K., 2003, *Religion and the Decline of Magic: Studies in Popular Beliefs in Sixteenth and Seventeenth-Century England*, Harmondsworth, Penguin.

Thomas, N., 2005, *Snail Down, Wiltshire: The Bronze Age Barrow Cemetery and Related Earthworks*, Devizes, Wiltshire Archaeological and Natural History Society.

Thomas, R., 1997, 'Land, Kinship Relations and the Rise of Enclosed Settlement in First Millennium BC Britain', *Oxford Journal of Archaeology* 16, 211–18.

Thorne, A. and M. Wolpoff, 1992, 'The Multiregional Evolution of Modern Humans', *Scientific American* 266, 28–33.

Thrane, H., 1984, *Lusehøj ved Voldtofte – en Sydvestfynsk Storhøj fra Yngre Broncealder*, Odense, Fynske Studier XIII.

Tilley, C., 1994, *A Phenomenology of Landscape*, Oxford, Berg Publishers.

Tilley, C., 2007, 'The Neolithic sensory revolution: monumentality and the experience of landscape', in Whittle, A. and V. Cummings (eds), *Going Over: The Mesolithic – Neolithic Transition in North-West Europe*, Oxford, Proceedings of the British Academy 144, 329–45.

Tiratsian, G., 1992, 'Découvertes Récentes en Arménie', *Les Dossiers D'Archeologie* 177, 32–9.

Todd, M., 1992, *The Early Germans*, Oxford, Blackwell.

Todorova, H., 1995, 'The Neolithic, Eneolithic and Transitional Period in Bulgarian prehistory', in Bailey, D. and I. Panayatov (eds), *Prehistoric Bulgaria*, Madison, Prehistory Press, 79–98.

Tooby, J. and L. Cosmides, 1992, 'The psychological foundations of culture', in Barkow, J., L. Cosmides and J. Tooby (eds), *The Adapted Mind: Evolutionary Psychology and the Generation of Culture*, Oxford, Oxford University Press, 19–136.

Topping, P., 2005, 'Shaft 27 revisited: an ethnography', in Topping, P. and M. Lynott (eds), *The Cultural Landscape of Prehistoric Mines*, Oxford, Oxbow, 63–93.

Torbrügge, W., 1970–71, 'Vor- und Frügeschichtliche Flußfunde zur Ordnung und Bestimmung einer Denmälergruppe', *Bericht der Römisch-Germanischen Kommission* 51–52, 1–145.

Tostevin, G. 2007, 'Social intimacy, artefact visibility and acculturation models of Neanderthal-modern human interaction', in Mellars, P., K. Boyle, O. Bar-Yosef and C. Stringer (eds), *Rethinking the Human Revolution*, Cambridge, McDonald Institute Monographs, 341–57.

Treherne, P., 1995, 'The Warrior's Beauty: The Masculine Body and Self-Identity in Bronze Age Europe, *Journal of European Archaeology* 3, 105–44.

Tresset, A. and J.-D. Vigne, 2007, 'Substitution of species, techniques and symbols at the Mesolithic-Neolithic transition in Western Europe', in Whittle, A. and V. Cummings (eds), *Going Over: The Mesolithic – Neolithic Transition in North-West Europe*, Oxford, Proceedings of the British Academy 144, 189–210.

Tringham, R., 2000, 'Southeastern Europe in the transition to agriculture in Europe: bridge, buffer, or mosaic', in Price, T.D. (ed.), *Europe's First Farmers*, Cambridge, Cambridge University Press, 19–56.

Tringham, R., 2005, 'Weaving house life and death into places: a blueprint for a hypermedia narrative', in Bailey, D., A. Whittle and V. Cummings (eds), *(Un)settling the Neolithic*, Oxford, Oxbow, 98–111.

Trinkus, E., 1983, *The Shanidar Neanderthals*, New York, Academic Press.

Turek, J., 2004, 'Craft symbolism in the Bell Beaker burial customs: resources, production and social structure at the end of Eneolithic period', in Besse, M. and J. Desideri (eds), *Graves and Funerary Rituals During the Late Neolithic and the Early Bronze Age in Europe (2700–2000 BC)*, Oxford, British Archaeological Reports (International Series) 1284, 147–57.

Turek, J., 2006, 'Beaker barrows and the houses of dead', in Šmedja, L. (ed.), *Archaeology of Burial Mounds*, Plzeň, University of West Bohemia.

Turk, I., J. Dirjec and B. Kavur, 1997, 'Description and explanation of the suspected bone flute', in Turk, I. (ed.), *Mousterian Bone Flute and Other Finds from Divje Babe 1 Cave Site in Slovenia*, Ljubljana, Založba ZRC, 157–78.

Tyler, C., 1978, 'Some New Entoptic Phenomena', *Vision Research* 18, 1633–9.

Udell, M. and C. Wynne, 2008, 'A Review of Domestic Dogs' (*Canis Familiaris*) Human-Like Behaviours: Or Why Behaviour Analysts Should Stop Worrying and Love Their Dogs', *Journal of Experimental Analysis of Behaviour* 89, 247–61.

Ustanova, Y., 1999, *The Supreme Gods of the Bosporan Kingdom*, Leiden, E.J. Brill.

Uytterschaut, H., 1990, 'De Veenlijken van Nederland', *Westerheem* 34, 185–95.

van de Noort, R., 2006, 'Argonauts of the North Sea – A Social Maritime Archaeology for the 2nd Millennium BC', *Proceedings of the Prehistoric Society* 72, 267–87.

van der Beek, Z., 2004, 'An ancestral way of burial: late Neolithic graves in southern Netherlands', in Besse, M. and J. Desideri (eds), *Graves and Funerary Rituals During the Late Neolithic and the Early Bronze Age in Europe (2700–2000 BC)*, Oxford, British Archaeological Reports (International Series) 1284, 157–94.

van der Sanden, W., 1988, 'The Ussen Project. Large Scale Settlement Archaeology of the Period 700BC–250AD, A Preliminary Report', *Analecta Praehistorica Leidensia* 20, 95–123.

van der Sanden, W., 1996, *Through Nature to Eternity: The Bog Bodies of Northwest Europe*, Amsterdam, Batavian Lion International.

van Vuure, C., 2005, *Retracing the Aurochs: History, Morphology and Ecology of an Extinct Wild Ox*, Sofia, Pensoft Publishers.

Vander Linden, M., 2006, 'For Whom the Bell Tolls: Social Hierarchy vs Social Integration in the Bell Beaker Culture of Southern France (Third Millennium BC)', *Cambridge Archaeological Journal* 16, 317–32.

Vandiver, P., O. Soffer, B. Klíma and J. Svoboda, 1989, 'The Origins of Ceramic Technology at Dolní Věstonice, Czechoslovakia', *Science*, 246, 1002–8.

Vanhaeren, M., F. d'Errico, C. Stringer et al., 2006, 'Middle Palaeolithic Shell Beads in Israel and Algeria', *Science* 312, 1785–8.

Verhart, L., 2008, 'New developments in the study of the Mesolithic of the Low Countries', in Bailey, G. and P. Spikins (eds), *Mesolithic Europe*, Cambridge, Cambridge University Press, 158–181.

Verlinde, A., 1985, 'Die Gräber und Grabfunde der späten Bronzezeit und frühen Eisenzeit in Overijssel IV', *Berichten van de Rijksdienst voor het Oudheidkundig Bodemonderzoek* 35, 231–411.

Vitebsky, P., 1995, *The Shaman*, Duncan Baird Publishers.

Vladár, J., 1973, 'Osteuropäische und Mediterrane Einflüsse im Gebiet der Slowakei Während der Bronzezeit', *Slovenská Archeológia* 21, 253–357.

Vlassa, N., 1963, 'Chronology of the Neolithic of Transylvania in the Light of the Tărtăria Settlement's Stratigraphy', *Dacia* 7, 485–94.

Vorren, Ø., 1985, 'Circular sacrificial sites and their function', in Bäckman, L. and Å. Hultkrantz (eds), *Saami Pre-Christian Religion: Studies on the Oldest Traces of Religion Among the Saamis*, Stockholm, Almqvist and Wiksell, 69–81.

Waddington, C., 1998, 'Cup and Ring Marks in Context', *Cambridge Archaeological Journal* 8, 29–54.

Wahl, J. and H. König, 1987, 'Anthropologisch – traumatologische Untersuchung der menschlichen Skelettreste aus dem bandkeramischen Massengrab bei Talheim, Kreis Heilbronn', *Fundberichte aus Baden-Württemberg* 12, 65–193.

Wainwright, G. and I. Longworth, 1971, *Durrington Walls: Excavations 1966–1968*, The Society of Antiquaries.

Walker, J., 1981, 'About Phosphenes: Luminous Patterns that Appear when the Eyes are Closed', *Scientific American* 244, 142–52.

Wallis, R., 2003, *Shamans/Neo-Shamans: Ecstasy, Alternative Archaeologies and Contemporary Pagans*, Routledge.

Wamser, L., 1984, 'Ein Bemerkenswerter Hortfund der Spätbronzezeit von Tauberbischofsheim-Hochhausen, Main-Tauber-Kreis', *Fundberichte aus Baden-Württemberg* 9, 23–40.

Warnier, J.-P., 2001, 'A Praxeological Approach to Subjectivation in a Material World', *Journal of Material Culture* 6: 5–24.

Warren, G., 2003, 'Life in the Trees: Mesolithic People and the Woods of Ireland', *Archaeology Ireland* 65, 20–3.

Warren, G., 2005, *Mesolithic Lives in Scotland*, Stroud, Tempus.

Warren, G., 2007, 'Mesolithic myths', in Whittle, A. and V. Cummings (eds), *Going Over: The Mesolithic – Neolithic Transition in North-West Europe*, Oxford, Proceedings of the British Academy 144, 311–28.

Waterbolk, H. and W. van Zeist, 1961, 'A Bronze Age Sanctuary in the Raised Bog at Bargeroosterveld (Dr.)', *Helinium* 1, 5–19.

Waterman, D., 1997, *Excavations at Navan Fort 1961–71, County Armagh*, Belfast, The Stationery Office.

Watson, A., 2001, 'The sounds of transformation: acoustics, monuments and ritual in the British Neolithic', in Price, N. (ed.), *The Archaeology of Shamanism*, Routledge, 178–92.

Watson, A. and D. Keating, 1999, 'Architecture and Sound: An Acoustic Analysis of Megalithic Monuments in Prehistoric Britain', *Antiquity* 73, 325–36.

Webley, L., 2007, 'Using and Abandoning Roundhouses: A Reinterpretation of the Evidence from late Bronze Age – Early Iron Age Southern England', *Oxford Journal of Archaeology* 26, 127–44.

Webster, J., 1999, 'At the End of the World: Druidic and Other Revitalisation Movements in Post-Conquest Gaul and Britain', *Britannia* 30, 1–20.

Wells, C. and D. Hodgkinson, 2001, 'A Late Bronze Age Human Skull and Associated Worked Wood from a Lancashire Wetland', *Proceedings of the Prehistoric Society* 67, 163–74.

Wels-Weyrauch, 1989, 'Mittelbronzezeitliche Frauentrachten in Süddeutschland (Beziehungen zur Hagenauer Gruppierung)', in Mordant, C. (ed.), *Dynamique du Bronze Moyen en Europe Occidentale*, Paris, Editions du Comité des Travaux Historiques et Scientifiques, 117–34.

Weyer, E., 1932, *The Eskimos: Their Environment and Folkways*, New Haven, Yale University Press.

Whimster, R., 1981, *Burial Practices in Iron Age Britain: A Discussion and Gazetteer of the Evidence c. 700 BC–AD 43*, Oxford, British Archaeological Reports (British Series) 90.

White, D., 1982, *The Bronze Age Cremation Cemeteries at Simon's Ground, Dorset*, Dorset Natural History and Archaeological Society Monograph Series, No. 3.

White, R., 1989a, 'Toward a contextual understanding of the earliest body ornaments', in Trinkaus, E. (ed.), *The Emergence of Modern Humans: Biocultural Adaptations in the Later Pleistocene*, Cambridge, Cambridge University Press, 211–31.

White, R., 1989b, 'Production Complexity and Standardisation in Early Aurignacian Bead and Pendant Manufacture: Evolutionary Implications', in Mellars, P. and C. Stringer (eds), *The Human Revolution: Behavioural and Biological Perspectives in the Origins of Modern Humans*, Edinburgh, Edinburgh University Press, 366–90.

White, R., 1993, 'Technological and social dimensions of "Aurignacian-age" body ornaments across Europe', in Knecht, H., A. Pike-Tay and R. White (eds), *Before Lascaux: The Complex Record of the Early Upper Palaeolithic*, Boca-Raton, CRC Press, 277–99.

White, R., 1997, 'Substantial acts: from materials to meaning in Upper Palaeolithic representation', in Conkey, M., O. Soffer, D. Stratmann and N. Jablonski. (eds), *Beyond Art: Pleistocene Image and Symbol*, San Francisco, California Academy of Sciences, 93–121.

White, R., 2003, *Prehistoric Art: The Symbolic Journey of Humankind*, New York, Abrams.

White, R., 2007, 'Systems of personal ornamentation in the early Upper Palaeolithic: methodological challenges and new observations', in Mellars, P., K. Boyle, O. Bar-Yosef and C. Stringer (eds), *Rethinking the Human Revolution*, Cambridge, McDonald Institute Monographs, 287–302.

Whitley, J., 2001, *The Archaeology of Ancient Greece*, Cambridge, Cambridge University Press.

Whittle, A., 1996, *Europe in the Neolithic: The Creation of New Worlds*, Cambridge, Cambridge University Press.

Whittle, A., 1997, *Sacred Mound, Holy Rings. Silbury Hill and the West Kennet Palisade Enclosures: A Later Neolithic Complex in North Wiltshire*, Oxford, Oxbow Monographs 74.

Whittle, A., J. Pollard and C. Grigson, 1999, *The Harmony of Symbols: The Windmill Hill Causewayed Enclosure*, Oxford, Oxbow.

Widholm, D., 1998, *Rösen, Ristningar och Riter*, Lund, Acta Archaeologica Lundensia.

Wieland, G., 1999, *Die Keltischen Viereckschanzen. Einem Rätsel auf der Spur*. Stuttgart, Konrad Theiss.

Wihlborg, A., 1977–78, 'Sagaholm. A Bronze Age Barrow with Rock-Carvings', *Meddelanden från Lunds Universitets Historiska Museum* 2, 111–28.

Wilhelm, M., T. Gerlach and K. Simon, 1990, 'Aunjetitzer Bestattung mit "Indirekter Leichenverbrennung" von Jeßnitz, Kr. Bautzen', *Ausgrabungen und Funde* 35, 21–9.

Williams, M., 2001, *Shamanic Interpretations: Reconstructing a Cosmology for the Later Prehistoric Period of North-Western Europe*, Unpublished PhD Thesis, University of Reading.

Williams, M., 2002, 'Tales from the dead: remembering the bog bodies in the Iron Age of north-western Europe', in Williams, H. (ed.), *Archaeologies of Remembrance: Death and Memory in Past Societies*, Kulwer.

Williams, M., 2003, 'Growing Metaphors: The Agricultural Cycle as Metaphor in the Later Prehistoric Period of Britain and North-Western Europe', *Journal of Social Archaeology* 3, 223–55.

Williams, M. and J. Creighton, 2006, 'Shamanic practices and trance imagery in the Iron Age', in de Jersey, P. (ed.), *Celtic Coinage: New Discoveries, New Discussion*, Oxford, British Archaeological Reports (International Series) 1532.

Wilson, C., 1981, 'Burials Within Settlements in Southern Britain During the Pre-Roman Iron Age', *Bulletin of the Institute of Archaeology* 18, 127–69.

Wilson, D., 1992, *Anglo-Saxon Paganism*, Routledge.

Winkelman, M., 1986, 'Trance States: A Theoretical Model and Cross-Cultural Analysis', *Ethos* 14, 174–203.

Woodward, A., 2002, 'Beads and Beakers: Heirlooms and Relics in the British Early Bronze Age', *Antiquity* 76, 1040–7.

Wright, D. and G. Gaskell, 1992, 'The construction and function of vivid memories', in Conway, M., D. Rubin, H. Spinnler and W. Wagenaar (eds), *Theoretical Perspectives on Autobiographical Memory*, London, Kluwer Academic, 275–92.

Wynn, T. and F. Coolidge, 2004, 'The Expert Neanderthal Mind', *Journal of Human Evolution* 46, 467–87.

Wynn, T. and F. Coolidge, 2007, 'Did a small but significant enhancement in working memory capacity power the evolution of modern thinking?', in Mellars, P., K. Boyle, O. Bar-Yosef and C. Stringer (eds), *Rethinking the Human Revolution*, Cambridge, McDonald Institute Monographs, 79–90.

Yates, D., 2001, 'Bronze Age agricultural intensification in the Thames Valley and estuary', in Brück, J. (ed.), *Bronze Age Landscapes: Tradition and Transformation*, Oxford, Oxbow, 65–82.

Yates, D., 2007, *Land, Power and Prestige: Bronze Age Field Systems in Southern England*, Oxford, Oxbow.

Yeates, S., 2008, *The Tribe of Witches: The Religion of the Dobunni and Hwicce*, Oxford, Oxbow.

York, J., 2002, 'The Life Cycle of Bronze Age Metalwork from the Thames', *Oxford Journal of Archaeology* 21, 77–92.

Zachrisson, I. and E. Iregren, 1974, *Lappish Bear Graves in North Sweden: An Archaeological and Osteological Study*, Stockholm, Early Norrland 5.

Zilhão, J., 2006, 'Genes, Fossils, and Culture. An Overview of the Evidence for Neanderthal-Modern Human Interaction and Admixture', *Proceedings of the Prehistoric Society* 72, 1–20.

Zimmermann, H., 1999, 'Why was cattle-stalling introduced in prehistory? The significance of byre and stable and of outwintering', in Fabech, C. and J. Ringtved (eds), *Settlement and Landscape*, Moesgård, Jutland Archaeological Society, 301–18.

Zubrow, E., 1989, 'The demographic modelling of Neanderthal extinction', in Mellars, P. and C. Stringer (eds), *The Human Revolution: Behavioural and Biological Perspectives on the Origin of Modern Humans*, Edinburgh, Edinburgh University Press, 212–31.

Zvelebil, M., 1994, 'Plant Use in the Mesolithic and its Role in the Transition to Farming', *Proceedings of the Prehistoric Society* 60, 35–76.

Zvelebil, M., 1997, 'Hunter-Gatherer Ritual Landscapes: Spatial Organisation, Social Structure and Ideology Among Hunter-Gatherers of Northern Europe and Western Siberia', *Analecta Praehistorica Leidensia* 29, 33–50.

Zvelebil, M., 1998, 'Agricultural frontiers, Neolithic origins, and the transition to farming in the Baltic Basin', in Zvelebil, M., R. Dennell and L. Domanska (eds), *Harvesting the Sea, Farming the Forest: The Emergence of Neolithic Societies in the Baltic Region*, Sheffield, Sheffield Academic Press, 9–27.

Zvelebil, M., 2003, 'People behind the lithics. Social life and social conditions of Mesolithic communities in temperate Europe', in Bevan, L. and J. Moore (eds), *Peopling the Mesolithic in a Northern Environment*, Oxford, British Archaeological Reports (International Series) 1157, 1–26.

Zvelebil, M., 2004a, 'Who were we 6000 years ago? In search of prehistoric identities', in Jones, M. (ed.), *Traces of Ancestry: Studies in Honour of Colin Renfrew*, Cambridge, McDonald Institute, 41–60.

Zvelebil, M., 2004b, 'Conclusion: the many origins of LBK', in Lukes, A. and M. Zvelebil (eds), *LBK Dialogues: Studies in the Formation of the Linear Pottery Culture*, Oxford, British Archaeological Reports (International Series) 1304, 183–205.

Zvelebil, M., 2008, 'Innovating hunter-gatherers: the Mesolithic in the Baltic', in Bailey, G. and P. Spikins (eds), *Mesolithic Europe*, Cambridge, Cambridge University Press, 18–59.

Zvelebil, M. and M. Lillie, 2000, 'Transition to agriculture in eastern Europe', in Price, T.D. (ed.), *Europe's First Farmers*, Cambridge, Cambridge University Press, 57–92.

Zvelebil, M. and P. Jordan, 1999, 'Hunter fisher gatherer ritual landscapes – questions of time, space and representation', in Goldhahn, J. (ed.), *Rock Art as Social* Representation, Oxford, British Archaeological Reports (International Series) 794, 101–27.

LIST OF ILLUSTRATIONS

All photographs are by the author except:

Colour plate 1: Neanderthal Child. Courtesy of http://commons.wikimedia.org/wiki/User:
Vugluskr.
Colour plate 1: Shanidar cave. Courtesy of http://commons.wikimedia.org/wiki/
User:JosephV.
Colour plate 2: Lion Man. Courtesy of Thomas Stephan, Ulmer Museum.
Colour plate 2: Lascaux Cave. © Norbet Aujoulat, Centre National du Préhistoire,
Perigueux.
Colour plate 3: Lepenski Vir head. Courtesy of http://commons.wikimedia.org/wiki/
User:Mazbln.
Colour plate 3: Reconstruction of Lepenski Vir. Courtesy of Giovanni Caselli.
Colour plate 5: Amesbury Archer. Courtesy of Wessex Archaeology and Jayne Brayne.
Colour plate 7: Gavrinis interior. Courtesy of http://commons.wikimedia.org/wiki/
User:Athinaios.
Colour plate 12: Sun Horse. Courtesy of John Lee, the National Museum of Denmark.
Colour plate 12: Fly agaric mushroom. Courtesy of http://commons.wikimedia.org/wiki/
User:onderwijsgek.
Colour plate 14: Gundestrup cauldron. Courtesy of Lennart Larsen, the National Museum of
Denmark.
Colour plate 14: Lindow Man. Courtesy of the British Museum.

All photographs used from Wiki Commons are reproduced under identical licences to those
that appear on the relevant web pages.

Every effort has been made to contact copyright holders for the images used in this edition.

INDEX

References to notes are in *italic* and references to colour plates are in **bold**.

Visit our website and discover thousands of other History Press books.

www.thehistorypress.co.uk